ENGLISH-GARO DICTIONARY

ENGLISH-GARO DICTIONARY

AMERICAN BAPTIST FOREIGN MISSION SOCIETY. GARO MISSION

COMPILER

M.C. MASON

Published by

FacsiMile Publisher
12 Pragati Market
Ashok Vihar, Ph-2
Delhi - 110052, India
Phone: 011-47034999
Email: www.facsimilepublishers.com
info@facsimilepublishers.com

Distribution Network
gyanbooks.com
India, USA, Canada, UK, Australia

ISBN: 978-93-3336-876-6 (HB)
First Published, 1905

2nd Impression 2025

Printed at: Gyan Press, Delhi.

ENGLISH-GARO DICTIONARY
Compiler: M.C. MASON

ENGLISH-GARO DICTIONARY

BY

MEMBERS OF THE GARO MISSION

OF THE

AMERICAN BAPTIST MISSIONARY UNION

TURA, ASSAM.

Published by the Garo Mission, American Baptist Missionary Union.

SHILLONG:

PINTED AT THE ASSAM SECRETARIAT PRINTING OFFICE.

1905.

PREFACE.

THIS Dictionary was prepared and published to meet an immediate demand in Garo School work, caused by substituting English text-books in place of the Bengali books formerly used, in the higher branches of study. Its preparation required haste, amidst the pressure of many other important duties. I therefore requested Modhunath Momin to draft definitions, in addition to his duties as teacher in the station school. This draft was corrected, modified and generally revised by Miss Ella C. Bond and myself with Modhunath. The pronunciation, introduction, and general editing have fallen to me. In the preparation of manuscript and reading of proofs, however, I have had the help of Miss Bond and Modhunath, also some help from Jon-sing Marak and Jobang Marak.

It was printed by the Assam Government at the Secretariat Press in Shillong, where no one knew the language. But we hope to find it fairly well adapted to the purpose for which it was prepared, namely, that of furnishing the pronunciations and Garo definitions of the more common English word

Tura, M. C. MASON.

November 1904.

Skisoani.

Englishko poraina sikgiparangna ia ki·tap dakchakbeani ong·gen ine anga ka·donga. Indiba ia ki·tapko jakkalna ia skisoaniko namedake skina nangohongmota. Aro maikai katarangko namedake aganna man·a; chong·motan maikai na·simang uina gita tale mingatna man·a iako skichengbo.

Gam·atani.

English katarangko nikarion mingatna man·jawa. Uni gimin ia Dictionaryo kataprakni ja·mano parenthesisni ning·o uko mingatna ua katapra kko setaiaha. Uni gimin katani gam·ako uina skode parenthesisni ning·o segiminko nibo.

Je katao silebel ge·sana bate donga, silebel ge·sanko rakkale mingatna nanga, aro basakoba silebel ge·gniko rakkale mingatna nanga. Mai silebelko rakatna nanga, uko ia chin ′ chi mesokronga, chong·motan silebelni ja·mano ua chinko nikode ua silebelko rakatbo. Ia gita do-ka′, gi-bok′, doka katao *ka*ko rakata, aro gibok katao *bok*ko rakata. Uandake je silebelni ja·mano ia ′ chinko nika, ua silebelko rakatbo. Ua chinko accent (ăk-sĕnt) minga. Aro silebelprakko uisrangna gita ua chin dongjaode silebelrangni gisepo ia chin - ko donronga. Skanggipa katako nibo, Ā-băn′dŭn, silebel ge·gitam; *a* silebel sa, *ban* silebel sa, aro *dun* silebel sa, aro jatohigipa *ban* ko rakatna nanga.

Aro ua oikorrang maikai gam·na nanga mesokani chinrang gnang, ua chinrangko gisiko donsrangbo. Ua gam·arangko iano mesoka.

ā ni gam·a bebe aro de ni e gita gam·a.

a ni gam·a ā gita ong·a, indiba on·titi kan·dikata; iano accent dongja.

ä ni gam·a A·chikni a gita ong·a.

å ni gam·a a gita ong·a, indiba on·titi kan·dikata; ianoba accent dongja.

ă ni gam·a Englishko Skichengani jak brio gnigipa a gita.

â ni gam·a ă ni gita ong·a, indiba una bate ro·bate gam·na nanga; aro uni ja·mano r dongronga, uni gimin uko on·titi dingtangata.

a ni gam·a bang·jabe; on·titisan a ko gam·ataibo.

ē ni gam·a A·chikni i gita ong·a.

e ni gam·a ē gita ong·a, indiba on·titi kan·dikata; iano accent dongja.

ĕ ni gam·a A·chikni *genni* e gita gam·a.

ê ni gam·a ĕ ni gam·a gita, indiba una bate ro·bata aro uni ja·mano r dongani gimin on·titi dingtangata.

e ni gam·a bang·jabe; on·titisan e ko gam·ataibo.

ī ni gam·a A·chikni ai gita.

i ni gam·a ī gita ong·a, indiba on·titi kan·dikata.

ĭ ni gam·a *jikni* i gita gam·a.

ō ni gam·a A·chikni skanggipa o gita, *do·o* ba *too* jokai o gam·a ugita.

o ni gam·a kosakni ō gita ong·a, indiba adita kan·dik·bate gam·a.

ô ni gam·a *bolo* donggipa o gita gam·a.

ŏ ni gam·a A·chikni a gita ong·a, indiba una bate kan·dikbatbea.

ū ni gam·a A·chikni iu gita gam·a.

u ni gam·a kosakgipa ū gita gam·a, indiba una bate on·titi kandakbata.

ŭ ni gam·a A·chikni u gita, indiba ro·bata, aro on·titi ū gita ong·a.

u ni gam·a A·chikni u kan·dikgipa gita ong·a.

ŭ ni gam·a A·chiko dongja, skigipa mesokna nanga. Indiba mi·rakko, ū ŏ gita ong jabe.

y ni gam·a ī ni gam·a gita. Iako katani bon·kamaosan scaha.

oi ni gam·a ŏ ī gita gam·a.

ou ni gam·a âu gita gam·a.

Da·o maikai na·simang iako rim·frangna man·gen, ia gam arangko jakkalko, aro skigipa ranta ka·atna nanga.

ā=āle, bāte, lā'bour, chā'os, chām'ber.

a=sen'ate, del'i-cate, cha-ot'ic, săl'u-ta-ry.

ä=ärm, fär, fä'THer, äh, ärt.

å=åsk, gråss, å-bout, A-mer'i-cå, so'få.

ă=ăm, făt, hăt, răt, ăt-tăck'.

â=câre, shâre, pâr'ent, com-pâre'.

a=fi'n*a*l, mad'*a*m, hus'b*a*nd.

ē=ēve, mēte, se-rēne', hēre.

e=so-ci'e-ty, e-pit'o-me.

ĕ=ĕnd, mĕt, shĕd, tĕnt, thĕm.

ê=hêr, hêrd, jêrk, vêrb, têrm, fêrm.

e=prudence, nov'el, rē'cent.

ī=īce, tīme, bīnd, fīve, līke, mīnd.

i=i-dea, tri-bu'nal.

ĭ=ĭll, pĭn, dĭsh, fĭsh, grĭt, hĭt, lĭft.

ō=ōld, nōte, bōld, ō'ver, rōpe, bōth.

o=o-bey', to-bac'co.

ô=ôrb, lórd, ôr'der, ab-hôr'.

ŏ=ŏx, ŏn, nŏt, drŏp, plŏd, hŏg, tŏp, hŏp.

ū=ūse, pūre, mūte, tūne, dūty.

u=u-nite', ac'tu-ate.

ṳ=rṳde, rṳ'mor, in-trṳde'.

ụ=fụll, pụt, pụsh, pụss.

ŭ=ŭp, ŭs, tŭb, bŭd, hŭnt, hŭt.

y=pit'y, in'ju-ry, dai'ly, ba'by.

oi=oil, boil, soil, coin, void, join.

ou=our, sour, noun, loud.

Ia oikorrang, chong·motan, b, d, g, h, j, k, l, m, n, p, r, s, t, w, A·chik ku·siko gam·a gita gam·a.

Ch. f. v. aro z, Englishko skichengani lesson 11 o mesoka gita gam·a. Th, balwani ong·a, thin, think, birth, ia katarango gam·a gita.

Th gam·ani ong·a, the, then, thy, with, father, ia katarango gam·a gita.

Parts of speech.

Parenthesisni ja·mano maiba oikorko seronga; ia gita, *n.* ba *ad.* Uarangni mangsonga, katani rokomko mesoka, chong·motan ua kata noun ong·a, ba verb ong·a, ba gipin gipin jeba ong·chong uko mesoka. Aro kata gimikni pal ia chinrangko seaiaha; aro ua chinrangni orto iarang.

a.=adjective.
adv.=adverb.
art.=article.
con.=conjunction.
int.=interjection.
n.=noun.
part.=participle.
pr.=pronoun.
prep.=preposition.
v.=verb.

Iarangko gisiktango donna nanga. Maina basakoba kata apsan ong·oba uni orto apsan ong·jawa. Fly *noun* ong·ode uni orto *tampi*; *verb* ong·ode uni orto *bila.* Bear *noun* ong·ode uni orto *mapil*; indiba *verb* ong·ode uni orto *ba·a* ba *kea* ba *chakchika.* Saw *noun* ong·ode uni orto *korat*; *verb* ong·ode uni orto *nikaha,* ba koratchi *raa.*

Bang·en kata orto dingtang dingtang, aro bang·en kata *verb* aro *noun* ong·a; ia gita, Act *v.* *Daka*; noun ong·ode uni orto *dakani* ong·a. Aro uandake adita bang·a kata ong·a. Skango *verbni* ortoko sea, jamanosa, *n.* sedapako basakoba nikgen. Unon ua kata nounba ong·a ine uibo; aro nounni ortoko sejaoba, verbni ortoko agandapode nounni ortoko uironggen. Iarang gita.

Hate, *v.* **Mitchia,** *n.* **mitchiani,**

Heed, *v.* **Knatima, mania,** *n.* **knatimani, maniani.**

Love, *v.* **Ka·saa,** *n.* **ka·saani.**

Lie, *v.* **Tol·a,** *n.* **tol·ani.**

Basakoba verbni biding ong·oba ni ong·jawa; ia gita *guide*, *v*. dila, *n*. dilgipa.

SUFFIXES.

Aro katani ortoko mesokman·o na·simang |basakoba basakoba katani tong·rangko nikgen; ia gita, -ment, -or, -tion, -ance, -al, -ant, -ent. Ia katani tong·rangko *suffix*rang minga. Ia katani tong·rang dingtango donge orto dongjaoba, gipin katani bon·kamachi sedapode ua katako dingtangata; ia gita, *Acknowledge*, *v*. ku·rachaka; *-ment*, *n*. ko sedapode *Acknowledgment* ong·gen; aro uni orto ku·rachakani.

Adhere, *v*. ma·gapa; -ence, *n*. sedapode *adherence* ong·gen; aro uni orto ma·gapani ong·gen. Uandake sedapani tong· bang·en ong·a. Katako mesoktokaha uandake ong·ja, on·titisan seaiaha. Mai tong· ua katao sedapna man·a, uko mesokna, ua katani tong·rangko gisimbatgipa oikorrangchi mitamko see donaha.

Sedapna man·gipa tong·rang mitamko iano sea. Uarangko aro uarangni ortorangko namedake skibo. -able, -ible, -ble, -ile. Iarangni orto ama, kraa; ia gita, *drink* ringa; *drinkable*, uko ringna ama, ringna kraa, ba ringna nama. *Endure*, chakchika, *endurable* uko chakchikna ama.

-ance, -ancy, -acy, -cy, -ence, -hood, -ion, -ment, -ness, -tion, -sion, -ion, ia pilakni orto -ni; dakani ba ong·ani.

-ed, -d; iarang past tenseko mesoka.

-er, -ar, -or; iaragni orto gipa, ba dakgipa.

-ful, -ous, -some; iarangni orto gapgimin; *hopeful*, *dangerous*.

-fy, -ise, -ize; iarang -at-; dakata, ong·ata.

-ish, -y; on·titi gnang, ba gita.

-kin, chongipa. -less, gri, dongja. -like, -ly, gita. -most, batgipa.

Iarangna agre bang·enga, indiba iarang jakkalbatgiparang ong·a.

Prefixes.

Suffixrangko katani bon·kamaosa seronga. Indiba katani mikkango donggipa tong·rang bang·a. Pilakkon sena man·ja, indiba mitamko jakkalrongbea; aro kata gimikko ia obidhano setokna man·ja. Uni gimin iarangko namedake skibo. Kata gimikko nikjaode aro a·bachengao ia tong·ni tong·sako sea gnangode, indide uni bangkiko gipin kata gita am·bo; iandake.

Unapt iako nikjaode *apt*ni ortoko am·bo, unon *unapt*ni ortoko uigen; maina *un*ni orto ja, gija ba ong·-ja; uandake *unapt*ni orto kragija, ong·ninggija ong·a ine uigen.

Inja·mano prefix mitamrangni ortorangko mesoka.

Ante-=skang.

Dis-=dingtang, -oni, -ja.

Ex-=-oni.

Mis-=guala, manija.

Over-, super-=kosak, bata, agre.

Pre-=skang, -so.

Re-=-tai, ba-pil·e.

Sub-=ka·mao, ning·o, ja·mano; aro **subter-, suc-, suf-, sug-, sup-, sur-, sus-**, iarangba *sub* gita ong·a.

Un-=gri, -ja, gija, kosako mesokaha gita; indiba verbo sesoode, ua verbni dakako bikpilatronga; ia gita, *untie*, *unload*. *Tie*ni orto kaa, *Untie*ni orto enga; *load*ni orto gatata, *unload*ni orto gatgimin balko ra·ona.

Iako nibo. Na·simang preffixko ra·e katao donsona man·jawa; maina uandake dakode gualbenaba donga. Preffixrangko donsotokaha, na·simang dongiminkosa skina nanga. Iano gualgniko uina man·a; *dis* aro *un*, ming gnini orto *ja* ong·a ong·ade, indiba *dislike* aro *unlike*ni orto dingtangbe; *dislike*ni orto *namnikja*; *unlike*ni orto *gita ong·ja*.

Irregular Verbs.

Verbo-ed ba-d sedapode past tenseko mesokronga, indiba mitam verbrang dingtang katachi past tenseko mesoka; ia gita, See, nika; saw, nikaha; have seen, nikmanaha. Do, daka; did dakaha; have done, dakmanaha. Uandakgipa verbrangni ja·mano past tenserangko seronagha; aro capital letterrangchisa seaha; ia gita, Abide *v.* ABODE, ABIDING. Abide, dongkama; abode, dongkamaha; Abiding, dongkamenga.

M. C. MASON.

ENGLISH-GARO DICTIONARY.

A.

A (ā), *art.* Sa, ge·sa, sanko mesokgipa.
Abandon (ă-băn′dŭn), *v.* Watgala. **-or**, *n.* **-ment**, *n.*
Abase (ă-bās′), *v.* Onata, chonata. **-ment**, *n.*
Abate (ă-bāt′), *v.* Komiata, chonata. **-ment**, *n.*
Abdomen (ăb-dō′-mĕn), *n.* Ok, okste.
Abhor (ăb-hôr′), *v.* Mitchia. **-rence**, *n.*
Abide (ă-bīd′), *v.* ABODE, ABIDING, Dongkama.
Ability (ă-bĭl′ĭ-ty), *n.* Bil, changani.
Able (ā′ b′l), *a.* Ama, bilgnang.
Abode (ă-bōd′), *n.* Dongram.
Abound (ă-bound′), *v.* Bang·bee ong·a.
About (ă-bout′), *adv.* Samtangtangchi, sepango ; gimin ; mang.
Above (ă-bŭv′), *adv.* Kosak.
Abrupt (ăb-rŭpt′), *adv.* Be·tonggimin ; chasronggipa dare, a·kuang. **-ion**, *n.*
Abscess (ăb′-sĕs), *n.* Bisi mina.
Absence (ăb′sens), *n.* Donggijani.
Absent (ăb′sĕnt), *a.* Dongja.
Absorb (ăb-sôrb′), *v.* Minoka, chipa.
Abstain (ăb-stān′), *v.* Maibaoniko a·tangko rakia.
Absurd (ăb-sêrd′), *a.* Ong·na kragija, ong·togija, ong·na amgija. **-ity**, *n.*
Abundance (ă-bŭn′dans), *n.* Chu·ongaranga.
Abundant (ă-bŭn′dant), *a.* Bang·a, namen, chu·onga.
Abuse (ă-būz′), *v.* Saia, namgija daka.
Accent (ăk′-sĕnt), *n.* Silebilo ku·rangko rakatani.
Accept (ăk-sĕpt′), *v.* Ra·chaka. **-ably**, *adv.* **ability**, *n.* **-ance**, *n.* **-ation**, *n.*
Accident (ăk′sĭ-dent), *n.* Uisogijani a·sel. **-al**, *a.*
Accommodate (ăk-kŏm′-medāt), *v.* Kraata, meliata, namnikata. **ion**, *n.*
Accompany (ăk-kŭm′-pă-ny), *v.* Baksa re·paa, re·chapa.
Accomplish (ăk-kŏm′-plĭsh), *v.* Chu·sokata. **-ment**, *n.*
Accord (ăk-kôrd′), *v.* Melia, meliata, ku·monggrika. *n.* **ska**tang. **-ance**, *n.* **-ant**, *a.*
Account (ăk-kount′), *v.* Chana, chane on·a. **-ability**, *n.* **-ant**, *n.*
Accumulate (ăk-kū′-mu-lāt), *v.* Chimonga, dandaka, man·dapa. **-or**, *n.* **-ion**, *n.* **-ive**, *a.*
Accurate (ăk′-ku-rat), *a.* Tik, guala gri.
Accuse (ăk-kūz′), *v.* Pota, matnanga. **-ation**, *n.*
Accustom (ăk-kŭs′-tŭm), *v.* Ranta ong·ata.
Ache (āk), *v.* Saa, saknaa, *n.*
Achieve (ă-chēv′), *v.* Daka, chu·sokata. **-ment**, *n.*
Acid (ăs′-id), *a.* Meseng, mesenggipa sam. **-ity**, *n.*

Acknowledge (ăk-nŏl′-ĕj), *v.* Ku·rachaka. **-ment**, *n.*

Acquaint (ăk-kwānt′), *v.* Uiata. **-ance**, *n.*

Acquire (ăk-kwīr′), *v.* Man·a. **-ment**, *n.*

Acquit (ăk-kwĭt′), *v.* Dos gri dakata, wata.

Acre (ā′-kêr), *n.* Ekar, bigha gitammang.

Across (ȧ-krôs′), *pr.* Nalsa, nalsachi; battonga; donpenga, dambenga.

Act (ăkt), *v.* Daka, ka·a. **-or**, *n.* **-rĕss**, *n.* **-ion**, *n.*

Act (ăkt), *n.* Dakani, ka·ani, ka·gimin.

Active (ăk′-tĭv), *a.* Bimchipa, gong·gipa. **-ĭty**, *n.*

Actual (ăk′-tu-al), *a.* Chong·-mot, beben. **-ĭty**, *n.*

Acute (ȧ-kūt′), *a.* Srama, mata.

Adapt (ȧ-dăpt′), *v.* Meliata, kraata. **-ȧbĭlĭty**, *n.* **-ation**, *n.*

Add (ăd), *v.* Chandima, nangdimata. **-ition**, *n.*

Addict (ăd-dĭkt′), *v.* Dakrongata.

Address (ăd-drĕs′), *n.* Tikana, kosako seani.

Address (ăd-drĕs′), *v.* Aganpraka, agana, bi·a.

Adept (ȧ-dĕpt′), *a.* Changgipa, sapgipa.

Adequate (ăd′-e-kwāt), *a.* Chu·onga.

Adhere (ăd-hēr′), *v.* Ma·gapa. **-ence**, *n.* **-ency**, *n.* **-ent**, *n.*

Adhesive (ăd-hē′-sĭv), *a.* Stapgipa, ma·gapninggipa.

Adhesion (ăd-hē′-zhŭn), *n.* Ma·-gapani, nangrimani.

Adjacent (ăd-jā′-sent), *a.* Sepang, chapchap, sepangbatgipa.

Adjective (ăd′-jĕk-tĭv), *n.* Noun-ni rokom ba gunko mesokgipa.

Adjourn (ăd-jêrn′), *v.* Dondika, dontonga. **-ment**, *n.*

Adjure (ăd-jūr′), *v.* Mikchetata.

Adjust (ăd-jŭst′), *v.* Namata, tariata, tik ong·ata. **-ment**, *n.*

Adjutant (ăd′-ju-tant), *n.* Hal-gila do·o; dal·batgipako dakchakgipa sipaini pamong.

Administer (ăd-mĭn′-is-têr), *v.* Maiba kamko dakata. **-trator**, *n.* **-tration**, *n.*

Admire (ăd-mīr′), *v.* Nitonika. **-ation**, *n.* **-ābly**, *adv.*

Admit (ăd-mĭt′), *v.* Napata, napna on·a; ku·rachaka. **-tance**, *n.*

Admission (ăd-mĭsh′-ŭn), *n.* Napatani, napna on·ani.

Admonish (ăd-mŏn′-ĭsh), *v.* Ka·sne manenge skia, mikrakata. **-tion**, *n.*

Adopt (ȧ-dŏpt′) *v.* Ra·chaka, ra·gata. **-ion**, *n.*

Adore (ȧ-dōr′) *v.* Olakibea, ka·-sabea, mande ra·bea. **-ation**, *n.*

Adorn (ȧ-dôrn′), *v.* On·dape nitoata, kraata. **-ment**, *n.*

Adrift (ȧ-drĭft′), *adv. a.* Karamoni gitchoa, balboa.

Adult (ȧ-dŭlt′), *a.* Briginin, bilsi chu·sokgimin.

Adulterate (ȧ-dŭl′-têr-āt), *v.* Brine namgija dakata. **-ion**, *n.*

Adulterer (ȧ-dŭl′-têr-êr), *n.* Til·ekgipa me·asa.

Adulteress (ȧ-dŭl′-têr-ĕs), *n.* Til·ekgipa me·chik.

Adultery (ȧ-dŭl′têr-y), *n.* Til·-ekani.

Advance (ăd-vāns′), *v.* Mikangchi re·ata, chuata, dakchakata; mikangchi re·a, chuoroa, nambatroroa. **-mĕnt**, *n.*

Advantage (ăd-văn'-tāj), *n.* Man·dapani, man·kalani. **-ous,** *a.*
Adventure (ăd-vĕn'-tur), *n.* Ong·ronggija dakani, kenani gnangko dakani.
Adverb (ăd'-vêrb), *n.* Verb, adjective ba adverbko dakchakgipa.
Adverse (ăd'-vêrs), *a.* Champenggipa, duk on·gipa, skako champenggipa.
Adversary (ăd'-vêr-sa-ry), *n.* Bobil, champenggipa.
Adversity (ăd-vêr'-sĭ-ty), *n.* Gimaani duk.
Advertise (ăd'-vêr-tīz), *v.* Pilakna uiata, aganprakata. **-mĕnt,** *n.*
Advice (ăd-vīs'), *n.* Skiani, patiani.
Advise (ăd-vīz'), *v.* Skia, patia, mikrakata, uiata. **-ability,** *n.*
Advocate (ăd'-vo-kat), *n.* Chakgipa, chake agangipa. *v.* **-ion,** *n.*
Adze (ădz), *n.* Bahila, bol sol·ani.
Afar (å-făr'), *adv.* Chel·ao.
Affair (ăf-fâr'), *n.* Ong·ani, kam.
Affect (ăf-fĕkt'), *v.* Dingtangata. **-ation,** *n.*
Affection (ăf-fĕk'-shŭn), *n.* Ka·saani, gisik nangani. **-ate,** *a.*
Affirm (ăf-fêrm'), *v.* Bebe ine agana. **-ation,** *n.*
Affix (ăf-fĭks'), *v.* (af'-fiks) *n.* On·dapa, ritchua, bon·kamao on·dapa, nangrimatdapa. **-ture,** *n.*
Afflict (ăf-flĭkt'), *v.* Duk on·a, duk on·chaa. **-ion,** *n.*
Afford (ăf-fōrd'), *v.* On·a, on·na bil gnang.

Afloat (ā-flōt'), *adv.* Gitchoa, balboa.
Afraid (ā-frād'), *a.* Kena.
After (ăft'ĕr), *pr.* Ja·mano.
Afternoon (aft'-ĕr-nụn'), *n.* Saljatchi paksa, atamgrochibara.
Afterward (âft'-ĕr-wêrd), *adv.* Ja mano, unja·mano.
√**Again** (ā-gĕn'), *adv.* Tai, pil·e, pil·taie, aro changsa.
Against (ā-gĕnst'), *pr.* Nangtinga, nangchaka, nangchapa, mikkangchaka, matnanga, champenga.
Age (āj), *n.* Tangani bilsi; bang·a bilsirangni tong·sa, chasong, bilsi bang·gipa. **-d,** *a.*
Agency (ā'-jen-sy), *n.* Ejentni kam.
Agent (ā'-jĕnt), *n.* Sakgipjnna kamko dakgipa.
Aggress (ăg-grĕs'), *v.* Chilchenga, pe·chenga.
Aggressive (ăg-grĕs'-sĭv), *a.* Chilchenggipa, pa·chenggipa.
Agile (ă'-jĭl), *a.* Bilchrokgipa, gong·rakgipa.
Agility (å-jĭl'-ĭ-ty), *n.* Ta·rakani, gong·rakani.
Agitate (ăj'-ĭ-tāt), *v.* Moata, tom·tomgija dakata. **-ion,** *n.* **-or,** *n.*
Agnostic (ăg-nŏs'-tĭk), *n.* Uijasranggipa, nastik.
Ago (ā-gō'), *adv.* Re·anggimin, batanggimin somoi.
Agony (ăg'-o-ny), *n.* Be·en ba gisikni saknaa.
Agree (ā-grē'), *v.* Ku·monga, ku·cholsan ong·a, ku·rachaka.
Agreeable (ā-grē'-å b'l), *a.* Name nikatani, kusi ong·atani. **-ably,** *adv.*

Agreement (å-grē′-mĕnt), *n.* Ku·rachakgrikani.
Aground (å-ground′), *adv.* A·ao nangtinga.
Ague (ā′-gū), *n.* Sawaka saa, sin·e be·en til·tile saa.
Aid (ād), *v.* Dakchaka, *n.*
Ail (āl), *v.* Saa, saknako man·a. **-mĕnt,** *n.*
Aim (ām), *v.* Mangsonga, nisan ka·a, *n.*
Air (âr), *n.* Bal, a·pal bangbang ; gitni sul ; mikim.
Aisle (īl), *n.* Giljao samtangtang asongchakani riting gisepni rama.
Ajar (å-jär′), *adv.* Samsa oa, oketchia.
Alarm (å-lärm′), *v.* Kenata, kenaniko uiata. **-ist,** *n.*
Alas (å-lȧs′), *int.* Himangai, skimani kata.
Alcohol (ăl′-ko-hŏl), *n.* Chuni ja·pång, chu ma·sa.
Alike (å-līk′), *a. adv.* Gita, apsan.
Alive (å-līv′), *a.* Tangenggipa, janggi gnang.
All (ôl), *a.* Pilak gimik.
Alligator (ăl′-lĭ-gā-tĕr), *n.* Aringga.
Allow (ăl-lou′), *v.* On·a, ku·rachaka. **-ance,** *n.*
Alloy (ăl-loi′), *v.* Brine gamchatako komiata, *n.*
Allure (ăl-lūr′), *v.* Kimala, gisikko sala. **-mĕnt,** *n.*
Ally (ăl-lī′), *v.* Nangrimata, bakrima, *n.*
Almanac (ôl′mȧ-năk), *n.* Ponjika.
Almighty (ôl-mīt′-y), *a.* Bilakbegipa, pilak bilni nokgipa.
Alms (ämz), *n.* Ka·sae on·ani.
Aloft (å-lŏft′), *adv.* Chuuo.
Alone (å-lōn′), *a.* Sasan, saksan.
Along (å-lŏng′), *adv. pr.* Joljol.
Aloud (å-loud′), *adv.* Rake, gam·e.
Already (ôl-rĕd′-y), *adv.* Da·on metchota, ong·angmanaha, dakmanaha ; da·oba.
Also (ôl′so), *adv.* Aro, ba, aroba.
Altar (ôl′-tĕr), *n.* Ganchi.
Alter (ôl′-tĕr), *v.* Dingtangata. **-ation,** *n.*
Alternate (ăl′-tĕr-nat), *v.* Pala bodol daka, pala· aree daka. *a. n.* **-ion,** *n.*
Although (ôl-THō′), *conj.* Oba.
Altitude (ăl′-tĭ-tūd), *n.* Chuani.
Altogether (ôl-tụ-gĕTH′ĕr), *adv.* Damsan.
Alum (ăl′-ŭm), *n.* Pitkiri.
Aluminium (ăl′-u-mĭn′-ĭ-ŭm), *n.* Sil ma·sa.
Always (ôl′-wāz), *adv.* Pangnan.
Am (ăm), *v.* WAS, BEEN. Ong·a.
Amaze (å-māz′), *v.* Aiao inata, dil·dil ong·ata. **-ment,** *n.*
Ambition (ăm-bĭsh′-ŭn), *n.* Chuna skani. **-ous,** *a.*
Ambuscade (ăm-bŭs-kād′) *n.* Timani biap.
Ambush (ăm′-bụsh), *n.* Timani biap.
Amiable (ā′-mĭ-å-b'l), *a.* Ka·sana kraa.
Amid (å-mĭd′), *pr.* Jatchio.
Amiss (å-mĭs′), *a. adv.* Namgija daka, dos daka.
Ammunition (ăm-mū-nĭsh′-ŭn), *n.* Dakgrikani guli barutrang.
Among (å-mŭng′), *pr.* Gisep.
Amount (å-mount′), *n.* Gimik.
Ample (ăm′-p'l), *a.* Chu·onga.
Amplify (ăm-plĭ-fy), *v.* Dak·ata.

Amputate (ăm′-pu-tāt), *v.* Be·-enni bakko rasota. **-ion**, *n.*
Amuse (å-mūz′), *v.* Kusi ong·-ata. **-mĕnt**, *n.*
An (ăn), *art.* Sako mesoka.
Analysis (å-năl′-ĭ-sĭs), *n.* Bakrangko dingtang dingtang dake mesokani.
Analyze (ăn′-å-līz), *v.* Bakrangko dingtang dingtang dake mesoka.
Anarchy (ăn′-ärk-y), *n.* Golmal dakani, rajani kosako chakatani, sason gri ong·ani.
Ancestor (ăn′-sĕs-têr), *n.* Ma·-gitcham, pagitcham.
Anchor (ăng-kêr), *n.* Siltin, *v.*
Ancient (ān′-shent), *a.* Skang chasongni.
And (ănd), *conj.* Aro.
Anew (å-nū′), *adv.* Pil·e, pil·taie.
Angel (ān′-jĕl), *n.* Salgini sa·gre.
Anger (ăng′-gêr), *n.* Ka·o-nangani.
Angle (ăng′-g′l), *n.* Ki·tik, lain ge·gnini ekgrikani.
Angle (ăng-g′l′, *v* Milsi pia. r, *n.*
Angry (ăng′-gry), *a.* Ka·o nanga, ka·o nanga gnang.
Anguish (ăng′-gwĭsh), *n.* Saknabeani.
Animal (ăn′-ĭ-mal), *n.* Janggi gnanggipa, *pl.* matrang.
Animate (ăn′-ĭ-māt), *v.* Tangata, an·saoata. **-ion**, *n.*
Ankle (ăng′-k′l), *n.* Ja·mik, ja·-gitok.
Anklet (ăng′-klĕt), *n.* Ja·gitoko gananı, ja·srang.
Annex (ăn-nĕks′), *v.* Nangdimatdapa. **-ation**, *n.*
Anniversary (ăn-nĭ-vêr′-sâry), *n.* Bilsianti soktaia sal.
Announce (ăn-nouns′), *v.* Parakata, uiata. **-mĕnt**, *n.*
Annoy (ăn-noi′), *v.* Jajrongata, dongtogija dakata, **-ance**, *n.*
Annual (ăn-u-al), *a.* Bilsiantini, bilsisani.
Anoint (å-noint′), *v.* To rudapa, to nongata.
Another (ăn-ŭth-êr), *a.* Gipin, dingtang, sákgipin.
Answer (ăn′-sêr), *v.* Aganchaka.
Ant (ănt), *n.* Chibrim ajengjo pilakan.
Antecedent (ăn-te-sēd′-ent), *a.* Skanggipa, re·sogipa, ong·so-gipa.
Antelope (ăn′-te-lōp), *n.* Matrong.
Antidote (ăn′-tĭ-dōt), *n.* Bisiko gimatgipa sam.
Antipathy (ăn-tĭp′-å-thy), *n.* Namnikgijani, mitchiani.
Antiquity (ăn-tĭk′-wĭ-ty), *n.* Skangni salrang.
Antler (ănt′-lêr), *n.* Matchok grongni bipek.
Anvil (ăn′-vĭl), *n.* Silkam.
Anxiety (ăng-zī′-e-ty), *n.* Jajrenganı, sinteani.
Anxious (ăngk′-shŭs), *a.* Jajrenggipa, sintegipa.
Any (ĕn′-y), *a.* Jeba, mamung.
Apart (å-pärt′), *adv.* Dingtang, ma·eka.
Apartment (å-pärt′-ment), *n.* Kuturi, nokdring.
Ape (āp), *n.* Huro aro ugita ki·me grigipa chadenge re·-gipa makreni jat pilakkon ape minga.
Ape (āp), *v.* Sninga.
Apiece (å-pēs′), *adv.* Sakantina, bakantina.
Apostle (å-pŏs′-s′l), *n.* Watata, sninggipa.

Appall (ăp-pôl'), *v.* Kenatbea, jagokata.
Apparel (ăp-păr'-ĕl), *n.* Ganding chinding.
Apparent (ăp-pâr'-ent), *a.* Nikchachaa gita.
Appeal (ăp-pēl'), *v.* Apil ka·a, sakgipinna bichal ka·china mol·mola, ba dakchakako bi·a.
Appear (ăp-pēr'), *v.* Nikata, parak ong·ata. **-ance,** *n.*
Appease (ăp-pēz'), *v.* Tom·tomata, namnikata. **-ment,** *n.*
Append (ăp-pĕnd'), *v.* On·dapa, nangdimata. **-age,** *n.*
Appetite (ăp'-pe-tīt), *n.* Okriani, cha·na skani.
Applaud (ăp-plôd'), *v.* Mitele jakpa doka ba inchroa.
Applause (ăp-plôz'), *n.* Mitelani, chuatani.
Apple (ăp'-p'l), *n.* Bol bite ma·sa, apple bite.
Apply (ăp-plī'), *v.* Dona, a·tangko on·a. **-iance,** *n.* **-ication,** *n.*
Appoint (ăp-point'), *v.* Dona, tik ka·a. **-mĕnt,** *n.*
Approach (ăp-prōch'), *n.* Sepangona re·baa.
Approve (ăp-prųv'), *v.* Mikchara, namnika, ra·chaka. **-al,** *n.*
April (ā'-pril), *n.* Bilsini brigipa ja.
Apron (ā'-pĕrn ba ā'-prŭn), *n.* Mikkangchi gandapani ba·ra.
Apt (ăpt), *a.* Kraa, dakninga, ong·naba donga, ong·ninga. **-itūde,** *n.*
Aqueduct (ăk'-we-dŭkt), *n.* Dongge, boi.
Arable (ăr'-å-b'l), *a.* Gamna kraa.
Arc (ärk), *n.* Dulni tong·a.
Arch (ärch), *n.* Kosakchi gongdole rikgimin.
Architect (är'-kĭ-tĕkt), *n.* Maidake rikgen uko daksogipa.
Ardent (är'-dĕnt), *a.* Gisik ding·gipa, an·saogipa.
Ardour (är'-dĕr), *n.* An·saoani.
Arduous (är'-du-ŭs), *a.* Dakna ambreja, neng·ani, rakani.
Are (är), *v.* WERE, BEEN. Ong·a.
Area (ā'-re-å), *n.* Arini ning·o donggipa biap kakket.
Argue (är'gū), *v.* Jegrika, ja·pangko mesoka. **-mĕnt,** *n.*
Arise (å-rīz'), *v.* Chåkata, uakata.
Arithmetic (å-rĭth'-me-tĭk), *n.* Chananiko uiani.
Ark (ärk), *n.* Ring nokma; sinduk.
Arm (ärm), *n.* Jakpong.
Armour (är'-mĕr), *n.* Champengna dondapani, silni gandapani.
Armpit (ärm'-pĭt), *n.* Påkkol.
Arms (ärmz), *n.* Silchidarerang.
Army (är'-my), *n.* Sipaini kotok.
Around (å-round'), *pr.* Samtangtangchi, dule.
Arouse (å-rouz'), *v.* De·mesaa, mikrakata.
Arrange (ăr-rānj'), *v.* Tarie dona, namedake dona. **-mĕnt,** *n.*
Array (ăr-rā'), *v.* Ganding chinding tarie nitoata.
Arrest (ăr-rĕst'), *v.* Rim·a, champenga, dondikata.
Arrive (ăr-rīv'), *v.* Soka. **-al,** *n.*
Arrow (ăr'-ro), *n.* Bra.
Art (ärt), *n.* Daka, rika aro ma·mantiko uiani ba changani.

Artery (är'-tĕr-y), *n.* Kan·-chokoniko an·chi jokatani ja·-dil.

Article (är'-tĭ-k'l), *n.* Bostu; a, an, the, iarangko article minga; mainiba gimin seani gimik.

As (ăz), *conj. adv.* Jekai, jedake, gita; miting.

Ascend (ăs-sĕnd'), *v.* Kosakchi doanga, gakata, doa. **-sion,** *n.*

Ascent (ăs-sĕnt'), *n.* Doangani, doani.

Ascertain (ăs-sĕr-tān'), *v.* Sandie uia, tik ka·a. **-ment,** *n.*

Ash (ăsh), *n.* Bol ma·sa.

Ashamed (ȧ-shāmd'), *a.* Kratcha·a.

Ashes (ăsh-ĕz), *n.* Tapra.

Aside (ȧ-sīd'), *adv.* Samsachi; mitino.

Ask (ȧsk), *v.* Singa, bi·a.

Asleep (ȧ-slēp'), *a.* Tusienga, tusimiting.

Aspire (ăs-pīr'), *v.* Chuna sikbea, man·na sikbea. **-ation,** *n.*

Ass (ȧs), *n.* Gada.

Assemble (ăs-sĕm'-b'l, *v.* Damsan tom·doka, chimonga.

Assembly (ăs-sĕm'bly), *n.* Tom·-dakgimin manderang.

Assent (ăs-sĕnt'), *v.* Ku·rachaka, namnika, oe ina.

Assert (ăs-sĕrt') *v.* Bebe ine agana. **-ion,** *n.*

Assess (ăs-sĕs') *v.* Gamchatako dona, kajana on·na nangata. **-mĕnt,** *n.*

Assign (ăs-sīn'), *v.* Dona, on·-skaa. **-ment,** *n.* **-ation,** *n.* **-ee,** *n.* **-or,** *n.*

Assist (ăs-sĭst'), *v.* Dakchaka. **-ance, -ănt,** *n.*

Associate (ăs-sō'-shĭ-āt), *n.* Ripeng nangrimgipa.

Association (ăs-sō-shĭ-ā'-shŭn basĭ-ā'-shŭn), *v.* Tom·daka, soba ka·a.

Assuage (ăs-swāj'), *v.* Saknaa, duk, ba ka·o nangako namata ba komiata.

Assure (ȧ-shur'), *v.* Ka·dongata, uiata. **-ance,** *n.*

Astonish (ăs-tŏn'-ĭsh), *v.* Aiao inata, dil·dil ong·ata. **-ment,** *n.*

Astound (ăs-tound'), *v.* Jagokata.

Astray (ȧ-strā'), *adv.* Branga.

Astride (ȧ-strīd'), *adv.* Ja·pak sepe asonga.

Astronomy (ăs-trŏn'-o-my), *n.* Sal, ja, askirangko uiani.

Asunder (ȧ-sŭn'-dĕr), *adv.* Stonga, den·tonga.

At (ăt), *pr.* Sepang, o.

Atlas (ăt'-lăs), *n.* Mapni ki·tap.

Atmosphere (ăt'-mŏs-fēr), *n.* Bal.

Atone (ȧ-tōn'), *v.* Nangrimata, nanmikata. **-mĕnt,** *n.*

Attach (ăt-tăch'), *v.* Kaa, kadapa, ma·gapa. **-mĕnt,** *n.*

Attack (ăt-tăk'), *v.* Rim·a, chaa, *n.*

Attain (ăt-tān'), *v.* Soka, chu·-soka, man·a. **-mĕnt,** *n.*

Attempt (ăt-tĕmpt'), *v.* Joton ka·a.

Attend (ăt-tĕnd'), *v.* Gisik on·a; dongpaa, re·paa; mania, knatima; dangdike on·a. **-ance,** *n.* **-ant,** *a.*

Attention (ăt-tĕn'-shŭn), *n.* Gisik on·ani, mikrakani.

Attire (ăt-tīr'), *v.* Ganat chinata, *n.* ganding chinding.

Attract (ăt-trăkt'), *v.* Sala, mikbokata. **-ion,** *n.* **-ive,** *a.*

Auction (ôk'-shŭn), *v.* Ilam ka·a. **-eer**, *n.* ilam ka·gipa.
Audible (ô'-dĭ-b'l), *a.* Knana man·gipa.
Audience (ô'-dĭ-*ens*), *n.* Knatimgipa jinma.
Auger (ô'-gêr), *n.* Puani bolma.
August (ô'-gŭst), *n.* Bilsini chetgipa ja.
Aunt (änt), *n.* Ma·detang, ma·jongtang, manitang.
Author (ô'thêr), *n.* A·bachengatgipa, ong·atgipa, ki·tapko dakgipa.
Authority (ô-thŏr'-ĭ-ty), *n.* Bil, bil gnangani, nokgipa ong·ani.
Autumn (ô'-tŭm), *n.* September, October aro November, ia ja gitam.
Avarice (ăv'-å-rĭs), *n.* Mikbokani, man·na skani.
Avenge (å-vĕnj'), *v.* Sasti on·skaa.
Average (ăv'-êr-aj), *n.* Gimikna suale apsan dakgimin, *a.*
Avoid (å-void'), *v.* Geela. **-ance**, *n.*
Await (å-wāt'), *v.* Sengsoa, nichaksoa.
Awake (å-wāk'), *v.* Mikraka.
Away (å-wā'), *adv.* Ang, gipinchi, chel·ao.
Awful (ô'-fṳl), *a.* Kenbeani.
Awhile (å-whīl'), *adv.* On·tisa, dikdiksa, on·tisa sal.
Awkward (ôk'-wêrd), *a.* Changgijagipa.
Awl (ôl), *n.* Silsrok, puani sil.
Axe (ăks), *n.* Rua, bol den·ani.
Axis (ăks'-ĭs), *n.* Ga·brong, wilwilchakani.
Axle (ăks'l), *n.* Gari chakani wilwilchakgipa sil ba bol.
Azure (ăzh'-ṳr ba ā'-zhṳr), *a.* Tangsima.

B.

Babble (băb'-b'l), *v.* Bokboka, indin agana, ja·pang gri agana.
Babe (bāb), *n.* Bakgitchak, odek.
Baboon (băb-ṳn'), *n.* Dal·gipa makre ma·sa, huro.
Baby (bā'-by), *n.* Bakgitchak, odek.
Bachelor (băch'-e-lêr), *n.* Pante, jik kimkujagipa me·asa.
Back (băk), *n.* Janggil, nokil, nokkisang.
Backbone (băk'-bōn'), *n.* Janggilni bolgro.
Backside (băk'-sīd'), *n.* Janggilchi, ki·sangchi.
Backslide (băk'-slīd'), *v.* Isoloni chel·anga.
Backward (băk'-wêrd), *adv.* Ki·sangchi bitine, bikpile.
Bacon (bā'-k'n), *n.* Wak gran.
Bad (băd), *a.* Namja, namgija.
Bade (băd), *v.* Ge·etaha.
Badge (băj), *n.* Kamni ba mande ra·ako mesokna ganani chin.
Bag (băg), *n.* Dokra, mona.
Baggage (băg'-gaj), *n.* Boa ba ripeani boksa, mal.
Bail (bāl), *v.* Jamin chaka.
Bail (bāl), *n.* Balti ba ketilni jak rim·ani nabak; jamin, jaminchakgipa.
Bail (bāl), *v.* Ko·a, we·a, sata.
Bait (bāt), *n.* Milsio jotani al, kimalani al.
Bake (bāk), *v.* Chu·dapni ning·o gope song·a.
Balance (băl'-*ans*), *n.* Tochakani; bangki, teria ong·ani.
Bald (bôld), *n.* Kodarok, skoo kni gri.
Bale (bāl), *n.* Dal·bea katomgimin.

Ball (bôl), *n.* Tom·betgipa, bol, robol.
Bamboo (băm-bụ'), *n.* Wa·a.
Banana (bå-nä'-nå), *n.* Te·rik ma·sa.
Band (bănd), *n.* Kaani; maiba kamni gimin nangrimgimin manderang.
Bandage (băn'-daj), *n.* Kadapani ba·ra ro·dinggipa.
Bandit (băn'-dĭt), *n.* Dokprete ra·gipa.
Banish (băn'-ĭsh), *v.* Songchelachi a·rikata, rikgalata. **-mĕnt,** *n.*
Bang (băng), *n.* Sugaka, doka.
Bank (băngk), *n.* Tangka chimongani bank nok; dram, rikam.
Banyan tree (băn'-yan), *n.* Giting bol.
Baptism (băp'-tĭz'm), *n.* Napbolani.
Baptist (băp'-tĭst), *n.* Ma·malsa Kristian, A·chikrang gita.
Baptize (băp-tĭz'), *v.* Napbola, napbolata.
Bar (băr), *n.* Tekani, kang·ani, champengani; kachario ukilrangni jegrikani biap, asamini chadengani biap; sona ba rupani bitin dalgap.
Barb (bärb), *n.* Milsi, bra ba sel·uni sre ku·chot.
Barbarian (bär-bā'-rĭ-an), *n.* Uigijagipa, ka·saninggija jat.
Barber (bär'-bêr), *n.* Kni rokgipa, hajam, napit.
Bare (bâr), *a.* Pindapani gri, bangbang, nagande.
Barely (bâr'-ly), *adv.* Mangmang, mangmangari, jenten.
Bargain (bär'-gĕn), *n.* On·srena ba sregrikna ku·mongani.
Bark (bärk), *n.* Bol bigil; maljuri gitamgipa, jahat bi·sa; achakni sing·a.
Bark (bärk), *v.* Achak sing·a.
Barley (bär'-ly), *n.* Job mi, mi ma·sa.
Barn (bärn), *n.* Mi, misi, megap, aro matchu gurerangko donani nok.
Barrack (băr'-rak), *n.* Sipairangni lain.
Barrel (băr'-rĕl), *n.* Pipa.
Barren (băr'-rĕn), *a.* Banji, bite nanggijagipa.
Barrier (băr'-rĭ-ĕr), *n.* Champengani, dongpengani.
Barter (bär'-têr), *v.* Sregrika, badinga.
Base (bās), *n.* Ja·pang, pangchakani, ka·magipa, a·achina pangchakram.
Base (bās), *a.* Choligijagipa ong·sigipa.
Bashful (băsh'-fụl), *a.* Kratcha·ninggipa.
Basin (bā'-s'n), *n.* Slemsi, sorea, donchakani; chibol, chikong, a·dap.
Basket (bås'-kĕt), *n.* Kok, kera, toka.
Bat (băt), *n.* Do·bak; bolko dokani go·ol.
Bath (băth), *n.* Auani.
Bathe (bāth), *v.* Aua.
Battle (băt'-t'l), *n.* Sipairangni dakgrikani.
Bazar (bä-zär'), *n.* Anti, bajal.
Be (bē), *v.* WAS, BEEN, Ong·a.
Bead (bēd), *n.* Ripok.
Beak (bēk), *n.* Do·oni ku·sik.
Beam (bēm), *n.* Bilbang.
Beam (bēm), *v.* Tong·sua.
Bean (bēn), *n.* Olasi, ka·ick, iarang.
Bear (bâr), *n.* Maptil.

Bear (bâr), *v.* BORE, BORN ba BORNE, Ripea; chakeh ka; bite nangs; ba'a.
Beard (bērd), *n.* Ku'simang.
Beast (bēst), *n.* Matburung, ba jillani, janggi gnanggipa.
Beat (bēt), *v.* BEAT, BEATEN, Doka; chaa; ama.
Beautiful (bū'-ti-fụl), *a.* Nitoa, nitobea.
Beauty (bū'-ty), *n.* Nitoani.
Because (bē-kôz'), *conj.* Maina, ni giminn.
Beckon (bĕk'-k'n), *v.* Jakjipa, chin dakata.
Become (be-kŭm'), *v.* BECAME, BECOME, Ong'l an.
Bed (bĕd), *n.* Tuchakani, biap.
Bed-bug (bĕd'-bŭg), *n.* Ru'dat.
Bedstead (bĕd'-stĕd), *n.* Palang, tuani kat.
Bee (bē), *n.* Bija, bia.
Beef (bēf), *n.* Matchu be'en.
Beer (bēr), *n.* Chū ma'sa.
Beetle (bē'-t'l), *n.* Bokehit aro ugita kosako rakgipa grangchi pindapgipa jatrang.
Before (be-fōr'), *pr.* Skango, mikkango.
Beg (bĕg), *v.* Bi'ama, mol'mola.
Beggar (bĕg'-gêr), *n.* Bi'amgipa, bi'ame cha'gipa.
Begin (be-gin'), *v.* A'bachenga.
Begrudge (be-grŭj'), *v.* Gipinni gam man'ako mikron dal'a.
Beguile (bē-gīl'), *v.* Tol'napa, tol'napachi kimala. **-ment,** *n.*
Behalf (be-häf'), *n.* Gipinni a'sel daka, chakpaa.
Behave (be-hāv'), *v.* Dakronga, bewal gita daka.
Behaviour (be-hāv'-yụr), *n.* Dakani bewal.
Behead (be-hĕd'), *v.* Sko rasota, sko sota.
Behind (be-hīnd'), *pr.* Ki'sangchi, ki'sango.
Behold (be-hōld'), *v.* BEHELD, BEHELD, Nia, nibo.
Belief (be-lēf'), *n.* Bebe ra'ani.
Believe (be-lēv'), *v.* Bebe ra'a, ka'donga.
Belittle (be-lit'-t'l), *v.* Chonnika, chonnikata.
Bell (bĕl), *n.* Konta, bel, ganti.
Belle (bĕl), *n.* Mikkang nitogipa me'chik.
Bellows (bĕl'-lŭs), *n.* Mul, wa'al jipani.
Bellow (bĕl'-lo), *v.* Matchu gita mikoa.
Belly (bĕl-ly) *n.* Ok, bikma.
Belong (be-lŏng'), *n.* -ni ong'a.
Beloved (be-lŭvd'), *part.* (bē-lŭv'-ĕd), *a.* Ka'sako man'gipa.
Below (be-lō'), *adv.* Ka'mao, ka'machi, onbataó.
Belt (bĕlt), *n.* Katongani.
Bench (bĕnch), *n.* Asongchakani am'pok ro'gipa.
Bend (bĕnd), *n.* Gongdela, gonggua, dol'a.
Beneath (be-nēth'), *pr* Ning'o, ka'mao.
Benediction (bĕn'-e-dik'-shŭn), *n.* Patiani, namgniko aganani, mitelani.
Benefactor (bĕn'e-făk'-têr), *n.* Namgniko dakgipa, dakchakgipa.
Beneficence (be-nĕf'-i-sens), *n.* Gipinna dakchakani, namgniko dakani.
Beneficent (be-nĕf'-i-sent), *a.* Namgniko ong'atgipa.
Beneficial (bĕn'-e-fish'-al), *a.* Namgniko ong'atgni.
Benefit (bĕn'-e-fit), *n.* Namgni.
Benevolent (be-nĕv'-o-lent), *a.* Namgniko dakna sikgipa, ka'sachakgipa.

Berry (bĕr′-ry), *n.* Miskuri, aro ugita chongipa nom·gipa biterang.
Beseech (be-sēch′), *v.* BESOUGHT, BESOUGHT, Bi·a, mol·-mola.
Beset (be-sĕt′), *v.* Champeng-dula, jajrengata. **-ment,** *n.*
Beside (be-sīd′), *pr.* Sepango, sambao; *adv.* bate, agre.
Besiege (be-sēj′), *v.* Champeng-du'a.
Best (bĕst), *a.* Nambata, nambatsranga.
Bestow (be-stō′), *v.* On·a. **-al,** *n.* **-ment,** *n.*
Bet (bĕt), *n.* Aramaria, bajimaria.
Betelnut (bē′-t'l-nŭt), *n.* Gue, supari.
Betimes (be-tīmz′), *adv.* Seng·-gnang.
Betray (be-trā′) *v.* Nampinike on·a.- **al,** *n.*
Betroth (be-trŏth′), *v.* Bia ka·na tik ka·a, bondobosto ka·a. **-al,** *n.* **-ment,** *n.*
Better (bĕt′-têr), *a.* Namkala, nambata.
Between (be-twēn′), *pr.* Gisepo, jatchio.
Betwixt (be-twĭkst′) *pr.* Gisepo, jatchio.
Beverage (bĕv′-êr-aj), *n.* Ringani.
Bewail (be-wāl′), *v.* Grapo kalima.
Beware (be-wâr), *v.* Gisik rakbo, mikrakbo.
Bewilder (be-wĭl′-dêr), *v.* Bingbangata, jajaata. **-mĕnt,** *n.*
Bewitch (be-wĭch′), *v.* Mani nangata, mikmalata. **-ment,** *n.*
Beyond (be-yŏnd′) *pr.* Nalsachi.
Bible (bī′-b'l), *n.* Torom sastro, Isolni ki·tap.
Bicycle (bī′-si-k'l), *n.* Chakagnigipa ja·achi re·atgipa gari.
Bid (bĭd), *v.* BADE, BIDDEN, On·-gen ine inata; ge·eta; okama. **-dêr,** *n.* -gipa.
Big (bĭg), *a.* Da·a.
Bigamy (bĭg′-ă-my), *n.* Sakgniko kimani.
Bile (bīl), *n.* Ka·kit.
Bill (bĭl) *n.* On·a nangarangko mesoke seani leka.
Bill (bĭl), *n.* Do·oni ku·sik.
Billion (bĭl′-yŭn), *n.* Amerika songo koti ritchasako billion minga, England songo kotian ritchasa hajalkosa billion minga.
Billow (bĭl′-lo), *n.* A·bri gita romtomgipa sagalni chipakore.
Bin (bĭn), *n.* Mi donani jam, bandal.
Bind (bīnd), *v.* FOUND, BOUND, Kaa.
Biped (bī′-pĕd), *n.* Ja·a samgnigipa.
Bird (bêrd), *n.* Do·o.
Birth (bêrth), *n.* Atchiani, mikkang nikani.
Biscuit (bĭs′-kĭt), *n.* Rakgipa ruti ma·sa, biskut.
Bisect (bi-sĕkt′), *v.* Apsan bakgni daka, ba apsangrik bakgni daka.
Bishop (bĭsh′-ŭp), *n.* Toromko skigipani pamong.
Bit (bĭt), *n.* Chonbea tong, chong·diksa; bolma chongipa; gure ku·siko chikapatgipa lagamni sil.
Bitch (bĭch), *n.* Achak jatranggni bima.

Bite (bīt), *v.* BIT, BITTEN, Chika.
Bitter (bĭt′-têr), *a.* Ka·a.
Black (blăk), *a.* Gisim, sima.
Blacksmith (blăk′-smĭth′), *n.* Sil dakgipa kamal.
Bladder (blăd′-dêr), *n.* Su·bu-tip.
Blade (blād), *n.* Bimik, rang-kogipa bijak; matgipa sil.
Blame (blām), *n.* Matnan-gani.
Bland (blănd), *a.* Ka·sina, rin-oka.
Blank (blănk), *a.* Sea grigipa, bangbang.
Blanket (blăn-kĕt), *n.* Kombol.
Blaspheme (blăs-fēm′), *v.* Isol-ko kal·stapa. **-y**, *n.*
Blast (blăst), *n.* Balwa ta·raka, begul ba singga sikani tong·-sa; barut goani.
Blaze (blāz), *v.* Wal·chaa, ching·chaa, *n.*
Bleach (blēch), *v.* Bokata, ko-bokata.
Bleat (blēt), *v.* Do·bok ba mesni mikoa.
Bleed (blēd), BLED, BLED, *v.* An·-chi ong·a.
Blend (blĕnd), *v.* Brina, brinata.
Bless (blĕs), *v.* Patia, mitela, rasong chaata.
Blind (blīnd), *a.* Mikgri.
Blindfold (blīnd′-fōld), *v.* Mik-ron katipa.
Blink (blĭngk), *v.* Mikjapa, mikelsi dake nia.
Bliss (blĭs), *n.* An·sengani, kusi ong·ani, katchaani.
Blister (blĭs′-têr), *n.* Tapinga, chibila.
Bloat (blōt), *v.* Boa, gangbua, sapinga.
Block (blŏk), *n.* Dotsa, tong·sa, chong·diksa.
Block (blŏk), *v.* Champenga, chipchanga, donpenga.
Blockade (blŏk-ād′), *v.* Cham-penga, chipchanga, donpenga.
Blockhead (blŏk′-hĕd), *n.* Goka-ong·gipa, gisik grigipa.
Blood (blŭd), *n.* An·chi.
Bloodhound (blŭd′-hound), *n.* Chikrakgipa achak ma·sa.
Bloodshot (blŭd′-shŏt), *a.* An·-chi kama.
Bloom (blụm), *v.* Balgawa, bala.
Blossom (blŏs′-sŭm), *n.* Bibal, pul.
Blot (blŏt), *v.* Daknanga; ipaka; kaliko ran·ata, chipata.
Blow (blō), *v.* BLEW, BLOWN, Spoa, jipa, bala, sika.
Blow (blō) *n.* Dokani; bibal balani.
Blue (blū), *a.* Tangsima.
Blunder (blŭn′-dêr), *n.* Simsak-gija gisikgrini gualani.
Blunt (blŭnt), *a.* Matgija, bin·a, boda changa.
Blur (blêr), *v.* Mrikmrak dak-ata.
Blush (blŭsh), *v.* Kratcha·e mik-kang gitchaka.
Boar (bōr), *n.* Wak bipa.
Board (bōrd), *n.* Tokta, bol-pleng.
Board (bōrd), *v.* Damko on·e miko cha·a; tangka ra·e cha·-aniko on·a.
Boast (bōst), *v.* Gaora de·e agana, rasong chae agana.
Boat (bōt), *n.* Ring.
Body (bŏd′-y), *n.* Be·en, bi-mang.
Bog (bŏg), *n.* A·bel, chibol.
Boil (boil), *n.* Gitot mina.
Boil (boil), *v.* Rita, song·a, chi-chara, bokbaka.

Boisterous (bois'-têr-ŭs), *a.* Gam·bee agangipa; ta·rakgipa.

Bold (bōld), *a.* Ka·donggipa, ka·sokgipa, kengijagipa.

Boll (bōl), *n.* Bitchri ra·chakram, kil bite.

Bolt (bōlt), *n.* Tekani, tekani sil.

Bombard (bŏm-bärd'), *v.* Topchi goa. **-ment,** *n.*

Bond (bŏnd), *n.* Kaani, ku·rachakani; tangka ra·chakako see on·ani leka.

Bondage (bŏnd'-aj), *n.* Nokol gita ong·ani.

Bondsman (bŏndz'-man), *n.* Jamin on·gipa.

Bone (bōn), *n.* Greng.

Bonnet (bŏn'-nĕt), *n.* Memrangni tupi ma·sa, ku·dipechi kaani donggipa.

Bonny (bŏn'-ny), *n* Nitogipa, milgipa, kusi ong·gipa.

Booby (bụ'-by), *n.* Goka, mamungkoba uigijagipa, do·o ma·sa.

Book (bụk), *n.* Ki·tap.

Boot (bụt), *n.* Ro·gipa juta, but.

Booth (bụth), *n.* Borang, jamdap, nok bi·sa.

Booty (bụt'-y), *n.* Ra·seke ra·gimin gam.

Borax (bō'răks), *n.* Suaka.

Border (bôr'-dêr), *n.* Sima, ari, simana, rikam.

Bore (bōr), *v.* A·kol pua, su·pua.

Born (bôrn), *v.* Atchigimin, atchiaha; *bearko nibo.*

Borrow (bŏr'-ro), *v.* Ra·chaka, sroa.

Bosom (bụz'-ŭm), *n.* Ka·bak.

Boss (bŏs), *n.* Ge·etgipa, kamko nitimgipa.

Both (bōth), *a.* Gnian, ge·gnian.

Bother (bŏTH'-êr), *v.* Golmal dakata, peng·pangata. **-ation,** *n.*

Bottle (bŏt'-t'l), *n.* Botol.

Bottom (bŏt'-tŭm), *n.* Mainiba onbatgipa ba ka·machini lak, ja·pang, ki·tik.

Bough (bou), *n.* Bolni cheksi.

Bound (bound), *v.* Tang·doa, tang·data, tang·pila bilchroka.

Boundary (bound'-â-ry), *n.* Sima, ari, simana.

Bounteous (boun'-te-ŭs), *a.* On·e cha·gipa, on·rakgipa.

Bountiful (boun'-tĭ-fụl), *a.* On·e cha·gipa, on·rakgipa.

Bow (bō), *n.* Chri.

Bow (bou), *v.* Olakia, gonggonga, bamgopa.

Bowels (bou'-ĕls), *n.* Bibikrang.

Bowl (bōl), *n.* Piala ba bati dal·gipa, serea.

Box (bŏks), *n.* Bakos, bakso.

Box (bŏks) *v.* Jaktome doka, satkapa.

Boy (boi), *n.* Me·a bi·sa.

Brace (brās) *n.* Singchakani.

Bracelet (brās'-lĕt), *n.* Jaksan.

Bracket (brăk'-ĕt), *n.* Maikoba skena pakmao rakatgipa bol ba sil; [ ] iakoba bracket minga.

Brag (brăg), *v.* Rasong chae, agana. **-gart,** *n.*

Brain (brān), *n.* Taning, kotaning.

Bramble (brăm-b'l), *n.* Bu·su granggipa, bol bi·sa.

Bran (brăn), *n.* Ginde.

Branch (brânch), *n.* Cheksi.

Brandish (brăn'-dish), *n.* Tonu-al ba churichi wingwanga.

Brandy (brăn'-dy), *n.* Chu ma·sa, barandi.

Brass (brâs), *n.* Sil ma·sa, pitolni sil. **-y,** *adv.*

Brave (brāv), *a.* Ka·donggipa, ka·sokgipa, kengijagipa. **-ry,** *n.*

Brazen (brā'-z'n), *a.* Pitolniko daka.

Bray (brā), *n.* Gadani mikoa, *v.*

Breach (brēch), *n.* Naponga, kolgipu.

Bread (brĕd), *n.* Ruti, pita; cha·ani.

Breadth (brĕdth), *n.* Gipeng.

Break (brāk), *v.* BROKE, BROKEN, Bē·a, be·ata, dingtangata. **-age,** *n.*

Breakfast (brĕk'-fast), *n.* Mepring, pringo cha·ani.

Breast (brĕst), *n.* Chef, ka·bak, sok.

Breath (brĕth), *n.* Rang·sitani bal.

Breathe (brēTH), *v.* Rang·sita, ka·spea.

Breech (brēch ba brĭch), *n* Ki·-sangchipak; ja·pang; slaini kunda.

Breeches (brĭch'-ĕz), *n.* Ja·skuona sokgipa pantaloon.

Breed (brēd), *v.* BRED, BRED, De atchiata, bi·sako ba·e ba pe·e alduo dal·ata, pe·ata.

Breeze (brēz), *n.* Ka·singipa balsrisri balgipa bal. **-y,** *a.*

Brethren (brĕTH'-rĕn), *n.* Jongadarang.

Brewery (brṳ'-ĕr-y), *n.* Chu dakani nok.

Brew-house (brṳ'-hous), *n.* Chu dakani nok.

Bribe (brīb), *n.* Ku·mutu, *v.* Ku·mutu on·a.

Brick (brĭk), *n.* It, ita.

Bride (brīd), *n.* Namchik gital, gital kimgipa me·chik. **-al,** *a.*

Bridegroom (brīd'-grṳm') *n.* Chawari gital, gital kimgipa me·asa.

Bridge (brĭj), *n.* Jang·rang, jal·ang,

Bridle (brī'-d'l), *n.* Gureni lagam.

Brief (brēf), *a.* Kan dika.

Brier (brī'-ĕr), *n.* Bu·su chagipa boldim.

Brigade (brĭ-gād'), *n.* Hajal gni ba una bate donggipa sipaini kotok.

Bright (brīt), *a.* Ching·a, seng·a.

Brilliant (brĭl'-yant), *a.* Ching·-chet ching·chet daka, ching·-bea, rong·chingbea. **-ance,** *n.*

Brim (brĭm), *n.* Riking.

Brimstone (brĭm'-stōn), *n.* Gondok.

Brindled (brĭn'-d'led), *a.* Brin brin.

Brine (brīn), *n.* Kari nanggipa chi.

Bring (brĭng), *v.* BROUGHT, BROUGHT, Ra·baa.

Brink (brĭnk), *n.* Dram chugipani rikam.

Bristle (brĭs'-s'l), *n.* Wak ba ugitani rakgipa kimil.

British (brĭt'-ĭsh), *a.* England songni.

Brittle (brĭt'-t'l), *a.* Srama, be·ninga.

Broad (brôd), *a.* Apala.

Broad-cloth (brôd'-klŏth), *n.* Banat, kimilni ba·ra.

Broil (broil), *v.* Wa·alo anga; jegrika, saigrika.

Broke (brōk), *v.* Be·aha; *break-ko nibo.*

Bronze (brŏnz ba brōnz), *n* Rang aro tama bringipa sil.

Brooch (brōch), *n.* Ka·bako ganani nitogipa pin.

Brood (brṳd), *v.* Bitchini kosako bama, *n.* Do·o sadipil.

Brook (brụk), *n.* Chiring.
Broom (brụm), *n.* Nok itrokani, sel·a.
Broth (broth), *n.* Me·chi, bitchi.
Brother (brŭTH'-êr), *n.* Jonggipa ba adatang.
Brother-in-law (brŭTH'-êr-ĭn-lô'), *n.* Boningtang, gumetang, sadutang, aro mosatang.
Brow (brou), *n.* Miksimang, miksikim; a·brini ku·chot.
Brown (broun), *a.* Gitchakmrang.
Bruise (brụz), *n.* Onjeta, matskoka, taprapa.
Brush (brŭsh), *n.* Burus; den·gimin cheksi chongiparang. *v.* Itroka, dokponga.
Brutal (brụ'-tal), *a.* Matburungrang gita ka·saninggijagipa. **-ity**, *n.* **-ize**, *v.*
Brute (brụt), *n.* Matburung, matburung gita ka·saninggijagipa. **-ish**, *a.*
Bubble (bŭb'-b'l), *n.* Chi do·chi dakgipa ka·spu rongprak.
Buck (bŭk), *n.* Do·bok, mes, matchok ba makgichak bipa.
Bucket (bŭk'-ĕt) *n.* Chi ko·chakani bolni baltin.
Buckle (bŭk'-k'l), *n.* Rakgrikatani sil, bakil.
Buckwheat (bŭk'-hwēt), *n.* Mi ma·sa.
Bud (bŭd) *n.* Manchoka, chong·kaa.
Buffalo (bŭf'-fâ-lō), *n.* Matma.
Bug (bŭg), *n.* Ru·dat, jo·ong.
Buggy (bŭg'-gy), *n.* Gurechi salgipa bagi gari.
Bugle (bū'-g'l), *n.* Begul, singga, adil.
Build (bĭld), *v.* BUILT, Rika.
Building (bĭld'-ing), *n.* Rikgimin nok.
Bulb (bŭlb), *n.* Tom·betgipa ja·dil.
Bulky (bŭl'-ky), *a.* Bimang dal·a.
Bull (bụl), *n* Matchu bipa.
Bulldog (bụl'-dŏg'), *n.* Matchu bipani sko gita sko dakgipa achak.
Bullet (bụl'-lĕt), *n.* Guli.
Bullfrog (bụl'-frŏg'), *n.* Gonggang, beng·blok dal·gipa.
Bullion (bụl'-yŭn'), *n.* Sona ba rupani bitin dotgimik.
Bullock (bụl'-lŭk), *n.* Matchu bolot.
Bump (bŭmp), *v.* Chagaka, chatinga, *n.* Chagakani, chatingani.
Bun (bŭn), *n.* Ruti ma·sa.
Bunch (bŭnch), *n.* Chokchim, katom.
Bundle (bŭn'-d'l), *n.* Katom, boksa.
Buoy (bwoi ba boi), *n.* Maiba chinko mesokna ba jahat kana chi ning·chi kae dongimin kosako balbogipa. **-ant**, *a.* **-ancy**, *n.* balboani, ritchengani, gitchoani.
Burden (bêr'-d'n), *n.* Bal, boja.
Burial (bĕr'-rĭ-al), *n.* Gopani.
Burial-ground (bĕr'-rĭ-al-ground'), *n.* Gopram, kobor kana.
Burn (bêrn), *v.* Kama, so·a.
Burrow (bŭr'-ro), *n.* Sapau ba ugita chongipa matburungrangni a·kol.
Burst (bêrst), *v.* BURST, BURST, Breta, goa.
Bury (bĕr'-ry), *v.* Gopa.
Bush (bụsh), *n.* Boldim, bol bi·sa.

Bushel (bush'el), *n.* Tik ka·gimin toani, merong muansamang chakgipa toka.
Bushy (bush'-y), *a.* Sombraa, chamila.
Busily (bĭz'-zĭ-ly), *adv.* Jakgitchagija ong·e.
Business (bĭz'-nĕs), *n.* Kam, a·sel.
Bust (bŭst) *n.* Ro·ongko mande dake cheltongdipet sol·gimiu.
Bustle (bŭs'-s'l), *v.* Skel bakel, sket baket, sketsketdaka.
Busy (bĭz'-zy), *a.* Kam ka·enggipa, kam ka·ronggipa.
Butcher (buch'-êr), *n.* Be·enko palna so·otgipa.
But (bŭt), *conj.* Indiba.
Butler (bŭt'-lêr), *n.* Kansama, mi on·timgipa.
Butt (bŭt), *v.* Kea.
Butt (bŭt), *n.* Ja·pangchini, ja·ta ; pipa.
Butter (bŭt'têr), *n.* Makkon. -y, *n.* makkonko donchakram.
Butterfly (bŭt'-têr-flī'), *n.* Me·pilip.
Buttermilk (bŭt'-têr-mĭlk') *n.* Makkon ra·mano dongrikgipa sok.
Buttock (bŭt'-tŭk), *n.* Ki·sangte.
Button (bŭt'-t'n), *n.* Butam, gudam.
Buttonhole (bŭt'-t'n-hōl'), *n.* Gudam tekani a·kol.
Buy (bi), *v.* BOUGHT, BOUGHT, Brea.
Buzz (bŭz), *v.* Ongonga, engenga, *n.* bijani mikoa.
By (bi), *pr.* Chi ; sepango, sambao.
By-and-by, *adv.* On·tisani ja·mano, tango, rutgijan.

C.

Cab (kăb), *n.* Chakagnigipa gari.
Cabbage (kăb'-baj), *n.* Kobi, me·su ma·sa.
Cabin (kăb'-in), *n.* Jahatni kuturi, nok bi·sa.
Cable (kā'-b'l) *n.* Budu dal·gipa, silni budu.
Cackle (kăk'-k'l), *v.* Do·bimani gogoteka.
Cactus (kăk'-tŭs), *n.* Su·che dal·gipa masa.
Cage (kāj), *n*, Gring, nol, kacha.
Cake (kāk), *n.* Chi·gipa cha·ani, ruti ma·sa.
Calamity (kă-lăm'-ĭ-ty), *n.* Duk, apod. **-itous**, *a.*
Calculate (kăl'-ku-lāt), *v.* Channa, hisab ka·a. **-tion**, *n.*
Calendar (kăl'-ĕn-dêr), *n.* Ponjika.
Calf (käf), *n.* Matchu bi·sa ; ja·pate.
Calico (kăl'-ĭ-ko), *n.* Chit ba·ra ma·sa.
Call (kôl), *v.* Okama.
Callous (kăl'-lŭs), *a.* Raka, gokrakrak daka.
Calm (käm), *a.* Tom·tomgipa.
Calmly (käm'-ly), *adv.* Tom·tom dake, ka·sindikdik dake.
Calvary (kăl'-vå-rĭ), *n.* Sko bikrok, Kristoko so·otram a·ding.
Calve (käv), *v.* Matchu dua ba ba·a.
Calyx (kā'-lĭks), *n.* Bibalni ganapak.
Cambric (kām'-brĭk), *n.* Se·engipa kildingni ba·ra ma·sa.
Camel (kăm'-ĕl), *n.* Ut.
Camera (kăm'-e-rå), *n.* Potograp dakani kol.

Camp (kămp), *n.* A·tip, tambu ping·ram.
Camphor (kăm'-fêr), *n.* Korpur.
Can (kăn), *n.* Tin, donchakani.
Can (kăn), *v.* Ama, bil gnang; sojachina chipata.
Canal (kâ-năl') *n.* Boi, dongge.
Cancel (kăn'-sĕl), *v.* Gimata, hisab ka·ao komiata. **-lation,** *n.*
Cancer (kăn'-sêr), *n.* Biati ma·sa pari daka. **-ate,** *v.* **-ous,** *a.*
Candid (kăn'-dĭd), *a.* Sronga, kakket, cha·chipila gri.
Candidate (kăn'-dĭ-dāt), *n.* Maiba kamko am·gipa ba bi·gipa, **-acy,** *n.*
Candle (kăn'd'l), *n.* Mom bati.
Candle-light (kăn'd'l-līt'), *n.* Chakini teng·a.
Candlestick (kăn'-d'l-stĭk') *n.* Mom batiko donchakani.
Cane (kān), *n.* Re', bet, gol·dik.
Canine (kâ-nīn'), *a.* Achakni jat gita dakgipa.
Canker (kăn'kêr), *n.* Ku·gisep soa.
Cannibal (kăn'-nĭ-bal), *n.* Mande cha·gipa.
Cannon (kăn'-nŭn), *n.* Slai nokma, top. **-eer,** *n.*
Cannonade (kăn'-nŭn-ād)', *v.* Topchi goa, ba po·a.
Canoe (kâ-nu'), *n.* Bol bigilni chongipa ring.
Canon (kăn'-ŭn), *n.* Toromni niam. **-ĭcal,** *a.*
Canteen (kăn'tēn'), *n.* Chu ba chiko ra·bitchakani; sipairangna chu aro ma·mantiko palram ba nok.
Canter (kăn'-têr), *n.* Gureni ka·sne kodom de·e re·ani, *v.*
Cantonment (kăn'-tŭn-ment), *n.* Sipairangni dongram.
Canvas (kăn'-vas), *n.* Son ba me·katchiko dakgipa ritchagipa ba·ra.
Cap (kăp), *n.* Tupi masa.
Capable (kā'-pâ-b'l), *a.* Ama, changa. **-ābĭlĭty,** *n.*
Capacious (kâ-pā'-shŭs), *a.* Chakbanggipa.
Capacity (kâ-păs'-ĭ-ty), *n.* Chakani bil. **-tate,** *v.*
Cape (kāp) *n.* A·kuchot; pakreko pindap.
Caper (kā'-pêr), *v.* Bilchokchoka.
Capillary (kăp'-ĭl-la-ry), *n.* Knding gita chonbegipa an·chi jokani ja dil.
Capital (kăp'-ĭ-tal), *n.* Skotong songjinma; skotonggipa; asoltangka, tangka bima.
Capsize (kăp'sīz'), *v.* Bikpila, chikkoppila, songtingpila.
Capsule (kăp'-sŭl), *n.* Jronggnigipa sam chipani wa·sing.
Captain (kăp'-tĭn), *n.* Jahatni pamong, sipai ritchasani pamong. **-cy,** *n.*
Captivate (kăp'-tĭ-vāt), *v.* Rim·gitanga; muni nangata. **-ion,** *n.*
Captive (kăp'-tĭv), *n* Rim·gimin, rim·gitanga mande. **-ĭty,** *n.*
Captor (kăp'-têr), *n.* Mandeko rim·gipa.
Capture (kăp'-tur), *v.* Mande ba songko rim·a.
Car (kär), *n.* Rel gari, maiba gari.
Caravan (kăr'-â-văn ba kăr-â-văn'), *n.* Rama re·gipa jinma; gari dal·gipa.
Carbine (kär'-bīn), *n.* Slai chongipa.

Carbon (kär'bŏn), *n.* Rongtalgipa anggal.
Carcass (kär'kas), *n.* Manggisi.
Card (kärd), *n.* Tas; leka ritchagipa namgipani tong.
Cardamom (kär'dă-mŭm), *n.* Elaich, elachi.
Cardinal (kär'dĭ-nal), *a.* Roman Katolikrangni pamongmu melapagipa.
Cardinal points (kär'dĭ-nal points'), *n.* Salaram, saliram, salgro, salgipeng, ia dam bri.
Care (kâr), *v.* Simsaka, sintea, jajrenga; nitimа.
Careful (kâr'fụl), *a.* Gisik rakgipa, simsakgipa.
Caress (kă-rĕs'), *v.* Ka·saako mesoka, doktopa, rim·roka, ku·dima.
Cargo (kär'go), *n.* Jahatni bal, boja.
Carnal (kär'nal), *a.* Be·enni biding. **-ity**, *n.*
Carnivorous (kär-nĭv'o-rŭs), *a.* Be·enko cha·gipa.
Carouse (kă-rouz'), *v.* Katchae chuko ringa, chu peka. **-al**, *n.*
Carpenter (kär'pĕn-têr), *n.* Bolni mistri. **-try**, *n.*
Carpet (kär'pĕt), *n.* Galicha, noko andapani ba·ra.
Carriage (kăr'rĭj), *n.* Gari.
Carrion (kăr'rĭ-ŭn), *n.* So·gimin be·en.
Carrot (kăr'rŭt), *n.* Gajol, me·su ma·si.
Carry (kăr'ry), *v.* Ra·bita, ola, ba·a, ripea, itchila.
Cart (kärt), *n.* Chaka gnigipa gari. **-age**, *n.*
Cartilage (kär'tĭ-laj), *n.* Bistil, nom·gipa greng.
Cartridge (kär'trĭj), *n.* Kartus.
Carve (kärv), *v.* Kita, konga, sol·a, repa.
Cascade (kăs-kād'), *n.* Chiringni dare.
Case (kās), *n.* Ra·chakani, chipani, bikop, chukop; ong·ani; mokordoma.
Cash (kăsh), *n.* Nogot tangka.
Cashier (kăsh-ēr'), *n.* Kajansi, tangka dontimgipa.
Cask (kåsk), *n.* Bolni pipa.
Cast (kåst), *v.* Goa, gala, rua; rue bimangko dakata.
Caste (kåst), *n.* Jat.
Castle (kăs''l), *n.* Guare, killa gnanggipa nok.
Caster (kăst'ĕr), *n.* Mainiba ja·choko tekani chongipa chaka.
Castor oil (kăs'têr oil'), *n.* Korondani to.
Castrate (kăs'trāt), *v.* Kasiata. **-ion**, *n.*
Cat (kăt), *n.* Menggo.
Catacombs (kăt'ă-kōmz), *n.* A·ningo manggisi donani biap.
Catalogue (kăt'ă-lŏg), *n.* Bigapon.
Cataract (kăt'ă-rŭkt), *n.* Chi dare dal·gipa.
Catarrh (kă-tär'), *n.* Gusu ginggre nangani ja·pang. **-al**, *a.*
Catch (kăch), *v.* CAUGHT. Rim·a; srapa.
Catechise (kăt'e-kīz), *v.* Sing·e skia. **-chist**, *n.*
Catechism (kăt'e-kĭz'm), *n.* Sing·e skiani ki·tap.
Caterpillar (kăt'êr-pĭl'lêr), *n.* Me·piliprangni jo·ong.
Cattle (kăt't'l), *n.* Matchurang; basakoba matchu, mes, jillanirangko minga.

Caucasian (kô-kā'shan), *n.* Europe aro Asiani bijatchio Kokesos a·bri sepango donggipa jat.
Cauliflower (kô'li-flou'êr), *n.* Pul kobi, me·su ma·sa.
Cause (kôz), *n.* Ja·pang, *v.* -at-.
Caution (kô'shŭn), *n.* Simsakani, gisik nangani. **-tious,** *a.*
Cavalier (kâv'ă-lēr), *n.* Gureo gakatgipa sipai.
Cavalry (kăv'ăl-ry), *n.* Gureo gakatgipa sipaini kotok.
Cave (kāv), *n.* Rong·kol, grim, a·kol.
Cavity (kăv'ĭ-ty), *n.* A·kol.
Caw (kô), *n.* Do·kani mikoa.
Cayenne (ka-ĕn' ba ki-en'), *n.* Jal·ik ma·sa.
Cease (sēs), *v.* Dondika, tipa.
Ceaseless (sēs'lĕs), *a.* Dondikgija, pangnan.
Ceiling (sēl'ing), *n.* Nok ning·chini nokking.
Celebrate (sĕl'e-brāt), *v.* Mingsingata. **-ion,** *n.*
Celery (sĕl'êr-y), *n.* Smilgipa samjak ma·sa.
Cell (sĕl), *n.* Chongipa kutori. **-ular,** *a.*
Cellar (sĕl'lêr), *n.* Nokkimani kutori, nokni ka·maoni gadang.
Cement (se-mĕnt'), *n.* Stapatani, ma·gapatani.
Cemetery (sĕm'e-têr-y), *n.* Gopram, koborkana.
Censure (sĕn'shur), *v.* Manenga, matnanga, namnikgijako mesoka, *n.*
Census (sĕn'sŭs), *n.* A·song gimikko chanani.
Cent (sĕnt), *n.* Bak ritchasani baksa; mitam songrangni paisa.
Centennial (sĕn-tĕn'nĭ-al), *a.* Bilsi ritchaprakni.
Center ba **Centre** (sĕn'têr), *n.* Jatchi, bijatchi.
Centipede (sĕn'ti-pēd), *n.* Snare.
Centurion (sĕn-tū'ri-ŭn), *n.* Ritchasani pamong.
Century (sĕn'tu-ry), *n.* Bilsi ritchasa.
Ceremony (sĕr'e-mo-ny), *n.* Niam gita dakbewal. **-al,** *n.* **-ous,** *a.*
Certain (sêr'tĭn), *a.* Tik, chong·mot; badiaba, aski. **-ty,** *n.*
Certificate (sêr-tĭf'ĭ-kat), *n.* Satibikot, sakini chiti.
Certify (sêr'-tĭ-fī), *v.* Bebe ine seata, aganata, saki on e uiata.
Chafe (chāf), *v.* Nata, nangtinggrika; ka·o nangata.
Chaff (châf), *n.* Cha·che.
Chain (chān), *n.* Sildeng, siliting.
Chair (châr), *n.* Choki, asongchakani.
Chairman (châr'man), *n.* So bani pamong, skotong.
Chalk (chôk), *n.* Korimati, seani chok.
Challenge (chăl'lĕnj), *n.* Susana ra·biani.
Chamber (chām'bêr), *n.* Nokdring, kesakgipa kutori.
Chamberlain (chām'bêr-lĭn), *n.* Rajani nokni pamong, tangka dontimgipa.
Chambermaid (chām'bêr-n āl') *n.* Nokol me·chik.
Chameleon (kă-mē'le-ŏn), *n.* Ganjapa.
Chamois (shăm'my ba shă-moi'), *n.* Burungni do·bok ma·sa.

Champ (chămp), *v.* Chikpneka, wak gita wagamko nangtinggrike gam·ata.

Champion (chăm'pĭ-ŭn), *n.* Dakchakna ba dakgrikchakna bilakbatgipa.

Chance (châns), *n.* Chol, nisogija ong·ani ; rasong.

Chancellor (chân'sĕl-lêr), *n.* Bichal ka·gipa pamong.

Change (chānj), *v.* Srea, dingtangata.

Channel (chăn'nĕl), *n.* Apalgipa chiapgitok, chi jokchakani biap, chikol.

Chant (chânt), *v.* Mangtata, doroa.

Chap (chăp), *v.* Jakpa breta.

Chapel (chăp'ĕl), *n.* Olakiani nok, gilja nok.

Chaplain (chăp'lĭn), *n.* Sorkarini doaa toromko skigipa.

Chapter (chăp'têr), *n.* Oidbai.

Character (kăr'ăk-têr), *n.* Cholon, mandeni chong·mot ong·ako mesokani ; oikar.

Charcoal (chär'kōl), *n.* Anggal.

Charge (chärj), *v.* Ge·eta ; damko bi·a ; matnanga ; ra·chakako s·rika.

Chariot (chăr'ĭ-ŏt), *n.* Dal·gipa gari, rot.

Charity (chăr'ĭ-ty), *n.* Ka·saani, ka sachakani ; ka·sae on·ani ba on·gimin.

Charm (chärm), *v.* Muni nangata.

Charm (chärm), *n.* Tabisi, madili.

Charming (chärm'ing), *a.* Nita, nama ; muni dakgipa.

Chart (chärt), *n.* Maikoba mesokani nop.

Chase (chās), *v.* Rika, ja·rika, sanna, sikar ka·a.

Chasm (kăz'm), *n.* Tu·e, dal·e aro ro·e bretgipa a·kol.

Chaste (chāst), *a.* Rongtala, marang gri.

Chasten (chā's'n), *v.* Doke skia.

Chastise (chăs-tīz'), *v.* Doke skia.

Chat (chăt), *v.* Bol·bola, gopo ka·a.

Chatter (chăt'têr), *v.* Wakengsisi daka.

Cheap (chēp), *a.* Dam nom·a, sosta.

Cheapen (chē'p'n), *v.* Dam nom·ata, komiata.

Cheat (chēt), *v.* Tol·napa, togia.

Check (chĕk), *v.* Dondikata, champenga.

Cheek (chēk), *n.* Pe.

Cheer (chēr), *v.* Ka·dongata, ka·dimeata, katchaata.

Cheerfully (chēr'ful-ly), *adv.* Kusi ong·e, katchae.

Cheese (chēz), *n.* Matchusokni tin·kagiminko daka ch·ani.

Chemise (she-mēz'), *n.* Me·chikrangni kamij.

Chemist (kĕm'ĭst), *n.* Ma·manti samni ja·pangko bak dake uina changgipa.

Cherish (chĕr'ĭsh), *v.* Ka·sae daka, ka·sae aldua.

Cherubim (chĕr'u-bĭm), *n.* Salgini sa·grerang.

Chest (chĕst), *n.* Chol ; dal·gipa bakos.

Chew (chū), *v.* Chikpneka, chobaia.

Chicken (chĭk'ĕn), *n.* Do·bisa, do·o.

Chicken-pox (chĭk'ĕn-pŏks'), *n.* Uri so·ep ma·sa.

Chide (chīd), *v.* CHID, CHIDDEN. Manenga.

Chief (chēf), *n.* Dal·batgipa, skitong, pamong, dal·gipa ge·etgipa.
Child (chīld), *n.* Mande bi·sa.
Children (chĭl'drĕn), *n.* Mande bi·sarang.
Chill (chĭl), *n.* Sin·a, sin·srika, sin·a napa. **-iness,** *n.* **-y,** *a.*
Chimney (chĭm'ny), *n.* Wal·ku jokatani.
Chin (chĭn), *n.* Ku·dil·ik, ku·dipe.
China (chī'nȧ), *n.* Chin song; chin bason, a·ani basonrang.
Chirp (chêrp), *v.* Chongipa do·oni mikoa, gukchuri aro asilikrangni mikoa.
Chisel (chĭz'ĕl), *n.* Batali, batal.
Choice (chois), *n.* Basegimin, segimin.
Choke (chōk), *v.* Rim·geka, rim·eka, rim·sota, kangdanga; rang·sitsokja, birang peng·a.
Cholera (kŏl'er-ȧ), *n.* Mariki saa.
Chop (chŏp), *v.* Gitaka, den·kninga, den·sota.
Chorus (kō'rŭs), *n.* Damsan ring·gipa adita mande; ring·taitaiani.
Christian (krĭs'chan), *n.* Kristoko ra·gipa.
Christmas (krĭs'mas), *n.* Kristoni atchiani sal, Dicember 25 sal.
Chronicle (krŏn'ĭ-k'l), *n.* Ma·chongko seani; Bongsaboli.
Chum (chŭm), *n.* Porairimgipa, rorima ripeng.
Chunk (chŭnk), *n.* Be·tonggimin tong·sa, dotsa.
Church (chêrch), *n.* Mondoli; gilja nok.
Churn (chêrn), *v.* Su·pokpoka, morokroka; makon dakata. *n.* Makon dakchakram ba dakchakani.
Chyle (kīl), *n.* Men·di, okningoni jronggini.in men·di.
Cigar (sĭ-gär'), *n.* Churut, ta·makurarako remremgipa.
Cigarette (sĭg'ȧ-rĕt), *n.* Sigaret, lekao remremgipa ta·maku.
Cinder (sĭn'dêr), *n.* Wal·miei, wal·ki, anggal. **-ous,** *a.*
Cinnamon (sĭn'nȧ-mŭn), *n.* Dalchini (daruchini), chi·gipa bol bigil ma·sa.
Cipher (sī'fĕr), *n.* Suino.
Circle (sêr'k'l), *n.* Dul.
Circular (sêr'ku-lêr), *a.* Dulgipa.
Circulation (sêr'ku-lā'shŭn), *n.* Jokruraani, on·rikrikani.
Circumcise (sêr'kŭm-sīz), *v.* Bigil rasota. **-ion,** *n.*
Circumference (sêr-kŭm'fêrĕns), *n.* Dului.
Circumscribe (sêr'kŭm-skrīb'), *v.* Saldula, arichi kachanga.
Circumstance (sêr'kŭm-stăns), *n.* Ong·ani.
Cistern (sĭs'têrn), *n.* Dal·gipa chi ra·chakani, pokri.
Citadel (sĭt'ȧ-del), *n.* Songjinmani killa.
Citizen (sĭt'ĭ-z'n), *n.* Songjinmao dongpagipa, songni dongpagipa.
City (sĭt'y), *n.* Songjinma.
Civet (sĭv'ĕt), *n.* Matchuri.
Civil (sĭv'ĭl), *a.* Mandeskana ka·sae dakgipa, mandera·gipa; Governmentni biding. **-ly,** *adv.*
Civilize (sĭv'ĭ-līz), *v.* Uigija, ka·saninggijagipa manderangko skie uiata. **-ation,** *n.*
Clabber (klăb'bêr), *n.* Matchusok tin·kagimin.
Clad (klăd), *part.* Gangimin, chingimin.

Claim (klām), *v.* Man·na nanga in· ina, angni ine ina, man·gni ong·a ine ina. **-ant**, *n.*
Clam (klăm), *n.* Gapchilek.
Clammy (klăm'my), *a.* Stapa gnang, ata gnang.
Clamour (klăm'ĕr), *n.* Jinmani rokrokani, jikjakani.
Clan (klăn), *n.* Ma·chong.
Clang (klăng), *v.* Imbike ba tengkrange birang chotgija teng ine gam·a.
Clap (klăp), *v.* Jakpa doktopa. *n.* Maibani doktopgrika gita gam·ani.
Clarify (klăr'ĭ-fī), *v.* Grikata, rongtalata.
Clash (klăsh), *v.* Nangtinggrika. **-ing**, *n.*
Clasp (klăsp), *v.* Rim·kata, gipaka.
Class (klâs), *n.* Ma·sannigipa-rang, sreni, klas.
Classify (klăs'sĭ-fī), *v.* Dingtang daka, ma·prakko dingtang dona, jatsanko sea.
Clause (klôz), *n.* Sentensni ba semni tong·sa.
Claw (klô), *n.* Jakskil, bu·su gita dagkipa jakskil.
Clay (klā), *n.* A·ste.
Clean (klēn), *a.* Rongtala. *v.* Rongtalata.
Cleanse (klĕns), *v.* Rongtalata.
Clear (klēr), *a.* Grika, brina gri, rongtala.
Cleave (klēv), *v.* Ma·gapa.
Cleave (klēv), *v.* CLEFT, CLEAVED ba CLOVEN. Pita.
Clemency (klĕm'ĕn-sy), *n.* Namgijagipana ba ongipana rinok rinok dakani, ka·sachakani.
Clergyman (klêr'jĭ-man), *n.* Toromko skigipa.
Clerk (klêrk), *n.* Setimgipa; paltimgipa.
Clever (klĕv'ĕr), *a.* Sapgipa, changgipa, uininggipa.
Click (klĭk), *n.* Tiktik ine gam·a.
Cliff (klĭf), *n.* Chugipa ro·ong dare.
Climate (klī'mat), *n.* Balchi, songni sin·a ba ding·ani, ba sosia ba ran·ani.
Climb (klīm), *v.* Maldoa, gakata. **-er**, *n.*
Cling (klĭng), *a.* CLUNG. Rim·kingkinga.
Clip (klĭp), *v.* Rasota.
Cloak (klōk), *n.* Krudapani chola.
Clock (klŏk), *n.* Ghori, baji.
Clod (klŏd), *n.* A·kinte.
Clog (klŏg), *v.* Peng·panga.
Close (klōz), *v.* Chipa, chipchanga.
Close (klōs), *a.* Chipgimin, sepang, chapchap, bing·a.
Closet (klŏz'ĕt), *n.* Chongipa kutori.
Clot (klŏt), *v.* Skana, tin·kaa, *n.*
Cloth (klôth), *n.* Ba·ra, kancha.
Clothe (klōTH), *v.* Ba·ra gana; ganata.
Clothes (klōTHz), *n.* Gana chinani.
Cloud (kloud), *n.* Aram, mikkasima.
Clove (klōv), *n.* Long, mosla ma·sa.
Cloven-footed (klō'v'n-fụt'ĕd), *a.* Ja·sipek, ja·skep pekgni dakgipa.
Club (klŭb), *n.* Manggot; danggina.
Clump (klŭmp), *n.* Adita sepanggrikgipa bolrang, eng·kalgipa bolgrim.

Clumsy (klŭm'zy), *a.* Re·togijagipa daktogijagipa. **-ily,** *adv.*
Cluster (klŭs'têr), *n.* Tom·dak, chokchim.
Coach (kōch), *n.* Chaka brigipa gari ma·sa.
Coagulate (ko-ăg'u-lat), *v.* Tin·kaa. **-ion,** *n.*
Coal (kōl), *n.* Koela, ro·ongni anggal.
Coarse (kōrs), *a.* Skakgipa, rakgipa; krabregijagipa.
Coast (kōst), *n.* Sagalni rikam.
Coat (kōt), *n.* Kot, chola kot.
Coax (kōks), *v.* Mol·mola.
Cob (kŏb), *n.* Me·raku ga·brong.
Cobra (kō'brå), *n.* Chipugam ba ugita bisi bang·begipa gitokko badalatna man·gipa chipu.
Cobweb (kŏb'wĕb'), *n.* Guang sringa.
Cock (kŏk), *n.* Do·bipa; me·gap dandaka, tongbol; slaini kora; *v.* Paia pe·a.
Cockatoo (kŏk'å-tụ'), *n.* Do·sik bapma dal·gipa.
Cockle (kŏk'k'l), *n.* Echaluk, echru.
Cockscomb (kŏks'kōm'), *n.* Do·oni gingmat; pul ma·sa.
Cocoanut (kō'ko-nŭt'), *n.* Narikel bite.
Cocoon (ko-kụn'), *n.* Muga, eria, aro ugita dakgipa jo·ongni bitip.
Cod (kŏd), *n.* Na·tok ma·sa.
Coerce (ko-êrs'), *v.* Draa. **-ion,** *n.* **-ive,** *a.*
Coffee (kŏf'fē), *n.* Kapi.
Coffer (kŏf'fêr), *n.* Tangka donani sinduk.
Coffin (kŏf' fin), *n.* Manggisi donani bakos.
Cog (kŏg), *n.* Chakao go·ol jotpengpanggipa.
Cohabit (kō-hăb'ĭt) *v.* Dongrima, turima.
Coheir (kō-âr'), *n.* Apsan man·rikpagipa.
Cohere (ko-hēr'), *v.* Nangrima, ma·gapa.
Coil (koil), *v.* Kon·a, rengkona. *n.*
Coin (koin), *n.* Silni tangka, paisa, iarang.
Coinage (koin'aj), *n.* Tangka dakani.
Coincide (kō'ĭn-sīd'), *v.* Melia, apsan ong·a. **-ence,** *n.*
Coir (koir), *n.* Narikelni bisring.
Cold (kōld), *a.* Siu·a, ka·sina, suri chika, *n.* **-ness.**
Colic (kŏl'ĭk), *n.* Okdita, ok chike saani.
Collapse (kŏl-lăps'), *v.* Be·gopa, be·prua, be·gipua.
Collar (kŏl'lêr), *n.* Gitoko ganani, kalar.
Colleague (kŏl'lēg), *n.* Ajsan kam ka·rimgipa.
Collect (kŏl'-lĕkt') *v.* Chimonga, gila, tom·a, **-ion,** *n.* **-ive,** *a.* **-ively,** *adv.*
College (kŏl'lĕj). *n.* Dal·gipa skul, chugipa skul.
Collide (kŏl-līd'), *v.* Chajekgrika, re·pekgrika.
Collier (kŏl'yêr) *n.* Koila cho·gipa.
Collision (kŏl-lĭzh'ŭn), *n.* Chapekgrikani, re·pekgrikani.
Colonel (kêr'nel), *n.* Sipaini pamong.
Colonize (kŏl'o-nīz), *v.* Adita bang·a manderang gital songdonga. **-ation,** *n.*

Colony (kŏl'o-ny), *n.* Songgipino tom·e donggipa manderang.

Color ba **Colour** (kŭl'ẽr), *n.* Rong.

Colt (kōlt), *n.* Gure bi·sa.

Column (kŏl'ŭm), *n.* Songdogipa krong; sipaini mitap dakgipa riting; kosakchini ka·maona riting.

Comb (kōm), *n.* Ki·chong; bija birangkap; gingmat.

Comb (kōm), *v.* Kni rokchita.

Combat (kŏm'băt ba kŭm'băt), *n.* Dakgrikani. **-ive,** *a.*

Combine (kŏm-bīn'), *v.* Nangdima, nangrima. **-ation,** *n.*

Combustible (kŏm-bŭs'tĭ-b'l), *a.* Kamninggipa, kamgnigipa.

Combustion (kŏm-bŭs'chŭn), *n.* Kamani.

Come (kŭm), *v.* CAME, COME. Re·baa.

Comedy (kŏm'e-dy), *n.* Ka·dingani, tamasani.

Comely (kŭm'ly), *a.* Nitoa. **-ness,** *n.*

Comet (kŏm'ĕt), *n.* Aski do·me.

Comfort (kŭm'fẽrt), *n.* Ka·dimeani, saknaaoni namani.

Comfortable (kŭm'fẽrt-a-b'l), *a.* Dongtoa, saknaa gri; *n.* Lep.

Comforter (kŭm'fẽrt-er), *a.* Ka·dimeatgipa; golabon.

Comic (kŏm'ĭk), *a.* Ka·dinggni, ka·dingatgipa.

Comical (kŏm'ĭ-kal), *a.* Ka·dinggni, ka·dingatgipa.

Comma (kŏm'mȧ), *n.* Koma, (,) ia chin.

Command (kŏm-mȧnd'), *v.* Ge·eta.

Commandment (kŏm-mȧnd'ment), *n.* Ge·etani.

Commence (kŏm-mĕns'), *v.* A·bachenga. **-ment,** *n.*

Commend (kŏm-mĕnd'), *v.* Mitela. **-ation,** *n.*

Comment (kŏm'mĕnt), *n.* Mesoke aganani, tika, ortoko seani.

Commentary (kŏm'mĕn-ta-ry), *n.* Mesoke aganani ki·tap.

Commerce (kŏm'mẽrs), *n.* Song chel·ao badinggrikani.

Commissary (kŏm'mĭs-sa-ry), *n.* Sipairangni cha·aniko chimonggipa.

Commission (kŏm-mĭsh'ŭn), *n.* Ka·ani; pakwatani; sakgipinna kamko ka·ani bhara.

Commissioner (kŏm-mĭsh'ŭn-ẽr), *n.* Rajani kamko chu·sokatna dongimin mande.

Commit (kŏm-mĭt'), *v.* Daka; on·a, pakwata.

Committee (kŏm-mĭt'te), *n.* Kamko chu·sokatna dongimin manderang.

Commodore (kŏm'mo-dōr'), *n.* Dakgrikani jahatrangni pamong.

Common (kŏm'mŭn), *a.* Ramram, ong·ronggipa; sorkarini.

Commonwealth (kŏm'mŭn-wĕlth'), *n.* Sason ka·ani gimin damsan nangrimgimin manderang.

Commotion (kŏm-mō'shŭn), *n.* Jinmani golmal.

Commune (kŏm-mūn'), *v.* Agangrika; gitelni dakbewalko manipaa. **-ion,** *n.*

Community (kŏm-mūn'ĭ-ty), *n.* Noksul songsul gimik.

Compact (kŏm-păkt'), *a.* Ma·keta. **-ness,** *n.*

Companion (kŏm-păn'yŭn), *n.* Ripeng, rorimgipa. **-able,** *a.*

Company (kŭm′pȧ-ry), *n.* Kotok, dams n ka·pagiparang.
Compare (kŏm-pâr′), *v.* To·usaa, togrika. **-ison,** *n.* **-ative,** *a.*
Compass (kŭm′pas), *n.* Dul·ni; salgroko tik ka·ani kol.
Compassion (kŏm-păsh′ŭn), *n.* Ka·sachakani, duk man·paani.
Compel (kŏm-pĕl′), *v.* Bilchi dakata, draata.
Compensate (kŏm′pĕn-sāt ba -pĕn′), *v.* On·skaa, gimaana on·dapa.
Compete (kŏm-pēt′), *v.* Susaa.
Competent (kŏm′pe-tent), *a.* Cha·onga, sapa, ama, kraa.
Competition (kŏm-pe-tĭsh′ŭn), *n.* Susaani.
Compile (kŏm-pīl′), *v.* Gipin ki·taprangoniko chimonga. **-ation,** *n.*
Complain (kŏm-plān′), *v.* Matnange agana.
Complaint (kŏm-plānt′), *n.* Duk ba matuanganiko agananí, dukni a·sel; biati.
Complement (kŏm′ple-ment), *n.* Matchctat.ni, chu·sokatani.
Complete (kŏm-plēt′), *v.* Matchita. *a.* Gimikgipa. **-ion,** *n.* **-ly,** *adv.*
Complex (kŏm′plĕks), *a.* Bang·a bak brina, brinbaoe. **-ity,** *n.*
Complexion (kŏm-plĕk′shŭn), *n.* Au·gil.
Complicate (kŏm′plĭ-kāt), *v.* Sakbrina, brine saka, brina nangrima. **-ion,** *n.* **-d,** *a.*
Comply (kŏm-plī′), *v.* Namnikpaa. **-ance,** *n.*
Compose (kŏm-pōz′), *v.* Chanchiako tom·dakata, banaia; tom·tomata. **-ition,** *n.* **-dly,** *adv.*
Compound (kŏm-pound′), *v.* Brina, dordima (kom′pound). *n. a.*
Comprehend (kŏm′pre-hĕnd′), *v.* Ma·sia, rim·a; man·gopa. **-sion,** *n.*
Compromise (kŏm′pro-mīz′), *v.* Bijatchi dako namgrikata, *n.*
Compute (kŏm-pūt′), *v.* Chana, hisab ka·e man·a. **-ation,** *n.*
Comrade (kŏm′răd ba kŏm′rad), *n.* Ripang, rorimgipa.
Conceal (kŏn-sēl′), *v.* Donua. **-ment,** *n.*
Conceit (kŏn-sēt′), *n.* A·tangko dal·nikani.
Conceive (kŏn-sēv′), *v.* Chanchichipa, ui·hipa; oko kea.
Concerning (kŏn-sêrn′ing), *part.* -ni gimin.
Concise (kŏn-sīs′), *a.* Bang·gija kat o orto bang·gipa.
Conclude (kŏn-klūd′), *v.* Tik ka·a, bon·kame chanchia. **-clusion,** *n.*
Concord (kŏn′kôrd), *n.* Nangrimani, m·ldiani.
Concubine (kŏn′ku-bīn), *n.* D·mui, gipin me·chikko adita salna ba on·tisa salna rakigipa jik.
Concur (kŏn-kêr′), *v.* Ku·cholsan, gisiksa ong·a. **-rence,** *n.*
Condemn (kŏn-dĕm′), *v.* Matnanga; sastina ge·eta. **-ation,** *n.* **-atory,** *adv.*
Condense (kŏn-dĕns′), *v.* Ma·ketata, chonata. **-ation,** *n.*
Condescend (kŏn′de-sĕnd′), *v.* Onate daka. **-sion,** *n.*
Condition (kŏn-dish′ŭn), *n.* Ong·ani, obosta. **-al,** *a.*
Condole (kŏn-dōl′), *v.* Gipinni duk ong·o duk ong·paa, duk man·rima. **-nce,** *n.*

Conduct (kŏn'dŭkt), *n*. Dakbewal, cholon.
Conduct (kŏn-dŭkt'), *v*. Re·dila, dakdila.
Conference (kŏn'fêr-ens), *n*. Ku·monggrikani.
Confess (kŏn-fĕs'), *v*. Ku·rachaka. **-ion**, *n*.
Confidence (kŏn'fi-dens), *n*. Ka·dongani, pangchakani. **-dential**, *a*. **-dentially**, *adv*.
Confine (kŏn-fīn'), *v*. Chipchanga. **-ment**, *n*.
Confirm (kŏn-fĕrm'), *v*. Mangrakata, katako mangrakata. **-ation**, *n*.
Confiscate (kŏn'fis-kāt ba kŏnfis'kāt), *v*. Korok ka·a. **-ion**, *n*.
Conflict (kŏn-flĭkt'), *v*. Jegrika, dokgrika. (kŏn'flikt), *n*.
Conform (kŏn-fôrm'), *v*. Apsan dakata. **-ation**, *n*.
Confound (kŏn-found'), *v*. Jajata, golmal dakata.
Confront (kŏn-frŭnt'), *v*. Mikkangchaka.
Confusion (kŏn-fū'zhŭn), *n*. Bildingbildang ong·ani, golmal ong·ani.
Congratulate (kŏn-grătu'-lāt), *v*. Katchipaako agana. **-ion**, *n*.
Congregate (kŏn'gre-gāt), *v*. Tom·a. **-ion**, *n*.
Conjugal (kŏn'ju-gal), *a*. Bia ka·ani biding.
Conjugate (kŏn'ju-gāt), *v*. Veron mood aro tensrangko mesoka. **-ion**, *n*.
Conjunction (kŏn-jŭngk'shŭn), *n*. Nangrimatgipa kata.
Connect (kŏn-nĕkt'), *v*. Nangrima, nangdima; nangrimata, nangdimata. **-ion**, *n*. **-ive**, *n*.
Conquer (kŏn'kêr), *v*. Ama, chea.
Conscience (kŏn'shens), *n*. Nama aro namgijako uiani gisik.
Conscious (kŏn'shŭs), *a*. Uiani gnang. **-ness**, *n*.
Consecrate (kŏn'se-krāt), *v*. Toromna on·kanga, maiba kamna dingtang dona, pakwata. **-ion**, *n*.
Consent (kŏn-sĕnt'), *v*. Ku·rachaka. *n*.
Consequence (kŏn'se-kwĕns), *n*. A·sodni Lite.
Consider (kŏn-sid'êr), *v*. Chanchia, chanchie nia. **-ation**, *n*.
Considerable (kŏn-sid'êr-ā-b'l), *a*. Adita bang a ba dal·a. **-ably**, *adv*.
Consign (kŏn-sīn'), *v*. Pakwate on·a. **-ment**, *n*.
Consist (kŏn-sist'), *v*. Ong·a, donga. **-ency**, *n*. **-ent**, *a*. **-ently**, *adv*.
Console (kŏn-sōl'), *v*. Ka·dimeata. **-ation**, *n*. **-atory**, *a*.
Consolidate (kŏn-sŏl'i-dāt), *v*. Mangrakata, rakata.
Consonant (kŏn'so-nant), *n*. Binjon borno, sor gri gam·na simgijagipa, b, c, d, f, g, h, j k, l, m, n, p, q, r, s, t, v iarang, w aro y ba basakoba ong·a
Conspire (kŏn-spīr'), *v*. Namgijana sriksrik ku·monga. *n*. Conspiracy (kŏn-spĭr'ā-sy).
Constable (kŭn'stā-b'l), *n*. Sibil polis.
Constant (kŏn'stant), *a*. Pangnan, dongdikgija, dingtanggija, mangraka.
Constellation (kŏn'stĕl-lā'-shŭn), *n*. Aski jinma.

Constipation (kŏn'sti-pā'shŭn), *n.* Bing·ani, a·pal bon ong·ani.

Constitution (kŏn'sti-tū'shŭn), *n.* Niamni ja·pang; be·enni aro gisikni bilni ja·pang.

Constrain (kŏn-strān'), *v.* Draata.

Construct (kŏn-strŭkt'), *v.* Rika, daka. **-ion,** *n.*

Consul (kŏn'sŭl), *n.* Songtangni badingani namgnina gipin songo rajani dongimin mande.

Consult (kŏn-sŭlt'), *v.* Gipinni chanchiako ku·monge ra·paa. **-ation,** *n.*

Consume (kŏn-sūm'), *v.* Cham·-ata, kamata, gimata.

Consumption (kŏn-sŭmp'shŭn), *n.* Ka·sopko cham·atgipa biati ma·sa.

Contact (kŏn'tăkt), *n.* Nangtingani, nangdikani.

Contagious (kŏn-tā'jŭs), *a.* Nangdikao batninggipa, batgipa biati. **-ion,** *n.*

Contain (kŏn-tān'), *v.* Chaka, man·gopa.

Contempt (kŏn-tĕmt'), *n.* Mitchinikani, chonnikani.

Contend (kŏn-tĕnd'), *v.* Jegrika, warachakgrika. **-tention,** *n.*

Content (kŏn-tĕnt'), *a.* Chu·-ongnikgipa, tom·tomgipa.

Contents (kŏn'tĕnts ba kŏntĕnts'), *n.* Gimik ning·o gnanggipa.

Contest (kŏn-tĕst'), *v.* Jegrika, dakgrika. **-ant,** *n.*

Contest (kŏn'tĕst), *n.* Jegrikani, dakgrikani.

Continent (kŏn'ti-nent), *n.* A·a dal·begipa, a·song dal·begipa.

Continue (kŏn-tĭn'u), *v.* Dongangkua, ong·angkua, dongkama. **-ation,** *n.*

Contract (kŏn-trăct'), *v.* Kom·-to·a; bon lobosto ka·a.

Contract (kŏn'tract), *n.* Bondobosto ka·ani.

Contractor (kŏn-trăk'têr), *n.* Tika ra·gipa mande.

Contradict (kŏn'trā-dikt'), *v.* Jechaka, inpila. **-ion,** *n.*

Contrary (kŏn'trā-ry ba kŏn'-tra-ry), *a.* Ong·gijagijako dakgipa, cholet rongret dakgipa.

Contrast (kŏn-trăst'), *v.* Dingtang ong·ako uina ba mesokna nisusa. (kŏn'trăst), *n.*

Contribute (kŏn-trĭb'ut), *v.* On·paa. **-ion,** *n.*

Contrive (kŏn-trīv'), *v.* Chanchisoa, chol daka. **-ance,** *n.*

Control (kŏn-trōl'), *v.* Skatang dakatna kosako bil man·a, maniata, *n.*

Convene (kŏn-vēn'), *v.* Tom·a, tom·ata.

Convenient (kŏn-vēn'yent), *a.* Jakkaltoa. **-ce,** *n.*

Convention (kŏn-vĕn'shŭn), *n.* Tom·ani, soba.

Converse (kŏn-vêrs'), *v.* Agangrika. **-ation,** *n.*

Convert (kŏn-vêrt'), *v.* Gisik pil·ata, dingtang ong·ata. **-version,** *n.*

Convex (kŏn'vĕks), *a.* Ki·sing janggil gita kom·chikgipa. **-ity,** *n.*

Convey (kŏn-vā'), *v.* Ra·anga, salanga, ripeanga, dingtangchi ong·ata. **-ance,** *n.*

Convict (kŏn-vikt'), *v.* Dosko uiata, dosi inata. **-ion,** *n.*

Convince (kŏn-vĭns'), *v.* Bebe ine uiata.

Convoke (kŏn-vōk'), *v.* Okamchimongata. **-vocation,** *n.*

Coo (kṳ), *v.* Do·kruni jokgrua.
Cook (kṳk) *v.* Song·a. *n.* Song·gipa.
Cool (kṳl), *a.* Ka·sina, sin·srika.
Cooly (kṳ'ly), *n.* Ku'i, begal
Coop (kṳp), *n.* Do·o jllani nok dornol.
Cooper (kṳp'ĕr), *n.* Bolni pipa dakgipa.
Cooperate (ko-ŏp'ĕr-āt), *v.* Apsan ka·paa, dakrimpaa. **-ion,** *n.*
Copper (kŏp'pĕr), *n.* Tama, paisani sil.
Copy (kŏp'y), *v.* Seskaa; gita daka. **-ist,** *n.*
Copy (kŏp'y), *n.* Seskagimin, seskaani.
Coral (kŏr'al), *n.* Probal minggipa sagalni jo·ong ma·sani bitip, sagalo chichang dakatgipa jo·ong ma·sa.
Cord (kôrd), *n.* Budu chongipa; ambolko toani, gro mik 5, gipeng mik 8 aro chua mik 3 ong ode cord samang ong·a.
Cordially (kôr'jal-ly), *adv.* Name chacha, stronge, cha·chipila gri onge.
Core (kŏr), *n.* Bijatchi ga·brong.
Cork (kôrk), *n.* Botolni kak, bongga.
Corkscrew (kôrk'skrṳ'), *n.* Botol kak okani pes.
Corn (kôrn), *n.* Me·raku, mi misirang.
Corner (kôr'nĕr), *n.* Kona, ki·tik.
Cornet (kôr'nĕt), *n.* Begul ma·sa.
Coronation (kŏr'o-nā'-shŭn), *n.* Rajako mukut stikatani.
Coroner (kŏro'nĕr), *n.* Rang·san ba maibakai siarangko bichal ka·gipa.
Corps (kŏr, pl. kŏrz), *n.* Sipai ka tok.
Corpse (kôrps), *n.* Mang·gisi.
Corpuscle (kôr'pŭs-s'l), *n.* Bisemsem.
Correct (kŏr-rĕkt'), *a.* Tik, guala gri. *v.* Guala gri ong·ata, namata.
Correspond (kŏr're-spŏnd'), *v.* Apsan ong·a, melia; chitiko segrika.
Corrode (kŏr-rōd'). *v.* Cham·ata, jrongata. **-rosion,** *n.*
Corrugate (kŏr'rṳ-gāt), *v.* Onding ondang chikare dake daka.
Corrupt (kŏr-rŭpt'), *v.* Soata, ong·siata **-ion,** *n.*
Cost (kŏst), *n.* Dam, on·gimin koroch.
Costly (kŏst'ly), *a.* Dam bang·gipa.
Costive (kŏs'tĭv), *v.* A·pal bon ong·a.
Costume (kŏs-tūm'), *n.* Ganding chindingni bewal.
Cot (kŏt), *n.* Tuchakani kat, palang.
Cottage (kŏt'taj), *n.* Chongipa nok, nok bi·sa.
Cotton (kŏt't'n), *n.* Kil.
Couch (kouch), *n.* Tue toani ga·ci.
Cough (kôf), *v.* Gusu chaa, so·ok nanga. *n.*
Council (koun'sil), *n.* Mela, melagiparang.
Counsel (koun'sĕl), *n.* Ku·mong·ani, chanchiani. *v.* Skia.
Count (kount), *v.* Channa. *n.* Europeni dal·a mande.

Countenance (koun'te-nans), *n.* Mikkang.
Counter (koun't'êr), *a.* Mikkang chakgipa, bobil dakgipa.
Counteract (koun'têr-ăct'), *v.* Bingbaugata.
Counterfeit (koun'têr-fit), *v.* Togina ine ma ba gita apsan dakata.
Countermand (koun'têr-mănd'), *v.* Ge'etako bikailata.
Counterpart (koun'têr-pärt'), *n.* Gita oag'gipa, apsan ong'-gipa ; jear.
Countersign (koun'têr-sīn), *v.* Be.e ong'a ine bimung sedap-a. *n.*
Countess (koun'tĕs), *n.* Count-ni jikgipa, rajani jikgipa.
Country (kŭn'try), *n.* Song, a'song, songjinma ong'gijani song, dogru, gitim.
County (koun'ty), *n.* District ba jila.
Couple (kŭp'l), *n.* Gni ba jora.
Courage (kŭr'aj), *n.* Ka'sokani, ka'dongani. **-ous,** *a.*
Course (kōrs), *n.* Katani, re'ani ba dakrongani rama.
Course (kōrs), *v.* Sikar ka'a, ja'rika, rika, sana.
Court (kōrt), *n.* Sara ; raja ba dal'gipa mandeni dongram ba nok; raja bak:a re'pagipa ; bichal ka'ram ; bichal ka'-ronggiparang.
Courteous (kêr'te-ŭs), *a.* Nam-nikatna changgipa, mande ra'-ronggipa.
Court-house (kōrt'hous'), *n.* Bichal ka'ram nok, kachari nok.
Cousin (kŭz''n), *n.* Ma'gipa pagipani jongada noabirangni de.
Cove (kōv), *n.* Chikongdik.
Covenant (kŭv'e-nant), *n.* Niam, ku'rachakgrikani, ku'mong-grikani.
Cover (kŭv'êr), *v.* Pin'apa, don-ana.
Covey (kŭv'y), *n.* Do'oni jak, do'jinma, do'o sudipil ; ma'-sanni bi'sa.
Cow (kou), *n.* Matchu bima.
Coward (kou'êrd), *n.* Ka'pong, kenrakgipa.
Coxcomb (kŏks'kōm), *n.* An'-tangko dal'nikgipa nigipa ine mesakgipa; do'oni gingmat.
Coy (koi), *a.* Kratchanninggipa.
Crab (krăb), *n.* Ang ke.
Crack (krăk), *v.* Breta, be'sria, be'ani gam'a. *n.*
Cradle (krā'd'l), *n.* Bi'sani ring-renggipa tuchakani.
Crafty (krâf'ty), *a.* Tol'rakgip-a, togigipa, chalaki dakgipa.
Crag (krăg), *n.* Ro'ong dare.
Cram (krăm), *v.* Agre gapata, gapatba a.
Cramp (krămp), *n.* Bi.itchu-ra'gni kom'tote'aani.
Crane (krān). *n.* Alabok ; bostu saldoani kol.
Cranium (krā'nĭ-ŭm), *n.* Sko bikrok.
Crank (krănk), *n.* Wilwilatani.
Crape (krāp), *n* Kalimako me-soksa ganani resomni ba'ra ma'sa.
Crash (krăsh), *n.* Be'kningani.
Crash (krăsh), *v.* Be'kninga.
Crater (krā'têr), *n.* Wa'alni a'brini wa'al ong'katani chol-kumang.
Crave (krāv), *v.* Mol'molbee bi'a, man'na sikbee bi'a.
Craven (krā'v'n), *n.* Kenrak-gipa, ka'pong.

Crawfish (krô'fish). *n.* Na'tik.
Crawl (krôl), *v.* Ma'ama.
Crayon (krā'ŭn), *n.* Pensil gita tarigiani chok.
Crazy (krā'zy), *a.* Pagila.
Cream (krēm), *n.* Matchusokni nambatgipa, kosako tin'kagipa.
Crease (krēs), *n.* Tem'ani chin, *v.*
Create (kre-āt'), *v.* Ong'ata. **-ion,** *n.*
Creator (kre-ā'têr), *n.* Ong'atgipa, Isol.
Creature (krē'tur), *n.* Ong'atgimin, janggi gnanggipa ong'atgimin.
Credit (krĕd'ĭt), *n.* Ka'dongna kraani, man'na nangani, ra'chakna on'ani.
Credit (krĕd'ĭt), *v.* Ka'donga, bebe ra'a.
Creditor (krĕd'ĭ-têr), *n.* Mahajon, gro nokgipa.
Credulous (krĕd'u-lŭs), *a.* Bebe ra'ninggipa, saki gri bebe ra'ninggipa.
Creed (krēd), *n.* Toromni gimin bebe ra'ani ja'pang.
Creek (krēk), *n.* Chiring dal'gipa; chongipa apchongipa sagal noksik.
Creep (krēp) *v.* CREPT. Ma'ama, ka'bakchi re'a.
Creeper (krēp'êr), *n.* Chongipa budu wegipa, malamgipa.
Crescent (krĕs'sent), *n.* Jajongni bak brini bak sani pal gita aro ugita dakgiparang pilakan.
Crest (krĕst), *n.* A'bri ku'chot, basu.
Crevice (krĕv'ĭs), *n.* Bretani a'kol chonbegipa.
Crew (krų), *n.* Jahatni kalasirang.
Cricket (krĭk'ĕt), *n.* Asilik.
Crime (krīm), *n.* Niamko pe'ani.
Criminal (krĭm'ĭ-nal), *n.* Niamko pe'gipa. *a.* **-ity,** *n.*
Crimson (krĭm'z'n), *n.* An'chi gita gitchakgipa.
Cripple (krĭp'p'l), *n.* Kora, lengra.
Crisis (krī'sĭs), *n.* Ong'gni uigijani sal, ka'dongtogijani sal, kenchakani sal, kamsba sia dingani baria ba komiani sal.
Critic (krĭt'ĭk), *n.* Nama namgijako mesokgipa.
Criticise (krĭt'ĭ-sīz), *v.* Nama namgijako nie mesoka.
Croak (krōk), *v.* Beng'blokni rera; namnikgijako agansoa.
Crock (krŏk), *n.* Dim'ak, dikmak.
Crockery (krŏk'êr-y), *n.* A'ako daka me'dik sam'dikrang.
Crocodile (krŏk'o-dīl), *n.* Gorial ma'sa.
Crook (krųk), *n.* Gonggeani.
Crooked (krųk-ed), *a.* Gonggea.
Crop (krŏp), *n.* Do'oni pechu; ragni nanggimin mi misi aro ma'manti biterang.
Crop (krŏp), *v.* Chiksota, cha'sota, rasota.
Cross (krŏs), *n.* Chisol.
Cross (krŏs), *v.* Battonga, re'sota.
Cross (krŏs), *a.* Ka'ting dakgipa.
Cross-examine (krŏs'ĕgz-ăm'ĭn), *v.* Pil'nipil sing'a, chem'chem sandie nia.
Crotch (krŏch), *n.* Bolnigpekkam.
Crouch (krouch), *v.* Bamgepa, bamgopa.
Croup (krųp), *n.* Golbera, gitokni biati ma'sa.

Crow (krō), *n*. Do·ka.
Crow (krō), *v*. Do·o gi·sika.
Crowd (kroud), *n*. Mande jinma.
Crown (kroun), *n*. Mukut; rokomsa tangka.
Crucifixion (krụ'sĭ-fĭk'shŭn), *n*. Chisolo so·otani.
Crucify (krụ'sĭ-fī), *v*. Chisolo so·ota.
Crude (krụd), *a*. Gitang, mingija, tarisogija.
Cruel (krụ'ĕl), *a*. Ka·saninggijagipa, duk on·na namnikgipa. **-ty**, *n*.
Crumb (krŭm), *n*. Biginchi.
Crumble (krŭm'b'l), *v*. Bnekata, biginchi changata.
Crush (krŭsh), *v* Onj·ta, bneka·a, kningata.
Crust (krŭst), *n*. A·palni rakgipa pindapani.
Crusty (krŭst'y), *a*. Ran·kapgimin; ka·sagijagipa.
Crutch (krŭch), *n*. Kora·angni pakolo sepe pangchake re·ani gol·dik.
Cry (krī), *v*. Grapa, chrika, inwata.
Crystal (krĭs'tal), *n*. Janera gita, grikbegipa janera ma·sa.
Cub (kŭb), *n*. Ma·cha ba mapllini bi·sa.
Cube (kūb), *n*. Gro, gipeng, chua pilakchin apsangipa.
Cubit (kū'bĭt), *n* Mik.
Cucumber (kū'kŭm-bêr), *n*. Te·mit.
Cud (kŭd), *n*. Cha·gimin samko bikotpile cha·ani; gue ba ta·maknko bil·ani.
Cudgel (kŭj'ĕl), *n*. Manggoteng, danggna, dokani.
Cuff (kŭf), *n*. Satkapani.
Cull (kŭl), *v*. Se·a bikota.
Culminate (kŭl'mĭ-nāt), *v*. Chua tiap ba ku·chotko man·a. **-ion**, *n*
Culprit (kŭl'prĭt), *n*. Matnangako man·gipa.
Cultivate (kŭl'tĭ-vāt), *v*. Wea, gama; dal·ata, bariata. **-ion**, *n*.
Culvert (kŭl'vêrt), *n*. Rama ning·ko chi jokangna gop dakgimin.
Cumber (kŭm'bêr), *v*. Maiba balchi champenga, ba·ko on·dapa, peng·panga; jajrengata.
Cumin (kŭm'ĭn), *n*. Jira, mosla ma·sa.
Cunning (kŭn'nĭng), *a*. Chalaki. *n*. Chalaki dakani.
Cup (kŭp), *n*. Piala, ringchakani.
Cupboard (kŭb'bêrd), *n*. Basonrangko donchakani almari.
Cur (kêr), *n*. Achak; chonnikgimin mande.
Curable (kūr'ā-b'l), *a*. An·sengatna amgni.
Curb (kêrb), *v*. Ta·rakako champenga.
Curd (kêrd), *n*. Dobi doi tin·ka pimin matchusok.
Curdle (kêr'd'l), *v*. Dobi dakata, tin·kaata.
Cure (kūr), *v*. An·sengata, namata.
Cure (kūr), *n*. An·sengatani.
Curious (kū'rĭ-ŭs), *a*. Aiao inmangni, nikronggijani, nina sikbegipa. **-osity**, *n*.
Curl (kêrl), *v*. Rengkota, kon·a.
Currant (kŭr'rant), *n*. Chongipa bite ma·sa.
Currency (kŭr'rĕn-sy), *n*. Cholienggipa tangka.

Current (kŭr'rent), *a*. Cholienggipa.

Current (kŭr'rent), *n*. Soolgipa jokgipa chi ba bal.

Curry (kŭr'ry), *n*. Bijak, holdi.

Curse (kêrs), *n*. Sao on·ani.

Curtain (kêr'tin), *n*. Purda, peng·ani ba·ra.

Curve (kêrv), *n*. Chri gita gongguani.

Cushion (kush'ŭn), *n*. Sko kam·ani ba asongchakani balis.

Custard (kŭs'têrd), *n*. Do·bitchi, chiui aro matchusok bringipa cha·ani ma·sa.

Custody (kŭs'to-dy), *n*. Koid ka·ani, chipchangani. **-ian,** *n*

Custom (kŭs'tŭm), *n*. Bewal; ra·napani kajai a.

Customer (kŭs'tŭm-êr), *n*. Saksanoniko breronggipa.

Cut (kŭt), *v*. Den·a, ras·a.

Cut (kŭt), *n*. Matani pari; rasotani waring.

Cutlass (kŭt'las), *n*. Tonual ma·sa, kukuri.

Cycle (sī'k'l), *n*. Gari ma·sa; wilwilsokani sal.

Cyclone (sī'klōn), *n*. Ta·rakgipa apalgipa balminduri. **-ic,** *a*.

Cylinder (sĭl'ĭn-dêr), *n*. Bim·ronge ro·gipa, wa·sing gita ro·dronggipa. **-drical,** *a*.

Czar (zär), *n*. Rusiani raja; uni jikgipako Czarina minga.

D.

Dagger (dăg'gêr), *n*. Kan·dikgipa su·ani, tonual ma·sa.

Daily (dā'ly), *adv*. Salanti.

Dainty (dān'ty), *a*. Cha·na toa, su·ua, nitoa rongtalako namnikgipa. *n*. Nama cha·ani.

Dairy (dā'ry), *n*. Gobali, matchusok seprram.

Daisy (dā'zy), *n*. A·bao chagipa bibal ma·sa.

Dale (dāl), *n*. A·bri giseppni a·kaoe.

Dam (dăm), *n*. Chiko kapengani, na·gil.

Damage (dăm'aj), *n*. Gimaani, namgijako man·ani, *v*.

Dame (dām), *n*. Nokni me·chik.

Damn (dăm) *v*. Sao on·a, nonokchi inata. **-ation,** *n*.

Damnable (dăm'nā-b'l), *a*. Sastie man·na kragipa, norokna kragipa.

Damp (dămp), *a*. Chijima.

Damsel (dăm'zĕl), *n*. Me·chik bi·sa, me·tra.

Dance (dāns), *v*. Chroka, mesara.

Dandruff (dăn'drŭf), *n*. Karoksi.

Danger (dān'jêr), *n*. A·sel nangani, a·sel ong·ani. **-ous,** *a*.

Dare (dâr), *v*. Ka·soka, ka·donga, kenja.

Dark (därk), *a*. Andala.

Darling (där'lĭng), *n*. Je a ka·sabea.

Darn (därn), *v*. Napongako wattapa, siktapa, kolapa.

Dart (därt), *n*. Sel·u ba bra.

Dart (därt), *v*. Goa, gochoka, chapaka.

Dash (dăsh), *v*. Chatinga, nanggaka satchima, chapraka.

Date (dāt), *n*. Tarik, sal; kejur bite aro bol.

Daub (dôb), *v*. Repia, nongmraka, nongmnika.

Daughter (dô'têr), *n*. Demechik.

Daughter-in-law (dô'têr-ĭn-lô), *n*. Deui jikgipa, namchiktang.

Dawn (dôn), *n*. Seng·baachibara, seng·uiichi mitchi.
Day (dā), *n*. Sal, salsa; chasong.
Dazzle (dăz'z'l), *v*. Ching·bea, nichakna amgija ching·a.
Deacon (dē'k'n), *n*. Mondolini me·apa, pamongna dakchakgipa, dangdike on·gipa.
Dead (dĕd), *a*. Sigimin, janggi gri.
Deaf (dĕf ka dēf), *a*. Ka'a, nachikol knagijagipa.
Deal (dēl), *n*. On·gimin, sua'gimin bak.
Deal (dēl), *v*. Daka; suale on·a.
Dear (dēr), *a*. Ka·sara; gamchata; man·na nangana bate dam raklata.
Dearth (dêrth), *n*. Bang·gija ong·ani, chu·onggija ong·ani.
Death (dĕth), *n*. Siani.
Debar (de-bär'), *v*. Champenga, beng·a.
Debase (de-bās'), *v*. Rasong be·ata, ŏnata. **-ment**, *n*.
Debate (de-bāt'), *v*. Jegrika, *n*.
Debauch (de-bôch'), *v*. Ong·siata.
Debility (de-bĭl'ĭ-ty), *n*. Bilgri ong·ani.
Debt (dĕt), *n*. Gro, on·na nangani. **-or**, *n*.
Decade (dĕk'ad), *n*. Chikung bi si.
Decalogue (dĕk'ă-l'g), *n*. Isolni ge·eta mingchikung.
Decapitate (de-kăp'ĭ-tāt), *v*. Sko sota. **-ion**, *n*.
Decay (de-kā'), *v*. Soa, sojronga, *n*.
Decease (de-sēs'), *n*. Siani, janggi galani.
Deceit (de-sēt'), *n*. Tol·napani.
Deceive (de-sēv'), *v*. Tol·napa.
December (De-sĕm'bêr), *n*. Ja chi·gnigipa, bilsini ben·kamgipa ja.
Decent (dē'sent), *a*. Kraa.
Deception (de-sĕp'shŭn), *n*. Tol·napani, tol·napako man·ani.
Decide (de-sīd'), *v*. Gisiko tik ka·a.
Decidedly (de-sīd'ĕd-ly), *adv*. Chong·mot, namen.
Decimal (dĕs'ĭ-mal), *a*. Bak chikung dakatgimin, dosomik.
Decision (de-sĭzh'ŭn), *n*. Tik ka·a, bon·kame ge·eta.
Deck (dĕk), *n*. Jahatni kosakbatgipa gadang, jahatni nokking.
Deck (dĕk), *v*. Nitoata, tar·ata.
Declaim (de-klām'), *v*. Boktrita ka·a, agana. **-lamation**, *n*.
Declaration (dĕk'lă-rā'shŭn), *n*. Uiatani, parakatani, mesokani, ce inatani, knaatani. **-ative**, *a*.
Declare (de-klâr'), *v*. Uiata, parakata.
Decline (de-klīn'), *v*. Jechaka; bil komia. **-ation**, *n*.
Decompose (dē'kŏm-pōz'), *v*. Jrongata, brina bostu dingtang ong·a; so·a **-ition**, *n*.
Decorate (dĕk'o-rāt), *v*. Nitoata. **-tion**, *n*.
Decoy (de-koi'), *v*. Kimala, *n*.
Decrease (de-krēs'), *n*. Komiani, onangani.
Decree (de-krē'), *v*. Ge·e'a.
Dedicate (dĕd'ĭ-kāt), *v*. Isolna ba toromna dingtang dona. **-ion**, *n*.
Deduct (de-dŭkt'), *v*. Katia, komia'a. **-ion**, *n*.
Deed (dēd), *n*. Dakgimin.
Deem (dēm), *v*. Chanchia.

Deep (dēp), *a.* Tu'a, ning'tua.
Deer (dēr), *n.* Matchok, me'-sam.
Deface (de-fās'), *v.* Bimang dingtangata, nitoatja. **-ment,** *n.*
Defame (de-fām'), *v.* Rasong be'ata. **-ation,** *n.*
Default (de-fôlt'), *n.* Dakna nangako dakgijani.
Defeat (de-fēt'), *v.* Ama, bing'-banga'a, *n.*
Defect (de-fěkt'), *n.* Namsrang-gijani, chu'sokgijani.
Defend (de-fěnd'), *v.* Warachake rakia. **-fence,** *n.*
Defer (de-fêr'), *v.* Dondika, don-tonga, ruuta'a.
Defiance (de-fī'ans), *n.* Dakgrik-na ra'biani, bamgijako mesok-ani.
Deficiency (de-fĭsh'-ěn-sy), *n.* Chu'onggijani, tikgijani.
Defile (de-fīl'), *v.* Marang nang-ata, rongtalgija ong'ata. **-ment,** *n.*
Define (de-fīn'), *v.* Tik ka'a; ariko tik ka'a; ortoko me-soka.
Definite (děf'i-nĭt), *a.* Tik, chong'mot.
Definition (děf'i-nĭsh'ŭn), *n.* Ortoko agmani.
Deform (de-fôrm'), *v.* Nitogija dakata, bimangko ong'siata. **-ity,** *n.*
Defraud (de-frôd'), *v.* Togia.
Defray (de-frā'), *v.* Koreehko on'a.
Defy (de-fī'), *v.* Dakgrikna ra'-bia. **-ance,** *n.*
Degrade (de-grād'), *v.* Salonata, onata. **-ation,** *n.*
Degree (de-grē'), *n.* Dulni bak 360 ni bak sa; gadang.
Deign (dān), *v.* A'tangko ona't-drae daka.
Deity (dē'ĭ-ty), *n.* Isol, mite.
Dejected (de-jěkt'ěd), *a.* Gisiko ka'donga grigipa, gisikko jrimatgimin. **-ion,** *n.*
Delay (de-lā'), *v.* Ruutata, dong-dikata, *n.*
Delegate (del'e-gat), *n.* Maini-ba gimin a'tangni pal mande-ko donata.
Deliberate (de-lĭb'êr-āt), *v.* Gisiko toe nia, bichal ka'a, namedake chanchia. **-ion,** *n.*
Delicate (děl'ĭ-kat), *a.* Se'enna, nitoa, rinoka, chona; bil bang'ja. **-cacy,** *n.*
Delicious (de-lĭsh'ŭs), *a.* Cha'na tobegipa, su'ubegipa.
Delight (de-līt'), *n.* Kusi ong'-ani, katchaani.
Delirium (de-lĭr'ĭ-ŭm), *n.* Ming'ming mang'mang daka-ni.
Delirium tremens (de-lĭr'ĭ-ŭm trē'měnz), *n.* Chuborot chaa-ni, chu peke pagla ong'ani.
Deliver (de-lĭv'êr), *v.* Jokata; an'paka; on'skaa. **-ance,** *n.*
Delude (de-lūd'), *v.* Gualata, togia, namgijachi ong'ata. **-lusion,** *n.*
Deluge (děl'uj), *n.* Chi dubiani.
Demand (de-mând'), *v.* Dabia, nangbea, *n.*
Demolish (de-mŏl'ish), *v.* Ruata, gimata, nisiata.
Demon (dē'mŏn), *n.* Mite, put. **-iacal,** *a.*
Demonstrate (děm'ŏn-strāt ba de-mŏn'strāt), *v.* Sakichi tik ka'a, ong'a ine tale mesoka. **-ion,** *n.*
Demoralize (de-mŏr'al-īz), *v.* Cholonko ong'siata. **-ation,** *n.*

Den (dĕn), *n.* Matburungrangni a·kol ba rong·kol ba turam.
Denial (de-nī'al), *n.* Jechakani.
Denote (de-nōt'), *v.* Maiba chinchi mesoka.
Denounce (de-nouns'), *v.* Pasake mainanga. **-ment,** *n.*
Dense (dĕns), *a.* Bing·gipa, dikegipa.
Dent (dĕnt), *v.* De·epa, *n.*
Dentist (dĕn'tĭst), *n.* Wagam tarigipa.
Denude (de-nūd'), *v.* Nagan.leata, pindapaniko gala.
Deny (de-nī'), *v.* Jechaka.
Depart (de-pärt'), *v.* Re·anga. **-ure,** *n.*
Department (de-pärt'ment), *n.* Maiba kamoi ba sasou ka·ani bak.
Depend (de-pĕnd'), *v.* Pangchaka. **-ence,** *n.* **-ent,** *a.* **-ency,** *n.*
Depict (de-pĭkt'), *v.* Tale agana, ku·sikchi noksa daka.
Deplore (de-plōr'), *v.* Kalima, duk man·chakako agana.
Depopulate (de-pŏp'u-lāt), *v.* Songko mande gri dakata. **-ion,** *n.*
Depose (de-pōz'), *v.* Kamoniko tang·ata. **-ition,** *n.*
Deposit (de-pŏz'ĭt), *v.* Dona, *n.*
Depôt (dē'po), *n.* Gam donram, bandal, gudam.
Deprave (de-prāv'), *v.* Namgija ong·ata, ong·siata. **-ity,** *n.*
Depress (de-prĕs'), *v.* Sinjeta, onata. **-ion,** *n.*
Deprive (de-prīv'), *v.* Gri ong·ata. **-ation,** *n.*
Depth (dĕpth), *n.* Tu·ani.
Depute (de-pūt'), *v.* A·tangni pal donata, watata. **-ation,** *n.*
Deputy (dĕp'u-ty), *n.* Saniba pal dongimin.
Derive (de-rīv'), *v.* Ong·katata, ja·pangoniko bikota. **-ation,** *n.*
Descend (de-sĕnd'), *v.* Ong·ona.
Descendent (de-sĕnd'ent), *n.* Derutchu, su·rutchu.
Describe (de-skrīb'), *v.* Katachi ba chinchi mesoka. **-scription,** *n.*
Desert (dĕz'ĕrt), *n.* A·gisi, morubhumi.
Desert (de-zĕrt'), *v.* Watga'a. **-tion,** *n.*
Deserve (de-zĕrv'), *v.* Man·na kraa.
Design (de-zīn'), *v.* Lekao daksoa; mangsonga, *n.*
Desire (de-zīr'), *v.* Man·na ska. *n.* **-ous,** *a.*
Desist (de-zĭst'), *v.* Wa'a, watga'a, dondika. **-ance,** *n.*
Desk (dĕsk), *n.* Sechakani mej.
Desolate (dĕs'o-lat), *a.* Mande grigipa.
Desolation (dĕs'o-lā'shŭn), *n.* Gima ong·ani.
Despair (de-spâr'), *n.* Ka·donga gri ong·ani.
Despatch (de-spăch'), *v.* Gong·rake watata, gong·rake daka; so·ota. *n.*
Desperate (dĕs'pêr-at), *a.* Ka·donga grini gimin simsakgijagipa. **-ion,** *n.*
Despise (de-spīz'), *v.* Mitchinika, chonika.
Despite (de-spīt'), *n.* Miknenga·ni, mitchiani, chonikani.
Despond (de-spŏnd'), *v.* Ka·dongjani gimin gisik jinma. **-ent,** *a.* **-ency,** *n.*

Despot (dĕs'pŏt), *n.* A·tang ska gita dakgipa raja ba nokgipa. **-ic,** *a.*

Destiny (dĕs'tĭ-ny), *n.* Ong·gniko tik dongimin, ong·gni, rasong.

Destitute (dĕs'tĭt-tut), *a.* Gri ong·a, kangal, gam gri, grisrang. **-ion,** *n.*

Destroy (de-stroi'), *v.* Rua, gimata, nisiata.

Destruction (de-strŭk'shŭn), *n.* Gimaani, nisiatani.

Detach (de-tăch'), *v.* Aktenga. **-ment,** *n.*

Details (dĕ'tālz ba detālz'), *n.* Chongipa ong·arang.

Detain (de-tān'), *v.* Rim·rika.

Detect (de-tĕkt'), *v.* Sandie uia. **-ion,** *n.*

Deter (de-têr'), *v.* Kenate kamko champenga. **-ent,** *a.* **-ence,** *n.*

Determine (de-têr'mĭn), *v.* Tik ka·a, mangsonga. **-ation,** *n.*

Detest (de-tĕst'), *v.* Mitchibea. **-ation,** *n.*

Develope (de-vĕl'ŏp), *v.* Naata, braata, pataktata, ka·sne dal·roroata. **-ment,** *n.*

Devil (dĕv''l), *n.* Diabol, Satan.

Devise (de-vīz'), *v.* Gisiko chanch·a, cholko daka.

Devoid (de-void'), *a.* Bangbang, gri.

Devote (de-vōt'), *v.* Boli on·a gita on·a, gisik nange on·a.

Devoted (de-vōt'ĕd), *a.* Gisik on·e olakigipa, gisik on·gipa.

Devour (de-vour'), *v.* Cha·minoka, minoka, nisiata, gima·a.

Devout (de-vout'), *a.* Isolna gisik nanggipa.

Dew (dū), *n.* Ripambchi.

Diadem (dī'ă-dĕm), *n.* Kadesil.

Diagonal (dī-ĭg'o-năl), *n.* Ki·tik·ni ki·tikoni dambenge salgimin.

Diagram (dī'ă-grăm), *n.* Sale mesokani.

Dial (dī'al), *n.* Ghori, compas ba ugita dakgiparangni mikkang.

Dialect (dī'ă-lĕkt), *n.* Ku·sikSanoni de·r·te agana ku·sik.

Dialogue (dī'ă-log), *n.* Agangrikani.

Diameter (di-ăm'e-têr), *n.* Maiba bostu tom·betani gipeng.

Diamond (dī'ă-mŭnd ba dī'mŭnd), *n.* Hira, gamchatbegipa ro·ong.

Diaphragm (dī'ă-frăm), *n.* Ka·prang, tingchangra.

Diarrhea (dī'ar-rē'ă), *n.* Ok re·ani.

Diary (dī'ă-ry), *n.* Salantini ong·ako seani.

Dictate (dĭk'tāt), *v.* Sena aganata; ge·eta.

Dictionary (dĭk'shŭn-a-ry), *n.* Obidhan.

Die (dī), *v.* Sia.

Diet (dī'ĕt), *n.* Cha·rongani.

Differ (dĭf'fêr), *v.* Dingtang ong·a, me'ija.

Difficult (dĭf'fĭ-kŭlt), *a.* Raka, dakna raka.

Dig (dĭg), *v.* DUG ba DIGGED. Cho·a.

Digest (dĭ-jĕst'), *v.* Ok ningo jrongata; gisiko tariata.

Digit (dĭj'ĭt), *n.* Saoni chikungona ongkorangko digit minga.

Dignify (dĭg'nĭ-fī), *v.* Rasong chaata, chuata.

Dignity (dĭg'nĭ-ty), *n.* Rasong, mikkim, mande ra·aui.

Digress (dĭ-grĕs'), *v.* Mingsong-aoni ekange dingtangni gimin agana.

Dilate (dī-lāt' ba di-lāt'), *v.* Gingbua, dal·ata.

Dilatory (dĭl'ā-to-ry), *a.* Jak su·utgipa, jak ru·utgipa.

Diligence (dĭl'ĭ-jens), *n.* Bimchhipani.

Diligent (dĭl'ĭ-jent), *a.* Bimchipgipa.

Dilute (dĭ-lūt'), *v.* Brina, bilko komiata, brine nom·a·a.

Dim (dĭm), *a.* Dimela, grikja, rongtalja.

Dimension (dĭ-mĕn'shŭn), *n.* Gro, gipeng, chuanba dal·a ong·ani.

Diminish (dĭ-mĭn'ĭsh), *v.* Komiata.

Diminutive (dĭ-mĭn'u-tĭv), *a.* Chona, chonbea, kan·dika, chakandika.

Dimple (dĭm'p'l), *n.* Daapa, kongdepa.

Din (dĭn), *n.* Knana man·pilgija gam·atani.

Dine (dīn), *v.* Mesal cha·a.

Dingy (dĭn'jy), *a.* Kaltapru, rongtalja, moila gnang.

Dinner (dĭn'nêr), *n.* Saljatebio cha·ani, mesal.

Dip (dĭp), *v.* Sim·bola ; we·a.

Diphthong (dĭf'thŏng ba dip'-), *n.* Vowel gegni mingsan gita gam·ani.

Direct (dĭ-rĕkt'), *v.* Dila, mesokata, cholko mesokata; ge·-eta.

Direct (dĭ-rekt'), *a.* Sronga.

Dirt (dêrt), *n.* Moila, jabol, an·-chnek.

Disadvantage (dĭs'ăd-vân'taj), *n.* Choljokgijani, champengani ong·ani.

Disappear (dĭs'ăp-pēr'), *v.* Chel·-anga, nikgija ong·a.

Disappoint (dĭs'ăp-point'), *v.* Ka·dongako bon·ata, ka·donga gri ong·ata.

Disapprove (dĭs'ăp-prūv'), *v.* Namnikja, ra·chakja.

Disarm (dĭs-ärm' ba dĭz-), *v.* Silchi lare gri ong·ata.

Disarrange (dĭs'ăr-rānj'), *v.* Bildingbildangata.

Disaster (dĭz-ăs'têr), *n.* Dukni, apodni, dal·bea dukni.

Discharge (dĭs-chärj'), *v.* Bal ba jrimako tang·ata ; kamoni tang·ata.

Disciple (dĭs-sī'p'l), *n.* Sninggipa.

Discipline (dĭs'sĭ-plĭn), *n.* Sason ka·ani, skiani.

Disclaim (dĭs-k'lām'), *v.* Jechaka, angni ong·ja ine jechaka. **-er,** *n.*

Disclose (dĭs-klōz'), *v.* Parakata. **-ure,** *n.*

Discolour, Discolor (dĭs-kŭl'-ĕr), *v.* Rongko dingtangata.

Discomfort (dĭs-kŭm'fĕrt), *n.* Dongtogijani, suk griani.

Disconnect (dĭs'kŏn-nĕkt'), *v.* Dingtangata, nangdimgija dakata.

Disconsolate (dĭs-kŏn'so-lat), *a.* Ka·dimea gri, ku·simtekgipa. **-ly,** *adv.* **-ness,** *n.*

Discontent (dĭs'kŏn-tĕnt'), *n.* Namnikgijani. chu·ongnikgijani. **-ed,** *a.*

Discontinue (dĭs'kŏn-tĭn'u), *v.* Dondika, bon·chongdika. **-ance,** *n.* **-ation,** *n.* **-ous,** *a.* **-ity,** *n.*

Discord (dĭs'kôrd'), *n.* Meligijani, jegrikani. **-ant,** *a.* **-ance,** *n.*

Discount (dĭs-kount'), *v.* Mitam komiata; Komison ra·a la on·a.
Discourage (dĭs-kŭr'aj), *v.* Ka·donga gri ong·ata. **-ment,** *n.*
Discourse (dĭs-kōrs'), *n.* Agangrikani, aganprakani.
Discover (dĭs-kŭv'ĕr), *v.* Nikchenga; parakata. **-y,** *n.*
Discredit (dĭs-krĕd'ĭt), *v.* Bebe ra·ja, ka·dongja; bebe ra·na ba ka·dongna man·gija ong·ata.
Discreet (dĭs-krēt'), *a.* Gisik gnanggipa, chanchisogipa, mikrakgipa. **-ly,** *adv.*
Discretion (dĭs-krĕsh'ŭn), *n.* Gisik gnangani, chanchisoani, mikrakani.
Discuss (dĭs-kŭs'), *v.* Jegrika, chanchigrika. **-ion,** *n.*
Disdain (dĭs-dān'), *v.* Oanika, chonnika. *n.*
Disease (dĭz-ēz'), *n.* Saa, rok, biati.
Disembark (dĭs'ĕm-bärk'), *v.* Ringoni ong·ona.
Disfigure (dĭs-fĭg'ur), *v.* Mikkang bimangko namgija dakata. **-ation,** *n.* **-ment,** *n.*
Disgorge (dĭs-gôrj'), *v.* Wakgala; on·pila.
Disgrace (dĭs-grās'), *v.* Chonata, onata, rasong griata, kratcha·ata. **-ful,** *a.* **-fully,** *adv.*
Disguise (dĭs-gīz'), *v.* Pindape uigija dakata, *n.* Mikkang dingtangatani.
Disgust (dĭs-gŭst'), *n.* Namnikgija ong·ani, mitchiaikani.
Dish (dĭsh), *n.* Cha·anirangko ra·chakani.
Dishearten (dĭs-här't'n), *v.* Ka·a be·ata, ka·donga griata.
Dishonest (dĭs-ŏn'ĕst ba dĭz-), *a.* Tol·napgipa, bebegijagipa.
Dishonour (dĭs-ŏn'ĕr ba dĭz-), *n.* Chonnikani, mande ra·gijaui, kratcha·ani, *v.*
Disjunction (dĭs-jŭngk'shŭn), *n.* Dingtang dakatani, ekatani.
Dislike (dĭs-līk'), *n.* Namnikgijani. *v.*
Dislocate (dĭs'lo-kāt), *v.* Biitchu ringreta, apjita. **-ion,** *n.*
Dislodge (dĭs-lŏj'), *v.* Ong·katata, arikata. **-ment,** *n.*
Disloyal (dĭs-loi'al), *a.* Gitelnga ka·sara grigipa, bama grigipa. **-ly,** *adv.*
Dismal (dĭz'mal), *a.* Sikdikdik, suk gri. **-ly,** *adv.*
Dismay (dĭs-mā'), *n.* Kenani.
Dismember (dĭs-mĕm'bĕr), *v.* Be·enni bakko rasota.
Dismiss (dĭs-mĭs'), *v.* Kamoni watata, nam katia. **-al,** *n.* **-ion,** *n.*
Dismount, (dĭs-mount'), *v.* Ong·ona.
Disobedient (dĭs'o-bē'dĭ-ent), *a.* Ge·etiko pe·gipa, manigijagipa. **-ance,** *n.* **-ly,** *adv.*
Disobey (dĭs'o-bā'), *v.* Ge·etako pe·a, manija.
Disoblige (dĭs'o-blīj'), *v.* Namnikgijako daka, namnika ba namgniko dakja. **-ing,** *a.*
Disorder (dĭs-ŏr'dĕr), *n.* Bildingbildang ong·ani, niam gita ong·gijani, golmal. **-liness,** *n.* **-ly,** *adv.*
Disorganize (dĭs-ŏr'gan-īz), *v.* Bildingbildang dakata.
Disown (dĭs-ōn' ba dĭz-), *v.* Nokgipa ong·ja ine jechaka.
Disparage (dĭs-păr'aj), *v.* Tosusae chonnikata.

Dispatch (dĭs-păch'), *n. Despatchko* nibo.

Dispel (dĭs-pĕl'), *v.* A·rikata, chel·ata.

Dispensary (dĭs-pĕn'sā-ry), *n.* Samko indin on·ani biap.

Dispense (dĭs-pĕns'), *v.* Suale on·a. **-er,** *n.* **-ation,** *n.*

Disperse (dĭs-pêrs'), *v.* Bilding-bildangata, dingtang ekata. **-ion,** *n.*

Displace (dĭs-plās'), *v.* Apjita, biaponi chel·ata.

Display (dĭs-plā'), *v.* Mesokata, parakata, *n.*

Displease (dĭs-p'ēz'), *v.* Nam-nikgija ong·ata. **-ure,** *n.*

Dispose (dĭs-pōz'), *v.* Tarie dona, namedake dona. **-al,** *n.*

Dispose of (dĭs-pōz'ŏv'), *v.* Pala, on·a.

Disposition (dĭs-po-zĭsh'ŭn), *n.* Bewal, cholon, ong·ani.

Dispute (dĭs-pūt'), *n.* Jegrikani, *v.* **-ant,** *n.* **-er,** *n.* **-able,** *a.*

Disqualify (dĭs-kwŏl'ĭ-fī), *v.* 'Kragija dakata, amgija dakata.

Disregard (dĭs're-gärd'), *v.* Mande minggija daka, chonnika, *n.*

Disrepute (dĭs're-pūt'), *n.* Namgija mingsingani. **-able,** *a.*

Disrespect (dĭs're-spĕkt'), *n.* Mande ra·gijani.

Dissatisfaction (dĭs-săt'ĭs-făk'-shŭn), *n.* Namnikgijani.

Dissect (dĭs-sĕkt'), *v.* Ratonge namedake nia.

Dissemble (dĭs-sĕm'b'l), *v.* Cha·-chipila, cha·chipile dingtangko mesoka.

Disseminate (dĭs-sĕm'ĭ-nāt), *v.* Sata, gipata.

Dissent (dĭs-sĕnt'), Chanchiao meligrikja, dingtang ong·-grika. **-sion,** *n.*

Dissipate (dĭs'sĭ-pāt), *v.* Rusia, gimata. **-ion,** *n.*

Dissolve (dĭz-zŏlv'), *v.* Jrongata. **-able, ent,** *a.*

Distance (dĭs'tans), *n.* Chel·a-ni, chel·grikani. **-ant,** *a.*

Distemper (dĭs-tem'pêr), *n.* Bi-ati, namgija cholon.

Distill (dis-til'), *v.* Cheka chu-daka. **-er,** *n.* **-ery,** *n.* **-ation,** *n.*

Distinct (dĭs-tĭngkt'), *a.* Ding-tang mancha, tala, ma·signi. **-ly,** *adv.*

Distinguish (dĭs-tĭng'gwĭsh), *v.* Dingtangko nia.

Distinguished (dĭs-tĭng'gwĭsht), *a.* Mande ra·ako man·gipa, mingsinggipa.

Distort (dĭs-tôrt'), *v.* Sakmrena, waengmikeng daka.

Distract (dĭs-trăkt'), *v.* Bing-bangata. **ion,** *n.*

Distress (dĭs-trĕs'), *n.* Duk, sa-knaa, apod, *v.*

Distribute (dĭs-trĭb'ut), *v.* Suale on·a. **-er,** *n.* **-ion,** *n.* **-ive,** *a.*

District (dĭs'trikt), *n.* A·song, song.

Distrust (dĭs-trŭst'), *n.* Ken-chakani, bebe ra·gijani, ka·danggijani. **-ful,** *a.*

Disturb (dĭs-têrb'), *v.* Jingjeng-ata. **-er, -ance,** *n.*

Disunite (dĭs'u-nīt') *v.* Ding-tang dakata, ekgrikata.

Ditch (dich), *n.* Chikare, boi, dongge.

Ditto (dĭt'to), *adv.* Uan, apsan, segimin ba agangimin gitan.

Diurnal (di-êr'nal), *a.* Salanti-ni.

Dive (dīv), *v.* Chio napa, chi ripa.

Diverge (dĭ-vêrj'), *v.* Ekanga. **-nce,** *n.* **-cy,** *n.* **-nt,** *a.*

Diverse (dī'vêrs ba dī-vêrs'), *a.* Dingtang ong'gipa. **-ify,** *v.*

Divert (dī-vêrt'), *v.* Gisikko ekata, kusi ong'ata. **-sion,** *n.* **-ive,** *a.*

Divest (dī-vĕst'), *v.* Gri ong'ata.

Divide (dī-vīd'), *v.* Suala, bak dakata, dingtangata.

Dividend (dĭv'ĭ-dĕnd), *n.* Sualgni.

Divine (dī-vīn'), *a.* Isolni biding.

Divine (dī-vīn'), *v.* Katchinike agana. **-ity,** *n.*

Divisible (dĭ-vĭz'ĭ-b'l), *a.* Sualna amgipa ba kraa.

Division (dĭ-vĭsh'ŭn), *n.* Sualani.

Divisor (dĭ-vī'zêr), *n.* Sualgipa.

Divorce (dĭ-vōrs'), *v.* Niam gita jik se galgrikata, *n.*

Divulge (dī-vŭlj'), *v.* Parakata.

Dizzy (dĭz'zy), *a.* Miksiwila, miksula.

Do (dŏ), *v.* DID, DONE. Daka, ka'a.

Dock (dŏk), *n.* Jahatrangko donani biap; kachario kodiko donani biap.

Doctor (dŏk'têr), *n.* Sam on'gip-a, oja, daktor.

Doctrine (dŏk'trĭn), *n.* Skiani. **-al,** *a.*

Document (dŏk'u-ment), *n.* Mesokani ba ge'etani chiti. **-ary,** *a.*

Dodge (dŏj), *v.* Gitchinge chak-a; pa'sika.

Doe (dō), *n.* Matchok ba sapau bima.

Dog (dŏg), *n.* Achak.

Dogged (dŏg'gĕd), *a.* Ku'boso-so dake manigijagipa, mikbel loklok dake chakchikgipa.

Doleful (dōl'fụl), *a.* Duk ong'a guang.

Doll (dŏl), *n.* Mande dakgipa kal'ani.

Dollar (dŏl'lêr). *n.* Sent 100 prako gong'sa ong'gipa, tang-ka ma'sa.

Dolphin (dŏl'fĭn), *n.* Sagalni na'tok ma'sa.

Domain (do-mān'), *n* Nokgipa-ni ning'o donggipa a'a, ba jeba.

Dome (dōm), *n.* Sangko chikopa gita gongdule dakgipa nok-king.

Domestic (do-mes'tĭk), *a.* Nok-tangni ba songtangni biding, jillani.

Domesticate (do-mes'tĭ-kāt), *v.* Noko jilla, mikmalata. **-ion,** *n.*

Dominate (dŏm'ĭ-nāt), *v.* Sason ka'a. **-ion,** *n.*

Domineer (dŏm'ĭ-nēr'), *v.* Gao-rade'e nokgipa daka, sason ka'a.

Dominion (do-mĭn'yŭn), *n.* Rai-jo, songnok, nokgipa ong'-ani.

Donate (dō'nāt), *v.* Ka'sae on'a. **-ion,** *n.* **-or,** *n.*

Done (dŭn), *v.* *Do*ko nibo.

Donor (dō'nŏr), *n.* Ka'sae on'-gipa.

Donkey (dŏng'ky), *n.* Gada.

Doom (dụm), *n.* Sastina ba gimatna ge'etani.

Door (dōr), *n.* Cholguga, do'ga-chol, do'ga.

Dormitory (dôr'mĭ-to-ry), *n.* Tu'mi nok ba kuturi, chatro-rangni lain.

Dose (dōs), *n.* Palasa, chang-prakna ringani sam.

Dost (dŭst), *v.* *Do* ni second person singular number.

Dot (dŏt), *n.* Su'tota, tota.

Doth (dŭth), *v.* *Do*ni third person singular number.
Double (dŭb''l), *a.* Dunagni, changgni.
Doubt (dout), *n.* Kenchakani. *v.*
Dough (dō), *n.* Nol·gimin moida.
Dove (dŭv), *n.* Do·kru, paroa, do·rek aro do·pilgim, iarang.
Dovetail (dŭv'tāl'), *n.* Do·kru ki·me gita wagam chite ritchugimin.
Dower (dou'ĕr), *n.* Segrini man·rikgni, se simano man·rikgni gam.
Down (doun), *adv.* Ka·machi, ka·mao, a·ao ; *n.* Ning·oni nom·gipa kinil.
Doze (dōz), *v.* Tusidimua.
Dozen (dŭz''n), *n.* Dojon, ge·chigni.
Drab (drăb), *a.* Kaltapru ma·sa.
Draft, Draught (drâft), *n.* Salani, salgimin ; ja·pangko sesoani ; tangkako man·ani chiti ; balwa jokpinggrikani.
Drag (drăg), *v.* Sala, salbrita.
Dragon (drag'ŭn), *n.* Mande·jangni aganronga granggnanggipa chipu ma·sa, ba Drakon.
Dragonfly (drăg'ŭn-flī'), *n.* Susuret, chuchuret.
Dragoon (drâ-gun'), *n.* Gureo gakatgipa sipai ma·sa.
Drain (drān), *v.* Chi lakwate wata, joksole tipata, sipata.
Drain (drān), *n.* Chikare, dongge.
Drake (drāk), *n.* Do·gep bipa.
Dram (drăm), *n.* Jrimako toani, adita jrimako mesokani.
Drank (drăngk), *v.* *Drink*ko nibo.
Draper (drā'pĕr), *n.* Ba·ra palgipa.
Drapery (drā'pĕr-y'), *n.* Ba·ra sikeani.
Draught (drâft), *n.* *Draft*ko nibo.
Draw (drô), *v.* DREW, DRAWN, Nok·a daka ; sala.
Drawer (drô'ĕr), *n.* Salokrurana man·gipa baks.
Draw-bridge (drô'brĭj'), *n.* Jitrurana man·gipa jang·rang.
Drawers (drô'ĕrs), *n.* Ning·o be·enchi an·pae kruani jama.
Drawl (drôl), *v.* Ka·sine arate agana.
Dread (drĕd), *v.* Kensoa ; *n.* Kensoani, kenbeani.
Dream (drēm), *v.* Jumang nika; *n.* Jumang.
Dreary (drēr'y), *a.* Sikdikdik.
Dredge (drĕj), *n.* Chi ning·ko kinani.
Dregs (drĕgs), *n.* Ki·tikchi skonggipa.
Drench (drĕnch), *v.* Sosiatsranga.
Dress (drĕs), *v.* Taria, ba·ra gana, *n.* Ganani ba·ra.
Dribble (drĭb'b'l), *v.* Tingtota, toktaka.
Drift (drĭft), *v.* Balwa ba chichi balpake dandaka.
Drill (drĭl), *v.* Skia, ranta ka·a ; a·kol pua.
Drink (drĭngk), *v.* DRANK, DRUNK, Ringa, *n.* Ringani.
Drip (drĭp), *v.* Jokrorota.
Drive (drīv), *v.* DROVE, DRIVEN, Moa, rika, chalaia, draa.
Drivel (drĭv''l), *v.* Ku·chi onga.
Drizzle (drĭz'z'l), *v.* Mikka wasisia.

Dromedary (drŭm'ē-dā-ry), *n.* Janggilo silchi ge·sasangipa Arabni ut ma·sa.
Drone (drōn), *n.* Bija bipa; aratgipa mande.
Droop (drōp), *v.* Oldawea, siboka; kom·chika.
Drop (drŏp), *v.* Tingtota, ga·akata, *n.* Tingtot.
Dropsy (drŏp'sy), *n.* Be·en boe saa.
Dross (drŏs), *n.* Silki.
Drought (drout), *n.* Mikka wagijani, sal rakchangani, akal ong·ani.
Drove (drōv), *n.* Moanggimin jak; *Drive*ko ba nibo.
Drown (droun), *v.* Chio dubie sia.
Drowsy (drou'zy), *a.* Tusina sikl ea.
Drudge (drŭj), *v.* Neng·bee kam ka·a,
Drug (drŭg), *n.* Sam.
Druggist (drŭg'gĭst), *n.* Samko palgipa, samko bringipa.
Drum (drŭm), *v.* Dama doka, *n.* Dama, nagra.
Drunk (drŭngk), *a.* Chu peka, chu pekgipa. **-ard,** *n.* Chupekronggipa mande.
Dry (drī), *v.* DRIED, Ran·ata, *a.* Ran·a, ringna ska.
Duck (dŭk), *v.* Sim·bola, *n.* Do·gep; ba·ra ma·sa.
Due (dū), *a* On·na nanga.
Duel (dū'ĕl), *n.* Sakgni dakgrikani.
Duet (du-ĕt'), *n.* Sakgni damsan ring·ani.
Dug (dŭg), *v* *Dig*ko nibo.
Duke (dūk), *n.* Jomidar ba raja gi·a dal·gipa mande.
Dull (dŭl), *a.* Gisikni goka, uininggijagipa; matgija, bin·a.
Dumb (dŭm), *a.* Ku·ma, ku·gri.
Dun (dŭn) *v.* Gro rika.
Dunce (dŭns), *n.* Uininggijagipa, gisik bang·gijagipa mande.
Dung (dŭng), *n.* Ki·i.
Dungeon (dŭn'jŭn), *n.* Patok nok, ning·oni andalgipa nokdring.
Duplicate (dū'plĭ-kat), *n.* Gita ba apsan dakani.
Durable (dū'rā-b'l), *a.* Ruute baigipa, rakgipa. **-ability,** *n.*
During (dūr'ing), *prep.* Mitingo.
Dusk (dŭsk), *n.* Atamsimsim, **-y,** *a.*
Dust (dŭst), *n.* A·dumu. **-y,** *a.*
Dutch (dŭch), *n.* Holand songoni mande.
Duty (dū'ty), *n* Dakna nanga kam; ra·napani kajana.
Dwarf (dwôrf), *n.* Mande bone, bone.
Dwell (dwĕl), *v.* Donga, dongkama.
Dwindle (dwĭn'd'l), *v.* Cham·roroa, komiroroa.
Dye (dī), *v.* Rong sim·a, rong on·a, *n.*
Dynasty (dī'nas-ty), *n.* Rajani ma·chong.
Dysentery (dĭ'sen-têr-y), *n.* Okgitchak saa.
Dyspepsia (dĭs-pĕp'sĭ-ā), *n.* Jronggijani ba goligijani saa.
Dyspeptic, *a.*

E

Each (ēch), *a. pro.* Prak, anti.
Eager (ē'gĕr), *a.* Sikbegipa.
Eagle (ē'g'l), *n.* Do·gandot.
Ear (ēr), *n.* Nachil, nachikol; kopsa, soksa.

Earl (êrl), *n.* England songni dal·a mande.
Early (êr'ly), *adv.* Seng·gnang.
Earn (êrn), *v.* Kam ka·e man·a, ba man·na kraa.
Earnest (êr'nĕst), *a.* Joton ka·gipa, bimchipgipa, gisik nanggipa, nachilakgija, *n.* Bahena on·a.
Earring (ēr'rĭng), *n.* Nachilo ganani, korea, sisa.
Earth (êrth), *n.* A·a, a·gimik.
Earthen (êrth''n), *a.* A·ako daka.
Earthquake (êrth'kwāk'), *n.* Banggria, a·a moani.
Earthworm (êrth'wêrm'), *n.* Kan·churi.
Ease (ēz), *n.* Neng gija ong·ani, ba saknaa gr·ani, tom tomani.
East (ēst), *n.* Salaiam.
Easter (ēs'têr), *n.* Kristoni chakatpilani salko maniani.
Easy (ēz'y), *a.* altua, nangraa.
Eat (ēt), *v.* ATE, EATEN, Cha·a.
Eaves (ēvz), *n.* Pangsone, sone.
Eaves-dropper (ēvz'drŏp'pêr), *n.* Gipinni aganako srik srik knatimgipa.
Ebb (ĕb), *v.* Rookanga, komianga.
Ebony (ĕb'ŭn-ny), *n.* Ablus bol, bol ma·sa.
Ebullition (ĕb'ŭl-lĭsh'ŭn), *n.* Chichara, bokbaka, gitna.
Eccentric (ĕk-sĕn'trĭk), *a.* Ong·ronggija, bewal gita ong·gijagipa.
Ecclesiastic (ĕk-klē'zĭ-ăs'tĭk), *n.* Toromko skigipa, *a.* Mondolini biding.
Echo (ĕk'o), *n.* Rong·kuchak, ra·chake gam·pilgipa ku·rang.
Eclipse (e-klĭps'), *n.* Sal ba jako nawang minokani.
Economize (e-kŏn'o-mīz), *v.* Simsake gamko jakkala. **-my, mist**, *n.* **-ical**, *a.*
Ecstatic (ĕk-stăt'ik), *a.* Namen ka·sroka.
Eczema (ĕk'ze-mā), *n.* Bigil saani biati ma·sa.
Eddy (ĕd'dy), *n.* Chiganduri.
Edge (ĕj), *n.* Riking, ku·chot.
Edible (ĕd'ĭ-b'l), *a.* Cha·na nama, cha·na kraa.
Edict (ē'dikt), *n.* Aganprakgimin ge etani.
Edifice (ĕd'ĭ-fĭs), *n.* Rikgimin, nok.
Edify (ĕd'ĭ-fī), *v.* Skia, skie namata, mangrakata.
Edit (ĕd'ĭt), *v.* Chapa ka·na tarisoa. **-or**, *n.* **-orial**, *a. n.*
Edition (e-dĭsh'ŭn), *n.* Changsano badita katapko chapa ka·a.
Educate (ĕd'u-kāt), *v.* Skia, pilakchin uigipa dakata, gisikni bilko dal·roroata. **-or, -ion**, *n.*
Eel (ēl), *n.* Asinta.
E'en (ēn), *adv.* Evenko kan·dikatgimin.
E'er (âr ba âr), *adv.* *Ever*ko kan·dikatgimin.
Efface (ĕf-fās'), *v.* Ripake gala, kimita. **-ment**, *n.*
Effeminate (ĕf-fĕm'ĭ-nat), *a.* Me·chik gita nom·gipa, bil grigipa, ka·donggijagipa.
Efficient (ĕf-fĭsh'ent), *a.* Kamni biteko nangatgipa ba chu·sokatgipa.
Effort (ĕf'fêrt), *n.* Joton ka·ani.
Egg (ĕg), *n.* Do·chi, bitchi.
Egotism (ē'go-tĭz'm), *n.* A·tangko de·mitelani, gaora de·ani. **-tist**, *n.*
Eight (āt), *a.* Chet, ge·chet.

Eighteen (ā'tēn'), *a.* Chi'chat.
Eighty (ā'ty), *a.* Sotchet, kolchanggbri.
Either (ē'THer, ba ī' THer), *a.* Gnini gisepo sa, ia ba ua.
Eject (e-jĕkt'), *v.* A'rikata, galata. **-or, -ion, -ment,** *n.*
Elapse (e-lăps'), *v.* Sal re'anga ba batanga.
Elastic (e-lăs'tĭk), *a.* Salkringo ro'e wato kom'totgipa, saloina man'gipa, rober gita.
Elate (e-lāt'), *v.* Gisikko kusi ong'ata.
Elbow (ĕl'bo), *n.* Jakskn, ba ugita dakgipa jeba, jakchik.
Elder (ĕl'dêr), *n.* Gipi, dal batgipa; me'apa, *a*
Elect (e-lĕkt'), *v.* Sea, mikchara. **-or, -ion,** *n.* **-ive,** *a.*
Electric (e-lĕk'trĭk'), *a.* Mikka riprapani bi ling.
Electricity (ē'lĕk-trĭs'ĭ ty), *n.* Mikka riprapani bil.
Elegance (ĕl'e-gans), *n.* Nitoani. **-gant,** *a.*
Elementary (ĕl'e-mĕn'tâ-ry), *a* Bringija, ong'telaigipa.
Elephant (ĕl'e-fant), *n.* Mongma.
Elevate (ĕl'e-vāt), *v.* Chuata. **-ion,** *n.*
Eleven (e-lĕv''n), *a.* Chi'sa, chi'gisa.
Eligible (ĕl'ĭ-jĭ-b'l), *a.* Donna kragipa.
Elocution (ĕl'o-kū'shŭn), *n.* Jinmani mikkango aganna sapa ba changani. **-ist,** *n.* **-ary,** *a.*
Eloquent (ĕl'o-kwent), *a.* Aganna changgipa, **-ce,** *n.*
Else (ĕls), *conj.* Ongjaoba; *a.* Gipin; *adv.* Agre, una agre.
Elsewhere (ĕls-hwâr'), *adv.* Gipino, gipin biapo.
Elude (e-lūd'), *v.* Pa'ske katanga. **-sive,** *a.*
Emaciate (e-mā'shĭ-āt), *v.* Ram'a, ram'ata. **-ion,** *n.*
Emancipate (e-măn'sĭ-pāt), *v.* Nokol itaoniko jokata. **-or, -ion,** *n.*
Embalm (ĕm-bäm'), *v.* Manggisi sojachina smilgipa moslako nonga. **-ment,** *n.*
Embargo (ĕm-bär'go), *v.* Jahat re'rurako chhampenga, *n.*
Embark (ĕm-bärk'), *v.* Jahato gakata, gakata. **-ation,** *n.*
Embarass (ĕm-băr'res), *v.* Jajrengata, gisikko bingbangata, champenga, **-ment,** *n.*
Embassader (ĕm-băs'sâ-dêr), *n.* *Ambassador*ko nibo.
Ember (ĕm'bêr), *n.* Wal'ki.
Emblem (ĕm'blĕm), *n.* Gipinko me okani noksa ba chin.
Embody (ĕm-bŏd'y), *v.* Bimang dakata.
Embrace (ĕm-brās'), *v.* Gipakagipakgrika. **-ment,** *n.*
Embroider (ĕm-broid'êr), *v.* Ba'rao pul de'a.
Emerald (ĕm'êr-ald), *n.* Gamchatgipa ro'ong ma'sa.
Emerge (e-mêrj'), *v.* Naa, ong'kata. **-nce,** n.
Emergency, *n.* Niksogija ong'ani; dakningna nangbeani.
Emigrant (ĕm'ĭ-grant), *n.* Songgipino dongna songtangko wate re'anggipa, song katgipa.
Eminence (ĕm'ĭ-nens), *n.* Chua biap; mande ra'ani.
Eminent (ĕm'ĭ-nent), *a.* Mingsinga, dal'batgipa, chugipa.
Emotion (e-mō'shŭn), *n.* Gisik moani, gisik nangani.

Emperor (ĕm′pêr-êr), *n.* Raja dal·gipa.

Emphasis (ĕm′fă-sĭs), *n.* K tako rakatani. **-size,** *v.*

Emphatic (ĕm-făt′ik), *a.* Katao raka gnang.

Empire (ĕm′pīr), *n.* Dal·gipa songnok, samraijo.

Employ (ĕm-ploi′), *v.* Kamo dona, jakkala. **-ment,** *n.* **-ee,** *n.*

Emporium (ĕm-pō′rĭ-ŭm), *n.* Dal·gipa badingani biap.

Empower (ĕm-pou′êr), *v.* Bil on·a, nokgipa ong·aniko on·a.

Empress (ĕm′prĕs), *n.* Rani dal·gipa.

Empty (ĕmp′ty), *a.* Rara, a i, bang·bang, mamungba gri.

Enable (ĕn-ā′b′l), *v.* Amata, bil on a.

Encamp (ĕn-kămp′), *v.* A·tip donga.

Enchain (ĕn-chān′), *v.* Sildengchi kaa, beri pata.

Enchant (ĕn-chânt′), *v.* Muni nangata. **-ment,** *n.*

Encircle (ĕn-sêr′k′l), *v.* Maikoba dula.

Enclose (ĕn-klōz′), *v.* Bare du·a, ning·o chipa, dim·dula.

Encompass (ĕn-kŭm′pas), *v.* Maikoba re·dula, du·a.

Encounter (ĕn-kount′êr), *v.* Mikkanggrika, dakgrika, *n.*

Encourage (ĕn-kŭr′aj), *v.* Ka·dongata, didiata. **-ment,** *n.*

End (ĕnd), *n.* Bon·kama; ku·chot; mangsongani.

Endanger (ĕn-dān′jêr), *v.* Duk ba gimaani ong·naba dongao dona, duk ba a·sel ong·gnio dona.

Endear (ĕn-dēr′), *v.* Ka·saata, ka·sagniko dakata.

Endeavour (ĕn-dĕv′êr), *n.* Joton ka ani, *v*

Endorse (ĕn-dôrs′), *v.* Janggilchi sohi ka·a; rosid see on·a.

Endow (ĕn-dou′), *v.* Namgnina pangnan jakkalna ba koroch ka·na bang·e on·a. **-ment,** *n.*

Endure (ĕn-dūr′), *v.* Chakchika, dongka na, mangrake donga. **-ance,** *n.*

Endwise (ĕnd′wīz), *adv.* Ku·chotchi, groe, ronggroe.

Enemy (ĕn′e-my), *n.* Bobil.

Energy (ĕn′êr-jy) *n.* Kam ka·ani bil, bimchipani. **-getic,** *a.*

Enfeeble (ĕn-fē′b′l), *v.* Bilgri dakata.

Enforce (ĕn-fōrs′), *v.* Bilchi dakata. **-ment,** *n.*

Engage (ĕn-gāj′), *v.* Bondobosto ka·a, tik ka·a; dakgrika. **-ment,** *n.*

Engender (ĕn-jĕn′dêr), *v.* Atchiata, ong·kata·a, ong·ata.

Engine (ĕn′jĭn), *n.* Bilko ong·katatgipa kol.

Engineer (ĕn′jĭ-nēr′), *n.* Kolko chalaigipa, kolni gimin nigippa ba jakkalgipa; rama, jang·rang aro kolni kamrangko changgipa.

English (ing′glĭsh), *a.* England songni.

Engrave (ĕn-grāv′), *v.* Konge ba kite sea ba noksa daka.

Enhance (ĕn-hâns′), *v.* Bariata, dal·ata.

Enjoin (ĕn-join′), *v.* Ge·eta.

Enjoy (ĕnjoi′), *v.* Kusi ong·nika, jakkala. **-ment,** *n.* **-able,** *a.*

Enkindle (ĕn-kĭn′d′l), *v.* Ching·ata.

Enlarge (ĕn-lärj′), *v.* Bariata, dal·ata. **-ment,** *n.*

Enlighten (ĕn-līt′′n), *v.* Teng·-suata, seng·ata, uiata. **-ment,** *n.*

Enlist (ĕn-list′), *v.* Sipaini kam-na bimung sea.

Enliven (ĕn-liv′′n), *v.* Kusi ong·-ata, an·sawata.

Enmity (ĕn′mĭ-ty), *n.* Mik-nengani, bobil ong·grikani.

Ennoble (ĕn-nō′b′l), *v.* Dal·ata, chuata, dal·gipa ba namgipa ong·ata, dal·gipa ma·chong dakata. **-ment,** *n.*

Enormous (e-nôr′mŭs), *a.* Agre dal bea, ba bang·bea. **-ity,** *n.*

Enough (e-nŭf′), *a.* Chū·onga.

Enrage (ĕn-rāj′), *v.* Ka·o nang-ata.

Enrich (ĕn-rĭch′), *v.* Gam gnang-ata; a·sal gnangata. **-ment,** *n.*

Enroll (ĕn-rōl′), *v.* Bohio sea, bimung gata. **-ment,** *n.*

Ensign (ĕn′sīn), *n* Chin, nisan.

Enslave (ĕn-slāv′), *v.* Nokol dakata. **-ment,** *n.*

Ensnare (ĕn-snâr′), *v.* Ja·gao nangata.

Ensue (ĕn-sū′), *v.* Ja·rika.

Entangle (ĕn-tăng′g′l), *v.* Bu-duo ke·a, remrema, buduchi bingbangata. **-ment,** *n.*

Enter (ĕn′têr), *v.* Napa.

Enterprise (ĕn′têr-prīz), *n.* Dal·-gipa joton ka·gni, raka ba neng·ani kam.

Entertain (ĕn′têr-tān′), *v.* Sok-gipa chaka, ala. **-ment,** *n.*

Enthrone (ĕn-thrōn′), *v.* Sing-hasono asongata, bilko on·ata. **-ment,** *n.*

Enthusiasm (ĕn-thū′zĭ-ăz′m), *n.* Maiba kamko kusi ong·e bim-chipe gisik ding·e dakani. **-st,** *n.* **astic,** *a.*

Entice (ĕn-tīs′), *v.* Mikbokata, kimala. **-ment,** *n.*

Entire (ĕn-tīr′), *a.* Gimik.

Entomb (en-tūm′), *v.* Gopa, gopramo dona.

Entrails (ĕn′tralz), *n.* Bibik-rang.

Entrance (ĕn′trans), *n.* Napa-ni cholrama.

Entrap (ĕn-trăp′), *v.* Ja·gaobi rim·a.

Entreat (ĕn-trēt′), *v.* Mol·mola, bi·bea. **-y,** *n.*

Entrust (ĕn-trŭst′), *v.* Gipinni jako ka·donge pakwata.

Entry (ĕn′try), *n.* Napani; napram; bohio gatani.

Entwine (ĕn-twīn′), *v.* Sakrem rema, remrema.

Enumerate (e-nū′mêr-āt), *v.* Chana. **-ion, or,** *n*

Envelop (ĕn-vĕl′ŏp), *v.* Dule pindapa, wendapa.

Envelope (ĕn′vĕl-ōp), *n.* Pindap-ani lepapa.

Environ (ĕn-vī′rŭn), *v.* Dula, kadula. **-ment,** *n.*

Envious (ĕn′vĭ-ŭs), *a.* Gipinni namana miknenggipa.

Envy (ĕn′vy), *n.* Miknengani, mikbokani.

Epidemic (ĕp′ĭ-dĕm′ĭk), *n.* Song-gimikna gipgipa sabisi.

Epiglottis (ĕp′ĭ-glŏt′tĭs), *n.* Atajipa.

Epilepsy (ĕp′ĭ-lĕp′sy), *n.* Tengu-ria ong·ani, kore chaani. **-tic,** *a.*

Epistle (e-pĭs′′l), *n.* Chiti.

Epitaph (ĕp′ĭ-tăf), *n.* Gopramni kosako segimin.

Epoch (ĕp′ŏk, ba ē′pŏk), *n.* Sōn, tik ka·gimin chanani sal.

Equal (ē′kwal), *a.* Apsan. **-ity,** *n.*

Equalize (ē'kwal-īz), *v.* Apsan dakata. **-ation,** *n.*
Equator (e-kwā'têr), *n.* A'ani ganduri, a'a jatchiko saltonggipa, a'ani seng'ki.
Equinox (ē'kwī-nŏks), *n.* Sal aro wal apsangrik ong'ani sal, March 21 aro September 22, ia salrang.
Equip (e-kwĭp'), *v.* Nangako onata. **-ment,** *n.*
Equity (ĕk'wĭ-ty), *n.* Kakket dakani, mikkang nigija dakani.
Equivalent (e-kwĭv'â-lent), *a.* Apsangipa. *n.*
Era (ē'râ), *n.* Son, bi'si.
Erase (e-rās'), *v.* Kimita, ipaka.
Ere (âr ba êr), *adv.* Skango. *conj.* Skang.
Erect (e-rĕkt'), *v.* Songdoa, rika, mangrakata. **-ion,** *n.*
Err (êr), *v.* Guala.
Errand (ĕr'rand), *n.* Watata mandeni chona kam.
Error (êr'rêr), *n.* Gualani, brangani.
Eruption (e-rŭp'shŭn), *n.* Bikpawani, ong'katani, namni.
Escape (ĕs-kāp'), *v.* Kate joka.
Escort (ĕs'kôrt), *n.* Re'mitingo rakigipa. *v.* (ĕs-kôrt').
Especial (ĕs-pĕsh'al), *a.* Dingtangmancha, mongsonggipa.
Espy (ĕs-pī'), *v.* Nia nika.
Esquire (ĕs-kwīr'), *n.* Mande ra'ani kata.
Essay (ĕs'sa), *v.* Joton ka'a. *n.* Rochona. **-ist,** *n.*
Essence (ĕs'sens), *n.* Maiba bostuni birong; nambatgipa bak.
Essential (ĕs-sĕn'shal), *a.* Namen nangbea, nangchongmota.
Establish (ĕs-tăb'lĭsh), *v.* Dona, tik ka'a, mangrakata. **-ment,** *n.*
Estate (ĕs-tāt'), *n.* Gam gimik, mangsongde a'a; ong'ani.
Esteem (ĕs-tēm'), *v.* Mande ra'a, gamchatnika.
Estimable (ĕs'ti-ma-b'l), *a.* Mandera ako man'gipa ba man'na kragipa.
Estimate (ĕs'tĭ-māt), *v.* Chanchihipa, koro hko ka'soe nia.
Estrange (ĕs-trānj'), *v.* Ka'saako dingtangata ba chel'ata.
Estuary (ĕs'tu-a-ry), *n.* Bibra, chibimani ku'sik.
Eternal (e-têr'nal), *a.* Jringjrotna bon'changgijagipa.
Eternity (e-ter'nĭ-ty), *n.* Jringjrotna ong'ani.
Etymology (ĕt'ĭ-mŏl'o-jy), *n.* Katani gam'ako uiani.
Eulogize (ū'lo-jīz), *v.* Sakoba mitelna sea ba aganpraka.
Eulogy (ū lo-jy), *n.* Sakoba mitelna seani, ba aganprakani.
Eunuch (ū'nŭk), *n.* Kasi mande.
Eurasian (u-rā'shan), *a.* Perenggi, saheb aro mande gisimni brine ong'katgipa. *n.*
European (ū'ro-pē'an), *a.* Europe songni, *n.*
Evade (e-vād'), *v.* Tol'napachi joka, bebeko geela.
Evangelist (e-văn'jĕl-ĭst), *n.* Nama katako aganprakgipa, procharok. **-ize,** *v.* **-ical,** *a.*
Evaporate (e-văp'o-rāt), *v.* Biba dake chadoanga. **-ion,** *n.*
Eve, evening (ēv, ēv'nĭng), *n.* Atam.
Even (ē'v'n), *a.* Tiktak, apsan, soman; *adv.* Aro, ba.
Event (e-vĕnt'), *n.* Ong'ani, a'sel ong'ani.
Ever (ĕv'êr), *adv.* Basakoba, pangnaba.

Evergreen (ĕv′ĕr-grēn), *a.* Pangnan tangsakgipa, *n.*
Everlasting (ĕv′ĕr-lȧst′ing), *a.* Jringjrotna donggipa.
Evermore (ĕv′ĕr-mŏr′), *adv.* Pangnan, jringjrot.
Every (ĕv′ĕr-y), *a.* Anti, prak.
Every-body (ĕv′ĕr-y-bŏd-y), *n.* Sakanti, sakprak.
Every one (ĕv′ĕr-y-wŭn), *n.* Sakanti, sakprak.
Every-where (ĕv′ĕr-y-hwĕr), *adv.* Pilak biapon, biap antion.
Evidence (ĕv′ĭ-dens), *n.* Saki.
Evident (ĕv′ĭ-dent), *a.* Nikninggni, uininggni.
Evil (ē′v′l), *a.* Namgija, namja.
Evolution (ĕv′o-lū′shŭn), *n.* Balgawani, dal·roroani.
Evolve (ē-vŏlv′), *v.* Balgawa, ra, opraka, ong·katata.
Ewe (ū), *n.* Mes bima.
Exact (ĕgz-ȧkt′), *a.* Tik, kakket.
Exaggerate (ĕgz-ăj′ĕr-āt), *v.* Ong·ana bate agana, dakdape agana, chobate agana. **-ion,** *n.*
Exalt (ĕgz-ôlt′), *v.* Chuata, rasong chaata.
Examine (ĕgz-ăm′ĭn), *v.* Porika ra·a, name lake nia. **-ation,** *n.*
Example (ĕgz-am′p′l), *n.* Dake mesokani.
Exasperate (ĕgz-ăs′pĕr-āt), *v.* Ka·onangbeata, ka·a ding·ata. **-ion,** *n.*
Excavate (ĕks′kȧ-vāt), *v.* Ning·ko cho·a, kongrua. **-ion,** *n.* **-or,** *n.*
Exceed (ĕk-sēd′), *v.* Agrea, badea, bata.
Excel (ĕk-sĕl′), *v.* Gipinna bate bata.
Excellent (ĕk′sĕl-lent), *a.* Nambegipa. **-ence,** *n.*
Except (ĕk-sĕpt′), *v.* Wata, ra·chakja. **-ion,** *n.*
Except (ĕk-sept′), *pre.* -na agre.
Excess (ĕk-sĕs′), *n.* Batani, agreani.
Excessive (ĕk-sĕs′ĭv), *a.* Agre, bata.
Exchange (ĕks-chānj′), *v.* Srĕa, bodola, *n.*
Excite (ĕk-sīt′), *v.* Gisikko ding·ata. **-ment,** *n.*
Exclaim (ĕks-klām′), *v.* Chrika, rake ag·ana.
Exclamation (ĕks-klȧ-mā′-shŭn), *n.* Aiao inmanako mesokani kata.
Exclude (ĕks-klūd′), *v.* Chipchanga, a·pal gala.
Exclusion (ĕks-klū′shŭn), *n.* Chipchangani, a·pal galani.
Excommunicate (ĕks′kŏm-mū′-nĭ-kāt), *v.* Mondolini a·pal ong·ata.
Excrement (ĕks′kre-ment), *n.* Be·enoni or g·katgimin, ki·i.
Excursion (ĕks-kĕr′shŭn), *n.* Rona bachiba re·ani.
Excuse (ĕks-kūz′), *v.* Wata; pa·ske agana; jechaka. (ĕks-kūs′), *n.*
Execute (ĕks′e-kūt), *v.* Chu·sokata; jinggi so·ota. **-ion,** *n.*
Executive (ĕgz-ĕk′u-tĭv), *a.* Kamko chu·sokatgipa, matchotatgipa, *n.*
Exegesis (ĕks′e-jē′sĭs), *n.* Sastroni ortoko parakatani.
Exemplify (ĕgz-ĕm′plĭ-fī), *v.* Kamchi dake mesoka.
Exempt (ĕgz-ĕmpt′), Wata, chanja. **-ion,** *n.* Watani, changijani.
Exercise (ĕks′ĕr-sīz), *v.* Ranta ka·ata; jakkalronga, *n.*
Exert (ĕgz-ĕrt′), *v.* Bilko on·ata, biltangchi ka·a.

Exhale (ĕks-hāl′ ba ĕgz-āl′), *v.* Balwako watata, bibako chakatata. **-ation**, *n.*

Exhaust (ĕgz-ôst′), *v.* Bilgriata, chon·ata, bangbangata. **-ion**, *n.* **-ive**, *a.*

Exhibit (ĕgz-ĭb′ĭt ba ĕks-hĭb′ĭt), *v.* Mesoka, parakata. **-tion**, *n.*

Exhort (ĕgz-ôrt′ ba ĕks-hôrt), *v.* Namako skie didia ba mol·mola, mikrakata. **-ation**, *n.*

Exile (ĕks′īl), *v.* Songtangoniko rikata, songgipinchi a·rikata, *n.*

Exist (ĕgz-ĭst′), *v.* Donga, ong·a, tanga. **-ence**, *n.*

Exodus (ks′o-dŭs), *n.* Re·chakatani, Mosini sea gnigipa ki·tap, Jatra.

Expand (ĕks-pănd′), *v.* Balgawa, barianga.

Expanse (ĕks-păns′), *n.* Dal·gapgap, bangbang.

Expect (ĕks-pĕkt′), *v.* Ka·dongsoa, sengsoa, nicbaksoa. **-ance, -ation**, *n.* **-ant**, *a.*

Expedient (ĕks-pĕ′dĭ-ent), *a.* Dakna kraa.

Expedite (ĕks′pe-dīt), *v.* Dakningata, bakbakata. **-ious**, *a.*

Expedition (ĕks′pe-dĭsh′ŭn), *n.* Bang·ani re·ani; bakbak dakani.

Expel (ĕks-pĕl′), *v.* A·rikata, ong·katata.

Expend (ĕks-pĕnd′), *v.* Koroch ka·ata, komiata. **-iture**, *n.*

Expense (ĕks-pĕns′), *n.* Dam ba koroch. **-ive**, *a.*

Experience (ĕks-pē′rĭ-ens), *n.* Bang·e nike ba dake nigimin.

Experiment (ĕks-pĕr′ĭ-ment), *n.* Nina dakani, dake niani.

Expert (ĕks-pêrt′), *a.* Changgipa, sapgipa, *n.*

Expire (ĕks-pīr′), *v.* Rang·sitaon·a, sia. **-ation**, *n.*

Explain (ĕks-plān′), *v.* Tale agane niata.

Explanation (ĕks′plā-nā′shŭn), *n.* Tale agane niatani.

Explode (ĕks-plōd′), *v.* Breta, goa. **-sion**, *n.* **-sive**, *a.*

Explore (ĕks-plōr′), *v.* Am·a, sandia. **-ation**, *n.*

Export (ĕks-pōrt′), *v.* Songtangoni ong·kata bostuko songgipinchi on·ata ba watata. **-ation**, *n.*

Expose (ĕks-pōs′), *v.* Mesokata, parakata. **-ition, -ure**, *n.*

Expositor (ĕks-pŏs′ĭ-têr), *n.* Ortoko mesokgipa, tika segipa.

Expound (ĕks-pound′), *v.* Ortoko pe·e mesoka.

Express (ĕks-prĕs′), *v.* Gisikko agana, mesoka. **-ion**, *n.* **-ive**, *a.*

Exquisite (ĕks′kwĭ-zĭt), *a.* Nambea.

Extend (ĕks-tĕnd′), *v.* Snila; gipanga; baria.

Extensive (ĕks-ten′sĭv), *a.* Dal·begipa, apalbegipa. **-ion**, *n.*

Extent (ĕks-tĕnt′), *n.* Bimang dal·ani ba ro·ani.

Exterior (ĕks-tē′rĭ-êr), *n.* A·pal·chini, *a.*

Exterminate (ĕks-têr′mĭ-nāt), *v.* Bon·changata, gimata, arikata. **-ion**, *n.*

External (ĕks-têr′nal), *a.* A·pal·chini.

Extinct (ĕks-tĭngkt′), *a.* Kimitgimin, sigimin.

Extinguish (ĕks-tĭng′gwĭsh), *v.* Kimita, gimata.

Extol (ĕks-tōl′), *v.* De·mitela.

Extort (ĕks-tôrt'), *v*. Drae ra'a, o ia dake ra'a. **-ion**, *n*.
Extra (ĕks trå), *a*. Bata, git cha a; nambatgipa.
Extract (ĕks-trăkt'), *v*. Salongkata, likot ta.
Extract (ĕks'trăkt), *n*. Bikotgim n.
Extraordinary (ĕks-trôr'dĭ-na-ry ba ĕks'trå-ôr'dĭ-na-ry), *a*. Ramram ong'gija, aiao inmanani.
Extravagant (ĕks-trăv'å-gant), *a*. Agre koroch ka'gipa. **-ance**, *n*.
Extreme (ĕks-trēm'), *a*. Bon'kamgipa, batsranggipa. **-ity**, *n*. Ku'chot, bon'kama.
Extricate (ĕks'trĭ-kāt), *v*. Jokata, ja'gaoni ba jajrengaoniko jokata.
Exult (ĕgz-ŭlt'), *v*. Ka'sroka. **-ant**, *a*. **-ation**, *n*.
Eye (ī), *n*. Mikron; bejini a kol.
Eyeball (ī-bôl'), *n*. Mikron ronggimik.
Eyebrow (ī-brou'), *n*. Mikskim.
Eyelash (ī-lăsh'), *n*. Miksimang.
Eyelet (ī'lĕt), *n*. Chongipa a'kol.
Eyelid (īlid'), *n*. Mikil.

F

Fable (fā'b'l), *n*. Kata a'jong, g lpo.
Face (fās), *n*. Mikkang, *v*. Mikkangchaka. **-cial**, *a*.
Facile (făs'ĭl), *a*. Altua, nengraa.
Facilitate (få-sĭl'ĭ-tāt), *v*. Altuata, nengraata.
Facility (få-sĭl'ĭ-ty), *n*. Altuani, nengraani; dakningani.
Facsimile (făk-sĭm'ĭ-le), *n*. Tiktak gita dakgimin.
Fact (făkt), *n*. Chong'mot ong'gimin.
Factory (făk'to-ry), *n*. Dakram, maikoba dakani nok.
Faculty (făk'ŭl-ty), *n*. Gun, gisikni bil; school ge'sani skigiparang.
Fade (fād), *v*. Rong re'a, sikrepa, dimela.
Fail (fāl), *v*. Chu'sokja, amja, be'gopa. **-ure**, *n*.
Faint (fānt), *v*. Siboka, neng'a, amchakja, *a*.
Fair (fâr), *a*. Nitoa; sakgitchak, sakgibok; simteka gri, rongtala.
Fair (fâr), *n*. Anti, mela.
Faith (fāth), *n*. Ka'dongani, bebe ra'ani.
Falcon (fô'k'n ba făl'kŭn), *n*. Do'rang ma sa.
Fall (fâl), *v*. FELL, FALLEN, Ga'aka.
False (fôls), *a*. Bebe ong'gija.
Fame (fām), *n*. Mingsingani.
Familiar (få-mĭl'yêr), *a*. Namedake uigimin.
Famine (făm'ĭn), *n*. Akal, karap.
Famish (făm'ĭsh), *v*. Okria si'a ba nom'a.
Famous (fā'mŭs), *a*. Mingsinggipa, de a man'gipa.
Fan (făn), *n*. Gijip, *v*. Gijip jipa.
Fancy (făn'sy), *n*. Gisikni chanchiani, namnikani, *v*.
Fang (făng), *n*. Bisi gnang'ripa wagam; chipu aro matcha gita wagam ro'gipa.
Far (fär), *a*. Chel'a. *adv*.

Fare (fâr), *n*. Re·ani dam, keria; cha·ani.
Farewell (fâr′wĕl′), *interj*. Ekgriknasio salam ka·ani kata.
Farm (färm), *n*. A·ba, ge·a, patal.
Farmer (färm′êr), *n*. A·a gamgipa, gam cha gipa.
Farrier (făr′rĭ-êr), *n*. Gurena sam tarigipa.
Farther (fär′THêr), *a*. Chel·bata. **-thest**, *a*.
Farthing (fär′THĭng), *n*. England songni paisa, pelsa baksi apsan.
Fashion (făsh′ŭn), *n*. Dakbewal, niam.
Fast (fåst), *v*. Okumu chika.
Fast (fåst), *a*. Gong·raka; kimkim; ma·gapgimin, *adv*.
Fasten (fås″n), *v*. Kaa, rakata, ma·gapata.
Fat (făt), *n*. Mitim.
Fat (fat), *a*. Mila, dal·a, mitima.
Fatal (fā′tal), *a*. Signi, gimatgni.
Fatality (fā-tăl′ĭ-ty), *n*. Janggi signini ong·ani.
Fate (fāt), *n*. Rasong, kopal.
Father (fä′THêr), *n*. Paa, pagipa, apa.
Father-in-law (fä′THêr-ĭn-lô), *n*. O·bite.
Fathom (făTH′ŭm), *n*. Tu·ako toani, mikbrini pal, pakkrangea, *v*.
Fathomless (făTH′ŭm-lĕs), *a*. Tu·l ea, tosokgija.
Fatigue (fā-tēg′), *n*. Neng·ani, *v*. Neng·ata.
Fatten (făt′t′n), *v*. Milata, dal·ata.
Faucet (fô′sĕt), *n*. Chi jokatani pes.
Fault (fôlt), *n*. Sokrijani, namsranggijani, namgij ni dos.
Favour (fā′vêr), *n*. Namnikani; ka·sae dakgimin.
Favourite (fā′vêr-ĭt), *n*. Ka·sara ba namnika mande.
Fawn (fôn), *n*. Matchok bi·sa, *v*. Mol·mola, gon·gona.
Fear (fēr), *v*. Kena, *n*. Kenani.
Feast (fēst), *n*. Alani, ala, *v*. Cha·bea, albea.
Feat (fēt), *n*. Dal·a ba bilakani kam.
Feather (fĕ′THêr), *n*. Do·kimil.
Feature (fē′tur), *n*. Mikkang ba bimangni maiba bak; mainil·a bak.
February (fĕb′ru-a-ry), *n*. Bilsini gnigipa ja.
Fed (fĕd), *v*. *Feed*ko nibo.
Fee (fē), *n*. Koraki, boton, boksis.
Feeble (fē′b′l), *a*. Bilgrigipa, bil bang·gijagipa.
Feed (fēd), *v*, FED, Ala, aldua.
Feel (fēl), *v*. FELT, Nangdika; duk sukko uia, te·euni ba gisikni uia.
Feet (fēt), *n*. Ja·arang, *foot*-rang.
Feign (fān), *v*. Cha·chipile daka.
Feint (fānt), *n*. Tol·napani, cha·chipile dakani.
Fell (fĕl), *v*. Den·pea; *Fall*ko nibo.
Fellow (fĕl′lō), *n*. Bipeng, chasonggrik ong·pagipa, mandeska, adjective dongjaode, basakoba chonnikaniko mesokani.
Fellowship (fĕl′lo-shĭp), *n*. Mandeskani nangrimani.
Felloe (fĕl′ly), *n*. Chakani a·achi nangchakgipa, dulni bol.

Felly, (fĕl'ly), *n*. Chakani a·achi nangchakgipa, dulni bol.
Felon (fĕl'ŭn), *n*. Niamko pe·gipa, namen namgijagipa mande; bisi minani.
Felony (fĕl'o-ny), *n*. Sina ba sinakrip patoko donna man·na kraa niamko pe·ani.
Felt (fĕlt), *n*. Kimilni ritchenggipa ba·ra. *v*. *Feel*ko nibo.
Female (fē'māl), *a*. Bima.
Fence (fĕns), *n*. Dileng, bari, guare.
Ferment (fêr-mĕnt'), *v*. Gangbua, chaa. **-ation**, *n*. **-ative**, *a*.
Fern (fĕrn), *n*. Su·sanat, sanat, me·konchek.
Ferocious (fe-rō'shŭs), *a*. Ka·saninggija, chikrakgipa.
Ferret (fĕr'rĕt), *n*. Rokomsa chuna.
Ferrule (fĕr'rĭl ba -rul), *n*. Nalwatani, sama chatani.
Ferry (fĕr'ry), *n*. Chi batram ghat; chobatani ring, *v*.
Fertile (fĕr'tĭl), *a*. A·sal gnang.
Fertilize (fêr'tĭ-līz), *v*. A·sal gnangata.
Fervent (fêr'vent), *a*. Gisik ding·gipa, gisik nanggipa, bimchipgipa.
Fervor (fĕr'vêr), *n*. Gisik ding·ani, bimchipani.
Fester (fĕs'têr), *v*. Mina, ripua, tottonga, chonchone ripua, *n*.
Festival (fĕs'tĭ'val), *n*. Ale cha·ani, kusi ong·ani sal.
Fetch (fĕtch), *v*. Ra·ea.
Fetid (fĕt'id ba fē'tĭd), *a*. Soa, seenga, soa gita seenga.
Fetlock (fĕt'lŏk), *n*. Gureni ja·aku ka·mao chagipa' kimil.
Fetter (fĕt'têr), *n*. Siliting, sildeng, beri, ja·dokdak kaani.

Feud (fūd), *n*. Ma·chong ba songni gisepo bobil dakgrikani.
Fever (fē'vêr), *n*. Be·en ding·e saa.
Few (fū), *a*. Adita, bang·gija.
Fiber, fibre (fī'bêr), *n*. Bisring, kilding.
Fickle (fĭk'k'l), *a*. Gisik dingtang ong·ninggipa.
Fiddle (fĭd'd'l), *n*. Behela.
Fidelity (fĭ-dĕl'ĭ-ty), *n*. Nokgipana ba dakna nangana kakket ong·gipa.
Field (fēld), *n*. Guare kadulgipa a·ba; dakgrikani biap.
Fiend (fēnd), *n*. Namen namgijagipa bobil; Soitan.
Fierce (fērs), *a*. Ka·onangrakgipa, ka·saninggijagipa.
Fiery (fī'êr-y ba fī'ry), *a*. Wal·gita ching·chagipa, gisik ding·gipa.
Fife (fīf), *n*. Bangsi.
Fifteen (fĭf'tēn), *a*. Chi·bonga.
Fifth (fĭfth), *a*. Bongagipa.
Fifty (fĭf-ty), *a*. Sotbonga, kolchanggni chikung.
Fig (fĭg), *n*. Te·wek bite, dumbur bite.
Fight (fīt), *v*. Dakgrika, dinggrika, *n*.
Figurative (fĭg'ur-â-tĭv), *a*. Toe mesokani gnang.
Figure (fĭg'ur), *n*. Bimang; ongko, *v*. Hisab ka·a.
File (fīl), *n*. Ret; riting riting tarie dongimin lekarang.
File (fīl), *v*. Retchi nata; riting dake re·a; tarie dona.
Filial (fĭl'yal), *a*. De gita dakgipa.
Fill (fĭl), *v*. Gapata, okkaata.
Filly (fĭl'ly), *n*. Gure bima bi·sa.

Film (film), *n.* Bisingkap, ba·gipa kaprang.
Filter (fil'têr), *v.* Chi cheka, *n.* Chi chekani.
Filth (filth), *n.* Moila; ki·i.
Fin (fin), *n.* Na·tokni gangching.
Final (fi'nal), *a.* Bon·kamgipa.
Finance (fi-năns'), *n.* Tangkako jakkalani. **-ial**, *a.* **-ier**, *n.*
Find (fīnd), *v.* FOUND, Nika, am·e man·a.
Fine (fīn), *n.* Jorimana ka·ani, *v. a* Nambea, nitobea, se·ena.
Finger (fing'gêr), *n.* Jaksi, *v.* Jaksichi nangdika.
Finish (fin'ish), *v.* Matchotata, chu·sokata, bon·ata.
Finite (fi'nīt), *a.* Bon·gnigipa, dongkamgijagipa.
Fire (fīr), *n.* Wa·al, *v.* Wa·al so·a; goa.
Firearm (fīr'ärm'), *n.* Slai.
Firebrand (fīr'brănd'), *n.* Wal·ki
Firefly (fīr'flī), *n.* Seng·wat, jonai.
Fire-proof (fīr'prụf'), *a.* Kamna amgijagipa.
Firework (fīr'wêrk), *n.* Wa·al kal·ani.
Firm (fêrm), *a.* Råka, kimkim, *n.* Badingani dol ba ma·mal.
Firmament (fêr'må-ment), *n.* Salgirang, bangbang.
First (fêrst), *a.* Skanggipa.
First-born (fêrst'bôrn'), *a.* Dejakra, atchichenggipa.
First-rate (fêrst'rāt), *a.* Nambatgiparangoni, nambegipa.
Fish (fish), *n.* Na·tok.
Fish-hawk (fish'hôk), *n.* Korua.
Fish-hook (fish'hụk'), *n.* Milsi.
Fissure (fish'ụr), *n.* Bretani.
Fist (fist), *n.* Jaktom.

Fit (fit), *v.* Kraata, ma·gapata, *n.* Matri saa, *a.* Kraa.
Five (fīv), *a.* Bonga.
Fix (fiks), *v.* Dona; rakata, niam daka; taria.
Flabby (flăb'by), *a.* Ma·ketgijagipa, olgrokgipa, dilwe dilwe dakgipa.
Flag (flăg), *n.* Misna, nisan; rong·pleng.
Flake (flāk), *n.* Ba·gipa ka·prang.
Flame (flām), *n.* Wal·sare.
Flank (flănk), *n.* Okil, ok·ambeng, ketchi.
Flannel (flăn'nĕl), *n.* Mes kimilni ding·gipa ba·ra ma·sa.
Flap (flăp), *v.* Gangpakpaka, gangchichia, *n.*
Flare (flâr), *v.* Jrao jrao dake ching·a.
Flash (flăsh), *v.* Delipa, riprapa.
Flat (flăt), *a.* Dalgapa, dalgepa.
Flatten (flăt'ten), *v.* Dalgapata, dalgepata.
Flatter (flăt'têr), *v.* Tol·e mitela.
Flatulent (flăt'u-lent), *a.* Okdita gnang.
Flaunt (flänt ba flônt), *v.* Gaora de·e paraka.
Flavour (flā'vêr), *n.* Su·uani; biba, *v.*
Flaw (flô), *n.* Silni pari, janerao be·chipilani.
Flax (flăks), *n.* Mosina, son.
Flea (flē), *n.* Su·tik.
Flee (flē), *v.* FLED, Kata, kene kata.
Fleece (flēs), *n.* Mesni kimil gimik, mongsongde rasotgimin, *v.*
Fleet (flēt), *n.* Jahat jinma, *a.* gong·rakgipa.

Flesh (flĕsh), *n.* Be'en, bitin.
Flew (flū), *v.* *Fly*ko nibo.
Flexible (flĕks'i-b'l), *a.* Dol'-ninggipa, gongdolningsipa.
Flicker (flĭk'ĕr), *v.* De'ip delip daka.
Flight (flīt), *n.* Bilani, katani.
Flimsy (flĭm'zy), *a.* Be'ninggipa, grinninggipa, ba'begipa.
Flinch (flinch), *v.* Salpila, donpila.
Fling (fling), *v.* FLUNG, Goata, galata.
Flint (flint), *n.* Wal'tot, rong'-silchi.
Flippant (flip'pant), *a.* Bol'bol-gipa, boklokgipa.
Flit (flit), *v.* Bilpakanga.
Float (flōt), *v.* Gitchoa, Ialboa, ba'paka.
Flock (flŏk), *n.* Mea, do bok ba do'orangni jak ba jinma.
Flog (flŏg), *v.* Go o! ka betchi doka.
Flood (flŭd), *n.* Chi dubi ani, bripani, bona re'ani.
Floor (flōr), *n.* Gan' ang, wa'se, dokta.
Floral (flō'al), *a.* Bibalni biding
Florin (flŏr'in), *n.* Rupani tangka ma'-a.
Florist (flŏr'ist), *n.* Bibalni bariko gamgipa.
Flounder (floun'dêr), *v.* Ronrom mital daka, il'eng pileng daka. *n.* Rokomsa na'tok.
Flour (flour), *n.* Moida, gomni ginde.
Flourish (flŭr'ish), *v.* Sila; wingwanga.
Flow (flō), *v.* Jokanga, so'olanga.
Flower (flou'êr), *n.* Bibal, pul.
Flown (flōn), *v.* *Fly*ko nibo.
Fluctuate (flŭk'tu-āt), *v.* Mo-raraa, wingwanga.
Fluent (flū'ent), *a.* Aganna sapgipa.
Fluid (flū'id), *n.* Jingjonggipa, chi dakgipa.
Flung (flŭng), *v.* *Fling*ko nibo.
Flush (flŭsh), *v.* Gitchakata; rang'san jokmrikata, *n.*
Flute (flūt), *n.* Bangsi.
Flutter (flŭt'têr), *v.* Gangpak-paka, gangchichia.
Fly (flī), *n.* Tampi.
Fly (flī), *v.* FLEW, FLOWN, Bila, kata.
Flyblow (flī'blō'), *n.* Tampini bitchi, *v.*
Fly-leaf (flī'lēf), *n.* Ki'tapni skanggipa aro bon'kanggipa mamungba sea grigipa jak.
Foal (fōl), *n.* Gu'ri bisa.
Foam (fōm), *n.* Ka'-pu.
Focus (fō'kŭs), *n.* Jeona salni renga'saako salchi monga.
Fodder (fŏd'dêr), *n.* Ran gimin jeng.
Foe (fō), *n.* Bobil.
Fog (fŏg), *n.* Guuri.
Foil (foil), *v.* Dakna skako chamtenga.
Fold (fōld), *v.* Dol'a, tem'a.
Fold (fōld), *n.* Nol, gisol, gohali.
Foliage (fō'li-aj), *n.* Bolni bijak-rang.
Folks (fōks), *n.* Manderang.
Follow (fŏl'lo), *v.* Ja'rika, rika; sninga.
Folly (fŏl'ly), *n.* Gokani, gisik grini.
Fond (fŏnd), *a.* Namnikgipa.
Food (fūd), *n.* Cha'ani.
Fool (fūl), *n.* Goka ba gisik grigipa mande.

Foolscap (fuls'kăp') *n.* L ka rokomsa.

Foot (fut), *n.* Ja'a, ja'ra; ja'-pang; inch 12.

Foot-path (fut'päth'), *n.* Rama chongipa.

Foot-step (fut'stĕp'), *n.* Ja'kol, ja'birang.

Footstool (fut'stul'), *n.* Ja'a don hokani, am'pok.

For (fôr), *pr.* Gimin, -na, maina, -ni p l.

Forasmuch (fôr'az-mŭch'), *con.* Maina, uni gimin.

Forbade (fŏr-băd'), *v.* *Forbid*-ko ni o.

Forbear (fŏr-bâr'), *v.* FORBORE, FORBEARS, FORBORNE, Dongdika; chakchika.

Forbid (fôr-bĭd'), *n.* FORBADE, FORBIDDEN, Beng'a, champenga.

Forebore (fŏr-bōr'), *v.* *Forbear*-ko nibo.

Force (fōrs), *n.* Bil; dakgrikna tarigimin sipairang.

Force (fōrs), *v.* Bilchi dakata, draata.

Forceps (fôr'sĕps), *n.* Sildangkep ma'sa.

Ford (fōrd), *v.* Ja'achi bata. *n.* Chi batram.

Fore (fōr), *adv.* Skango, mikkangchipak.

Forearm (fōr-ärm'), *v.* Nangana skang silchida'e hi tarisoa, *n.* Jak, jakwang.

Forbode (fōr-bōd'), *v.* Maiba namgijana kensoa ba chanchisoa.

Forecast (fōr-kâst'), *v.* Mikkangchiniko niksoa, chanchisoa.

Forecastle (fōr'kas''l), *n.* Jahatni mikkangchinipak.

Forefathers (fōr'fäth'ērs), *n.* Pagitchamrang.

Forefinger (fōr'fĭng'gēr), *n.* Ja' si atra.

Forefoot (fōr'fut'), *n.* Matchu ba do'bokni mikkangchini jak.

Forehead (fŏr ĕd), *n.* Mikking.

Foreigner (fŏr'ĭn-ēr), *n.* Songgipini mande.

Forelock (fōr'lŏk'), Mikkingni kni.

Foreman (fōr'man), *n.* Mohori; nitimgipa, kam ka'ako mesokgipa.

Foremost (fōr-mōst), *a.* Pilakna skangbatgipa.

Forenoon (fōr'nun'), *n.* Pringchibara.

Foreskin (fōr'skĭn'), *n.* Ma'ani ku'dimani bigil ku'chot.

Forest (fŏr'ĕst), *n.* Bolgrim.

Forever (fŏr ĕv'ēr), *adv.* Jringjrotna, pangran bon'gija.

Forfeit (fôr'fĭt), *n.* Namgijako dakani gimin gnangako ba gamko gimatani.

Forgave (fŏr-gāv'), *v.* *Forgive*-ko nibo.

Forge (fōrj), *n.* Sil dakani chanskol.

Forgery (fōr'jēr-y), *n.* Jal daka, gita daka, togie daka ba sea.

Forget (fŏr-gĕt'), *v.* FORGOT, FORGOTTEN, Gua'a, jamanga.

Forgive (fŏr-gĭv'), *v.* FORGAVE, FORGIVEN, Kima ka'a, wata.

Forgot (fŏr-gŏt'), *v.* *Forget*-ko nibo.

Fork (fôrk), *n.* Be'en jote cha'ani silni bu'su, sil chonggeng, rekam.

Forlorn (fôr-lôrn'), *a.* Watgalgimin.

Form (fôrm), *n.* Bimang. *v.* Bimang daka. **-ation,** *n.*
Formal (fôr'mal), *a.* Niam gita, nanga gita.
Former (fôr'mêr), *a.* Skanggip-a.
Formidable (fôr'mĭd-â-b'l), *a.* Kenbegni.
Formula (fôr'mu-lâ), *n.* Dakbewal ba niamko mesokani.
Fornication (fôr'nĭ-kā'shŭn), *n.* Jik se gri pante me'tra til'ekani.
Forsake (fŏr-sāk'), *v.* Watgala.
Forsooth (fŏr-sṳth'), *adv.* Bebe.
Forswear (fŏr-swâr'), *v.* Tol'e mikcheta.
Fort (fōrt), *n.* Killa.
Forth (fōrth), *adv.* A'palchi, mikkangchi, mikkangchipak.
Forthwith (fōrth-wĭth' ba -with), *adv.* Rang'san, ruutgijan, bakbakan.
Fortieth (fôr'tĭ-ĕth), *a.* Sotbrigipa.
Fortitude (fôr'tĭ-tud), *n.* Chakchikani bil.
Fortnight (fôt'nīt' ba -nit), *n.* Anti gni.
Fortress (fôr'trĕs), *n.* Killa.
Fortune (fôr'tun), *n.* Rasong; gam. **-ate,** *a.*
Fortune-teller (fôr'tun-tĕl'êr), *n.* Gonok, jakko nie ong'gniko agangipa.
Forty (fôr'ty), *a.* Sotbri, kol changgni, wakma gni.
Forward (fôr'wêrd), *v.* Mikkangchi ong'ata ba dakata, *a.* Mikkangchipak, dakninggipa, gonggipa.
Fossil (fŏs'sil), *n.* Mainiba ro'ong pil'gimin.
Foster (fŏs'têr), *v.* Aldua; mittanga; ka'dongata.
Foster-brother (fŏs'têr-brŭth'er), *n.* Soksanchi aldua man'rimgipa gipin mande.
Foster-child (fŏs'têr-chīld'), *n.* Aldua ba mittanga de.
Foster-father (fŏs'têr-fä'thêr), *n.* Aldugipa mittanggipa paa.
Fought (fôt), *v.* *Fight*ko nibo.
Foul (foul), *a.* Moila gnanggipa, mitchigni.
Found (found), *v.* Ja'pangko dona, rika; *Find*ko ba nibo.
Foundation (foun-dā'shŭn), *n.* Rikchakani ja'pang.
Founder (found'êr), *v.* Chio dubiata; gureko koraata, *n.* Rikchenggipa, donchenggipa.
Foundery (found'êr-y), *n.* Silko ruani biap.
Fountain (foun'tĭn), *n.* Chimik.
Four (fōr), *a.* Bri, ge'bri.
Fourfold (fōr'fōld'), *a.* Duna bri.
Four-square (fōr'skwâr'), *a.* Samtangtang sambri apsangipa.
Fourteen (fōr'tēn'), *a* Chi bri.
Fourth (fōrth), *a.* Brigipa.
Fowl (foul), *n.* Do'orang, mongsongde do'nok.
Fox (fŏks), *n.* Peru ma'sa.
Fraction (frăk'shŭn), *n.* Bak, tong, pe'raronani.
Fracture (frăk'tur), *n.* Be'ani, greng be'ani pari.
Fragile (fră'jĭl), *a.* Be'ninggipa, sramgipa.
Fragment (frăg'ment), *n.* Be'tong giminni tong'sa.
Fragrant (frā'grant), *a.* Simila. **-nce,** *n.*
Frail (frāl), *a.* Gimaninggipa, baigijagipa, be'ninggipa. **-ty,** *n.*

Frame (frām), *n.* Rikgniko mangrakatani, pindapgni rikani.
Frank (frăngk), *a.* Cha·chipila grigipa.
Frantic (frăn'tik), *a* Kene ba mainiba gimin pagla gita ong·gipa.
Fraternal (fră-têr'nal), *a.* Jongada gita.
Fraud (frôd), *n.* Tol·napani. **-ulent,** *a.*
Freak (frēk), *n.* Indinari ba a·sel gri gisik dingtang ong·-ani.
Free (frē), *a.* Jakgitel.
Freedom (frē'dŭm), *n.* Jakgitel ong·ani.
Freethinker (frē'thingk'êr), *n.* Ska gita chanchiaigipa, bebe ra·gijagipa.
Freeze (frēz), *v.* FROZE, FROZEN, Sin·nana tin·kaa ba tin·daka.
Freight (frāt), *n.* Ringni bhara; gatgimin mal.
French (frĕnch), *a.* France songni.
Frequent (frē'kwent), *a.* Pil·-nipil.
Fresh (frĕsh), *a.* Gital, daldal; kari nanggijagipa.
Fret (frĕt), *v.* Tikitiki ina.
Friction (frik'shŭn), *n.* Natgrikani.
Friday (frī'da), *n.* Sukrobar, Sukulbar.
Fried (frīd), *v.* *Fry*ko nibo.
Friend (frĕnd), *n.* Ripeng. **-ship,** *n.*
Fright (frīt), *n.* Rang·sın kenbeani.
Frighten (frīt''n), *v.* Rang·sankenatbea.
Frigid (frij'id), *a.* Ka·sinbea, sin·bea.
Frill (fril), *n.* Skeme kodapgimin ba·ra riking.
Fringe (frinj), *n.* Ba·ra ja·te.
Frisk (frisk), *v.* Bilchroka, bila.
Frith (frith), *n.* Sagal noksik.
Frivolous (friv'o-lŭs), *a.* Gisik ritchenggipa.
Frock (frŏk), *n.* Krudapani cho'a.
Frog (frŏg), *n.* Beng·blok, beng·bek.
Frolic (frŏ'lik), *n.* Ka·srokani, kal·ani. *v.*
From (frŏm), *prep.* -oni.
Front (frŭnt), *n.* Mikkang, mikkangchini.
Frontier (frŏn'tēr), *n.* Songni ku·chot, sima.
Frost (frŏst), *n.* Suuri.
Froth (frŏth), *n.* Ka·spu.
Frown (froun), *v.* Mikskemachi ba niachi namnikgijako mesoka.
Frozen (frōz''n), *v.* *Freeze*ko nibo.
Frugal (frụ'gal), *a.* Nanga gita korochi ka·aigipa. **-ity,** *n.* (fru-găl'i-ty).
Fruit (frụt), *n.* Bite.
Frustrate (frŭs'trāt), *v.* Ong·gramaiata, bingbangata.
Fry (frī), FRIED, *v.* So·a, jo·a.
Fuel (fū'ĕl), *n.* Wa·alko so·ani, am·bol.
Fugitive (fū'ji-tiv), *n.* Joke katgipa.
Fulfil (fụl-fil'), *v.* Chu·sokata.
Full (fụl), *a.* Gapgimin.
Fuller (fụl'lêr), *n.* Ba·rako kom·-totatgipa. *a* Gapbatgipa.
Fumble (fŭm'b'l), *v.* Rim·nolnola.
Fume (fūm), *v.* Wal·kuata, bibi chakatata. *n.*

Fumigate (fū'mi-gāt), *v*. Bisiko gimatna ba chel atna wal·ku mika.
Fun (fŭn), *n*. Ka·dingani, kal·gaikani.
Fund (fŭnd), *n*. Maiba kamni gimin chimonge dongimin gam.
Fundamental (fŭn'dā-mĕn'tal), *a*. Ja·rangni ba pangchakani biding.
Funeral (fū'nêr-*a*l), *n*. Mande gopao pilak dakanirang.
Funnel (fŭn'nĕ), *n*. Ruchakani, silni chochoki; wal·ku jakatani noli.
Funny (fŭn'ny), *a*. Ka·dingatani, ba ka·dingatgipa.
Fur (fêr), *n*. Nom·gipa, seengipa, rinokgipa kimil, matrangni kimil.
Furious (fū'ri-ŭs), *a*. Namen ka·onangbegipa.
Furlong (fêr'long), *n*. Mailsani bak chetni bak sa, mik 440 mang.
Furlough (fêr'lo), *n*. Kamoni adita watako man·ani chuti.
Furnace (fêr'nas), *n*. Wa·al sikram, chinko'.
Furnish (fêr'nish), *v*. Nangako on·a.
Furniture (fêr'ni-tur), *n*. Nokni bostu·ang.
Furrow (fêr'ro), *n*. A·a weo nanggrini chikare dake matanggipa biap; be·enni chikare.
Further (fêr'THêr), *adv*. Chel·ao, chel·bato.
Further-more (fêr'THêr-mōr'), *adv*. Iana agreba, aroba.
Fury (fū'ry), *n*. Namen ka·o nangani.
Fuse (fūz), *v*. Ding·ate jrongata, jrongate nangrimata. -**ion**, *n*.
Fuse (fūz), *n*. Barut nonggimin killing ba badu, ka·sne kamangchina ro·ong goao bisnal dongipa.
Fuss (fŭs), *n*. Golmal ba mel·mel mul·mul dakani.
Futile (fū'til), *a*. Bite gri, ong·gramaia.
Future (fū'tur), *a*. Ong·gni ba ong·gni sal.
Fuzz (fŭz), *n*. Seengipa kimil, bisimak.

G.

Gabble (găb'b'l), *v*. Bil·bil bal·bal dake rongtalgija agana.
Gable (gā'b'l), *n* Sone samtangtangni gisepo biap.
Gag (găg), *v*. Ku·sikko rim·tipe dondikata, wakalna sikata, ka·rekata.
Gage (gāj), *n*. Toani.
Gauge (gāj), *n*. Toani.
Gaiety (gā'e-ty), *n*. Katchaani, kusi ong·ani.
Gayety (gā'e-ty), *n*. Katchaani, kusi ong·ani.
Gaily (gā'ly), *adv*. Katchae, kusi ong·e.
Gayly (gā'ly), *adv*. Katchae, kusi ong·e.
Gain (gān), *v*. Man·dapa, *n*.
Gainsay (gān'sā'), *v*. Jechaka.
Gait (gāt), *n*. Re·ani bewal.
Gaiter (gā'têr), *n*. Juta ma·se, ja·gitokko pindapani.
Galaxy (găl'ăks-y), *n*. Aski jinma; matma ja·kol.
Gale (gāl), *n*. Balwa ta·rakani, balwa rakani.

Gall (gôl), *n.* Ka·gipa bitchi; ka·kit

Gallant (gal'lant), *a.* Ka·dong-gipa, bilakgipa.

Gallant (găl-länt'), *a.* Me·chik-rangna rinoke dakgipa.

Gallery (gal lêr-y), *n.* Nokning-oni srek, baranda.

Gallon (găl'ŭn), *n.* Jronga bostuko toani ma·sa, sel bri.

Gallop (găl'lŭp), *n.* Dabraia-ni. *v.*

Gallows (găl'lŭs ba -loz), *n.* Pa-si on·ani bol.

Galoche, Galoshe (gâ-lŏsh'), *n.* Robolni juta.

Gamble (găm'b'l), *v* Joa kal·a.

Gambol (găm'bŏl), *v.* Chroka, bilchroka, kal·grika. *n.*

Gambrel (găm brĕl), *n.* Mat-chu ba do·bokrangni ja·sku.

Game (gām), *n.* Kal·ani; sikar ka·e goa do·o ba matrang.

Gander (găn'dêr), *n.* Rajahas bipa.

Gang (găng), *n.* Damsan ka·-gipa mande jinma.

Gangway (găng'wā'), *n.* Ja-bato napani chol.

Gaol (jāl), *n.* Patok nok. **Jail** seode nambata.

Gap (găp), *n.* Bretani; napong-grikani.

Gape (gäp), *v.* Ajama; nitata.

Garb (gärb), *n.* Ganani ba·ra.

Garbage (gär'baj), *n.* Cha·spa, re·cham.

Garden (gär'd'n), *n.* Bari, bagi-ja.

Gargle (gär'g'l), *v.* Chiko bil·-bite songdoe gitokko su·sranga.

Garland (gär'land), *n.* Bibalni ripok.

Garlic (gär'lik), *n.* Rasin gip-bok.

Garment (gär'ment), *n.* Ganani ba·ra.

Garner (gär'nêr), *n.* Jam, bandal, mi donani, *v.*

Garnish (gär'nish), *v.* Nitoata. **·ment,** *n.*

Garret (găr'rĕt), *n.* Nokni ko-sakbatgipa kutori ba gadang.

Garrison (găr'ri-s'n), *n.* Killa-ni sipairang.

Garter (gär'têr), *n.* Muja rak-atani.

Gas (găs), *n.* Biba, balwa ma·-sa.

Gash (găsh), *v.* Ning·tue mata. *n.* Matgimin.

Gasp (gâsp), *n.* Ka·tapo, ka·ta-po dakani, *v.*

Gate (gāt), *n.* Barini do·ga.

Gather (găTH'ĕr), *v.* Chimong-a, tom·a; ba·rako skema.

Gaunt (gänt), *a.* Ram·sisigipa.

Gauge (gāj), *n.* *Gage*ko ni-bo.

Gauze (gôz), *n.* Ba·begipa, nik-senggipa, daka a·sikgijagipa ba·ra.

Gave (gāv), *v.* *Give*ko nibo.

Gavial (gā'vi-al), *n.* Gorial.

Gay (gā), *a.* Kusi ong·gipa, ka·-dingrakgipa; rongchinggipa.

Gaze (gāz), *v.* Miksonge nia, nitata.

Gazette (gă-zĕt'), *n.* Kobor ka-goj ma·sa. Songbad.

Gecko (gĕk'o), *n.* Bapme.

Gelding (gĕld'ing), *n.* Kasi, mongsongde gure.

Gem (jĕm), *n.* Gamchatbegipa ripok.

Gender (jĕn'dêr), *n.* Bima bipa-ko mesokani kata.

Genealogy (jĕn'e-ăl'o-jy), *n.* Ma·chongko seani ba mesoka-ni.

General (jĕn'ĕr-al), *a.* Ramram, minggopgipa. *n.* Sipairangni pamong.
Generate (jĕn'ĕr-āt), *v.* Ong·katata, atchiata.
Generation (jĕn'ĕr-ā'shŭn), *n.* Chasong.
Generous (jĕn'ĕr-ŭs), *a* On·rakgipa, jaksramgipa.
Generosity (jĕn'ĕr-ŏs'i-ty), *n.* Jaksramani.
Genesis (jĕn'e-sis), *n.* Sastro a·bachengani.
Genial (jēn'yal ba jēn'i-al), *a.* Ripeng gita dakgipa, kusi ong·e ripeng dakgipa.
Genitive (jĕn'i-tiv), *a.* Nokgipa ong·ako mesokgipa karok. (Possessive kes).
Genius (jēn'yŭs), *n.* Gun, changani, skigija man·talaiani.
Gentile (jĕn'til), *a.* Jihudi ong·gijagipa, kritgipa.
Gently (jĕnt'ly), *adv.* Rinoke, name, mikmale.
Gentility (jĕn-til'i-ty), *n.* Namao atchiani; namgipani mikkim.
Genuine (jĕn'u-in), *a.* Ong·telaigipa, brina grigipa.
Geography (je-ŏg'rā-fy), *n.* Bhugol, a·ani kosakni gimin uiani.
Geology (je-ŏl'o-jy), *n.* A·a ning·oni gimin uiani.
Geometry (je-ŏm'e-try), *n.* Toaniko skiani.
Germ (jêrm), *n.* Bimik, bitchri.
German (jêr'man), *n.* Germany songni.
Germinate (jêr'mi-nāt), *v.* Bimik naa.
Gesture (jĕs'tur), *n.* Be·enchi dak·e mesokani chin.
Get (gĕt), *v.* GOT, GOTTEN, Man·a.
Ghost (gōst), *n.* Me·mang; put; gisik.
Giant (ji'ant), *n.* Bimang dal·begipa mande.
Gibberish (gib'bêr-ish), *n.* Bol·bolani.
Gibe (jib), *v.* Ka·dingsteka, kal·stapa.
Giblets (jib'lĕts), *n.* Bika, ka·rongte, kan·chok, iarang.
Giddy (gid'dy), *a.* Miks·wila, miksula; gisik to.n·tongijagipa.
Gift (gift), *n.* Indinari ba ka·sae on·gimin, on·gimin.
Gig (gig), *n.* Gure mangsanchi salgipa chaka gnigipa gari.
Gigantic (ji-găn'tik), *a.* Dal·bea.
Giggle (gig'g'l), *v.* Kikkikari ka·dinga.
Gild (gild), *v.* GILDED ba GILT, Sonachi rubripa ba repidapa.
Gill (gil), *n.* Natokni pekuare; do·oni pedupuo olwegipa gingmat.
Gill (jil), *n.* Pint sani ¼, chotak gni gita aps.n toani.
Gilt (gilt), *n.* Sonachi rubripgimin, repigimin.
Gimlet (gim'lĕt), *n.* Chongipa puani, borma bi·sa.
Gin (jin), *n.* Chu ma·sa; ja·ga; kil jetani kol.
Ginger (jin'jêr), *n.* E·ching.
Giraffe (ji-răf'), *n.* Jirap, gitok ro·tegipa matburung ma·sa.
Gird (gêrd), *v.* GIRT ba GIRDED, Kang·kare.
Girdle (gêr'd'l), *n.* Kang·kare kani.
Girdle (gêr'd'l), *v.* Den·janginga, den·jangjota, den·dula.

Girl (gêrl), *n.* Me·chik bi·sa.
Girth (gêrth), *n.* Gurek chelo katongani; dulako toani.
Give (giv), *v.* GAVE, GIVEN, On·a.
Gizzard (gĭz'zêrd), *n.* Do·oni ka·rongte.
Glacier (glā'shêr ba glăs'ĭ-êr), *n.* Suurini so·olgipa chibima.
Glad (glăd), *a.* Kusi ong·a.
Glade (glād), *n.* Bolgri ni jatchibini bangbanggipa biap.
Gladiator (glăd'ĭ-ā'têr), *n.* Boksisna tonualchi dakgrikgipa.
Glance (glâns), *v.* Niroka, niketchia; nangketchia, su·sketa, *n.*
Gland (glănd), *n.* Be·eno ba chagipao bitchi ong·katitani.
Glare (glâr), *v.* Jrao jrao ching·a.
Glass (glâs), *n.* Janera; ringchakani.
Glaze (glāz), *v.* Ching·chet ching·chet dakata, rinokata.
Gleam (glēm), *v.* Riprapa gita ching·chet ching·chet daka, *n.*
Glean (glēn), *v.* Mi lang·teta.
Glee (glē), *n.* Kusi ong·aniko mesokani, katchaani.
Glen (glĕn), *n.* A·bri ge·gnini gisep, a·kongkep.
Glide (glīd), *v.* Neng·mangija sol·solanga gita re·anga ba jokanga.
Glimmer (glĭm'mêr), *v.* Dimel dimel daka, *n.*
Glimpse (glimps), *n.* On·tisa nia, on·tisa ching·a, niksketa.
Glisten (glĭs''n), *v.* Jrao jrao ching·a.
Glitter (glĭt'têr), *v.* Gisep gisep jrao jrao dake ching·a, *n.*
Gloat (glōt), *v.* Miktnatgija nia, miksonge nia.
Globe (glōb), *n.* Tom·betgipa, a·tombet, a·gimik.
Globular (glŏb'u-lêr), *a.* Tom·betgipa.
Gloom (glōm), *n.* Andalsisi dakani; duk ong·ani.
Glorify (glō'rĭ-fī), *v.* Mitela rasong chaata.
Glory (glō'ry), *n.* Rasong, mitelani.
Glorious (glō'rĭ-ŭs), *a.* Rasong gnanggipa.
Gloss (glŏs), *n.* Rimil trittrit ching·gipa, natani ching·gimin. **-y**, *a.*
Glove (glŭv), *n.* Jak-i ge·antina koa gnanggipa jako kruani.
Glow (glō), *v.* Wal·chaa, ching·chaa.
Glowworm (glō'wêrm'), *n.* Sang·wat, jonai.
Glue (glū), *n.* Rakgipa stapgipa ata.
Glutton (glŭt't'n), *n.* Cha·betbong, cha·betbonggipa.
Gnash (năsh), *v.* Wagam chikmijila.
Gnat (năt), *n.* Gangguा.
Gnaw (nô), *v.* Tina.
Go (gō), *v.* WENT, GONE, Re·a.
Goad (gōd), *n.* Su ani silchonggeng, loru.
Goal (gōl), *n.* Amani ba cheani biap, jeona mang·onge susaa.
Goat (gōt), *n.* Do·bok.
Gobble (gŏb'b'l), *v.* Minokketa; tarke do·o gita mikoa.
Gobblet (gŏb'blĕt), *n.* Ja·chokgnanggipa ringchakani.
Goblin (gŏb'lin), *n.* Me·mang, put.
God (gŏd), *n.* Isol.
Goiter, Goitre (goi'têr), *n.* Gitok bel·bugipa.
Gold (gōld), *n.* Sona.

Golden (gōld'n), *a.* Sonani, sonako daka.
Goldfinch (gōld'fínch'), *n.* Rimitgipa do·o ma·sa.
Goldleaf (gōld'lēf'), *n.* Ba·begipa sona, sona bijak.
Goldsmith (gōld'smith'), *n.* Sonari, sona dakgipa.
Gone (gŏn), *v.* *Go*ko nibo.
Gong (gŏng), *n.* Rang, konta.
Good (gud), *a.* Nama.
Goodbye, goodby, (gud'bī'), *n.* Chel·achi re·nasio salam ka·ani.
Goods (guds), *n.* Bostu·rang, gamrang.
Goose (gus), *n.* Rajahas, rajahas bima ; gisik bang·gijagipa.
Gooseberry (guz- ba gus'b r-ry), *n.* Chongipa bite ma·sa.
Gore (gōr), *n.* An·chi, mongsongde tin·kagimin, *v.* Grongchi kea.
Gorge (gôrj), *n.* Gitok, gitokbu, chigitok.
Gorgeous (gôr'jŭs), *a.* Nitogipa, ching·chipgipa.
Gorilla (go-ril'lå). *n.* Mande gita dal·begipa bilakgipa makkre ma·sa.
Gosling (gŏz'lĭng), *n.* Rajahas bi·sa.
Gospel (gŏs'pĕl), *n.* Jisu Kristoni Nama kata, Mati, Mark, Luk, aro Johan, iarang.
Gossip (gŏs'sip), *n.* Gopo ka·ani, mitakani.
Got (gŏt), *v.* *Get*ko nibo.
Gouge (gouj ba guj), *n.* Batali ma·sa, chikong dakgipa batali.
Gourd (gōrd ba gurd), *n.* Lau.
Govern (gŭv'ẽrn), *v.* Nokgipa daka, sason ka·a. **-ment,** *n.* **-or,** *n.*
Gown (goun), *n.* Dal·gipa jraugipa chola.
Grab (grăb), *v.* Chagrope rim·a.
Grace (grās), *n.* Kragijana ka·saani, ka·sachakani.
Grade (grād), *n.* Gadang ; apsan chua ba onani.
Gradually (grăd'u-al-ly), *adv.* Ka·sne ka·sne.
Graduate (grăd'u-āt), *v.* Schoolko matchota, pas ka·a ; batroroangako suala, *n.*
Graft (gráft), *n.* Kadapgimin cheksi, kolom on·gimin, *v.*
Grain (grān), *n.* Mimisi ; mi ba misini birong rongsa, ginchi rongsa ; bolni bisring, birim rongprak.
Grammar (grăm'mẽr), *n.* Biakron, sea ba aganani niamrang. **-ian,** *n.*
Granary (grăn'å-ry), *n.* Mi donram, jam, bandal.
Grand (grănd), *a.* Nama aro dal·a.
Grandchild (grănd'chīld'), *n.* Su·gipa, su·tang
Grandeur (grănd'ur), *n.* Nitoani, rasong, bil.
Granddaughter (grănd'dô'têr), *n.* Su·gipa me·chik.
Grandfather (grănd'fäTH'ẽr), Atchutang, budetang.
Grandmother (grănd'mŭTH'ẽr), *n.* Ambitang, bitchitang.
Granite (grăn'ĭt), *n.* Rakgipa ro·ong ma·sa.
Granivorous (grå-niv'o-rŭs), *a.* Mi misiko cha·e tanggipa.
Grant (grănt), *v.* On·a.
Grape (grāp), *n.* Draka bite.
Graphic (grăf'ik), *a.* Namedake talo segimin, noksa gita dakgimin.
Grasp (grásp), *v.* Rake rim·a, rim·kepa.
Grass (grås), *n.* Samsi, sam.

Grasshopper (grȧs'hŏp'pêr), *n.* Guk, aguk.
Grate (grāt), *v.* Skakgipa rakgipachi nata, *n.* Silni ritchokchi dakgimin pengani.
Grateful (grāt'ful), *a.* *Gratitude*ko nibo.
Gratify (grăt'ĭ-fī), *v.* Namnikata.
Gratitude (grăt'ĭ-tūd), *n.* Namgniko maa·ani gimin gisiko mitelani, *a.* **Grateful.**
Grave (grāv), *n.* Gopani a·kol, *a.* Jrima, nangbea.
Gravel (grăv'ĕl), *n.* Rong·srek; samitcheng saa.
Graveyard (grāv'yärd'), *n.* Gopram.
Gravitate (grăv'ĭ-tāt), *v.* Bidimolona sala.
Gravitation (grăv'ĭ-tā'shŭn), *n.* Salopani.
Gravity (grăv'ĭ-ty), *n.* A·ani salopani bil.
Gravy (grā'vy), *n.* Me·chi.
Gray (grā), *a.* Kaltapru, gisim aro gipbok brina.
Graze (grāz), *v.* Cha·ama.
Grease (grēs), *n.* Mitim.
Great (grāt), *a.* Dal·a.
Great-grandchild (grāt'grănd'-chīld'), *n.* Su·tangni de.
Great-grandfather (grāt'-grănd'fä'thêr), *n.* Atchutangni pagipa, ambitangni pagipa.
Great-grandmother (grāt'-grănd'mŭth'êr), *n.* Ambitangni ma·gipa, atchutangni ma·-gipa.
Greedy (grēd'y), *a.* Cha·betbonggipa, mikbokgipa.
Green (grēn), *a.* Tangsek; mingija; gitang; brigija.
Greet (grēt), *v.* Salam ka·a.
Grew (grụ), *v.* *Grow*ko nibo.
Greyhound (grē'hound'), *n.* Sikori achak ma·sa.
Grief (grēf), *n.* Kalimani duk.
Grieve (grēv), *v.* Duk on·a, kalimata; kalima. **-ous,** *a.* **-ance,** *n.*
Grim (grĭm), *a.* Kengni, mongsongde mikkang.
Grimace (grĭ-mās'), *n.* Mikkang ka kusikchi namnikgijako mesokani chon.
Grimy (grīm'y), *a.* Dimak nanggipa, moila nanggipa.
Grin (grĭn), *v.* Wakicheng daka.
Grind (grīnd), *v.* GROUND, GROUND, Na·a, wil·a.
Grindstone (grīnd'stōn'), *n.* Wilwigipa natani ro·ong.
Grip (grĭp), *v.* Rike rim·a, rim·-kepa, rim·kotkota, *n.*
Gripe (grīp), *v.* Ok chike saa, *n.* Rimkepani.
Grist (grĭst), *n.* Changsano natgimin mimisi.
Gristle (grĭs''l), *n.* Nom·gipa greng, su·utgipa ja·dil.
Grist-mill (grĭst'mil'), *n.* Natani kol.
Grit (grĭt), *n.* An·cheng; jotking dakani gisik, watgalgijani gisik.
Grizzled (grĭz'z'ld), *n.* *Grey*ni biding; rong ma·sa.
Groan (grōn), *v.* Ma·ama, *n.*
Grocer (grōs'êr), *n.* Cha·anirangko palgipa, dokandar.
Groin (groin), *n.* Ja·pak.
Groom (grụm), *n.* Gure nirikgipa, sohis.
Groove (grụv), *v.* Ro·e chikare dake kita, *n.*
Grope (grōp), *v.* Dangrokroke am·a.

Gross (grōs), *n*. Dojon chi·gni, ba 144.

Gross (grōs), *a*. Agre dal·a ba mila; goka, dal·gopgrangaigipa.

Grotto (grŏt'tō), *n*. Grim, a·kol.

Ground (ground), *n*. A·a; *grind*-koba nibo.

Group (grup), *n*. Jinma, tom·-daka.

Grove (grōv), *n*. Bolgrim.

Grovel (grŏv''l), *v*. A·o malam-a.

Grow (grō), *v*. GREW, GROWN, Chan, dal·roroa.

Growl (groul), *v*. Ran linga.

Grub (grŭb), *v*. Cho·a, p·ka, *n*. Bokchit pil·gipa jo·ong.

Grudge (grŭj), *n*. Mikuengani.

Gruel (gru'ĕl), *n*. Men·di.

Grumble (grŭm'b'l), *v*. Miteng miteng ina, namnikgijako mesoka.

Grunt (grŭnt), *v*. Wak gita huk huk ine ina.

Guarantee (găr'ăn-tē'), *n*. Jamin, *v*.

Guard (gärd), *v*. Nitime maiba ong·gnieniko rakia, *n*. Nitimegipa, rakigipa.

Guava (gwä'vä), *n*. Kompiram.

Guess (gĕs), *v*. An las ka·a; gita nika.

Guest (gĕst), *n*. Sokgipa.

Guide (gīd), *n*. Dilgipa, ramako mesokgipa, *v*. Dila. **-ance**, *n*.

Guile (gīl), *n*. Change tol·napani, cha·chipilani.

Guilt (gĭlt), *n*. Dos, namgija.

Guinea (gĭn'e), *n*. England songni sonani tangka, siling 21.

Guitar (gĭ-tär'), *n*. Salgija jakchi moaiani behela.

Gulf (gŭlf), *n*. Sagal noksik; a·kong.

Gullet (gŭl'lĕt), *n*. Gitokbu, mirama, mi napani chol.

Gulp (gŭlp), *v*. Mi nokk·ta, *n*.

Gum (gŭm), *n*. Wagamni waring, waja·ong; sti.

Gun (gŭn), *n*. Sloi, chandal.

Gunny (gŭn'ny), *n*. Chalja.

Gunpowder (gŭn'poud'ẽr), *n*. Barut.

Gunstock (gŭn'stŏk'), *n*. Sloi kunda, sloini ga·tong.

Gurgle (gẽr'g'l), *v*. Brok brok ine gam·a, jokani gam·a.

Gush (gŭsh), *v*. Chini ta·rake ong·kata ba joka.

Gust (gŭst), *n*. Rang·san ta·rake balani; ka·o nangdatani.

Gut (gŭt), *n*. Bibik.

Gutter (gŭt'tẽr), *n*. Dongge, chikare, boi.

H.

Ha (hä), *int*. Aiao inmananiko mesokani.

Habit (hăb'ĭt), *n*. Dakrongani, dakbewal.

Habitable (hăb'ĭt-ȧ-b'l), *a*. Mande dongna kraa.

Habitation (hăb'ĭ-tā'shŭn), *n*. Dongani biap, nok.

Habitual (hȧ-bĭt'u-al), *a*. Dakrongani biding.

Hack (hăk), *v*. Den·gitaka; ka·sne gusua, *n*. Gari ma·-sa.

Had (hăd), *v*. *Have*ko nibo.

Hag (hăg), *n*. Nitogijagipa namgijagipa buchuma.

Haggard (hăg'gard), *a*. Saa ba dukni gimin ram·sisigipa.

Haggle (hăg'g'l), *v*. Den·chemchema.

Hail (hāl), *int*. Patiani ba mitelani kata.

Hail (hāl), *v.* Salam ka·a; okama.
Hail (hāl), *n.* Stil.
Hair (hâr), *n.* Kni, matchu gurerangni kimil.
Hair-brush (hâr'brŭsh'), *n.* Kni chitani burus.
Hairy (hâr'y), *a.* Kimil gnang.
Hale (hāl), *a.* An·senga, saa ding·a gri, bilaka.
Half (häf), *n.* Gimikni samsa, bak gnini bak sa.
Half-witted (häf'wĭt'tĕd), *a.* Gisik sokgija ba kan·dikgipa.
Hall (hôl), *n.* Nokni kutori dal·gipa.
Halleluiah (hăl'le-lū'yâh), *n.* Isolko mitelani.
Halloo (hăl-lų'), *v.* Rake okama.
Hallow (hăl'lo), *v.* Rongtalata.
Halt (hôlt), *v.* Dong·lika.
Halter (hôl'têr), *n.* Gureni skoo sikkroke moani matbigil ba budu.
Halve (häv), *v.* Samgni ba bak gni dakata.
Ham (hăm), *n.* Ja·ping; kari nonge ripoe ran·atgimin wakni ja·ping.
Hamlet (hăm'lĕt), *n.* Chongipa gitim.
Hammer (hăm'mêr), *n.* Ture, hature.
Hammock (hăm'mŏk), *n.* Tue rochakani, ba wingwange roani chek.
Hamper (hăm'pêr), *v.* Ja·dokdak kaa, *n.*
Hand (hănd), *n.* Jak.
Handcuff (hănd'kŭf'), *n.* Hatkora, jako kaani silleng.
Handful (hănd'fụl), *n.* Jakkapsa, jakkamsa.
Handiwork (hănd'i-wêrk), *n.* Jakchi dakgimin kam.
Handkerchief (hăng'kêr-chĭf), *n.* Rumal, ipakani chongipa ba·ra.
Handle (hăn'd'l), *v.* Jakdangdika, *n.* Rim·chakani, nabak.
Handmaid (hănd'mād), *n.* Nokol me·chik.
Handsome (hăn'sŭm), *a.* Nitoa.
Handwriting (hănd'rīt'ing), *n.* Jakni sea.
Handy (hănd-y), *a.* Changgipa, sapgipa; nambea, jakkaltoa.
Hang (hăng), *v.* Sikea, alaia, dingdea; pasi on·a.
Hanker (hang'kĕr), *v.* Man·n a sikbea.
Hapless (hăp'lĕs), *a.* Rasong grigipa, kopal grigipa.
Happen (hăp'p'n), *v.* Maiba a·sel ong·a, maiba dukni ong·a, ghotona ong·a.
Happy (hăp'py), *a.* Kusi ong·gipa. **-ness**, *n.*
Harass (hăr'as), *v.* Neng·ata, jajrengata.
Harbour (här'bêr), *n.* Bondor, ja·hat karam biap.
Hard (härd), *a.* Raka, neng·gni.
Hardly (härd'ly), *adv.* Neng·dike, jenten.
Hardware (härd'wâr'), *n.* Silko dakgimin song·chak ritchakanirang.
Hardy (härd'y), *a.* Rakgipa, bilakgipa, ka·donggipa.
Hare (hâr), *n.* Sapau.
Harem (hā'rĕm), *n.* Me·chikrangko chipchange donram; sak ani chipchanggimin me·chikrang.
Hark (härk), *int.* Knatimbo.
Harlot (här'lŏt), *n.* Dari, noti.

Harm (härm), *n*. Namgija ba duk ong·atgimin, *v*.
Harmony (här'mo-ny), *n*. Nang-rimani, me·liani, ma·gapani. **-ous**, *a*.
Harness (här'nĕs), *n*. Gari salna gureko tariani mathigilrang.
Harp (härp), *n*. Knal.
Harpoon (här-poon'), *n*. Sel·u, sre gnanggipa sel·u.
Harrow (hăr'ro), *n*. Mul ba ugita dakgipa rokomsa, *v*.
Harsh (härsh), *a*. Skaka, raka, rinokja.
Hart (härt), *n*. Rokomsa matchok bipa.
Harvest (här'vĕst), *v*. Mi raa, biteko chimonga, *n*.
Has (hăz), *v*. *Have*ni 3rd person singular number.
Hashish (hăsh ish), *n*. Ganja, bhang.
Hasp (hăsp), *n*. Talako sikkrokani nabak.
Haste (hāst), *n*. Sketbaket dakani.
Hat (hăt), *n*. Tupi.
Hatch (hătch), *v*. Do·chi peॱa.
Hatchet (hătch'et), *n*. Chongipa rua.
Hate (hāt), *v*. Mitchia.
Hath (hăth), *v*. *Have* ni 3rd person singular number sastroni.
Hatred (hā'trĕd), *n*. Mitchiani.
Haughty (hô'ty), *a*. Onnikgipa, chonnikgipa.
Haul (hôl), *v*. Sala.
Have (hăv), *v*. HAD. Man·a, -o gnang.
Haven (hā'v'n), *n*. Jahat ma·chakani biap.
Havoc (hăv'ŏk), *n*. Nisiatani, gimaat ni.
Hawk (hôk), *n*. Do·rang atore mosa.
Hay (hā), *n*. Ran·gimin sam jong.
Haze (hāz), *n*. Guuri mikmik dakani. **-y**, *adv*.
He (hē), *pr*. Ua (bipa).
Head (hĕd), *n*. Sko; skotong; pamong.
Headache (hĕd'āk'), *n*, Sko saani.
Headland (hĕd'lănd'), *n*. A·sko, a·kuchot.
Headlong (hĕd'lŏng'), *adv*. Songchoke; chanchibewalgija.
Headquarters (hĕd'kwôr'têrs), *n*. Skotongni biap, skotong song.
Headstrong (hĕd'strŏng'), *a*. Manigija, kata ra·gija, ska gita dakgipa.
Heal (hēl), *v*. An·sengata, namata.
Health (hĕlth), *n*. An·sengani.
Heap (hēp), *n*. Dandakgimin, tom·dakgimin.
Hear (hēr), *v*. HEARD. Knaa, knatima; mania.
Hearken (härk''n), *v*. Knatimbo, gisik on·bo.
Hearse (hêrs), *n*. Manggisiko salani gari.
Heart (härt), *n*. Kan·chok; ka·tong.
Hearth (härth), *n*. Chu·dan, wa·al sikchakani.
Heartily (härt i-ly), *adv*. Gisik nange, kusi onge.
Heat (hēt), *v*. Di·ng·ata, *n*.
Heathen (hē'then), *n*. Mitedakak, olak gija, kritgipa songsarik. **-ism**, *n*. **-ish**, *a*. **-dom**, *n*.
Heave (hēv), *v*. HEAVED ba HOVE, HOVE. Bil on·e de·doa.
Heaven (hĕv''n), *n*. Salgi; kosakni bangbang.

Heavy (hĕv'y), *a*. Jrima.
Hebrew (hē'bru), *n*. Ibri mande.
Hector (hĕk'têr), *v*. Jongkria.
Hedge (hĕj), *n*. Boldimni guare, bari, tanggipa bol bi·sani dileng.
Hedgehog (hĕj'hŏg'), *n*. Okupu.
Heed (hēd), *v*. Gisik on·a, *n*.
Heel (hēl), *n*. Ja·pa ki·tik.
Heifer (hĕf'êr), *n*. Matchu bima bi·sa, karoli, damri.
Height, hight (hīt), *n*. Chuani.
Heir (âr), *n*. Gamko man·rikgnigipa, nokdongrikgnigipa.
Held (hĕld), *v*. *Hold*ko nibo.
Hell (hĕl), *n*. Norok.
Helm (hĕlm), *n*. Ringko pe·atgipa, ringni ki·me.
Help (hĕlp), *v*. Dakchaka, *n*. Dakchakani.
Helpmate (hĕlp'māt'), *n*. Dakchakgipa ripeng.
Helpmeet (hĕlp'mēt'), *n*. Dakchakna kragipa, jikgipa.
Helter-skelter (hĕl'têr-skĕl'têr), *adv*. Skel bakel, bilding bildang.
Helve (hĕlv), *n*. Rua bipong.
Hem (hĕm), *v*. Tem·a, *n*. Tem·e kogimin.
Hemisphere (hĕm'ĭ sfēr), *n*. Tom·betani samsa.
Hemp (hĕmp), *n*. Son ba me·katchi ma·sa.
Hen (hĕn), *n*. Do·bima.
Hence (hĕns), *adv*. Ianoni; iani gimin; a·sel.
Henceforth (hĕns'fōrth'), *adv*. Da·ontal.
Hencoop (hĕn'kup), *n*. Do·nol chongipa.
Henpecked (hĕn'pĕkt), *a*. Jikna bamgipa, senokol.
Henroost (hĕn'rust), *n*. Do·oni turam.

Heptagon (hĕp'tă-gŏn), *n*. Riking samsngipa.
Her (hêr), *pr*. Uni ba uko (bima).
Herald (hĕr'ald), *n*. Maiba uiatani katako aganrorogipa.
Herb (êrb), *n*. Bilsiprakna tangaigipa, me·su samjak.
Herd (hêrd), *n*. Matchu, matma ba mongmarangni jak.
Here (hēr), *adv*. Iano, iachi ianona.
Hereabouts (hēr'â-bouts'), *adv*. Ia jolo.
Hereafter (hēr-âf'têr), *adv*. Ian ja·mano.
Hereby (hēr-bī'), *adv*. Iachi.
Heretofore (hēr'tu-fōr'), *adv*. Ina skang, skangon.
Hereditary (he-rĕd'ĭ-ta-ry), *a*. Ma·a paoni man·rikgimin.
Hermit (hêr'mĭt), *n*. Burungo donggipa, soinasi.
Hermitage (hêr'mĭt-aj), *n*. Soinasini dongram.
Hero (hē'rō), *n*. Ka·donggipa kengniko chakchike namgniko dakgipa.
Heroine (hĕr'o-ĭn), *n*. Ka·donggipa me·chik, *hero* me·chik.
Heroism (hĕr'o-iz'm), *n*. Ka·donggipani dakani.
Heron (hĕr'ŏn), *n*. Alabok ma·sa.
Herring (hĕr'rĭng), *n*. Chongipa na·tok ma·sa.
Hers (hêrs), *pr*. Unin (bima).
Hesitate (hĕz'ĭ-tāt), *v*. Dongdika, kenchaka gita daka.-**ion**, *n*.
Hew (hū), *v*. Sol·a.
Hexagon (hĕks'ă-gŏn), *n*. Riking dok gnanggipa.
Hiccough (hĭk'kŭp), *n*. Ti·ika.
Hid (hĭd), *v*. *Hide*ko nibo.

Hide (hīd), *n.* Matbigil.
Hide (hīd), *v.* HID, HIDDEN. Donnua. dongnua.
Hideous (hĭd'e-ŭs), *a.* Kenbegnini, nina mi·ilgni.
Hie (hī), *v.* Gong·rake re·a, re·na dilia.
Hieroglyphic (hī'êr-o-glĭf'ĭk), *n.* Bimang ba noksa dakachi seani.
High (hī), *a.* Chua.
Highly (hī ly), *adv.* be-, namen.
Hight (hīt), *n.* Chuani.
Highway (hī'wā'), *n.* Rama sorkari, sorok.
Hill (hĭl), *n.* A·ding, a·chu, a·bri.
Hillock (hĭl'ŭk), *n.* A·timbo.
Hilt (hĭ t), *n.* Tonualni bipong.
Him (hĭm), *pr.* Uko (bipa).
Himself (hĭm-sĕlf'), *pr.* Ua a·tangkon, a·tangan (bipa).
Hind (hīnd), *n.* Matebok buna, *a.* Ki·sangchigipa.
Hinder (hĭn'dêr), *v.* Champeng·a. **-drance**, *n.*
Hinge (hĭnj), *n.* Kopja.
Hint (hĭnt), *v.* Chin daka, mai·chiba uiata.
Hip (hĭp), *n.* Ki·sning.
Hire (hīr), *v.* Bhara ra·a.
His (hĭz), *pr.* Uni (bipa).
Hiss (hĭs), *v.* Chipu gita sao ine gam·ata, mitchianiko mesoka.
Hist (hist), *int.* Jrip, ba knabo.
Historian (hĭs-tō'ri-an), *n.* Itihasko segipa.
History (hĭs'tō-ry), *n.* Itihas. **-ical**, *a.*
Hit (hĭt), *v.* HIT, HIT. Nanga ba doka.
Hitch (hĭtch), *v.* Juria, nangrimata, salusuka.
Hither (hĭth'êr), *adv.* Iachi, ianona.
Hitherto (hĭth'êr-to'), *adv.* Iana kingking.
Hive (hīv), *n.* Bijakolko jilani baks.
Hoar (hōr), *a.* Boka, budepa kni bokgimin.
Hoary (hōr'y), *a.* Boka, budepa kni bokgimin.
Hoard (hōrd), *n.* Donkamna chimonggimin, chimonggimin gam.
Hoarse (hōrs), *a.* Gitok dela.
Hoax (hōks), *v.* Togia, nachilaka, pa·ska.
Hobble (hŏb'b'l), *v.* Keng·be, keng·be dake re·a.
Hobnail (hŏb'nāl), *n.* Jutao datgipa dal·dalgipa silni busu.
Hoe (hō), *n.* Gitchima, *v.* Bak·a cho·a, sua, subaka.
Hog (hŏg), *n.* Wak.
Hoggish (hŏg'gĭsh), *a.* Wak gita, moila, namgija, cha·gap-na ba man·gopna sikgipa.
Hogshead (hŏgz'hĕd), *n.* Muan bonga sel kolgrik chet chakgipa pipa.
Hoist (hoist), *v.* De·doata, songdoata.
Hold (hōld), *v.* HELD. Rim·a, rim·rika; chaka.
Hole (hōl), *n.* A·kol.
Holiday (hŏl'ĭ-dā), *n.* Chutini sal.
Hollow (hŏl'lo), *a.* Konggranggrang, bangbang; a·kongdapgipa, *n.*
Holy (hōl'y), *a.* Toromni gimin rongtala. **-iness**, *n.*
Homage (hŏm'aj), *n.* Mande ra·ani, olakiani.
Home (hōm), *n.* Songtang, noktang, noktangni manderangni dongram.

Homely (hōm'ly), *a*. Nitogijagipa, daknanggijagipa.
Home-ward (hōm'-wêrd), *adv*. Songtang ba nok·angchi mikkange.
Honest (ŏn'ĕst), *a*. Kakketgipa, cha·chipila grigipa. **-y**, *n*.
Honey (hŭn'y), *n*. Bija bitchi.
Honey-comb (hŭn ī-kōm'), *n*. Bija birangkap.
Honor, honour (ŏn'êr), *v*. Mande ra·a, dal·nika.
Hood (hụd), *n*. Skoo pindapani.
Hoof (hụf), *n*. Gure, matchu, aro ugita dakgipa jat rangni ja·skil. nail
Hook (hụk), *n*. Akura ; milsi.
Hoop (hụp ba hụp), *n*. Sil ba bolko daka wentongani ; dule dakgimin.
Hop (hŏp), *v*. Ga·dengdenge re·a, do·oni aro beng·bekni re·agita re·a.
Hop (hŏp), *n*. Wegipa sam ma·sa.
Hope (hōp), *v*. Ka·donga.
Hopper (hŏp'pêr), *n*. Rongrongatchakani.
Horizon (hō-rī'zŭn), *n*. Salgi aro a·a jeo nangrima ba chikopgrika gita nikgipa biap.
Horn (hôrn), *n*. Grong.
Hornet (hôr'nĕt), *n*. Bijasik ma·sa.
Hornpipe (hôrn'pīp'), *n*. Rokomsa bangsi.
Horrible (hŏr'rĭ-b'l), *a*. An·skitatgni.
Horrid (hŏr'rĭd), *a*. Kenmanbegni.
Horrify (hŏr'rĭ-fī), *v*. Kenata.
Horror (hŏr'rêr), *n*. An·skitmanpile kenani.
Horse (hôrs), *n*. Gure.
Horseback (hôrs'băk'), *n*. Gure janggil ; gureo gakate dongani.
Horse dealer (hôrs-dēl'êr), *n*. Gure badinggipa.
Horse-fly (hôrs'flī), *n*. Chap.
Horse shoe (hôrs'shụ), *n*. Gureni ja·ao datgipa sil.
Hosanna (hō-zăn'nâ), *n*. Isolko mitelani.
Hose (hōz), *n*. Rokomsa muja ; budu gita nom·gipa chi jokani noli.
Hospitable (hŏs'pĭ-tâ-b'l), *a*. Sokgipa chakronggipa.
Hospital (hŏs'pĭ-tal), *n*. Haspatal, sagiparangko sanani biap.
Host (hōst), *n*. Algipa, sokgipa chakgipa.
Hostile (hŏs'tĭl), *a*. Bobil dakgipa, warachakgipa. **-ity**, *n*.
Hostler (hŏs'lêr ba ŏs'lêr), *n*. Gureko nitimgipa, sohis.
Hot (hŏt), *a*. Ding·a.
Hotel (ho-tĕl'), *n*. Damko ra·e sokgipa chakani nok.
Hound (hound), *n*. Sikari achak.
Hour (our), *n*. Konta.
House (hous), *n*. Nok.
Housebreaker (hous'brāk'êr), *n*. Nokko cho·ponge cha·ugipa.
Household (hous'hōld'), *n*. Nokgimikni mande. **-er**, *n*.
Housemaid (hous'mād'), *n*. Nokol me·chik.
Housewife (hous'wīf'), *n*. Nokmong, nokni skotonggipa me·chik.
Hove (hōv), *v*. *Heave*ko nibo.
Hovel (hŏv'ĕl), *n*. Namgijagipa nok bi·sa.
Hover (hŭv'êr), *v*. Meraa, wenwena.
How (hou), *adv*. Maidake, maikai.
However (hou-ĕv'êr), *adv*. Indiba ; indioba ; jeba ong·chong.

Howl (houl), *v*. Achak ba peru gita grape mikoa.
Hub (hŭb), *n*. Chakani jatchi.
Huddle (hŭd'd'l), *v*. Damsan tom·a, sepanggrik chimonga.
Hue (hū), Rongni dingtang ong·ani, chikbata ba dimelani.
Hug (hŭg), *v*. Gipakkota.
Huge (hūj), *a*. Dal·begipa.
Hull (hŭl), *n*. Jahatni bimang gimik; bikap, bigil.
Hum (hŭm), *v*. Bijani ong-onga.
Human (hu'man), *a*. Mandeni biding.
Humane (hu-mān'), *a*. Ka·sae dakgipa.
Humankind (hū'man-kīnd'), *n*. Mande jat.
Humble (hŭm'b'l), *a*. A·tangko onnikgipa, sontolgipa.
Humblebee (hŭm'b'l-bē'), *n*. Bombaneng.
Humbug (hŭm'bŭg), *n*. Tol·napani.
Humiliation (hu-mĭl'ĭ-ā'shŭn), *n*. Kratcha·anichi onatani.
Hummingbird (hŭm'mĭng-bérd), *n*. Bibalni bitchiko op-gipa chonbegipa do·o.
Humorous (hū'mêr-ŭs), *a*. Etal-gipa, ka·dingatgipa.
Hump (hŭmp), *n*. Silchi, simchi, janggil kom·chikani.
Hundred (hŭn'dred), *n*. *a*. Rit-chasa.
Hung (hŭng), *v*. *Hang*ko nibo.
Hunger (hŭng'gêr), *n*. Okriani, cha·na sikani.
Hunt (hŭnt), *v*. Sikar ka·a; am·a.
Hurl (hêrl), *v*. Rake goata, gal-ata.
Hurra, Hurrah (hur-rä'), *int*. Ka·srokeinchroani kata.
Hurricane (hŭr'rĭ-kān), *n*. Ta·rakbegipa balwa.
Hurry (hŭr'ry), *v*. Babbak daka.
Hurt (hêrt), *v*. Matata, saknaata, namgija dakata.
Husband (hŭz'band), *n*. Segipa.
Husbandman (hŭz'band-man), *n*. A·a gamgipa.
Hush (hŭsh), *v*. Jripata, jrip dongbo.
Husk (hŭsk), *n*. Bikap, bigil, bitchrini bikap, *v*. Bigil oa.
Hut (hŭt), *n*. Nok bi·sa, jam-dap.
Hydrant (hī'drant), *n*. Chi jokatani kol.
Hydrophobia (hī'dro-fō'bĭ-å), *n*. Achak paglani chike pagla ong·ani.
Hyena (hi-ē'nå), *n*. Se·el gita dakgipa matburung ma·sa.
Hygiene (hī'jĭ-ēn), *n*. An·senga-ni gimin skiani.
Hymn (hĭm), *n*. Ring·ani, torom git.
Hyphen (hī'fĕn), *n*. Katako bak dakani chin, (-) ian.
Hypocrisy (hĭ-pŏk'rĭ-sy), *n*. Cha·chipilani.
Hypocrite (hĭp'o-krĭt), *n*. Cha·chipilgipa.
Hypotheses (hi-pŏth'e-sĭs), *n*. Chanchichipani.
Hysterics (hĭs-têr'iks), *n*. Duga ka·dinge ba grape pagla gita ong·pilani.

I.

I (ī), *pr*. Anga.
Ibex (ī'bĕks), *n*. Ramsagol, dal·gipa do·bok ma·sa.
Ice (īs), *n*. Stil gita tin·kagiminchi.

Icicle (ī'sī-k'l), *n.* Chi tingtotnasigipa tin·karikrikange ro·o go·ol gita tin·kagipa.
Idea (i-dē'ă), *n.* Gisiko chanchibchipani.
Identical (i-dĕn'tĭ-kal), *a.* Uan, apsan.
Identify (i-dĕn'tĭ-fī), *v.* Uan ong·a ine mesoka. **-ication,** *n.*
Idiom (ĭd'ĭ-ŭm), *n.* Aganani b·wal ba niam.
Idiot (ĭd'ĭ-ŏt), *n.* Gokagipa, jaragipa, mamungba uigijagipa. **-ic,** *a.*
Idle (ī'd'l), *a.* Aratgipa, kam ka·gijagipa, roaigipa.
Idol (ī'dŏl), *n.* Mite dakgimin ba sol·gimin.
Idolater (i-dŏl'a-têr), *n.* Mite kritgipa, mite dakako olakigipa.
Idolize (ī'dŏl-īz), *v.* Miteko gita olakia, agre mande ra·a ba ka·saa, agre dal·nika.
If (ĭf), *con.* -ode.
Ignite (ĭg-nīt'), *v.* Wa·al sika, ba so·baka.
Ignoble (ĭg-nō'b'l), *a.* Ongipa, mande ra·na kragijagipa.
Ignorant (ĭg'no-rant), *a.* Uigijagipa, skia man·gijagipa. **-ce,** *n.*
Ignore (ĭg-nōr'), *v.* Chonnika, uina jechaka.
Ill (ĭl), *a.* Saa ; namgija.
Illegal (ĭl-lē'gal), *a.* Niam gita ong·gija, niamko pe·a.
Illegible (ĭl-lĕj'ĭ-b'l), *a.* Poraina man·gija, sea rongtalgija.
Illegitimate (ĭl'le-jĭt ĭ-mat), *a.* Niam gita kimgrikgija, niam gita ong·gija depatchi.
Ill-favoured (ĭl'fā'vêrd), *a.* Nitogija, daknanggija.
Illiterate (ĭl-lĭt'êr-at), *a.* Lekapora grigipa, skia man·gijagipa.
Ill-natured (ĭl-nā'turd'), *a.* Ka·onangninggipa, kusi ong·gijagipa.
Illuminate (ĭl-lū'mĭ-nāt), *v.* Ching·ata, teng·suata.
Illusion (ĭl-lū'zhŭn), *n.* Ong·gijako ong·a gita nikani.
Illustrate (ĭl-lŭs'trāt), *v.* Noksa dake mesoka, toe mesoka. **-ion,** *n.*
Illustrious (ĭl-lŭs'trĭ-ŭs), *a* Dal·gipa, mingsinggipa, rasong chagipa.
Ill will (ĭl'wĭl'), *n.* Namgijako dakna ska, miknengani.
Image (ĭm'aj), *n.* Bimang dakgimin, gisiko dakgimin noksa.
Imagine (ĭm-ăj'in), *v.* Chanchia, banaia. **-ation,** *n.*
Imitate (ĭm'ĭ-tāt), *v.* Gita daka, ja·rika, sninga.
Immaculate (ĭm-măk'u-lat), *a.* Marang gri, matnanga gri.
Immature (ĭm'mā-tūr), *a.* Brigija.
Imeasurable (ĭm-mĕzh'ur-â-b'l), *a.* Tona amgija, tosokgija.
Immediately (im-mē'dĭ-at-ly), *adv.* Rang·san, bakan.
Immense (im-mĕns'), *a.* Namen dal·bea. **-ity,** *n.*
Immerse (ĭm-mêrs'), *v.* Dubiata, napbolata. **-ion,** *n.*
Immigrate (ĭm'mĭ-grāt), *v.* Songo dongkamna re·baa.
Immigrant (ĭm'mĭ-grant), *n.* Songo dongkamna re·bagipa.
Imminent (ĭm'mĭ-nent), *a.* Ong·nasigipa, sepangbagipa kengni.
Immoderate (im-mŏd'êr-at), *a.* Agre dakgipa.

Immodest (ĭm-mŏd'ĕst), *a.* Kratcha·ninggijagipa. **-y,** *n.*

Immoral (ĭm-mŏr'al), *a.* Kraako dakgijagipa, namgijagipa, niamko manigijagipa. **-ity,** *n.*

Immortal (ĭm-môr'tal), *a.* Sigijagipa, jringjrotna donggipa. **-ity,** *n.*

Immovable (ĭm-mṳv'ȧ-b'l), *a.* Il·engatna ba jitna amgija.

Imp (ĭmp), *n.* Chongipa put.

Impair (ĭm-pâr'), *v.* Bil gri ong·ata, namgija ong·ata.

Impale (ĭm-pāl'), *v.* Jotprota.

Impart (ĭm-pärt'), *v.* Uiatpaa, bak on·paa.

Impartial (ĭm-pär'shal), *a.* Kakket, mikkang nigijagipa.

Impassable (ĭm-păs'ȧ-b'l), *a.* Batna amgija.

Impatience (ĭm-pā'shens), *n.* Chakchikna sikgijani, chakchikgijani.

Impeach (ĭm-pēch'), *v.* Matnanga, nalis ka·a, jechaka. **-ment,** *n.*

Impede (ĭm-pēd'), *v.* Champenga, peng·panga. **-ment,** *n.*

Impel (ĭm-pĕl'), *v.* Didiata, mikkangchi re·ata.

Impend (ĭm-pĕnd'), *v.* Namgija ba duk on·naba donga.

Impenetrable (ĭm-pĕn'e-trȧ-b'l), *a.* Napna amgija.

Imperfect (ĭm-pêr'fĕkt), *a.* Chu·sokgija, namsranggija. **-ion,** *n.*

Impertinent (ĭm-pêr'tĭ-nent), *a.* Inchakgipa, ga·kragijagipa, ga·nanggijagipa.

Impious (ĭm'pĭ-ŭs), *a.* Isolko mande ra·gijagipa.

Impiety (ĭm-pī'e-ty), *n.* Otorom.

Implement (ĭm'ple-ment), Jakkalani.

Implore (ĭm-plōr'), *v.* Mol·mola.

Imply (ĭm-plī'), *v.* Parake agangija, maichiba uiata.

Import (ĭm-pōrt'), *v.* Songgipinoniko songtangona ra·baa. **-ation,** *n.*

Important (ĭm-pôr'tant), *a.* Mongsonggipa, nangbegipa. **-ance,** *n.*

Impose (ĭm-pōz'), *v.* Pakwata, balko on·a; tol·napata. **-ition,** *n.*

Impossible (ĭm-pŏs'sĭ-b'l), *a.* Amgija.

Impost (ĭm'pōst), *n.* Kajana.

Impostor (ĭm-pŏst'êr), *n.* Tol·napgipa.

Impotent (ĭm'po-tent), *a.* Bilgri.

Impoverish (ĭm-pŏv'êr-ish), *v.* Gam griata, kangalata, bilgriata.

Impregnate (ĭm-prĕg'nāt), *v.* Oko keata.

Impress (ĭm-prĕs'), *v.* Sinjete chinko dakata, chin robiata; gisiko nangata. **-ion,** *n.*

Imprint (ĭm-prĭnt'), *v.* Sinjete chapa ka·ata.

Imprison (ĭm-prĭz''n), *v.* Chipchanga, patoko chipa. **-ment,** *n.*

Improbable (ĭm-prŏb'ȧ-b'l), *a.* Ong·na kragija, jeko ong·jasusu nika.

Improper (ĭm-prŏp'êr), *a.* Kragija, nitogija.

Improve (ĭm-prṳv'), *v.* Namroroa, namroroata, name jakkala. **-ment,** *n.*

Imprudent (ĭm-prṳ'dent), *a.* Chanchisogijagipa, mikraksogijagipa, simsaksogijagipa.

Impudent (ĭm'pu-dent), *a.* Kratchagijagipa, inchakgipa.
Impulse (im'pŭls), *n.* Rang·san re·ata ba dakatani.
Impure (im-pūr'), *a.* Rongtalgijagipa, moila ba marang gnang.
In (ĭn), *prep. adv.* Ning·o.
Inability (ĭn'ă-bĭl'ĭ-ty), *n.* Amgijani.
Inaccessible (ĭn'ăk-sĕs'ĭ-b'l), *a.* Man·na amgija, sokna amgija.
Inaccurate (ĭn-ăk'ku-rat), *a.* Tik ong·gija, guala gnang.
Inactive (ĭn-ăk'tĭv), *a.* Arata, joton ka·a grigipa.
Inanimate (ĭn-ăn'ĭ-mat), *a.* Janggi grigipa, gisik grigipa.
Inarticulate (ĭn'är-tik'u-lat), *a.* Bil·bil bal·bal.
Inasmuch (ĭn'ăz-mŭch'), *adv.* Indakani gimin.
Inattention (ĭn'ăt-tĕn'shŭn), *n.* Gisik on·gijani.
Inaudible (ĭn-ô'dĭ-b'l), *a.* Gam·-ja, knana mangija.
Inauguration (in-ô'gu-rā'shŭn), *n.* Kamna pakwatani; a·bachengani.
Incarnate (ĭn-kär'nāt), *v.* Bimangko ra·dapata.
Incautious (ĭn-kô'shŭs), *a.* Gisik rakgija, simsakgija.
Incense (ĭn-sĕns'), *v.* Ka·onangata.
Incense (ĭn'sĕns), *n.* Smilgipa cha·chat.
Incentive (ĭn-sĕn'tĭv), *n.* Didiatani.
Incessant (ĭn-sĕs'sant), *a.* Matchotgija, dondikgija.
Inch (ĭnch), *n.* Put (foot) sani bak chi·gnini bak sa.
Incident (ĭn'sĭ-dent), *n.* Ong·-ani.

Incite (ĭn-sīt'), *v.* Didiata.
Incline (ĭn-klīn'), *v.* So·onchoka; gonga, ska.
Include (ĭn-klūd'), *v.* Man·gopa, man·chapa.
Income (ĭn'kŭm'), *n.* Man·a tangka, dorma·ba.
Incommunicable (ĭn-kŏm-mu'-nĭ-kă-b'l), *a.* Uiatna ba aganna amgija.
Incomparable (ĭn-kŏm'păr-ă-b'l), *a.* Tona ampilgija.
Incompatible (ĭn-kŏm-păt'ĭ-b'l), *a.* Meligija, nangrimgija.
Incomplete (ĭn-kŏm-plēt'), *a.* Matchotgija.
Incomprehensible (ĭn-kŏm'pre-hĕn'sĭ-b'l), *a.* Uisokgija, chanchisokgija, ning·tua.
Inconceivable (ĭn'kŏn-sēv'ă-b'l), *a.* Uisokgija, aiao inmangni.
Inconsiderable (ĭn'kŏn-sĭd'êr-ă-b'l), *a.* Chona, channa kraja.
Inconsiderate (ĭn'kŏn-sĭd'êr-at), *a.* Chanchigija, gisik rakgija.
Inconsistent (ĭn'kŏn-sĭs'tent), *a.* Bikpil bawil dakgipa ba agangipa.
Inconstant (ĭn-kŏn'stant), *a.* Dongtomgija, tom·tomgija.
Inconvenient (ĭn'kŏn-vēn'yent), *a.* Jakkaltogija.
Incorporate (ĭn-kôr'po-rāt), *v.* Dakdima, nangnima. **-ion,** *n.*
Incorrect (ĭn'kŏr-rĕkt'), *a.* Guala gnang.
Incorrupt (ĭn'kŏr-rŭpt'), *a.* Nama, guala ba ong·sia gri.
Increase (ĭn-krēs'), *v.* Baria, bariata.
Incredible (ĭn-krĕd'ĭ-b'l), *a.* Bebe ra·na kragija.
Incubate (ĭng'ku-bāt), *v.* Do·-bima gita bama, bame pe·ata. **-ion,** *n.*

Incur (ĭn-kêr'), *v.* Tekia, gronanga.
Incurable (ĭn-kūr'ȧ-b'l), *a.* An·songatna amgija.
Indebted (ĭn-dĕt'ĕd), *a.* Grognanggipa.
Indeed (ĭn-dēd'), *adv.* Oe, beben, nanggo, chong·mot.
Indefensible (ĭn'de-fĕn'sĭ-b'l), *a.* Kraako me·okna amgija.
Indefinite (ĭn-dĕf'ĭ-nĭt), *a.* Tik ong·gija.
Indelible (ĭn-dĕl'ĭ-b'l), *a.* Kimitna ba gimatna amgija.
Indemnify (ĭn-dĕm'nĭ-fī), *v.* Gimaako on·pila.
Independent (ĭn'de-pĕnd'ent), *a.* Gipino pangchakgijagipa.
Indescribable (ĭn'de-skrīb'ȧ-b'l), *a.* Aganna ba toe mesokna amgija.
Index (ĭn'dĕks), *n.* Suchi mesokani; kitapni japangrangko mesokani.
Indian corn (ĭn'dĭ-an ba ĭnd'-yan kôrn), *n.* Me·raku.
India rubber (ĭn'dĭ-ȧ rŭb'bêr), *a.* Rangket.
Indicate (ĭn'dĭ-kāt), *v.* Mesoka.
Indifferent (ĭn-dĭf'fêr-ent), *a.* Simsakgijagipa.
Indigestion (ĭn-dĭ-jes'chŭn), *n.* Oko goligijani, jrongijani.
Indignant (ĭn-dĭg'nant), *a.* Ka·onanggipa.
Indignity (ĭn-dĭg'nĭ-ty), *n.* Mande ra·gijani, chonnikani.
Indigo (ĭn'dĭ-go), *n.* Neri.
Indirect (ĭn'dĭ-rĕkt'), *a.* Srong-gija, gonggea.
Indiscreet (ĭn'dĭs-krēt'), *a.* Chanchigijagipa, gisik rakgijagipa.
Indissoluble (ĭn-dĭs'so-lu-b'l), *a.* Jrongna amgija.

Indistinct (ĭn'dĭs-tĭngkt'), *a.* Nikna ba knana rongtalgija.
Individual (ĭn'-dĭ-vĭd'u-al), *n.* Saksan, *a.* Dingtanggipa.
Indivisible (ĭn'dĭ-vĭz'ĭ-b'l), *a.* Sualna amgija.
Indolent (ĭn'do-lent), *a.* Aratgipa.
Indorse (ĭn-dôrs'), *v.* Bimungko sedapa, sain ka·a.
Induce (ĭn-dūs'), *v.* Didiata, skie dila. **-ment,** *n.*
Indulge (ĭn-dŭlj'), *v.* Skako dakna on·a, namnikata, lai o·na. **-nce,** *n.*
Industrious (ĭn-dŭs'trĭ-ŭs), *a.* Gong·gipa, bimchipgipa.
Industry (ĭn'dŭs-try), *n.* Kam, maikoba dakani kam; bimchipani.
Inebriate (ĭn-ē'brĭ-āt), *v.* Chupekata. *n.* Chupekronggipa.
Inefficient (ĭn'ĕf-fĭsh'ent), *a.* Chu·sokgija.
Inequality (ĭn'e-kwŏl'ĭ-ty), *n.* Apsan ong·gijani.
Inestimable (ĭn-ĕs'tĭ-mȧ-b'l), *a.* Gamchatbea, tona amgija gamchata.
Inevitable (ĭn-ĕv'ĭ-tȧ-b'l), *a.* Champengna amgija.
Inexcusable (ĭn'ĕks-kūz'ȧ-b'l), *a.* Kema ka·na ba watna amgija.
Inexhaustible (ĭn'ĕgz-ôst'ĭ-b'l), *a.* Bon·na man·gija, bangbangatna man·gijagipa.
Inexpedient (ĭn'ĭks-pē'dĭ-ent), *a.* Kragija, daktogija.
Inexperienced (ĭn'ĕks-pē'rĭ-enst), *a.* Bang·e nike uikujagipa.
Inexpressible (ĭn'ĕks-prĕs'ĭ-b'l), *a.* Aganna ba parakna amgija.

Inextinguishable (ĭn'ĕks-tĭng'-gwĭsh-ă-b'l), *a.* Kimitoa amgija.

Infallible (ĭn'făl'lĭ-b'l), *a.* Guala gri.

Infamous (ĭn'fă-mŭs), *a.* Namgija ba kratcha·gnini gimin mingsinggipa.

Infancy (ĭn'fan-sy), *n.* Bi·samiting.

Infant (ĭn'fant), *n.* Bakgitchak, odek, menga.

Infanticide (ĭn-făn'tĭ-sīd), *n.* Bakgitchakko so·otani.

Infantry (ĭn'fan-try), *n.* Ja·achi re·gipa sipairang.

Infect (ĭn-fĕkt'), *v.* Nangdike bisi nangata, saata, ba rongtalgija ong·ata. **-ion,** *n.* **-ious,** *a.*

Infer (ĭnfêr'), *v.* Chanchichipa, ine chanchia. **-ence,** *n.*

Inferior (ĭn-fē'rĭ-êr), *a.* Onbatgipa, chonbatgipa; nambrogijagipa.

Infernal (ĭn-fêr'nal), *a.* Norokna kragipa ba norokni biding.

Infertile (ĭn-fêr'tĭl), *a.* A·salgri; ranji.

Infest (ĭn-fĕst'), *v.* Duk on·gipachin gapata.

Infidel (ĭn'fĭ-del), *n.* Toromko bebe ra·gijagipa. **-ity,** *n.*

Infinite (ĭn'fĭ-nĭt), *a.* Ari gri, bon·changgijagipa.

Infirmary (ĭn-fêrm'ă-ry), *n.* Bilgrigipa sagiparangko sanram, haspital.

Infirm (ĭn-fêrm'), *a.* Bilgri, mangrakgijagipa. **-ity,** *n.*

Inflame (ĭn-flām'), *v.* Ching·chaata, kamata, ka·onangata, ding·ata.

Inflammation (ĭn'flăm-mā'shŭn), *n.* Be·enni ding·a ba kamani.

Inflate (ĭn-flāt'), *v.* Gangbuata, tapingata. **-ion,** *n.*

Inflexible (ĭn-flĕks'ĭ-b'l), *a.* Doina man·gija. **-bility,** *n.*

Inflict (ĭn-flĭkt'), *v.* Duk on·a, sasti on·a. **-ion,** *n.*

Influence (ĭn'flu-ens), *n.* Gipinni kosako cholonni bil, mande ong·ani bil.

Influenza (ĭn'flu-ĕn'za), *n.* Serdi nangani, pilakna gipgipa saa ma·sa.

Inform (ĭn-fôrm'), *v.* Uiata knaata, skia.

Informal (ĭn-fôrm'al), *a.* Niam gita dakgija, dakronga gita ong·gija. **-ity,** *n.*

Information (ĭn'fôrm-ā'shŭn), *n.* Uiatani, kobor.

Infrequent (ĭn-frē'kwent), *a.* Ong·ronggijagipa, basakobasangija.

Infuse (ĭn-fūs') *v.* Gisiko chinapata, gisiko nangata. **-ion,** *n.*

Ingenious (ĭn-jēn'yŭs), *a.* Dakna ba rikna changgija, chu·suk at na sapgipa.

Inglorious (ĭn-glō'rĭ-ŭs), *a.* Rasong chagijagipa.

Ingot (ĭn'gŏt), *n.* Sona ba maiba silni jronggija tong.

Ingratitude (ĭn-grăt'ĭ-tūd), *n.* Dakchakako ba namgniko ku·rachakgija ba chanchigijani.

Ingulf (ĭn-gŭlf'), *v.* Sagalo dubiata; bripata.

Inhabit (ĭn-hăb'ĭt), *v.* Songdonga, dongkama. **-ant,** *n.* Dongkamgipa.

Inhale (ĭn-hāl'), *v.* Rang·eita, salopa.

Inherit (ĭn-hĕr'ĭt), *v.* Ma·a paaoni man·rika, gamko man·rika. **-ance,** *n.*

Inhospitable (ĭn-hŏs'pĭt-å-b'l), *a*. Sokgipa chakgijagipa, chakna sikgijagipa.
Inhuman (ĭn-hū'man), *a*. Ka·-saninggijagipa.
Iniquity (ĭn-ĭk'wĭ-ty), *n*. Namgija, pap.
Initial (ĭn-ĭsh'al), *n*. Katani ba bimungni skanggipa oikor.
Injection (ĭn-jĕk'shŭn), *n*. Ning·chi chipatani, selka mariani.
Injure (ĭn'jur), *v*. Gimata, namgija ong·ata. -**ious**, *a*.
Injustice (ĭn-jŭs't s), *n*. Kakket ong·gijani, onia dakatani.
Ink ('ngk), *n*. Kali.
Inkstand (ingk'stănd), *n*. Doat, kali donchakani.
Inland (ĭn'land), *a*. Sagaloni che·gipa.
Inlet (ĭn'lĕt), *n*. Apchongipa napram chol.
Inmate (ĭn'māt'), *n*. Dongrimpagipa, noksano dongpagipa.
Inmost (ĭn'mōst'), *a*. Pilakna bate ning·batgipa.
Inn (ĭn), *n*. Waltuani nok, alda.
Inner (ĭn'nêr), *a*. Ning·tukalgipa.
Innocent (ĭn'no-sent), *a*. Dosgri.
Innumerable (ĭn-nū'mêr-å-b'l), *a*. Channa amgija.
Inoculate (ĭn-ŏk'u-lāt), *v*. Tika sua, kolom on·a.
Inoffensive (ĭn'ŏf-fĕn'sĭv), *a*. Namnikgijani gri.
Inquest (ĭn'kwĕst), *n*. Kuni todonto ka·ani, sorkarini bil gnanggipani saudie niani.
Inquire (ĭn-kwīr'), *v*. Sing·e nia, sandie nia.
Inquisitive (ĭn-kwĭz'ĭ-tĭv), *a*. Sing·rakgipa, sing·na sikbegita.
Insane (ĭn-sān'), *a*. Pagila. -**ity**, *n*.
Insatiable (ĭn-sā'shå-b'l), *a*. Chu·ongnikgijagipa, mikokaninggijagipa.
Inscribe (ĭn-skrīb'), *v*. Konge sedapa.
Inscription (ĭn-skrĭp'shŭn), *n*. Konge sedapgimin.
Insect (ĭn'sĕkt), *n*. Jo·ong, gukrang, bima.
Insecure (ĭn'se-kūr'), *a*. Kenchakani gri ong·ja.
Insensible (ĭn-sĕn'sĭ-b'l), *a*. Uiani gri.
Inseparable (ĭn-sĕp'å-rå-b'l), *a*. Dingtangatna man·gijagipa.
Insert (ĭn-sêrt'), *v*. Gipinni ning·o ba gisepo dona.
Inside (ĭn-sīd'), *adv*. Ning·o, ning·chi.
Insight (ĭn'sīt), *n*. Ning·tue niani ba uiani.
Insignificant (ĭn'sĭg-nĭf'ĭ-kant), *a*. Simsakna kragija, gamchatgija.
Insincere (ĭn'sĭn-sēr'), *a*. Srong-gijagipa, cha·chipilgipa.
Insinuate (ĭn-sĭn'u-āt), *v*. Ka·sne uiata, chinchi uiata.
Insipid (ĭn-sĭp'ĭd), *a*. Su·ua gri.
Insist (ĭn-sĭst'), *v*. Nangchongmota ine ina.
Insnare (ĭn-snâr'), *v*. Ja·gao nangata.
Insolent (ĭn'so-lent), *a*. Gipinko chonnike gaora de·gipa.
Insoluble (ĭn-sŏl'u-b'l), *a*. Jronggija, goligija.
Insomuch (ĭn'so-mŭch'), *adv*. Indake ong·ani gimin.
Inspect (ĭn-spĕkt'), *v*. Name dake nia, porika ka·e nia. -**ion**, *n*.
Inspire (ĭn-spīr'), *v*. Balwako salopa; didia, an·saoata. -**ation**, *n*.

Inspirit (in-spir'it), *v.* Ka·dongata.
Instability (in'stă-bil'i-ty), *n.* Tom·tomgijani.
Instance (in'stans), *n.* Mesokani, ong·ani.
Instant (in'stant), *n.* Dikdik, on·titi sal, da·o.
Instead (in-stĕd'), *adv.* Pal.
Instep (in'stĕp), *n.* Ja·pa janggilni ja·gitok sambaoni daapgipa.
Instigate (in'sti-gāt), *v.* Didiata, mongsongde namgijana didiata.
Instinct (in'stingkt), *n.* Ba·kapaonin uiani gisik.
Institute (in'sti-tūt), *v.* A·bachengata, dona, tik ka·a. **-ion,** *n.*
Instruct (in-strŭkt'), *v.* Skia, uiata, ge·eta. **-ion,** *n.*
Instrument (in'stru-ment), *n.* Jakkalani, silchidare. **-al,** *a.*
Insubordinate (in'sŭb-ôr'di-nat), *a.* Bamgijagipa. **-ation,** *n.*
Insufferable (in-sŭf'fêr-ȧ-b'l), *a.* Chakchikna amgija.
Insufficient (in'sŭf-fish'ent), *a.* Chu·onggija, tikgija.
Insult (in-sŭlt'), *v.* Chonnika, kratcha·ata, saia. (in'sŭlt) *n.*
Insuperable (in-sū'pêr-ȧ-b'l), *a.* Batna ba amna amgija.
Insupportable (in'sŭp-pōrt'ȧ-b'l), *a.* Chakna amgija.
Insure (in-shur'), *v.* Chong·mot ong·ata ; gimajana gita maikoba daksoa ; gimaako man·pilna tik ka·soa. **-ance,** *n.*
Insurrection (in'sŭr-rĕk'shŭn), *n.* Golmal, governmentni kosako chakatani.
Integer (in'te-jêr), *n.* Chu·gimik ongko.
Integrity (in-tĕg'ri-ty), *n.* Kakket ong·ani.
Intellect (in'tĕl-lĕkt), *n.* Uiani bil. **-ual,** *a.*
Intelligent (in-tĕl'li-jent), *a.* Uiani bil gnanggipa. **-gence,** *n.*
Intelligible (in-tĕl'li-ji-b'l), *a.* Rongtale uigni.
Intemperate (in-tĕm'pêr-at), *a.* Cha·a ringani gimin nangana agre dakgipa.
Intend (in-tĕnd'), *v.* Mangsonga.
Intense (in-tens'), *a.* Gisik kringa, bimchipa, namen.
Intention (in-tĕn'shŭn), *n.* Mangsongani.
Inter (in-têr'), *v.* Gopa.
Intercede (in'têr-sēd'), *v.* Gipinni gimin bi·chaka, baltia.
Intercept (in'têr-sĕpt'), *v.* Re·angako doodikata.
Intercession (in'têr-sĕsh'ŭn), *n.* Bi·chakani.
Interchange (in'têr-chānj'), *v.* On·grika, sregrika.
Intercourse (in'têr-kōrs), *n.* Rorimgrikani.
Interdict (in'têr-dikt'), *v.* Beng·a, champenga.
Interest (in'têr-ĕst), *v.* Gi·ik nangata, nangrimata. *n.* Sut, tangkani bi·sa.
Interfere (in'têr-fēr'), *v.* Jak dangdikpaa ; nangtinggrika.
Interior (in-tē'ri-êr), *a.* Ning·o donggipa. *n.* Ning·oni.
Interleave (in'têr-lēv'), *v.* Leka segijako ki·tapo gisep gisep jakprak kodapa.
Interline (in'têr-lin'), *v.* Ritingni gisepo sea.
Interlock (in'têr-lŏk'), *v.* Binggrika.

Intermarry (ĭn'têr-măr'ry), *v.* Kimgrika, bia ka·grika.
Intermeddle (ĭn'têr-mĕd'd'l), *v.* Gipinni kamo jak daogdikpaa.
Intermediate (ĭn'têr-mē'dĭ-āt), *a.* Ma·jatchigipa.
Intermingle (ĭn'têr-mĭng'g'l), *v.* Brina.
Intermit (ĭn'têr-mĭt'), *v.* Dondika, donchanga. **-tent,** *a.*
Intermix (ĭn'têr-mĭks'), *v.* Brina. **-ture,** *n.*
Internal (ĭn-têr'nal), *a.* Ning·ni biding.
Interpose (ĭn'têr-pōz'), *v.* Bijatchiona on·a ; baltia.
Interpret (ĭn-têr'prĕt), *v.* Pe·e agana, uiata.
Interrogate (ĭn-t·r'ro-gāt), *v.* Sing·a. (ĭn-têr-rŏg'ȧ-tiv) *a.*
Interrupt (ĭn'têr-rŭpt'), *v.* Dondikata, dontongata, golmal dakata. **-ion,** *n.*
Intersect (ĭn'têr-sĕkt'), *v.* Battonggrika.
Intertwine (ĭn'têr-twīn'), *v.* Sakmrena, saka.
Interval (ĭn'têr-val), *n.* Gisepni sal ba biap.
Interview (ĭn'têr-vū), *n.* Grongani, agangrikani.
Intestines (ĭn-tĕs'tins), *n.* Bibikrang.
Intimate (ĭn'tĭ-mat), *a.* Naugrimbegipa.
Intimate (ĭn'tĭ-māt), *v.* Chanchiata, ba on·titi uiata.
Intimidate (ĭn-tĭm'ĭ-dāt), *v.* Kenata.
Into (ĭn'tų), *prep.* Ning·chi.
Intolerable (ĭn-tŏl'êr-ȧ-b'l), *a.* Chaktogija, chakna amgija.
Intolerant (ĭn-tŏl'êr-ant), *a.* Chakchikgi jagipa.
Intoxicate (ĭn-tŏks'ĭ-kāt), *v.* Chupekata.
Intrench (ĭn-trĕnch'), *v.* Dule cho·dula.
Intrepid (ĭn-trĕp'ĭd), *a.* Kengija, ka·donggipa.
Intricate (ĭn'trĭ-kat), *a.* Bil·dik bil·dak.
Intrigue (ĭn-trēg'), *v.* Melaprua, srik srik ku·monga.
Introduce (ĭn'tro-dūs'), *v.* Uiata, napata, a·bachengata. **-tion,** *n.*
Intrude (ĭn-tr̤d'), *v.* Hukum ba okama gri napa.
Intrusion (ĭn-tr̤'zhŭn), *n.* Hukum ba okama gri napani.
Intrust (ĭn-trŭst'), *v.* Gipinni jako ka·donge on·a, pakwata.
Inundate (ĭn-ŭn'dāt), *v.* Chi dubiata. **-ion,** *n.*
Invade (ĭn-vād'), *v.* Dakgrikna ba bobil ong·na napa.
Invalid (ĭn'vȧl-ĭd), *n.* Sagipa. (ĭn-văl'ĭd) *a.* Bil gri.
Invaluable (ĭn-văl'u-ȧ-b'l), *a.* Gamchatbegipa, aganna ampilgija gamchata.
Invariable (ĭn-vā'rĭ-ȧ-b'l), *a.* Pangnan dingtanggija.
Invasion (ĭn-vā'zhŭn), Bobil ong·na napani.
Invent (ĭn-vĕnt'), *v.* Dakchenga, bikotchenga, ong·ata.
Inverse (ĭn-vêrse'), *a.* Bikpilgimin bikpilgrikgimin.
Investigate (ĭn-vĕs'tĭ-gāt), *v.* Ja·pangko sandie nia. **-ion,** *n.*
Invigorate (ĭn-vĭg'êr-āt), *v.* Bilakata.
Invincible (ĭn-vĭn'sĭ-b'l), *a.* Pilaknibа amako man·gijagipa.
Invisible (ĭn-vĭz'ĭ b'l), *a.* Nikna amgija, jeko nikna amja.
Invite (ĭn-vīt'), *v.* Okama, nimontron ka·a. **-ation,** *n.*

Invoice (in'vois'), *n.* Bostu on·ataniko sea mesokatani list.

Involuntarily (in-vŏl'ŭn-ta-rily), *adv.* Chanchisoa ba mangsongsoa gri draani gimin daka.

Inward (in'wêrd), *adv.* Ning·chi. *a.* Ning ogipa.

Iris (ī'ris). *n.* Mikron birong, nonoriko dule donggipa.

Irish (ī'rish), *a.* Ireland songni.

Iron (ī'ŭrn), *n.* Silgrak, sil.

Irony (ī'rŭn-y), *n.* Namgijako nama inn·ike ka·dingstekani.

Irradiate (ir-rā'di-āt), *v.* Ching·ata.

Irregular (ĭr-rĕg'u-lêr), *a.* Niam gita ong·gija.

Irreligion (ir're-lij'ŭn), *n.* Torom gri ong·ani.

Irreproachable (ir're-prōch'ă-b'l), *a.* Matnangako man na amgija.

Irresistible (ir're-zist'i-b'l), *a.* Champengna ba warachakna amgija.

Irresolute (ĭr-rĕz'o-lūt), *a.* Gisik gnigipa, tiktak maugsonggijagipa.

Irrespective (ir're-spĕk'tiv), *a.* Nangrima gri.

Irresponsible (ir're-spŏn'si-b'l), *a.* Dai gri.

Irreverence (ĭr-rĕv'êr-ens), *n.* mande ra·gijani.

Irreversible (ir're-vêrs'i-b'l), *v.* Bikpilatna man·gija.

Irrigate (ĭr'rĭ-gāt), *v.* Ge·aona chi bakwata, boi cho·e ra·anga. **-ion,** *n.*

Irritate (ir'ri-tāt), *v.* Natgrike ding·ata, ka·onangata.

Irruption (ĭr-rŭp'shŭn), *n.* Bikpawani, a·tangan ong·katani.

Is ('z), *v.* AM, WAS, BEEN. Donga ba ong·a. Beni third person, singular number.

Island (ī'land), *n.* Chichang.

Isle (īl), *n.* Chichang.

Isolate (ī'so-lāt ba is'-o-), *v.* Ge·san ba saksan dongata, a·te dongata.

Issue (ish'ū), *v.* Ong·kata.

Isthmus (is'mŭs ba ist'mŭs), *n.* Chi gisepni a·gitok.

It (it), *pr.* Ia, ua, iako, uako.

Italic (i-tăl'ik), *a.* Gitchinge segipa oikor.

Itch (itch), *v.* Mitpa, ka·kita. *n.* Kasi ba am·bol cha·a.

Itself (it-sĕlf'), *pr.* An·tangan.

Ivory (ī'vo-ry), *n.* Mongma wagam.

Ivy (ī'vy), *n.* Budu wegipa sam ma·sa.

J.

Jabber (jăb'bêr), *v.* Bokboka, bol·bola, bel·bela.

Jack (jăk), *n.* Jabatni nisan chongipa; dakchakani maiba chongipa kol.

Jackal (jăk'ôl'), *n.* Peru.

Jackass (jăk'ăs), *n.* Gada bipa.

Jackdaw (jăk'dô'), *n.* Do·ka ma·sa.

Jacket (jăk'ĕt), *n.* Kan·dikgipa be·enna kakket ong·gipa chola.

Jackknife (jăk'nīf'), *n.* Kipoa man·gipa jepo ra·bitani chongipa churi.

Jade (jād), *n.* Mamungnaba choligijagipa guru; ripok do·katchi.

Jade (jād), *v.* Neng·ata.

Jaguar (jä-gwär'), *n.* Amerikan matcha ma·sa.

Jail (jāl), *n*. Jelkana, patok nok.

Jailbird (jāl'bêrd'), *n*. Patokonigipa, patokoni joka man'-gipa mande.

Jam (jăm), *n*. Chini baksa song·e bon ka·e dongimin bite.

Jam (jăm), *v*. Sinjeta, mande jinmao sikchepchepa.

January (jăn'u-a-ry), *n*. Bilsini skanggipa ja.

Japanese (jă'pă-nēz' ba -nēs'), *n*. Japan songni mande. *a*.

Jar (jär), *n*. Ku·sik dal·gipa a·ani tikili.

Jar (jär), *v*. Rang·san moata, tim·jil dakata.

Jaundice (jôn'dĭs), *n*. Holdia sop saani, sop saani.

Javelin (jăv'lĭn), *n*. Chongipa selu.

Jaw (jô), *n*. Chengkna.

Jay (jā), *n*. Do·chai.

Jealous (jĕl'ŭs), *a*. Mikbua, mikron dal·a.

Jeer (jēr), *v*. Ka·dingsteke sminga.

Jehovah (je-hō'vä), *n*. Isolni bimung, Jihova.

Jelly (jĕl'ly), *n*. Biteni bitchriko chinimu tarie tin·kaatgimin.

Jelly fish (jĕl'ly-fĭsh'), *n*. Sagalni nom·begipa na·tok ma·-sa.

Jenny (jĕn'ny), *n*. Kilding rikani kol.

Jerk (jĕrk), *v*. Rang·san sala ba morereka, cha·sua, sutika gita dakata.

Jest (jĕst), *n*. Ka·dingatani kata. *v*.

Jester (jĕst'êr), *n*. Ka·dingatgipa.

Jesuit (jĕz'u-ĭt), *n*. Roman kato likni ma·malsa, tol·gipa, togigipa.

Jesus (Jē'zŭs), *n*. Jisu.

Jet (jĕt), *n*. Rong gisim.

Jew (jū ba jụ), *n*. Jihudi.

Jewel (jū'ĕl ba jụ'ĕl), *n*. Gamchatgipa ripok.

Jew's-harp (jūz' ba jụz'härp), *n*. Silni gomina.

Jingle (jĭng'g'l), *v*. Sreng sreng ba srang srang ine gam·a.

Job (jŏb), *n*. Kam mingsa, tika ra·gimin kam gimik.

Jog (jŏg), *v*. Jakskuchi su·tinga, ka·sne jitpaka.

Join (join), *v*. Ritchua, nangrimata.

Joint (joint), *n*. Biritchu.

Joke (jōk), *n*. Etalani, mangkalani, nachilakani.

Jolly (jŏl'ly), *a*. Katchagipa, ka·srokgipa.

Journal (jêr'nal), *n*. Salantini ong·aniko seani; songbadni bimung.

Journey (jêr'ny), *v*. Re·a, re·roa. *n*.

Joy (joi), *n*. Kusi ong·ani, katchaani. *v*.

Jubilee (jū'bĭ-lē), *n*. Bilsi sotbongaprako kusi ong·e maniani; dal·a kusi ong·ani sal.

Judaism (jū'da-ĭz'm), *n*. Jihudini torom.

Judge (jŭj), *v*. Bichal ka·a, *n*. Bichal ka·gipa. **-ment**, *n*.

Judicial (ju-dĭsh'al), *a*. Bichal ka·ani biding.

Judicious (ju-dĭsh'ŭs), *a*. Nama ba kakketko chanchigipa.

Jug (jŭg), *n*. Ku·sik chongipa dal·gipa a·ani botol.

Juggle (jŭg'g'l), *v*. Beliki dak-a.

Juice (jūs), *n*. Bitchi. -**y**, *a*.
July (jū-lī'), *n*. Bilsini snigipa ja.
Jumble (jŭm'b'l), *v*. Bilding bildang brinbawe daka.
Jump (jŭmp), *v*. Bila, bilchroka, bilbata.
Junction (jŭngk'shŭn), *n*. Nangdimani biap, bibra.
June (jūn), *n*. Bilsini dokgipa ja.
Jungle (jŭng'g'l), *n*. Burung, bolgrim.
Junior (jūn'yêr), *n*. Bilsi chonbatgipa.
Jupiter (jū'pi-têr), *n*. Brihospoti minggipa grobo; Romrangni mite dal·batgipa.
Jurisdiction (jū'ris-dĭk'shŭn), *n*. Gam ba a·ani nokgipani ning·o man·a gimik.
Jury (jū'ry), *n*. Bichal ka·na dongimin manderang.
Just (jŭst), *a*. Kakket, bebe, tik. -**ice**, *n*.
Justify (jŭs'ti-fī), *v*. Dos gri mesoka, matnangaoniko jokat-a, toromi ina. -**ication**, *n*.
Jut (jŭt), *v*. Ro·chokgipa ku·chot dakata.
Jute (jūt), *n*. Me·katchi.
Juvenile (jū've-nīl), *a*. Pantegipa, pantena ba bi·sana kragipa.

K.

Kangaroo (kăng'gå-rū), *n*. Jakna bate ja·a ro·robatgipa aro bi·siko chipo ra·ani ka·bakchi mona donggipa Ostrelia songni mathurung ma·sa.
Katydid (kā'tĭ-dĭd'), *n*. Gukchuri.
Keel (kēl), *n*. Ringni janggil matchi.
Keen (kēn), *a*. Sramgipa, matgipa; uininggipa.
Keep (kēp), *v*. Rakia, dona, sogija dona.
Keg (kĕg), *n*. Pipa chongipa.
Kerosene (kĕr'o-sēn), *n*. Korasin to.
Kettle (kĕt't'l), *n*. Chi ritani ba song·ani silni me·dik.
Key (kē), *n*. Chabi; sulni ja·-pang ba ochenggipa, sulni nangrimani ja·pang.
Keyhole (kē'hōl'), *n* Chabini a·kol.
Keyboard (kē'bōrd'), *n*. Piano, bajona ba ugita maibao jaksichi sinjete moanirang.
Keystone (kē'stōn'), *n*. Kosak chi gongdole rikaniko rakatan ro·ong, chong·motan ki·tikni skotong.
Kick (kĭk), *v*. Ga·teka, ga·tinga. *n*.
Kid (kĭd), *n*. Do·bok bi·sa.
Kidnap (kĭd'năp'), *v*. Mandeko cha·ua.
Kidney (kĭd'ny), *n*. Gila, ka·-rongte.
Kill (kĭl), *v*. So·ota.
Kiln (kĭl), *n*. A·ani dakgiminrangko so·chakani biap.
Kin (kĭn), *n*. Bak, chatchi.
Kind (kīnd), *a*. Ka·sae dakgipa.
Kind (kind), *n*. Rokom, ma·-a.
Kindle (kĭn'd'l), *v*. Wa·al so·-baka, snama.
Kindred (kĭn'drĕd), *n*. Bak chong·mot; nangrimgipa, biding apsangipa.
King (kĭng), *n*. Raja.
Kingdom (kĭng'dŭm), *n*. Raijo, songnok.
Kingfisher (kĭng'fĭsh'ĕr), *n*. Muslengga do·o.
Kiss (kis), *v*. Ku·dima. *n*.

Kit (kĭt), *n*. Mistrini jakkalani silrang gimik.
Kitchen (kĭch'ĕn), *n*. Song·ram biap ba kutori.
Kite (kīt), *n*. Do·reng ; leka do·reng.
Kitten (kĭt't'n), *n*. Menggo bi·sa.
Knack (năk), *n*. Changani, sap·ani.
Knave (nāv), *n*. Denggugipa, namgijagipa.
Knead (nēd), *v*. No·a.
Knee (nē), *n*. Ja·sku.
Kneel (nēl), *v*. KNELT, KNEELED. Ja·sku dem a, ja·chik dipana.
Knew (nū), *v*. *Know* ko nibo.
Knickerbockers (nĭk'ĕr-bŏk'ĕrs), *n*. Ja·skuona sokaigipa pentalun.
Knife (nīf), *n*. Churi, chakku.
Knit (nĭt), *v*. Sika.
Knob (nŏb), *n*. Rim·chakani nagong.
Knock (nŏk), *v*. Doka, doktika.
Knot (nŏt), *n*. Kaani bistit.
Know (nō), *v*. KNEW, KNOWN. Uia.
Knowledge (nŏl'ĕj), *n*. Uiani.
Knuckle (nŭk'k'l), *n*. Jaksi ganti.
Knuckle (nŭk'k'l), *v*. Bama, ning·o ong·a.

L.

Label (lā'bĕl), *n*. Kadapani ba tapani bimung segimin leka.
Labor, labour (lā'bĕr), *v*. Kam ka·a.
Labor, labour (lā'bĕr), *n*. Kam; an·pakani saknaa.
Laborious (lā-bō'rĭ-ŭs), *a*. Kam ka·begipa, neng·atgnigipa.
Lac (lăk), *n*. Laha.
Lace (lās), *n*. Juta kaani lulu ; chongipa ro·dinggipa rikingo ko·lapaoi ba·ra.
Lack (lăk), *v*. Chu·ongja, tikja.
Lad (lăd), *n*. Me·a bi·sa, pante bi·sa.
Ladder (lăd'dĕr), *n*. Jano·ke, do·jaleng.
Lade (lād), *v*. Bal gata, boja gata.
Ladle (lā'd'l), *n*. Koncholi, chamos dal·gipa.
Lady (lā'dy), *n*. Mande ra·a man·gipa me·chik.
Ladylike (lā'dy-lik'), *a*. Kragipa me·chik gita.
Lag (lăg), *v*. Ja·man chaka, ka·sne r·a. -**gard**, *n*.
Laid (lād), *v*. *Lay* ko nibo.
Lain (lān), *v*. *Lie* ko nibo.
Lair (lâr), *n*. Matburungrangni dongram ba turam.
Lake (lāk), *n*. Hrud, dal·begipa chibol, chongipa sagal gita.
Lamb (lăm), *n*. Mes bi·sa.
Lame (lām), *a*. Kora.
Lament (lă-mĕnt'), *v*. Duk ong·a, kaiina.
Lamp (lămp), *n*. Chaki, tochi, lamp.
Lampblack (lămp'blăk'), *n*. Chakini wal·kusi, simgipa dim·ak.
Lance (lăns), *n*. Sel·a ma·sa.
Lancet (lăn'sĕt), *n*. Mandeni be·enko raani chongipa matgipa churi.
Land (lănd), *n*. A·a.
Landholder (lănd'hōld'ĕr), *n*. A·a man·gipa. a·a nokgipa.
Landing (lănd'ĭng), *n*. A·gaona gakatram ba cng·onram biap.
Landlord (lănd'lôrd), *n*. A·a ba nokni nokgipa.

Landmark (lănd'märk'), *n.* A·a sima·ani chin.
Landscape (lănd'skāp), *n.* Nikwatgipa a·a.
Landslide (lănd'slīd'), *n.* A·a sol·solgimin; a·a sol·solani.
Landtax (lănd'tăks'), *n.* A·ani kajana.
Lane (lān), *n.* Dilengrangni ba nokrangni gisepo chongipa rama.
Language (lĭng'gwāj), *n.* Agananí ku·sik.
Languid (lăng'gwĭd), *a.* Be·en jrima ba a·ata.
Languish (lang'gwĭsh), *v.* Neng·roroa, sikreproroa.
Lank (lăngk), *a.* Okjolwewe dakgipa, manle mangchenggiamgipa.
Lantern (lăn'têrn), *n.* Ra·bite re·ani chaki, lenten.
Lap (lăp), *v.* Cha·sraka; dondapa, pindapa, tem·a. *n.*
Lap (lăp), *n.* Ja·ping.
Lap dog (lăp'dŏg'), *n.* Ja·pingo gakatgipa achak chongipa jat.
Lapse (lăps), *v.* Simsakgija ba uirikgija batanga.
Lapwing (lăp'wing), *n.* Chio iogipa do·o ma·sa.
Lard (lärd), *n.* Wak mitim.
Large (lärj), *n.* Dal·a.
Lark (lärk), *n.* Do·o ma·sa, saru gitimang dal·a.
Larva (lär'vå), *n.* Ja·mano me·pilip ba maiba bilgipa pil·gipa jo·ongrang.
Larynx (lăr'ingks), *n.* Gitokbu, gitoko mikoani bakos ba kol.
Lash (lăsh), *n.* Ku·choto budu ba matbigiko kagipa betsmit.
Lass (lås), *n.* Me·chik bi·sa, me·tra bisa.
Lassitude (lăs's·-tūd), *n.* Be·enni manga·ani, bilgri ong·ani.
Last (låst), *v.* Baia.
Last (lås:), *a.* Bon·kamgipa; *n.* Jutako sikkroke gojal datchakani bolko sol·gimin.
Latch (lăch), *n.* Do·gako rakatani ba tekani.
Late (lāt), *a.* Ruutgipa; sigimin, sagi; gipinrangna ja·mangipa, tik salo sokgijagipa, ka·singipa.
Lately (lāt'ly), *adv.* Da·osin, ruutkoja·on, daldal.
Lathe (lāTH), *n.* Maikoba kundaina jakchi wilwi ani.
Lather (lăTH'êr), *n.* Sabonni ka·spu.
Latin (lăt'in), *n.* Skangni Romrangni agananí ku·sik.
Latter (lăt'têr), *a.* Gipinni gisepo bon·kame ba ja·man jeni gimin agana.
Laud (lôd), *v.* Mitela, rasong chaata.
Laugh (läf), *v.* Ka·dinga.
Launch (länch), *v.* Gitchoata.
Laundress (län'drĕs), *n.* Ba·ra sa·gipa me·chik.
Laundry (län'dry), *n.* Ba·ra su·ani nok.
Lava (lä'vå), *n.* Wa·al a·brioni sil aro ma·manti jronga ong·katgipa.
Lave (lāv), *v.* Chidaro chake aua, su·ringa.
Lavender (lăv'ĕn-dêr), *n.* Smilgipa bol ma·sa.
Lavish (lăv'ĭsh), *v.* Indira i koroch ka·e gimata, agre koroch ka·a.
Law (lô), *n.* Niam.
Lawful (lô'fụl), *a.* Niam gita ong·a ba kraa.
Lawless (lô'lĕs), *a.* Niam gri, niamko manigijagipa.

Lawn (lôn), *n*. Se·engipa ba·ra ; rongtala a·ba ba sara.
Lawsuit (lô'sūt'), *n*. Mokordoma ka·ani.
Lawyer (lô'yêr), *n*. Ukil.
Lax (lăks), *a*. Olgroka.
Lay (lā), *v*. LAID. Dona, chi·a (do·o bitchi chi·a). *Lie* koba nibo.
Lazy (lā'zy), *a*. Aratgipa, roaigipa.
Leach (lēch), *n*. Katchi cholani dengreng.
Lead (lēd), *v*. LED. Dila.
Lead (lĕd), *n*. Sisa.
Leaf (lēf), *n*. Bijak.
League (lēg), *n*. Nangrimgrikani ; kros sa adhani pal bokroako toani.
Leak (lēk), *n*. Selani a·kol. *v*. Chisela, selå.
Lean (lēn), *v*. Dengdala, dan·-dana.
Leap (lēp), *v*. Bila, bilchroka.
Leap-frog (lēp'frŏg'), *n*. Beng·-blok dake bile roani ka·'·grikani.
Leap-year (lēp'yēr'), *n*. Salsa batgipa bilsi, chong·motan bilsi bri brini ja·mano February jani salsa batgipa bilsi.
Learn (lêrn), *v*. Skia, poraia.
Learned (lêrn'ĕd), *a*. Skia man·-gipa.
Lease (lēs), *n*. Pata, bhara on·-ani, bagua on·ani.
Least (lēst), *a*. Chonbatgipa.
Leather (lĕTH'êr), *n*. Tarigimin bigil.
Leave (lēv), *n*. Chuti ; watgrikani ; hukum on·ani.
Leave (lēv), *v*. LEFT. Wata, watanga, donanga.
Leaven (lĕv''n), *n*. Wanti.
Lecture (lĕk'tūr), *v*. Skia, boktrita ka·a.
Ledger (lĕj'êr), *n*. Kata bohi, dokandarrangni bisab rakiani.
Lee (lē), *n*. Balmitin, baljanggil.
Leech (lēch), *n*. Ru·at.
Leek (lēk), *n*. Rasin gipbok ma·sa.
Leer (lēr), *v*. Mikdambenge nia, mikbrao dake nia.
Leeward (lē'wôrd), *adv*. Baljanggilchi.
Left (lĕft), *a*. Jakasi ; *Leave*-koba nibo.
Leg (lĕg), *n*. Ja·a.
Legacy (lĕg'â-sy), *n*. Sinasion on·angani, sigipani on·angani.
Legal (lē'gal), *a*. Niam gita.
Legalize (lē'gal-iz), *v*. Niam gita dakata ba ong·ata.
Legatee (lĕg'â-tē), *n*. Sianggipani on·anga gamko man·rikgipa.
Legation (le-gā'shŭn), *n*. Gipin songchi watata montri ba uni dongram.
Legend (lĕj'ĕnd ba lē'jĕnd), *n*. Agalrikrikani kata gitcham.
Legible (lĕj'i-b'l), *a*. Poraina nama, poraitoa.
Legion (lē'jŭn), *n*. Sipaini kotok ; bang·bea mande jinma.
Legislate (lĕj'is-lāt), *v*. Niamko daka.
Legislature (lĕj'is-lā'tūr), Niamko dakgipa manderang.
Legitimate (le-jĭt'i-mat), Niam gita ba kraa.
Leisure (lē'zhur), *n*. A·sel jokani, kam bang·gijani.
Lemon (lĕm'ŭn), *n*. Te·matchi.
Lemonade (lĕm'ŭn-ād'), *n*. Te·matchi bitchiko chi aro chini ba' sa bringimin ringani.
Lend (lĕnd), *v*. LENT. Ra·chakna on·a.
Length (lĕngth), *n*. Gro, ro·ani.

Lengthwise (lĕngth'wīs'), *adv.* Groe.

Lengthen (lĕngth''n), *v.* Ro·ata, bakroata.

Lens (lĕnz), *n.* Jatchio chutinge ba kongdape dakgimin janera.

Lent (lĕnt), *v.* *Lend*ko nibo.

Leopard (lĕp'ĕrd), *n.* Matchapong, matcha chongipa.

Leper (lĕp'ĕr), *n.* Konchi ritamgipa.

Leprosy (lĕp'ro-sy), *n.* Konchi, konchi ritam biati.

Less (lĕs), *a.* Komibata.

Lesson (lĕs's'n), *n.* Poraiani leson.

Lest (lĕst), *conj.* -jana gita.

Let (lĕt), *v.* Ona·a, dakna on·a.

Lethargy (lĕth'ăr-jy), *n.* Tusidumuani, aratani, gisik on·gijani.

Letter (lĕt'têr), *n.* Chiti; oikor.

Lettuce (lĕt'tis), *n.* Samjak ma·sa, salad.

Level (lĕv'ĕl), *v.* Apsan dakata. *n.* Apsan dakatani, *a.* Apsan ong·a.

Lever (lē'vêr ba lĕv'êr), *n.* Bostu ba maikoba saldoani go·ol.

Levite (lē'vīt), *n.* Lebi mande.

Levity (lĕv'ĭ-ty), *n.* Gisik ritchengani, jrimgijani.

Lewd (lūd), *a.* Til·ekrakgipa.

Lexicon (lĕks'ĭ-kŏn), *n.* Obhidhan ma·sa.

Liable (lī'ȧ-b'l), *a.* Ong·naba donggipa.

Liar (lī'ĕr), *n.* Tol·gipa.

Libel (lī'bĕl), *n.* Tol·e matnangani.

Liberal (lĭb'ĕr-*al*), *a.* On·rakgipa, jakseramgipa.

Liberate (lĭb'ĕr-āt), *v.* Jokata, jakgitel ong·ata.

Liberty (lĭb'ĕr-ty), *n.* Jakgitel ong·ani.

Librarian (li-brā'ri-*an*), *n.* Ki·tap donarangko nitimgipa.

Library (lī'bra-ry), *n.* Ki·tap donani nok.

Lice (līs), *n.* *Louse*ni plural number, tikrang.

License (lī'*sens*), *n.* On·gimin hukum ba bil, laison.

Lick (lĭk), *v.* Cha·sraka.

Licorice (lĭk'o-rĭs), *n.* Chi·gipa bolni ja·dil, josti modu.

Lid (lĭd), *n.* Sikani, pindapani; miksimang.

Lie (lī), *v.* LAY, LAIN. Tua.

Lie (lī), *v.* Tol·a. *n.*

Lieu (lū), *n.* Pal.

Lieutenant (lu-tĕn'*ant*), *n.* Sipaini pamong.

Life (īf), *n.* Janggi; janggi tangani bilsi.

Lifeguard (līf'gärd'), *n.* Rajako nitimgipa sipai.

Lift (lĭft), *v.* De·doa, saldoa, de·toma.

Ligament (lĭ'gȧ-m*ent*), *n.* Biritchuni grengrangko nangdimatgipa ja·dil.

Light (līt), *n.* Seng·a, teng·ani.

Light (līt), *a.* Ritchenga, chikbregija, rongchingbreja.

Light (līt), *v.* Ching·ata, so·a.

Lighten (līt''n), *v.* Teng·ata; ritchengata; teng·suako man·a; mikka riprapa.

Light-footed (līt'fut'ĕd), *a.* Gong·rakgipa, ja·a ritchenggipa, ja·a teng·gipa.

Light-headed (līt'hĕd'ĕd), *a.* Bel·belgipa.

Light-hearted (līt'härt'ĕd), *a.* Kusi ong·gipa, katchagipa, siutea grigipa.

Lighthouse (lit'hous), *n*. Jahatrang nikchina sagal rikamo chaki so·e donani nok.
Lightning (lit'ning), *n*. Mikka riprapa.
Like (lik), *a*. Gita, apsan.
Like (lik), *v*. Namnika.
Likely (lik'ly), *a*. Ong·naba donga, ong·susu.
Liken (lik''n), *v*. Togrika, tosusaa.
Likeness (lik'nĕs), *n*. Apsan bimang; noksi.
Likewise (lik'wiz'), *adv*. Indake, apsan, gita.
Lily (lil'y), *n*. Bibal ma·sa, rasin gita bijak aro bita dakgipa sam aro bibalrang.
Limb (lim), *n*. Cheksi; mandeni jak ba ja·a.
Limber (lim'bêr), *a*. Dol·ninggipa
Lime (lim), *n*. Meseng bite; chun.
Limit (lim'it), *n*. Sima, ari, rikam.
Limp (limp), *v*. Keng·be keng·be teng·dik teng·dik dake re·a, koragipani re·a.
Limp (limp), *a*. Dol·ningipa, non·gipa.
Limpid (lim'pid), *a*. Rongtala, grika.
Line (lin), *n*. Riting; salsrete; chongipa budu.
Lineage (lin'e-aj), *n*. Ma·chong, biding.
Linen (lin'ĕn), *n*. Mosina ba·ra. *a*.
Linger (ling'gêr), *v*. Ruuta.
Linguist (ling'gwist), *n*. Ma·manti ku·sikko uigipa.
Liniment (lin'i-ment), *n*. Be·eno nongani ba nol·ani sam, liniment.
Lining (lin'ing), *n*. Ba·rani ning·chi an·pae kodapgimin.
Link (lingk), *n*. Sildengni ba silitingni rit hugrikgipa tong·prak.
Linseed (lin'sēd), *n*. Mosina bitchil.
Lint (lint), *n*. Kadapani rinokgipa ba·ra ba kil.
Lion (li'ŏn), *n*. Singho.
Lip (lip), *n*. Ku·chil.
Liquefy (lik'we-fi), *v*. Jrongata, chi cakata.
Liquid (lik'wid), *n*. Bitchi, chi gita dakgipa, jingjonggipa.
Liquor (lik'ĕr), *n*. Chu.
Lisp (lisp), *v*. Sni pal thko gam·ate agana.
List (list), *n*. Sulsul ba riting riting seani, talika.
List (list), *v*. Knaa; ska.
Listen (lis''n), *v*. Knatima, gisik on·a.
Listless (list'lĕs), *a*. Ska gri, gi·ik on·a gri, gong·gija.
Literal (lit'êr-al), *a*. Oiko·ni orto gita, tik.
Literature (lit'êr-â-tur), *n*. Ki·lak segaminrang, sahito.
Lithography (li-thŏg'râ-fy), *n*. Rongchi chapa ka·ani.
Litigate (lit'i-gât), *v*. Nalis ka·grika.
Litter (lit'têr), *n*. Sa·sanni bi·sa gi·nik; bilding bildang dongani.
Little (lit't'l). *a*. Chona, on tisa.
Live (liv), *v*. Tanga, donga.
Live (liv), *a*. Janggi gnang.
Liver (liv'êr), *n*. Bika.
Liver-complaint (liv'êr-kŏm-plānt'), *n*. Ka·a saa, bika saa.
Lively (liv'ly), *a*. Gong·rakgipa, ta·rakgipa.

Living (liv'ing), *n.* Janggi tangani.

Lizard (l z'ẽrd), *n.* Ben·chidik, bapme aro mannni jatrang.

Lo (lō), *int.* Nibo.

Load (lōd), *n.* Gatgimin bal ba boja.

Load ('ōd), *v.* Bal gatata.

Loaf (lōf), *n.* Ruti dotgimik.

Loaf (lōf), *v.* Indinari salko re·ata.

Loam (lōm), *n.* A·sal.

Loan (lōn), *v.* Ra·chakna on·a.

Loath (lōth), *a.* Namnikgija, sikgija.

Loathe (lōTH), *v.* Mitchinika.

Lobster (lŏb'stẽr), *n.* Sagalni na·tik dal·gipa.

Local (lō'ka.), *a.* Biapni biding. **-ity**, *n.*

Locate (lō'kāt), *v.* Dona.

Location (lo-kā'shŭn), *n.* Donani ba dongani biap.

Lock (lŏk), *n.* Tala, tekani; kni tom·daksa.

Lock (lŏk), *v.* Chabi teka, bon ka·a.

Locomotion (lō'ko-mō'shŭn), *n.* Biap gipinona re·ani.

Locomotive (lō'ko-mō'tĭv), *n.* Bibachi re·ani kol.

Locust (lō'kŭst), *n.* Gukrori.

Lodge (lŏj), *v.* Waltua.

Lodging (lŏj'ing), *n.* Waltuani biap.

Lofty (lôft'y), *a.* Chua.

Log (lŏg), *n.* Boltong, tum.

Logic (lŏj'ik), *n.* Chanchiani pangchakako skiani, mingsaoni mingsaona chanchina uiani.

Loin (loin), *n.* Kang·kare.

Loiter (loi'tẽr), *v.* Ruuta, mel·mela.

Loll (lŏl), *v.* Neng·ani sre ong·kata; dengdala, dan·dana.

Lonely (lōn'ly), *a.* Saksan, ripeng gri.

Long (lŏng), *a.* Ro·a, bakroa.

Long (lŏng), *v.* Sikbea.

Longevity (lŏn-jĕv ĭ-ty), *n.* Janggi tangbangani, ruute tangani.

Longitude (lŏn'jĭ-tūd), *n.* Biapsaoni salaram ba saliramchi chel·ani.

Look (lụk), *v.* Nia.

Looking-glass (lụk'ing-glȧs), *n.* Mikkang niani janera.

Look out (lụk'out'), *v.* G·sik rakbo.

Loom (lụm), *n.* Ba·ra dakani tat.

Loop (lụp), *n.* Dola bika, genga.

Loophole (lụp'hol'), *n.* Kila ba jabato slai goatani a·kol.

Loose (lụs), *v.* Enga, wata.

Loose (lụs), *a.* Olgroka.

Loot (lụt), *v.* Raseke cha·ua, dakait ka·a.

Lop (lŏp), *v.* Olimea, denkrea, cheksiko den·e gala ba ritama.

Loquacious (lo-kwā'shŭs), *a.* Aganrakgipa, betbetgipa.

Lord (lôrd), *n.* Git·l, nokgipa.

Lose (lụz), *v.* LOST. Gimara.

Loss (lŏs), *n.* Gimaani.

Lot (lŏt), *n.* Kopal; bak; kadulgimin a·ba.

Lotion (lō'shŭn), *n.* Bigilo nongani sam.

Lottery (lŏt'tẽr-y), *n.* Tangka ba gamna chiti kal·e on·ani.

Loud (loud), *a.* Gam·begipa.

Lounge (lounj), *v.* Arate salko re·ata.

Louse (lous), *n.* Tik, plural LICE (lis).

Lousy (louz'y), *a.* Ti kgnang.

Love (lŭv), *v*. Ka·sara.
Lovely (lŭv'ly), *a*. Nitoa, nambea.
Low (lō), *a*. Ona, tu·a, chona.
Low (lō), *v*. Matchuni mikoa.
Lowland (lō'land), *n*. Ongipa a·a, a·kawe.
Low-spirited (lō'spĭr'ĭt-ĕd), *a*. Ku·bososo dakgipa.
Loyal (loi'al), *a*. Rajani ge·etako dakgipa, rajako manigipa; ripeng ong·ako watgalgijagipa.
Lubricate (lū'brĭ-kāt), *v*. Rimilata. **-ant, -tion**, *n*.
Luck (lŭk), *n*. Rasong, kopal.
Lug (lŭg), *v*. Jrimako ra·togija ra·anga, olanga ba ripeanga.
Luggage (lŭg'gaj), *n*. Ra·bita mal, boksa.
Lukewarm (lūk'wôrm'), *a*. Ding·boma, bo·om bo·om ding·a.
Lumber (lŭm'bêr), *n*. Ragimin bol, tokta.
Luminous (lū'mĭ-nŭs), *a*. Teng·sugipa.
Lump (lŭmp), *n*. Dotgimik.
Lunar (lū'nêr), *a*. Jani biding.
Lunatic (lū'na-tik), *n*. Pagila ong·gipa, kore chagipa.
Lunch (lŭnch), *n*. Mesal, tipin.
Luncheon (lŭnch'ŭn), *n*. Mesal, tipin.
Lungs (lŭngs), *n*. Ka·sop.
Lurch (lūrch), *v*. Pakwaka.
Lure (lūr), *v*. Mikbokata, kimala.
Lurk (lêrk), *v*. Dongnue tima.
Luscious (lŭsh'ŭs), *a*. Chi·bea, su·abea, cha·tobea.
Lust (lŭst), *n*. Namgijana sikbeani, gang·ani.
Lustful (lŭst'ful), *a*. Ti·ekrakgipa, gang·gipa.
Lustre (lŭs'têr), *n*. Ching·ani, teng·suani, nitoani.
Lusty (lŭst'y), *a*. Bilakgipa.
Luxuriant (lŭgz-ū'rĭ-ant), *a*. Silbegipa. **-ance**, *n*.
Luxury (lŭk'shu-ry), *n*. Nokma chae man·e cha·a, maha maha dakani.
Lye (lī), *n*. Katchi nanggipa chi.
Lying (lī'ing), *n*. Tol·e aganani; tuani.

M.

M (ĕm), *n*. English oikor mingsa; hajalsako mesokani.
Ma (mä), *n*. Ma·gipa.
Macadamize (măk-ăd'am-īz), *v*. Ro·ongko dokpneke ana.
Macaroni (măk'ă-rō'nĭ), *n*. Moidaoniko dakgimin cha·ani ma·sa.
Mace (mās), *n*. Joitri minggipa mosla ma·sa.
Machine (mȧ-shēn'), *n*. Kol.
Machinery (mȧ-shēn'êr-y), *n*. Kolni bakrang.
Machinist (mȧ-shēn'ĭst), *n*. Kolko dakgipa.
Mackintosh (măk'ĭn-tŏsh), *n*. Sosijana gita kosako krudapani.
Mad (măd), *a*. Pagilagipa; ka·onangbegipa.
Madam (măd'am), *n*. Me·chikko mande ra·ani kata.
Madden (măd'd'n), *v*. Ka·onangata; pagila ong·ata.
Made (măd), *v*. *Makeko* nibo.
Magazine (măg'ȧ-zēn'), *n*. Bandal, silchidare donram hiap; songbat ma·sa.
Maggot (măg'gŭt), *n*. Tatapini jo·ong.

Magi (mā'ji), *n*. Paroisoni uigipa mande.
Magic (măj'ik), *n*. Bheliki, montol dakani.
Magician (mâ-jĭsh'*an*), *n*. Bheliki dakgipa.
Magistrate (măj'is-trāt), *n*. Governmentni bichal ka·gipa.
Magnet (măg'nĕt), *n*. Chumbok, salopgipa sil.
Magnificent (măg-nĭf'i-sent), *a*. Rasong gnang, bil gnang, ching·a gnang. **-ce**, *n*.
Magnify (măg'nĭ-fī), *v*. Dal·e nikata, dal·ata.
Magnitude (măg'nĭ-tūd), *n*. Dal·ani.
Magpie (măg'pī), *n*. Do·pasi.
Mahomedan (mâ-hŏm'ĕd-*an*), *n*. Musolman.
Maid (mād), *n*. Me·tra ; nokol me·chik.
Maiden (mād''n), *n*. Me·tra.
Mail (māl), *n*. Dak.
Maim (mām), *v*. Kora ong·ata, matata.
Main (mān), *a*. Mongsonggipa, skanggipa, bimonggipa.
Maintain (man-tān'), *v*. Allua, rakia.
Maintenance (mān'te-n*a*ns), *n*. Aldumitangani.
Maize (māz), *n*. Me·raku.
Majesty (maj'ĕs-ty), *n*. Rajani mikim. **-ic**, *a*.
Major (mā'jêr), *n*. Kaptinna bate dal·batgipa sipaini pamong.
Majority (mâ-jŏr''-ty), *n*. Bang·batan, samsana baten.
Make (māk), *v*. MADE. Daka.
Malady (măl'â-dy), *n*. Biati rok.
Malaria (mâ-lā'rĭ-â), *n*. Be·en ding·e saatani bisi, jor saatgipa, sawaka saatgipa.
Malcontent (măl'kŏn-tĕnt'), *a*. Namnikgija, chu·ongnikgija. *n*.
Male (māl), *a*. Bipa. *n*.
Malediction (măl'e-dĭk'shŭn), *n*. Sao on·ani.
Malefactor (măl'e-făk'têr), *n*. Dos dakbegipa, miamko pe·gipa.
Malevolent (mâ-lĕv'o-lent), *a*. Namgijako ong·atna sikgipa.
Malice (măl's), *n*. Miknengani, gipinna namgijako ong·atna skani.
Malicious (mâ-lĭsh'ŭs), *a*. Miknenggipa, miknengani gisik gnanggipa.
Malign (mâ-līn'), *v*. Mitaka. **-ant**, *a*. **-ancy**, *n*.
Malleable (mal'le-â-b'l), *a*. Sil suutgipa.
Mallet (măl'lĕt), *n*. Bolni ture.
Malt (môlt), *n*. Chi dim·e ran·atgimin job mi.
Maltreat (măl-trēt'), *v*. Duk on·a, namgija dakata.
Mamma (mâ-mä' ba mä'mâ), *n*. Ama, ma·gipa.
Mammal (măm'm*a*l), *n*. Sok kangipa janggi gnanggipa.
Mammon (măm'mŭn), *n*. Gam; gamni mite.
Man (măn), *n*. Mande ; me·asa.
Manacles (măn'â-k'ls), *n*. Hatkora, jakko kaani sil.
Manage (măn'aj), *v*. Maniata, dilata ; chu·sokata.
Mandarin (mân'dâ-rēn'), *n*. Chin songni dal·a mande.
Mandate (măn'dat), *n*. Bil gnanggipani ge·eta.
Mane (mān), *n*. Merang.
Manfully (măn'ful-ly), *adv*. Mandeni krae.
Mange (mānj), *n*. Kawak, achakrangko cha·gipa kawak.

Manger (măn'jêr), *n.* Alani chikong, jengko donchakani bakos.

Mangle (măng'g'l), *v.* Den·mitcheka; rolarchi istri on·a.

Mango (măng'go), *n.* Te·gatchu.

Manhood (măn'hụd), *n.* Mande ong·ani.

Maniac (mā'nĭ-ăk), *n.* Pagila mande.

Manifest (măn'ĭ-fĕst), *a.* Parakong·gipa. *v.* Talata, uiata.

Manifold (măn'ĭ-fōld), *a.* Ma·manti, bang·en.

Manikin (măn'ĭ-kĭn), *n.* Chongipa mande, mande bone; pilak bakrangko dake mande dakgimin.

Manipulate (må-nĭp'u-lāt), *v.* Jakchi jakkala.

Mankind (măn'kīnd'), *n.* mande jat.

Manly (măn'ly), *a.* Me·asa gita, me·asana kraa.

Manner (măn'nêr), *n.* Dakrongani bewal.

Man of war (măn'ŏv-wär'), *n.* Dakgrikani jahat.

Mansion (măn'shŭn), *n.* Dal·gipa nok.

Manslaughter (măn'slô'têr), *n.* Mangsonggija mandeko so·otani.

Mantis (măn'tĭs), *n.* Gang·gi.

Mantle (măn't'l), *n.* Chinani.

Manual (măn'u-al), *n.* Chongipa ki·tap.

Manual (măn'ū-al), *a.* Jakchi dakani biding.

Manufacture (măn'u-făk'tur), *v.* Kolchi ba jakchi dakata.

Manure (må-nūr'), *n.* A·sal. *v.* A·sal gnangata.

Manuscript (măn'u-skrĭpt), *n.* Jakchi segimin.

Many (mĕn'y), *a.* Bang·a.

Map (măp), *n.* Songrangko mesokna dakgimin noksa, map.

Mar (mär), *v.* Matata, ong·siata.

Marauder (må-rôd'êr), *n.* Ra·sekna re·rorogipa.

Marble (mär'b'l), *n.* Namgipa, bokgipa, rakgipa ro·ong ma·sa.

March (märch), *v.* Riting dake re·a, ja·ku damsan ga·e re·a.

March (märch), *n.* Bilsini gitamgipa ja.

Mare (mâr), *n.* Gure bima.

Margin (mär'jĭn), *n.* Rikam, sima, ari.

Marine (må-rēn'), *a.* Sagalni biding.

Marine (må-rēn'), *n.* Dakgrikani jahatrang; dakgrikani jahatni sipai.

Mariner (măr'ĭ-nêr), *n.* Jahat chogipa, kalasi.

Mark (märk), *n.* Chin, salsretani.

Mark (märk), *v.* Chin o·na; gisik on·a.

Market (mär'kĕt), *n.* Anti, bajal, bostu palram.

Marketable (mär'kĕt-å-b'l), *a.* Palna kraa.

Marksman (märks'man), *n.* Goe nangrakgipa, gona changgipa.

Marquis (mär'kwĭs), *n.* England, France ba Germanini dal·gipa mande.

Marriage (măr'rĭj), *n.* Bia ka·ani.

Married (măr'rĭd), *a.* Bia ka·gimin.

Marrow (măr'ro), *n.* Greng ning·oni geu.

Marrowbone (măr'ro-bōn'), *n.* Geu donggipa greng.

Marry (măr'ry), *v.* Bia ka·a; kima

Mars (märz), *n.* Dakgrikani mite; Mongol groho.

Marsh (märsh), *n.* Chidipek dakgipa biap, drop.

Mart (märt), *n.* Anti.

Martial (mär'shal), *a.* Dakgrikani biding.

Martyr (mär'têr), *n.* Toromni gimin so·ota man·gipa.

Marvel (mär'vĕl), *v.* Aiao inmana.

Marvellous (mär'vĕl-ŭs), *a.* Aiao inmangni.

Masculine (măs'ku-lĭn), *a.* Bipa, me·asa; bilakgipa.

Mash (măsh), *v.* Rinnikata, binnekata.

Mask (măsk), *n.* Mikkangko pindapani. *v.* Pindapa, uigija dake dongnua.

Mason (mā's'n), *n.* Ro·ongni mistri.

Masonry (mā's'n-ry), *n.* It ba ro·ongchi rikgimin.

Mass (mås), *n.* Chong·a, dana, jinma.

Massacre (măs'så-kêr), *n.* Bang·a manderangko mikkang nigija so·otani.

Massive (mås'sĭv), *a.* Namen dal·begipa.

Mast (måst), *n.* Jahatni malju-ri.

Master (mås'têr), *n.* Skigipa, nokgipa.

Masticate (măs'ti-kāt), *v.* Chobaia, chikpneka.

Mat (măt), *n.* Am.

Match (mătch), *n.* Dislai; apsangipa.

Match (mătch), *v.* Apsan dakata, nangrimata.

Matchless (mătch'l's), *a.* Jora gri, apsan ong·a gri.

Mate (māt), *n.* Jora, jik ba se, rorimgipa, ripeng.

Material (må-tē'ri-al), *n.* Bostu ko dakani ja·pang.

Maternal (må-têr'na'), *a.* Ma·a gita, ma·ani biding.

Mathematics (măth'e-măt'iks), *n.* Hisab ka·ani.

Matter (măt'têr), *n.* Ong·ani ja·pang.

Mattress (măt'trĕs), *n.* Tosok.

Mature (må-tūr'), *a.* Bria, ja·dela; mina.

Maul (môl), *v.* Doka. *n.* Bolni dal·gipa ture.

Maund (mänd ba mônd), *n.* Muan.

Maw (mô), *n.* Atom, pechu, bimema.

May (mā), *n.* Bilsini bongagipa ja.

May (mā), *v.* MIGHT. Ama, dakna man·a.

Mayor (mā'êr), *n.* Songjinmani pamong.

Me (mē), *pr.* Angko, angna.

Mead (mēd), *n.* Samsi gnanggipa bakra a·ba.

Meadow (mĕd'o), *n.* Samsi gnanggipa bakra, a·ba.

Meal (mēl), *n.* Patisa ba changsa cha·ani; ginde, moida.

Mean (mēn), *a.* Rasong gri, mande ra·a gri; bijatchigipa. *n.*

Mean (mēn), *v.* Mangsonga.

Meander (mē-ăn'dêr), *v.* Gonggeske dake re·a.

Meaning (mēn'ing), *n.* Mangsongani; orto.

Means (mēns), *n.* Jechi daka; chimonggimin gam.

Meantime (mēn'tīm'), *adv.* Unomiting.

Measles (mē'z'lz), *n*. Urį se·ep.
Measure (mĕzh'ur), *v*. Toa. *n*. Toani.
Meat (mēt), *n*. Cha·ani; bitin, be·en.
Mechanic (me-kăn'ĭk), *n*. Mistri.
Medal (mĕd'*a*l), *n*. Boksisna tangka gita dakgimin.
Meddle (mĕd'd'l), *v*. Gipinni kamo jak dangdikpaa. **-r**, *n*. **-some**, *a*.
Mediate (mē'dĭ-āt), *v*. Baltia, namgrikata. **-or**, *n*. **-tion**, *n*.
Medical (mĕd'i-k*a*l), *a*. Samni biding.
Medicine (mĕd'ĭ-sĭn), *n*. Sam.
Meditate (mĕd'ĭ-tāt), *v*. Chanchibewala.
Mediterranean (Mĕd'ĭ-tĕr-rā'ne-*a*n), *a*. A·ani jatchigipa sagalni bimung.
Medium (mē'dĭ-ŭm), *n*. Ma·jatchigipa, bijatchigipa; jechi daka.
Meek (mēk), *a*. Sontol.
Meet (mēt), *v*. MET. Gronga, gronggrika,
Meet (mēt), *a*. Kraa.
Meeting (mēt'ing), *n*. Mandeni tom·a, grongrikani.
Melancholy (mĕl'ăn-kŏl-y), *n*. Ku·bosoo dakani gisik. *a*. Kusi ong·ani gri.
Mellow (mĕl'lo), *a*. Mingimin bite gita nom·a, tapua.
Melody (mĕl'o-dy), *n*. Knatogipa ring·ani, sul. **-ious**, *a*.
Melon (mĕl'ŭn), *n*. Te·e.
Melt (mĕlt), *v*. Jronga, jrongata.
Member (mĕm'bĕr), *n*. Bak ong·gipa; gimikoni saksa; ge·sa ba tong·sa.
Membrane (mĕm'brān), *n*. Bisring, bichingchrap.
Memory (mĕm'o-ry), *n*. Gisik ra·ani.
Memorandum (mĕm'o-răn'-dŭm), *n*. Gisiko rakina segimin.
Men (mĕn), *n*. Manderang.
Menace (mĕn'as), *v*. Ka·mikena. *n*. Ka·mikenani.
Mend (mĕnd), *v*. Taris, namata.
Mendicant (mĕn'dĭ-k*a*nt), *n*. Bi·ame cha·gipa.
Menstrual (mĕn'strų-*a*l), *a*. Jaanti ong·gipa, me·chikrangni jaantini ong·bewalni biding.
Mental (mĕn't*a*l), *a*. Gisikni biding.
Mention (mĕn'shŭn), *v*. Janapa.
Mercantile (mêr'kăn-tĭl), *a*. Badingani biding.
Mercenary (mêr'se-na-ry), *a*. Dormahanasa ka·aigipa.
Merchandise (mêr'ch*a*n-dīz), *n*. Badingani bosturang.
Merchant (mêr'ch*a*nt), *n*. Badinggipa, mahajon.
Merchantman (mêr'ch*a*nt-m*a*n), *n*. Badingani jahat.
Merciful (mêr'sĭ-fųl), *a*. Ka·sachakgipa.
Mercury (mêr'ku-ry), *n*. Jingjonggipa sil ma·sa, para; grobo ge·sa; Romrangni manigipa mite mingsa.
Mercy (mêr'sy), *n*. Ka·saani, ka·sachakani.
Mere (mēr), *a*. Aia, ari, san.
Merely (mēr'ly), *adv*. Aia, ari, san.
Merge (mêrj), *v*. Sripa, dubia.
Meridian (me-rĭd'ĭ-*a*n), *n*. Mapo salgrochini salgipengchina a·ako dule saldulgipa lain; salaram, saliram biaprangni chel·grikako toani; Dragbima, salni bijatchini biding, saljatchi.

Merit (mĕr'ĭt), *v.* Mande ra·ako ba boksisko man·na kraa. *n.*

Mermaid (mêr'mād), *n.* Buga me·chik; tong·sa me·chik tong·sa na·tok dakgipa.

Merrily (mer'ri-ly), *adv.* Katchae.

Merry (mer'ry), *a.* Katchagipa, kusi ong·gipa. **-iment,** *n.*

Mesh (mĕsh), *n.* Chekni a·kol.

Mess (mes), *v.* Cha·paa, cha·rima. *n.* Cha·ani; cha·rimgiparang; golmal ong·ani; biliing bildang dake nangbrine namgija ong·atgimin.

Message (mĕs'saj), *n.* Aga·ata kata.

Messenger (mĕs'sĕn-jêr), *n.* Sa·gre; katako ra·anggipa mande.

Messiah (mĕs-sī'å), *n.* Mosiho, nonggimin, Kristo.

Met (mĕt), *v.* *Meet*ko nibo.

Metal (mĕt'*a*l ba mĕt''l), *n.* Sil.

Metallic (me-tăl'ĭk), *a.* Silni biding, sil gita dakgipa.

Metaphor (mĕt'å-fêr), *n.* Mesokani ba toani kata ma·sa.

Meteor (mē'te-êr), *n.* Chual, bilgipa aski.

Meter (mē'têr), *n.* Toani kol ma·sa.

Method (mĕth'ŭd), *n.* Niam gita dakani.

Methodist (mĕth'o-dĭst), *n.* Kristan toromko ra·gipa ma·malsa.

Metropolis (me-trŏp'o-lĭs), *n.* Skotonggipa songjinma, rajani dongram; a·songni gisepo dal·batgipa songjinma.

Mew (mū), *v.* Menggo gita mikoa.

Mica (mī'kå), *n.* So·re.

Mice (Mīs), *n.* Menggotchirang. *Mouse*ko nibo.

Microbe (mī'krōb ba mĭk'rōb), *n.* Nikna amgija biatini jo·ong.

Microscope (mī'kro-skop ba mĭk'ro-), *n.* Chonbeako dal·bee nikatgipa janerani kol.

Mid (mĭd), *a.* Bijatchi, jatchi.

Midst (mĭdst), *n.* Bijatchiogipa.

Middle (mĭd'd'l), *a.* Bijatchi.

Midwife (mĭd'wīf'), *n.* An·nigipa, kamal me·chik.

Mien (mēn), *n.* Mikkang bimang.

Might (mīt), *n.* Bil. **-y,** *a.* **ily,** *adv.*

Might (mīt), *v.* *May*ko nibo.

Migrate (mī'grāt), *v.* Gipin songchi re·ange donga. **-ion,** *n.* **-ory,** *a.*

Mikado (mĭ-kä'do), *n.* Japan songni rajako mingani.

Milch (mĭlch), *a.* Jilani sok ong·mitinggipa.

Mild (mīld), *a.* Rinoka, nom·a, ka·sina.

Mile (mīl), *n.* Mail, kros sani simsa.

Military (mĭl'ĭ-ta-ry), *a.* Sipaini biding.

Militia (mĭ-lĭsh'å), *n.* Songtango donggipa nangani salosa dakaigipa sipairang.

Milk (mĭlk), *n.* Matchu ba ma·manti janggi gnanggiparangni sepgimin sok. **-y,** *a.*

Milkmaid (mĭlk'mād'), *n.* Sok sepgipa me·chik, goala me·chik.

Milky way (mĭlk'ĭ-wā'), *n.* Matma ja·kol, gai kopini ja·kol, aski jinma.

Mill (mĭl), *n.* Jata, natani kol natram nok.

Millet (mĭl'lĕt), *n*. Misi.
Milliner (mĭl'li-nêr), *n*. Me·chikrangni tupiko dakgipa ba palgipa.
Million (mĭl'yŭn), *n*. Lak chikung.
Millstone (mĭl'stōn'), *n*. Jatani ro·ong.
Minaret (mĭn'ă-rĕt), *n*. Musolmanrangni olakiani nok ba gilja nokni ku·chot, protchong.
Mince (mĭns), *v*. Den·kninga, den·chemchema.
Mind (mīnd), *n*. Gisik, *v*. Gisik on·a; chanchia; mania.
Mine (mīn), *pr*. Angnin.
Mine (mīn), *n*. Silko cho·e bikotani a·kol.
Miner (mīn'êr), *n*. Silko cho·e bikotgipa, a·kolo kam ka·gipa.
Mineral (mĭn'êr-*a*l), *n*. Sil. *a*.
Mingle (mĭng'g'l), *v*. Brina; brinata; nangrimgrika.
Minion (mĭn'yŭn), *n*. Tol·e mitelachi ka·saa ba namnikako man·gipa.
Minimum (mĭn'ĭ-mŭm), *n*. Kombatgipa.
Minister (mĭn'ĭs-têr), *n*. Dangdike on·gipa; toromko skigipa; montri.
Minister (mĭn'ĭs-têr), *v*. Dangdike on·a.
Minor (mīn'êr), *a*. Chonkalgipa.
Minor (mīn'êr), *n*. A·tang jakgitel ong·aona bilsi sokgijagipa, England aro America songo bilsi 21 ong·gijagipa.
Minority (mĭ-nŏr'ĭ-ty), *n*. Uigijamiting, bi·samiting; samsana bate komigipa.
Minstrel (mĭn'strĕl), *n*. Dokgipa, dam·gipa ba ring·gipa.
Mint (mĭnt), *n*. Tangka dakram; podina, moela ma·sa.
Minuend (mĭn'u-ĕnd), *n*. Jeoniko biog ka·na nanga, biog ka·gni.
Minus (mī'nŭs), *a*. Komiatani kata, biog ka·ani chinko minus minga.
Minute (mī-nūt'), *a*. Bisemsem chonbegipa.
Minute (mĭn'ĭt), *n*. Minit, kanta sani bak sotdokni bak sa.
Miracle (mĭr'ă-k'l), *n*. Aiao inmanani kam.
Miraculous (mĭ-răk'u-lŭs), *a*. Isolni daka aiao inmanpilgni.
-**ly**, *adv*.
Mirage (me-răzh'), *n*. Chel·beaoni jagringko ia·bae sepango gita nikatgipa.
Mire (mīr), *n*. A·bel.
Mirror (mĭr'rêr), *n*. Mikkang niani janera.
Mirth (mêrth), *n*. Kusi ong·a ba katchaani jikjaka.
Mis (mĭs-), Ian kata a·bachengani tong·sa, ia dongode ong·gijako, nanggijako ba guale dakako mesoka.
Miscarry (mĭs-kăr'ry), *v*. Sal sokgija an·paka, dugala.
Miscellaneous (mĭs'sĕl-lā'ne-ŭs), *a*. Ma·manti, brinbawe.
Mischief (mĭs'chĭf), *n*. Namgija ong·atani.
Mischievous (mĭs'che-vŭs), *a*. Namgija ong·atgipa.
Misconceive (mĭs'kŏn-sēv'), *v*. Guale chanchia.
Misconception (mĭs'kŏn-sĕp'-shŭn), *n*. Guale chanchiani.
Miscreant (mĭs'kre-*a*nt), *n*. Denggugipa, bebe ra·gijagipa
Miser (mī'zêr), *n*. Rubegipa, kirpin.
Misery (mĭz'êr-y), *n*. Duk ong·beani, saknabeani.

Misfortune (mĭs-fôr'tun), *n*. Kopal griani, rasong griani.

Miss (mĭs), *n*. Me·tra, bia ka·kuja me·chik.

Miss (mĭs), *v*. Nisano nangja, mikgranggrang daka, mikruangruang daka.

Missile (mĭs'sĭl), *n*. Jeko goata, jakoni ro·ong ba sel·u.

Mission (mĭsh'ŭn), *n*. Watatani kam.

Missionary (mĭsh'ŭn-a-ry). *n*. Toromko skina watata mande.

Missive (mĭs'sĭv), *n*. Watatgimin chiti ba kata.

Mist (mĭst), *n*. Guuri; mikka wasisiani.

Mistake (mĭs-tāk'), *v*. Guala, gua·e daka.

Mister (mĭs'têr), *n*. Me·asako mande ra·ani kata, iani pal, **Mr.** ko seronga.

Mistress (mĭs'trĕs), *n*. Nokgipa me·chik; kimgimin me·chikko mande ra·ani kata, iani pal, **Mrs.** ko seronga.

Mistrust (mĭs-trŭst'), *v*. Kenchaka, ka·dongja.

Misuse (mĭs-ūz'), *v*. Namgija daka, duk on·a.

Mite (mīt), *n*. Bisemsem; chonbegipa jo·ong.

Mitigate (mĭt'ĭ-gāt), *v*. Dukko ka·sinata ba tom·tomata.

Mitten (mĭt'tĕn), *n*. Jako kruani muja.

Mix (miks), *v*. Brina.

Mixture (mĭks'tur), *n*. Bringimin.

Moan (mōn), *v*. Ma·ama.

Moat (mōt), *n*. Chikare ba boi dake killako dule cho·gimin a·kol.

Mob (mŏb), *n*. Jinmani golmal; namgijako dakgipa jinma.

Mock (mŏk), *v*. Ka·dingsteka, chonnika, chonnike ba ka·dinge sning·a.

Mode (mōd), *n*. Dakani ba ong·ani rokom.

Model (mŏd'ĕl), *n*. Mesokani, nomuna.

Moderate (mŏd'êr-at), *a*. Agregija, duga dakgija.

Moderate (mŏd'êr-at), *v*. Duga dakaoni komiata. **-or**, *n*. tom·ani pamong. **-ion**, *n*.

Modern (mŏd'êrn), *a*. Da·ororoni, da·o chasongni.

Modest (mŏd'ĕst), *a*. A·tangko dal·nikgijagipa, gaora de·gijagipa; krae dakgipa.

Modify (mŏd'ĭ-fī), *v*. Dingtang ong·ata.

Modulate (mŏd'u-lāt), *v*. Ku·rangko meliata.

Mohammedan (mo-hăm'mĕd-*a*n), *n*. Musolman. *a*.

Moist (moist), *a*. Chijimgipa, ontiti sosia. **-ure**, *n*.

Moisten (mois''n), *v*. Sos·ata, chijimata.

Molar (mō'lêr), *n*. Wama.

Molasses (mo-lăs'sĕz), *n*. Mitai bitchi.

Mold, mould (mōld), *v*. Dimita, me·gumu chaa; bimangko daka.

Mold, mould (mōld), *n*. Bimang gita dake dakatani ba ruani; burungni a·sal; dimita megumu.

Mole (mōl), *n*. Me·mang so·dika; a·ao bitgipa gipi ma·sa.

Molest (mo-lĕst'), *v*. Jajrengata, duk on·ata. **-ation**, *n*.

Mollify (mŏl'li-fī), *v*. Nom·ata, ka·dimeata, tom·tomata.

Mollusk (mŏl'lŭsk), *n*. Ka·prang, grengni be·enarigipa jo·ongrang.

Molt (mōlt), *v.* Gilsrea, kimil gitcham go·oka.
Moult (mōlt), *v.* Gilsrea, kimil gitcham go·oka.
Molten (mōl't'n), *a.* Jronggimin.
Moment (mō'ment), *n.* Dikdiksa, on·tisa sal.
Momentary (mō'men-ta-ry), *a.* Dikdiksa dongaigipa, on·tisa sal dongaigipa.
Monarch (mŏn'ärk), *n.* Raja.
Monastery (mŏn'ăs-têr-y), *n.* Toromni gimin gipinoni ekanggipa manderangni chimonge dongram.
Monday (mŭn'da), *n.* Sombar.
Monetary (mŏn'e-ta-ry), *a.* Tangkani biding.
Mongoose (mŏn'go͞os), *n.* Chuna.
Monk (mŭngk), *n.* Soinasi, toromni gimin mandeskaoni dingtang ekanggipa mande.
Monkey (mŭng'ky), *n.* Makre ba ugita dakgipa jatrang.
Mono- (mŏn-ō-), Iako gipin katana skang seode sa sanko mesoka.
Monopoly (mo-nŏp'o-ly), *n.* Saksan ba jatsan badinggopani. **-ize**, *v.*
Monosyllable (mŏn'o-sil'lă-b'l), *n.* Selebil ge·sangipa kata.
Monotony (mo-nŏt'o-ny), *n.* Gam·a apsan ong·ani, uanuan, mingsan ong·ani. **-ous**, *a.*
Monsoon (mŏn-so͞on'), *n.* Indiani sagalo ta·rakgipa balgipa ma·sa.
Monster (mŏn'stêr), *n.* Bimang dal·begipa ba skal. **-ous**, *a.*
Month (mŭnth), *n.* Ja, jasa.
Monument (mŏn'u-ment), *n.* Gisik ra·na tarie songgimin ro·ong, it ba silni krong, rikgimin nok.
Mood (mo͞od), *n.* Gisikni dingtang dingtang ong ani rokom.
Moon (mo͞on), *n.* Jajong, ja.
Moonbeam (mo͞on'bēm'), *n.* Jasenga, jatenga.
Moonlight (mo͞on'līt'), *n.* Jani seng·a.
Moonshine (mo͞on'shīn'), *n.* Ja teng·a.
Moor (mo͞or), *n.* Dul bari, samsi chagipa chidipbek biap; Morocco songni mande.
Mop (mŏp), *n.* Wa·se ba toktako rim·roprope su·srangna go·olo kagimin ba·ra suri.
Mope (mōp), *v.* Simsakgija indin salko re·ata ba donga.
Moral (mŏr'al), *a.* Niamni biding, namako dakani biding.
Morbid (môr'bĭd), *a.* An·senggija, gisik an·senggija.
More (mōr), *a.* Bata, bang·bata, *adv.*
Morn, morning (môrn, môrn'-ĭng), *n.* Pring.
Morocco (mo-rŏk'ko), *n.* Matbigil ma·sa; Afrikani song damsa.
Morose (mo-rōs'), *a.* Ka·onangninggipa, gisik jrimgipa, kusi ong·gijagipa, mikbamjiljil dakgipa.
Morrow (mŏr'ro), *n.* Salgipin ba knal.
Morsel (môr'sĕl), *n.* Ku·sa, chong·diksa, tong·sa.
Mortal (môr'tal), *a.* Siatgipa; *n.* signigipa. **-ly**, *adv.*
Mortar (môr-têr), *n.* Su·pnekchakani; sa·am, cha·sam; slai nokma; surkini moala.
Mortgage (môr'gaj), *v.* Bondok dona, *n.*
Mortify (môr'tĭ-fī), *v.* Sigiminni soa; so·ota; kratcha·ata.

Mortise (mŏr'tĭ), *n*. Siktekani a·kol.

Mosque (mŏsk), *n*. Musolmanrangni olakiani nok, ba uamang·ni torom nok.

Mosquito (mŏs-kē'to), *n*. Ganggua.

Moss (mŏs), *n*. Bol ba ro'ongrango chagatgipa chongipa rinokgipa samsi, bol ku·simang.

Most (mōst), *a*. Bata, bang·bata

Mote (mōt), *n*. Bisemsem, chonbegipa dak.

Moth (mŏth), *n*. Wa·alo bilnapgipa chongipa me·pilip.

Mother (mŭTH'ēr), *n*. Ma·gipa, ma·a.

Mother-in-law (mŭTH'ēr-'n-lô'), *n*. Niotang.

Motion (mō'shŭn), *n*. Re·ani, il·engani; namnikako mesokani.

Motive (mō'tĭv), *n*. A·sel, mangsongatani.

Motor (mō'têr), *n*. Moatgipani bil, kol.

Motto (mŏt'tō), *n*. Ja·pang kata.

Mould (mōld), *v*. *Mold* ko nibo.

Mound (mound), *n*. A·timbo, dal·bee gatgimin a·ali.

Mount (mount), *n*. A·bri.

Mount (mount), *v*. Gakata, gadoa.

Mountain (moun'tĭn), *n*. A·bri, a·chu.

Mountaineer (moun'tĭn-ēr'), *n*. A·brio donggipa mande.]

Mountainous (moun'tĭn-ŭs), *a*. A·briraragipa.

Mourn (mōrn), *v*. Kalima, duk ong·a.

Mouse (mous), *n*. Mese menggotchi, plural *mice*.

Moustache (mŭs-tăch'), *n*. Kosakchini ku·simang, singgera.

Mouth (mouth), *n*. Kŭ·sik; bibra; ku mang.

Move (mōv), *v*. Moa, il·enga; il·engata, jitata.

Mow (mō), *v*. Atchili, ba kolchi samsiko raa.

Mr. *Mister* ko nibo.

Mrs. *Mistress* ko nibo.

Much (mŭch), *adv*. Bang·en. *a*. Banga.

Mucilage (mū'sĭ-laj), *n*. Stapgipa ata ma·sa.

Mucus (mū'kŭs), *n*. Stapgipa ku·chi; ginggre; do·chi bigipbok gita.

Mud (mŭd), *n*. A·dubek.

Muddle (mŭd'd'l, *v*. Kimongata, muingmrang daka.

Muff (mŭf), *n*. Jakko sikkrokani.

Muffle (mŭf'f'l), *v*. Pingripa.

Mug (mŭg), *n*. Ringchakani piala ma·sa.

Muggy (mŭg'gy), *a*. Rang·sitna ambregija chijimgipa bal gnang.

Mulatto (mu-lăt'to), *n*. Mande gipbok baksa Nigroni brine ong·katgipa.

Mulberry (mŭl'bĕr-ry), *n*. Miskuri.

Mule (mūl), *n*. Kochor, gure aro gadaoni brine ong·katgipa ba atchigipa.

Multiple (mŭl'tĭ-p'l), *n*. Chakgipa, changsana agre bang·kigri chakgipa.

Multiplicand (mŭl'tĭ-plĭ-kănd'), *n*. Chantaitaigni.

Multiplier (mŭl'tĭ-plī'ēr), *n*. Chantaitaigipa.

Multiply (mŭl'tĭ-plī), *v.* Chantaitaia.

Multitude (mŭl'tĭ-tūd), *n.* Jinma, bang·a.

Mum (mŭm), *a.* Agangijagipa, jrip donggipa.

Mumble (mŭm'b'l), *v.* Ku·chilko ogija agana.

Mummy (mŭm'my), *n.* Soatgija dake dong·imin manggisi.

Mumps (mŭmps), *n.* Pe ripimani, pebo nangani, pebo saani.

Munch (mŭnch), *v.* Ku·sik gape ku·bol ku·bol dake cha·a.

Municipal (mu-nĭs'ĭ-pal), *a.* Songjinmani biding.

Murder (mêr'dêr), *v.* Mangsonge mandeko so·ota.

Murmur (mêr'mŭr). *n.* Miteng miteng, mitu mitu, bru bru inani. *v.*

Muscle (mŭs''l), *n.* Be·enarigipa ja·dil, be·en bitin.

Muse (mūz), *v.* Gisik nange chanchia, chanchibewala.

Museum (mu-zē'ŭm), *n.* Ma·manti aiao inmanani, ma·manti sigimin manggisirangko donram ba mesokchakani nok, (jadu nok).

Mush (mŭsh), *n.* Ritgimin ginde.

Mushroom (mŭsh'rụm), *n.* Me·gumu.

Music (mū'zĭk), *n.* Knatoani gam·a.

Musician (mu-zĭsh'an), *n.* *Musicko* dakgipa, ring·na changgipa.

Musk (mŭsk), *n.* Grong grigipa matchok ma·sani smilgipa gandil.

Musket (mŭs'kĕt), *n.* Slai ma·sa.

Musk melon (mŭsk mĕl'ŭn), *n.* Rokomsa te·e.

Muslin (mŭz'lĭn), *n.* Molmol ba·ra, rinokgipa ba·ra ma·sa.

Musquito (mŏs-kē'to), *n.* Ganggua.

Muss (mŭs), *n.* Bilding bildang ong·ani.

Mussel (mŭs's'l'), *n.* Gapchilek.

Mussulman (mŭs'sŭl-man), *n.* Musolman.

Must (mŭst), *v.* Nanga, nangchongmota.

Mustache (mŭs-tåsh'), *n.* Kosakchini ku·simang, singgera.

Mustard (mŭs'têrd), *n.* Besual.

Muster (mŭs'têr), *v.* Chimonga, tom·daka.

Muster roll (mŭs'têr-rōl'), *n.* Sipairangni bimungko seani leka.

Musty (mŭs'ty), *a.* Mi sima, sima.

Mutable (mū'tȧ-b'l), *a.* Dongkamgijagipa, dingtang ong·gnigipa.

Mute (mūt), *a.* Ku·ma, ku·gri.

Mutilate (mū'tĭ-lāt), *v.* Be·enni maiba bakko pe·tonga, aktonga. **-or, -ion,** *n.*

Mutineer (mū'tĭ-nēr'), *n.* Bamgijagipa, rajani kosako chakatgipa.

Mutiny (mū'tĭ-ny), *n.* Bang·a mandeni bamgija dakani. *v.*

Mutter (mŭt'têr), *v.* Aganmitua.

Mutton (mŭt't'n), *n.* Mesni be·en.

Mutual (mū'tu-al), *a.* Grik, nangrimgrikgipa.

Muzzle (mŭz'z'l), *n.* Ku·sikko katipani; slai nolni ku·mang; matburungni ku·sik.

My (mī), *pr.* Angni.

Myriad (mĭr'ĭ-*a*d), *n.* Hajal chikung, ojut sa; namen bangani.

Myself (mi-sĕlf', ba mī-sĕlf'), *pr.* Anga a·tangan.

Mystery (mĭs'têr-y), *n.* Ning·-tuani, dongnuani, uisokgija-ni.

Mysterious (mĭs-tē'rĭ-ŭs), *a.* Ning·tugipa, dongnua gnang-gipa, uisokgija.

Mythology (mī-thŏl'o-jy), *n.* Miteni gimin uiani.

N.

Nab (năb), *v.* Ra·seke ra·a, rimseka.

Nadir (nā'dêr), *n.* A·ani kokkima, ka·madingding.

Nag (năg), *n.* Gure chongipa.

Nag (năg), *v.* Dondikgija ma-nenga.

Nail (nāl), *n.* Jakskil, ja·skil; gojal.

Naked (nā'kĕd), *a.* Nagande, ba·ra gri.

Name (nām), *n.* Bimung.

Namely (nām'ly), *adv.* Chong·-motan.

Nap (năp), *n.* Tusidumuani, on·-tisa tusiani; ba·rani kimil, bismak.

Nape (nāp), *n.* Kil·ok.

Napkin (năp'kĭn), *n.* Cha·mano ku·sikko ipakani jaron chon-gipa.

Narrate (năr-rāt' ba năr'rat), *v.* Katako agana. **-or, -ion,** *n.* **-ive,** *n.*

Narrow (năr'ro), *a.* Apchona, apchangket, apalgija.

Narrow-minded (năr'ro-mīnd'-ĕd), *a.* Apale chanchigijagipa.

Nasal (nā'z*a*l), *a.* Gingtingni biding.

Nasty (nås'ty), *a.* Moila gnang-gipa, moilabegipa.

Nation (nā'shŭn), *n.* Raja saksanni ning·o donggipa mande gimik ba jat. **-ality,** *n.* **-al,** *a.*

Native (nā'tĭv), *n.* Atchiram songni mande. *a.*

Nativity (nā-tĭv'ĭ-ty), *n.* At-chiani.

Natural (năt'u-r*a*l), *a.* Skangin-talan ong·gipa, ong·telaigipa, ba ba·kapa intal ong·gipa.

Nature (nā'tur), *n.* Dakgimin gimik; bewal.

Naught (nôt), *a.* Mamungba ong·gija, suino. *a.* Namgija.

Naughty (nô'ty), *a.* Namgija-gipa.

Nausea (nô'she-å ba nô'shå), *n.* Ka·rekani.

Nautical (nô'tĭ-k*a*l), *a.* Sagalni gimin.

Naval (nā'v*a*l), *a.* Dakgrikani jahatni biding.

Navel (nā'v'l), *n.* Gandil, gan-duri.

Navigate (năv'ĭ-gāt), *v.* Chiko choe re·a, **-or, -ion,** *n.*

Navy (nā'vy), *n.* Dakgrikani jahat aro manderang.

Nay (nā), *adv.* Ong·ja.

Near (nēr), *adv.* Sepang, chel·-gija.

Nearly (nēr'ly), *adv.* Ong·nasi-pile.

Nearsighted (nēr'sīt'ĕd), *a.* Se-pangonikosan nikaigipa, chel·e nikgijagipa.

Neat (nēt), *a.* Rongtala, taria.

Necessaries (nĕs'ĕs-sa-rĭz), *n.* Nanganirang.

Neck (nĕk), *n.* Gitok.

Necklace (něk'las), *n.* Gitoko ganani ripbok ba chondrohar.
Need (nēd), *v.* Nanga.
Needle (nē'd'l), *n.* Biji.
Needy (nēd'y), *a.* Gam grigipa, kangalgipa.
Ne'er (nēr ba når), *adv.* *Never*-ko kandikotgimin.
Negative (něg'å-tĭv), *n.* Jechakani.
Neglect (něg'lěkt'), *v.* Simsakgija daka.
Negligent (něg'li-jent), *a.* Simsakgijagipa.
Negotiate (ne-gō'shĭ-āt), *v.* Ku·rachakgrika, badinga, sondhi ka·a.
Negro (nē'gro), *n.* Afrikani mande, simbegipa mande ma·sa.
Neigh (nā), *n.* Gureni mikoa. *v.*
Neighbour (nā'bêr), *n.* Noksŭl, songsŭl.
Neighbourhood (nā'bêr-hud), *n.* Sepangjol, sepanggipa biap, sambagipa biap.
Neither (nē'THêr ba nī THêr), *con.* Iaba uaba ong·ja, gni ba bang·ani gisepo mingsaba ong·ja.
Nephew (něf'u), *n.* Gritang; jonggipa, adatang, nogipa ba abitangni dogipa.
Nerve (nêrv), *n.* Uiani ja·dil, bil, ka·donga.
Nest (nĕst), *n.* Bitip, do·ni bitip.
Net (nĕt), *n.* Chek.
Nether (nĕTH'êr) *a.* Ka·magipa.
Nettle (nĕt't'l), *n.* Gil·mat.
Neuralgia (nū-răl'ji-å), *n.* *Nerve*ni saknaani.
Neuter (nū'têr), *n.* Bima bipa ong·gijani.
Neutral *a.* Pilakchiba, chakgijagipa.
Never (nĕv'êr), *adv.* Mamung saloba ong·ja, pangnaba ong·ja.
Nevertheless (nĕv'êr-the-lĕs'), *con.* Indioba
New (nū), *a.* Gital.
News (nūz), *n.* Kata gital, knaani kata, songbad.
Next (nĕkst), *a.* Sepangbatgipa, sambaogipa.
Next (nĕkst), *adv.* Unikoa, unja·mano.
Nib (nĭb), *n.* Ku·chot; do·oni ku·sik; silni pen.
Nibble (nĭb'b'l), *v.* Cha·rikgepa, on·tiprak chiktete cha·a.
Nice (nīs), *a.* Nama, toa, nitoa, cha toa. **-ly**, *adv.*
Niche (nĭch), *n.* Pak·na ba guareo najokgija on tisa kongrue gop dakgipa biap
Nick (nĭk), *v.* Rikel rikel dak ata, den·rikeka, den·t ka.
Nickel (nĭk'el), *n.* Bokgipa sil ma·sa.
Nickname (nĭk'nām'), *n.* Mingjitani, mingjeani, mingkalakani bimung.
Niece (nēs), *n.* Namchiktang; adatang, jonggipa, nogipa ba abitangni demechik.
Niggard (nĭg'gêrd), *n.* Onninggijagipa, rubegipa, mikbokgipa.
Nigh (nī), *a.* Sepang, samba.
Night (nīt), *n.* Wal.
Nightingale (nīt ĭn-gāl), *n.* Walo mikogipa do·o ma·sa.
Nightmare (nīt'mâr), *n.* Mangsinani, marakasinani.
Nighthawk (nīt'hôk'), *n.* Do·bakchrit, do·bakchil, alsia do·o
Nimble (nĭm'b'l), *a.* Goslekgipa, bilchokchokgipa.

Nine (nīn), *a.* Sku, ge·sku.
Ninefold (nīn'fōld'), *a.* Dunasku.
Nineteen (nīn'tēn'), *a.* Chi·sku.
Ninety (nīn'ty), *a.* Sotsku, kolchang bri chikung.
Ninny (nĭn'ny), *n.* Gokagipa, gisik grigipa.
Ninth (nīnth), *a.* Skugipa.
Nip (nip), *v.* Tikota, se·eta; chikta.
Nipple (nip'p'l) *n.* Sokkute, sok ku chot.
Nit (nit), *n.* Chonbegipa jo·ongni bitchi.
Niter ba **Nitre** (nī'tẽr), *n.* Kari ma·sa, songra.
No (nō), *adv.* Ihing, ong·ja.
Noble (nō'b'l). *a.* Dal·gipa, mande ra·ako man·na kragipa.
Nobody (nō'bŏd-y), *n.* Pilakba ong·ja, mande ong·jo.
Nocturnal (nŏk-tẽr'-nal), *a.* Walni biding.
Nod (nŏd), *v.* Denggoka, gongjoka, skochi chin daka.
Noise (noiz), *n.* Gam·ani, -y, *a.*
Noisome (noi'sm), *a.* Seenggipa, saatgnigipa.
Nominal (nŏm'ĭ-nal), *a* Bimungna mangmang, bimungarigipa, bimungni biding, -ly, *adv.*
Nominate (nŏm'ĭ-nāt), *v.* Bimungko donata ba mingata, -or, -ion, *n.*
Nominative (nŏm'ĭ-nā-tĭv), *n.* Dakgipako mesokgipa, (kes ma·sa).
None (nŭn), *a.* Pilakba ong·gija, mamungba ong·gija, ge·saba saksaba donggija.
Nonplus (nŏn'plŭs), *v.* Jajaata.
Nonsense (nŏn'sĕns), *n.* Gisik grini kata, orto grini kata.
Noodle (nụ'd'l), *n.* Bokbokgipa, gisik grigipa.
Nook (nụk), *n.* Kona, bitip, dongnuani biap.
Noon (nụn), *n.* Saljatchi.
Noonday (nụn'dā), *n.* Saljatchi.
Noose (nụs ba nụz), *n.* Dola bikani.
Nor (nôr), *con.* Iaba uaba ong·ja.
Normal (nôr'mal), *a.* Bewal gita, sronga.
North (nôrth), *n* Salgro.
North-east (nôrth ēst'), *n.* Salgro salaramni gisep.
Northern (nôrth'ẽrn), *a.* Salgrochinigipa.
North-west (nôrth-wĕst), *n.* Salgro saliramni gisep.
Nose (nōz), *n.* Gingting.
Nose-ring (nōz'rĭng'), *n.* Gingtingo ganani, not.
Nostril (nŏs'trĭl), *n.* Gingkol.
Not (nŏt), *adv.* Ong·ja, -ja.
Notable (nōt'ȧ-b'l), *a.* Mingsinggipa.
Notation (no-tā'shŭn), *n.* Ongkchi seani.
Notch (nŏch), *n.* Rikel rikel dakani, den·tekani.
Note (nōt), *n.* Chin; ku·rang; chiti; groko ku·rachakani leka; tomusuk.
Note (nōt), *v.* Gisik on·a; gisik rakia; see rakia.
Noted (nōt'ĕd), *a.* Mingsinggipa.
Nothing (nŭth'ĭng), *n.* Mamungba ong·gijani, mamungba griani.

Notice (nō'tĭs), *n.* Gisik rakatani, ba gisik ra·atani, uiatani, bigapon.

Notice (nō'tĭs), *v.* Nia, nie gisik on·a.

Notification (nō'tĭ-fĭ-kā'shŭn), *n.* Uiatani, knaatani.

Notify (nō'tĭ-fī), *v.* Uiata.

Notion (nō'shŭn), *n.* Chanchichipani.

Notorious (no-tō'rĭ-ŭs), *a.* Mingsinggipa, mangsongde namgijani gimin.

Notwithstanding (nŏt'wĭth-stănd'ĭng), *con.* Indikba, minggija.

Nought (nôt), *n.* Gun griani, mamungba ong gijani, **Naught**, gita apsan.

Noun (noun), *n.* Bimungko mesokgipa kata.

Nourish (nŭr'ĭsh), *v.* Aldumitanga, dal·ata. **-ment**, *n.*

Novel ((nov'el), *n.* Golpo ki·tap. *a.* Ong·ronggijagipa, gital, **-ist**, *n.*

November (no-vĕm'bĕr), *n.* Bilsini skugipa ja.

Novice (nŏv'ĭs), *n.* A·bachenggipa, chang·kujagipa.

Now (nou), *adv.* Da·o.

Now-a-days (nou'ā-dāz), *adv.* Da·ororo.

Nowhere (nō'hwâr), *adv.* Pilakoba gri, mamung biapoba gri.

No way (nō'wā'), *adv.* Mamung dakeba ong·ja.

Nowise (nō'wīz'), *adv.* Mamung dakeba ong·ja.

Nozzle (nŏz'z'l), *n.* Ku·chot, nageng.

Nucleus (nū'kle-ŭs), *n.* Dal·gnigipa bostuni bitchri.

Nude (nūd), *a.* Nagande, ba·ragri. **-ity**, *n.*

Nudge (nŭj), *v.* Jakskuchi su·tinga.

Nugget (nŭg'gĕt), *n.* Gamchatgipa silni til·ong.

Nuisance (nū'sans), *n.* Jajrengatani, neng·atani.

Null (nŭl), *a.* Orto grigipa, bil grigipa, chollgija, **-ify**, *v.*

Numb (nŭm), *a.* Goka ong·gipa, gokachanggipa.

Number (nŭm'bĕr), *n.* Chanani rasi, bang·a, adita.

Numeral (nū'mĕr-al), *a.* Chanani ba rasini biding.

Numerator (nū'mĕr-ā'tĕr), *n.* Pe·raronani mesokgipa.

Numerous (nū'mĕr-ŭs), *a.* Bang·a, bang·bea.

Numskull (nŭm'skŭl'), *n.* Gokagipa, uigijagipa mande.

Nun (nŭn), *n.* Sainasi me·chik, toromni gimin mandeskaoni dingtang ekanggipa.

Nunnery (nŭn'nĕr-y), *n.* Sainasi me·chikrangni dongram biap.

Nuptial (nŭp'shal), *a.* Bia ka·ani biding.

Nurse (nêrs), *v.* Bi·sako sok kane aldua; saako sana.

Nurse (nêrs), *n.* Kamal me·chik; saako sangipa.

Nursery (nêrs'ĕr-y), *n.* Bi·sarangko alduani biap; bitchri chaatani bari.

Nut (nŭt), *n.* Bite rakgipa.

Nutcracker (nŭt'krăk'ĕr), *n.* Rakgipa biteko bretatani, ba dokpretani.

Nutmeg (nŭt'mĕg), *n.* Joipol.

Nutrition (nu-trĭsh'ŭn), *n.* Cha·ani namgni, dal·roroatani.

Nutshell (nŭt'shĕl'), *n.* Rakgipa biteni bikap.

O.

O (ō), *int.* Wai ba o, ine okamani.

Oak (ōk), *n.* *Ok* 'minggipa dal'gipa bol ma'sa.

Oakum (ōk'um), *n.* Ring bretao dattekani budu.

Oar (ōr), *n.* Ring choani boita kewal.

Oasis (ō'ā-sĭs ba o-ā'sĭs), *n.* A'gisini gisepo a sal gnanggipa a'a.

Oath (ōth), *n.* Mikchetani; Isolni bimungko indinari mingani.

Oats (ōts), *n.* Mi ma sa.

Obedience (o-bē'dĭ-*e*ns), *n.* Bamani, ning'o donga ba maniani.

Obedient (o-bē'dĭ-*e*nt), *a.* Ge'eta ra'gipa, bamgipa.

Obeisance (o-bē'*sa*ns ba o-bā'-), *n.* Olakiani, salam ka'ani.

Obey (o-bā'), *v.* Ge'etako ra'a, mania.

Obituary (o-bĭt'u-a-ry), *n.* Sigimin mandeni gimin seani.

Object (ŏb-jĕkt'), *v.* Jechaka. **-or, -ion,** *n.*

Objective case (ŏb-jĕkt'iv-kās'), *n.* Daka man'ako mesokgipa, 'ako daka uko mesokgipa.

Oblige (o-blīj'), *v.* Ka'sae dakachi gro nanggipa ong'ata.

Oblique (ŏb-lĕk'ba lĭk'), *a.* Gitchinggipa, chingkrenggipa.

Obliterate (ŏb-lĭt'ĕr-āt), *v.* Kimita, gimaata.

Oblivion (ŏb-lĭv'ĭ-ŭn), *n.* Gualani, gimaani.

Oblong (ŏb'lŏng), *a.* Gipengna bate gro ro'batgipa.

Obnoxious (ŏb-nŏk'shŭs), *a.* Mitchigni.

Obscene (ŏb-sēn'), *a.* Ku'atogija, aganna kragija. **-ity,** *n.*

Obscure (ŏb-skūr'), *a.* Andalao; donggipa; rongtalgija; mingsinggija. *v.* **-ity,** *n.*

Observe (ŏb-zĕrv'), *v.* Gisik on'a, nia; mania.

Observatory (ŏb-zĕrv'ā-to-ry), *n.* Niwatani biap ba nok; sal, ja. askirangko niani nok.

Obsolete (ŏb'so-lēt), *a.* Jakkalani ong'jahagipa.

Obstacle (ŏb'stā-k'l), *n.* Champengani.

Obstinate (ŏb'stĭ-nat), *a.* Ong'gijana kimkim mangsonggipa.

Obstruct (ŏb-strŭkt'), *v.* Champenga. **-ion,** *n.*

Obtain (ŏb-tān'), *v.* Man'a.

Obtuse (ŏb-tūs'), *a.* Uininggijagipa, jadagipa; petckokgijagipa.

Obvious (ŏb'vĭ-ŭs), *a.* Nikchachagni, tale nikgni.

Occasion (ŏk-kā'zhŭn), *n.* Nama chol ong'ani. **-al,** *a.*

Occasion (ŏk-kā'zhŭn), *v.* Ong'ata.

Occident (ŏk'sĭ-d*e*nt), *n.* Saliramni. **-al,** *a.*

Occupy (ŏk'ku-pī), *v.* Donga, gipa, nokgipa daka. **-ant, -ancy,** *n.*

Occur (ŏk-kĕr'), *v.* Ong'a, gisik naa. **-rence,** *n.*

Ocean (ō'sh*a*n), *n.* Sagal dal'gipa.

Octagon (ŏk'tā-gŏn), *n.* Ki'tik chetgipa, rikam chet apsan gnanggipa.

Octangular (ŏk-tăng'gu-lêr), *a.* Ki'tik chet gipa, kona chet gipa.

Octavo (ŏk-tā'vo), *n.* Leka kingsako tem'chet tem'ode badita dal'a ukon actavo minga.

October (ŏk-tō'bêr), *n.* Bilsini chikunggipa ja.

Ocular (ŏk'u-lêr), *a.* Mikronchi nikchachagipa; mikronni biding.

Oculist (ŏk'u-lĭst), *n.* Mikron saako tarigipa daktor.

Odd (ŏd), *a.* Jora gri; ramram ong'gija, nikronggija.

Odds (ŏds), *n.* Apsangijani, dingtang ong'ani.

Odor (ō'dêr), *n.* Simila, ba seengani bisak.

Odorous (ō'dêr-ŭs), *a.* Similgipa, seenggipa.

Of (ŏv), *prep.* -ni.

Off (ŏf), *adv.* -oni, chel'ao.

Offal (ŏf'fal), *n.* Jabol, galgni, namgijani.

Offend (ŏf-fĕnd'), *v.* Dos daka, ka'o nangata, **-er**, *n.*

Offense (ŏf-fĕns'), *n.* Namgijani, ka'onangatani, **-ive**, *a.*

Offer (ŏf'fêr), *v.* On'na, ba dakna ku'rachaka, ba janapa.

Offering (ŏf'fêr-ing), *n.* Boli on'ani.

Office (ŏf'fĭs), *n.* Sorkarini kam ba biap, apis.

Officer (ŏf'fĭ-sêr), *n.* Sorkarini maiba kamko ka'gipa; apiso kam ka'gipa.

Official (ŏf-fĭsh'al), *a.* Apisni biding.

Officiate (ŏf-fĭsh'ĭ-āt), *v.* Apismi kamko ka'a.

Officious (ŏf-fĭsh'ŭs), *a.* Sing'gija ba namnikgija gipinni kamo dangdikpagipa.

Off-scouring (ŏf'skour-ing), *n.* Galgimin.

Offset (ŏf'sĕt'), *n.* Bolni cheksini ja'dil su'skaani; apsan gitani pal dongimin. (ŏf-sĕt'), *v.*

Offspring (ŏf'spring'), *n.* Ong'katskagipa ba desu'rang.

Oft, often (ŏft, ŏf'n), *adv.* Changni chang, pilnipil.

Oh (ō), *inter.* A ba u inani pal.

Oil (oil), *n.* Tō, tochi.

Ointment (oint'ment), *n.* Nong'ani.

Old (ōld), *a.* Bilsi bang'gipa; gitchamgipa.

Olive (ŏl'ĭv), *n.* Jit bol, joitun bol.

Omelet (ŏm'e-lĕt ba ŏm'lĕt), *n.* Do'chi aro matchu sok brine jo'gimin.

Omen (ō'mĕn), *n.* Ong'gniko mesokani chin.

Omission (o-mĭsh'ŭn), *n.* Gualani, watchangani.

Omit (o-mĭt'), *v.* Watchanga.

Omnipotent (ŏm-nĭp'o-tent), *a.* Pilakni kosako bilko man'gipa.

Omnipresent (ŏm-nĭ-prĕz'ent), *a.* Pilakon gipgipa, pilakon donggipa.

Omniscient (ŏm-nĭsh'ent), *a.* Pilakkon uigipa.

Omnivorous (ŏm-nĭv'o-rŭs), *a.* Pilak rokomkon cha'gipa.

On (ŏn), *prep.* Kosak, -o.

On (ŏn), *adv.* -ang, mikkangchi.

Once (wŭns), *adv.* Changsao, skango. **At once** (ăt'wŭns), *adv.* Rang'san.

One (wŭn), *a.* Sa, ge'sa.

One (wŭn), *n.* Sangipa.

One by one (wŭn'bĭ-wŭn'), *adv.* Saksa saksa, sakprakprak, ge'prakprak.

Onion (ŭn'yŭn), *n.* Rasin.
Only (ōn'ly), *adv.* Mangmang, san.
Onward (ŏn'wẽrd), *adv.* Mikkangchi.
Ooze (ụz), *v.* Sipa, tingtota, ka·-sne ong·kata.
Opaque (o-pāk'), *a.* Nikprotna ba seng·protna man·gijagipa.
Open (ō'p'n), *v.* Oa, badala, parakata.
Open-handed (ō'p'n-hănd'ĕd), *a.* Jaksramgipa, on·rakgipa.
Open-hearted (ō'p'n-härt'ĕd), *a.* Cha·chipila grigipa.
Opening (ō'p'n-ĭng), *n.* Chol, kolgipu; a·bachengani.
Operate (ŏp'ẽr-āt), *v.* Kamko dakata, kamko ka·a. *a.* **-ion, -or,** *n.* **-ive,** *a.*
Ophthalmic (ŏf-thăl'mĭk), *a.* Mikronni gimin, ba mikronnì biding.
Opiate (ō'pĭ-at), *n.* Tusiatgipa sam.
Opinion (o-pĭn'yŭn), *n.* Chanchiani, chanchichipani.
Opium (ō'pĭ-ŭm), *n.* Aping, kani.
Opponent (ŏp-pō'nent), *n.* Warachakgipa, bobil.
Opportunity (ŏp-pŏr-tū'nĭ-ty), *n.* Chol.
Oppose (ŏp-pōz'), *v.* Warachaka, champenga.
Opposite (ŏp'po-zĭt), *a.* Mikangdingdinggipa, mikkangchakgrikgipa.
Oppress (ŏp-prĕs'), *v.* Onia daka, duk on·a. **-or, -ion,** *n.* **-ive,** *a.*
Optical (ŏp'tĭ-kal), *a.* Mikronni ba nikani biding.
Optic (ŏp'tĭk), *a.* Mikronni ba nikani biding.
Optician (ŏp-tĭsh'an), *n.* Chosma ba mikronchi niani gipin janerarangko dakgipa.
Option (ŏp'shŭn), *n.* Ska ba mangsongani see ra·ani ba skatangko dakani bil.
Opulent (ŏp'u-lent), *a.* Man·e cha·gipa.
Or (ôr), *con.* Ba.
Oracle (ŏ'rā-k'l), *n.* Gisik gnanggipa katako agangipa.
Oral (ō'ral), *a.* Ku·sikarichi.
Orange (ŏr'ĭnj), *n.* Chi·gipa narang, amrik.
Orangoutang (o-răng'ụ-tăng'), *n.* Mande burung, bilakbegipa dal·begipa makkre ma·-sa.
Oration (o-rā'shŭn), *n.* Mande jinmana aganna tarisogimin kata.
Orator (ŏr'â-têr), *n.* Mande jinmana aganna changgipa, oration ko agangipa.
Orb (ôrb), *n.* Tom·betgipa, salgio donggipa, sal, ja, askirang.
Orbit (ôr'bĭt), *n.* A·gilsak, sal, ja, ba askirangni re·ani rama.
Orchard (ôr'chẽrd), *n.* Bite nanggipa bolni bari.
Orchestra (ôr'kĕs-trâ), *n.* Bebela aro ugita dakgiparangko damsan salgiparang.
Orchid (ôr'kĭd), *n.* Bolo chagatgipa ma·manti rokom dake balgipa balgitorang.
Ordain (ôr-dān'), *v.* Dona, tik ka·a.
Ordeal (ôr'de-al), *n.* Wa·al aro ma·mantichi porika ka·e nia-ni.
Order (ôr'dẽr), *n.* Ge·etani; bewal gita biaptangtango dona-ni.

Order (ôr'dêr), *v.* Ge·eta.
Ordinal (ôr'dĭ-nal), *a.* Sulsul ba ja·pang intal chaoani.
Ordinance (ôr'dĭ-nans), *n.* Ge·-etani, niam, tiktak niam gita dakbewal.
Ordinary (ôr'dĭ-na-ry), *a.* Ram-ram.
Ordination (ôr'dĭ-nā'shŭn), *n.* Toromni kamo donani, pa-mongni kamo donani.
Ore (ōr), *n.* A·aoni ro·ong baksa bringipa aro rongtalatkuja-gipa sil.
Organ (ôr'gan), *n.* Bajona; jechi kam chu·sokata; be·enni kam ka·gipa bakrang chong-motan kan·chok, bika, ka·sop aro iarangna agre mongsong-gipa bakrang.
Organize (ôr'gan-īz), *v.* Kamko chu·sokatna taria.
Orient (ō'rĭ-ent), *n.* Salaram; ba Asiani songrang. **-al**, *a.*
Orifice (ŏr'ĭ-fĭs), *n.* A·kolni ku·-mang.
Origin (ŏr'ĭ-jĭn), *n.* A·bachenga-ni, ba ja·pang. **-al**, *a.*
Originate (o-rĭg'ĭ-nāt), *v.* A·ba-chengata, ong·katata.
Oriole (ō'rĭ-ōl), *n.* Do·o ma·sa.
Ornament (ôr'na-ment), *n.* Ni-toatani; *v.* Nitoata. **-al**, *a.*
Orphan (ôr'fan), *n.* Ma·a paa gri bi·sa.
Orthodox (ôr'tho-dŏks), *a.* Sas-troni sea gita bebe ra·gipa.
Orthography (ôr-thŏg'ra-fy), *n.* Oikorni gimin uiani.
Oscillate (ŏs'sĭl-lāt), *v.* Wing-wanga.
Ossify (ŏs'sĭ-fī), *v.* Greng pil·a, greng pilata.
Ostentation (ŏs'tĕn-tā'shŭn), *n.* A·tangko rasong chaatna mesokani.
Osteology (ŏs'te-ŏl'o-jy), *n.* Grengrangni gimin uiani.
Ostrich (ŏs'trĭch), *n.* Ustro do·o.
Other (ŭth'êr), *a.* Gipin, ding-tang.
Otherwise (ŭth'êr-wīz'), *adv.* Gipin dake; ong·jaode.
Otter (ŏt'têr), *n.* Matram.
Ottoman (ŏt'to-man), *n.* Tu-roskoni mande; rokomsa asongchakani.
Ought (ôt), *v.* Dakna nanga.
Ounce (ouns), *n.* Toani ma·sa, adha chotakni pal; matbu-rung ma·sa.
Our (our), *pr.* Chingni ba a·-chingni.
Ours (ourz), *pr.* Chingnin ba a·chingnin.
Ourselves (our-selvz'), *pr.* Chinga a·tangtangan.
Oust (oust), *v.* Biaponi a·rikata ba jitata.
Out (out), *adv.* A·pal, a·palo.
Out of (out'ŏv'), *prep.* -oni.
Outbreak (out'brāk'), *n.* Na-prake ong·katani, golmal; saa bang·e ong·katani.
Outcast (out'kȧst'), *n.* Jatoniko galgimin, branggipa.
Outcry (out'krī'), *n.* Chrika, jikjaka.
Outdo (out-dụ'), *v.* Bate daka.
Outdoors (out'dōrz'), *adv.* Nokni a·pal.
Outer (out'êr), *a.* A·palchigipa, nikrangrachigipa.
Outermost (out'êr-mōst'), *adv.* Pilakna bate a·palbatgipa.
Outfit (out'fĭt'), *n.* Kamko dakna a·bachengna nangani-rang.
Outgo (out-gō'), *v.* Bate re·a. *n.* Koroch ka·ani.

Outgrow (out-grō′), *v.* Bate dal·a.

Outhouse (out′hous), *n.* A·palni nok.

Outlast (out-lâst′), *v.* Bate baia.

Outlaw (out′lô′), *n.* Niam pe·ani gimin galako man·gipa.

Outlay (out′lā′), *n.* Koroch ka·ani.

Outlet (out′lĕt′), *n.* Ong·katani rama.

Outline (out′līn′), *n.* Noksani arirangko dakani. *v.* Adita noksako dake mesoka.

Outlive (out-liv′), *v.* Bate tangbata.

Outlook (out′luk′), *n.* Niwatani, niwatani biap, ong·gniko nisoani.

Outlying (out′lī′ing), *a.* A·palchi batao donggipa, chel·batao donggipa.

Outnumber (out′nŭm′bêr), *v.* Chanao bate bata, bangbata.

Outpost (out′pōst′), *n.* Sipai jinmani tambuoni chel·ao nitimani biap.

Outrage (out′raj), *v.* Mandena namen namgijako daka. **-ous,** *a.*

Outride (out-rīd′), *v.* Gureo gakate katseka.

Outright (out′rīt′), *adv.* Da·on, rang·san, srang.

Outrun (out-rŭn′), *v.* Katseka.

Outset (out′sĕt′), *n.* A·bachengani.

Outside (out′sīd′), *n.* A·palchi. *a.*

Outskirt (out′skêrt′), *n.* Songni rikam.

Outstretch (out-strĕch′), *v.* Badala.

Outward (out′wêrd), *a.* A·palchigipa, nikrangrachigipa. *adv.* A·palchi.

Outweigh (out-wā′), *v.* Bate jrima.

Outwit (out-wĭt′), *v.* Bate togia.

Oval (ō′val), *a.* Do·chi gita ro·ronggipa.

Ovary (ō′vâ-ry), *n.* Sa·tip, bitchi dakram.

Oven (ụv′′n), *n.* Chankol, chu·dap.

Over (ō′vêr), *prep.* Kosak, kosakchi ; nalsachi ; bate.

Overalls (ō′vêr-ôlz), *n.* Kosako krudapani pantelun.

Overarch (ō′vêr-ärch′), *v.* Kosako arch daka. *Arch*ko nibo.

Overawe (ō′vêr-ô′), *v.* Agre dabi on·a, mikkimchi kenata.

Overbalance (ō′vêr-băl′ans), *v.* Jrimachi bata.

Overbear (ō′vêr-bâr′), *v.* Agre bamata ba sinjeta.

Overboard (ō′vêr-bōrd′), *adv.* Jahatni a·palchi chio.

Overbold (ō′vêr-bōld′), *a.* Agre ka·donggipa.

Overcast (ō′vêr-kăst′), *v.* Aram simdapa ; koremrema.

Overcharge (ō′vêr-chäj′), *v.* Agre dam chata.

Overcloud (ō′vêr-kloud′), *v.* Aram simdapa.

Overcoat (ō′vêr-kōt′), *n.* Kosako krudapani chola.

Overcome (ō′vêr-kŭm′), *v.* Ama, chea.

Overdo (ō′vêr-dụ′), *v.* Agre daka.

Overdue (ō′vêr-dū′), *a.* On·ani sal batgipa.

Overfeed (ō′vêr-fēd′), *v.* Agre cha·a ; agre ala.

Overflow (ō'vêr-flō'), *v.* Suaka, chi jokmrika, dubia.
Overgrow (ō'vêr-grō'), *v.* Dikpripa, wepripa.
Overhang (ō'vêr-hăng'), *v.* Kosakchi kadea, niondapa.
Overhaul (ō'vêr-hôl'), *v.* Srapa; namedake nisranga.
Overhead (ō'vêr-hĕd'), *adv.* Sko kambechi, sko kosakchi.
Overhear (ō'vêr-hēr'), *v.* Knabata, knawata, knadata, knagaka.
Overheat (ō'vêr-hēt'), *v.* Agre ding'ata.
Overjoy (ō'vêr-joi'), *v.* Agre kusi ong'a.
Overleap (ō'vêr-lēp'), *v.* Bate bila.
Overlay (ō'vêr-lā'), *v.* Rubripa, dondapa, pa'dapa.
Overlook (ō'vêr-luk'), *v.* Nikchanga, nibadea, nikbata.
Overmatch (ō'vêr-mătch'), *v.* Bilbatgipa ong'a.
Overmuch (ō'vêr-mŭch'), *a.* Agre bata.
Overnight (ō'vêr-nīt'), *adv.* Walgimik.
Overpay (ō'vêr-pā'), *v.* Damna agre on'a.
Overpower (ō'vêr-pou'êr), *v.* Bil man'bata bil batachi ama.
Overrate (ō'vêr-rāt'), *v.* Agre gamchatnika.
Overreach (ō'vêr-rēch'), *v.* Tol'-napa, togia.
Overrule (ō'vêr-rul'), *v.* Sason ka'draa.
Overrun (ō'vêr-rŭn'), *v.* Wepripa, dikpripa, gipanga; bamata; suaka.
Oversee (ō vêr-sē'), *v.* Niroka, nitima.
Overset (ō'vêr-sĕt'), *v.* Bikpilata.
Overshadow (ō'vêr-shăd'o), *v.* Salakimdapata.
Oversight (ō'vêr-sīt'), *n.* Nitimani, nirikani; nikbadeani.
Oversleep (ō'vêr-slēp'), *v.* Tusidapa, agre tusia.
Overtake (ō'vêr-tāk'), *v.* Srapa.
Overthrow (ō'vêr-thrō'), *v.* Bikpilata, nisiata.
Overturn (ō'vêr-têrn'), *v.* Bikpilata.
Overwhelm (ō'vêr-hwĕlm'), *v.* Dubiata, pripata; sinjeta.
Overwise (ō'vêr-wīz'), *a.* A'tangko gaora de'gipa.
Overwork (ō'vêr-wêrk'), *v.* Bilna agre kam ka'a, bilbee kam ka'a.
Owe (ō), *v.* Gro nanga.
Owl (oul), *n.* Do'po.
Own (ōn), *a.* A'tangni, a'tang.
Own (ōn), *v.* Nokgipa ong'a; ong'a ine ku'rachaka.
Owner (ōn'êr), *n.* Nokgipa.
Ox (ŏks), *n.* Matchu bolot.
Oxygen (ŏks'i-jĕn), *n.* Rokomsa *gas*, janggi gnanggipa-rangna nangchongmotgipa balwa ma'sa.
Oyster (ois'têr), *n.* Gapchilek ma'sa.

P.

Pa (pä), *n.* Apa, paa.
Pace (pās), *n.* Ja'ku
Pace (pās), *v.* Ja'ku de'e re'a.
Pacific (pȧ-sĭf'ĭk), *a.* Tom'tomgipa, tom'tomatgipa, rinokgipa.
Pacification (pȧ-sĭf-ĭ-kā'shŭn), *n.* Tom'tomatani. -or, *n.*

Pacify (păs'ĭ-fī), *v.* Tom·tomata, ka·sinata, ka·dimeata.
Pack (păk), *v.* Katoma, tom·a; sikata, gapata.
Package (păk'āj), *n.* Katom, bosta.
Packet (păk'ĕt), *n.* Katom chongipa.
Packhorse (păk'hôrs'), *n.* Bal ra·gipa gure.
Pack thread (păk'thrĕd'), *n.* Bosta kaani kilding.
Pad (păd), *n.* Rinokgipa pa·ani; bilating ba maiba leka.
Paddle (păd'd'l), *n.* Boita, kewal.
Paddle (păd'd'l), *v.* Jak ba ja·achi chiko jipa.
Paddy (păd'dy), *n.* Mi gil gnang.
Padlock (păd'lŏk'), *n.* Chabi tekani tala.
Pagan (pā'gan), *n.* Mite kritgipa, Kristian ong·gijagipa. *a.*
Paganism (pā'gan-ĭz'm), *n.* Mite kritako maniani.
Page (pāj), *n.* Ki·tapni jaksani samsa, ki·tapni jak.
Pagoda (pȧ-gō'dȧ), *n.* Baudhorangni olakiani nok.
Pail (pāl), *n.* Balti, baltin.
Pain (pān), *n.* Saani, saknaani.
Pain (pān), *v.* Duk on·a, saknaata. **-ful**, *a.*
Pains (pāns), *n.* Gisik nange dakani.
Paint (pānt), *n.* Rong, *v.* Rong nonga.
Painting (pānt'ing), *n.* Rong nongani; rong nonge noksa dakani.
Pair (pâr), *n.* Jora.
Pair (pâr), *v.* Nangrima, ripeng ong·a, bia ka·a.
Palace (pă'las), *n.* Rajani nok.
Palanquin, palankeen (păl'angkēn'), *n.* Mande ripeani palki.
Palate (păl'at), *n.* Chikak.
Palatial (pȧ-lā'shal), *a.* Palace ni biding.
Pale (pāl), *a.* Bokdalgepa, delbua, dimela.
Paling (pāl'ing), *n.* Bolplengko date bera dakgimin.
Palliate (păl'lĭ-āt), *v.* Namgijako pindapa, ritchengata.
Pallid (pal'lid), *a.* Bokdalgepa.
Palm (päm), *n.* Jakpa; gue, sawe, narikol aro ugita dakgipa bolrangko, palm minggopa.
Palmerworm (päm'ĕr-wêrm'), *n.* Mi ja·pangko tingipa jo·ong.
Palpitate (păl'pĭ-tāt), *v.* Til·tila, jiljila, dekdeka. **-ion**, *n.*
Palsy (pôl'zy), *n.* An·ma goka ong·ani.
Paltry (pôl'try), *a.* Gamchata grigipa.
Pamper (păm'pêr), *v.* Okkaata.
Pamphlet (păm'flĕt), *n.* Chongipa ki·tap.
Pan (păn), *n.* Chi donchakani ba su·srangchakani sorea ma·sa.
Panacea (păn'ȧ-sē'ȧ), *n.* Pilak saako gimatgipa sam.
Pane (pān), *n.* Do·ga ba kerkio donani janera.
Panel (păn'ĕl), *n.* Do·gao dingtang kopgipa bol.
Pang (păng), *n.* Dikdiksana saknabeani.
Panic (păn'ik), *n.* Rang·san ba indinari jinmani kenani.
Panorama (păn'o-rä'mȧ), *n.* Bang·a noksarangko chong·mot gita nikatgipa, noksa dal·begipa ma·sa.

Pansy (păn'zy), *n*. Bibal ma·sa.
Pant (pănt), *v*. Neng bea gita, rang·sita, ka·tapo ka·tapo daka.
Pantaloon (păn'tâ-lụn'), *n*. Ja·o kruani jama, saheb me·asarangni ganani.
Pantheism (păn'the-ĭz'm), *n*. Ĭ ilak dakgiminrang Ĭsol ong·-a ine bebe ra·ani.
Panther (păn'thêr), *n*. Matchapeng dal·gipa ma·sa.
Pantry (păn'try), *n*. Cha·anirangko donram.
Pap (păp), *n*. Sok ku·te; bi·sa chongipani cha·ani.
Papa (pâ-pä' ba pä'pâ), *n*. Paa, apa, baba.
Papacy (pā'pâ-sy), *n*. Roman Katolikrangni pamongni kam.
Papal (pā'pal), *a*. Popeni kamni biding.
Paper (pā'pêr), *n*. Leka.
Papist (pā'pĭst), *n*. Roman Katolik mande.
Par (pär), *n*. Apsan ong·ani.
Parable (păr'â-b'l), *n*. Toe aganani.
Parachute (păr'â-shụt), *n*. Belunoni ong·onbaani chata gita dakgipa ma·sa.
Parade (pâ-rād'), *v*. Re·e ba dake mesoka.
Paradise (păr'â-dĭs), *n*. Salgi; sukni biap; Eden bari.
Paradox (păr'â-dŏks), *n*. Ong·-oba ong·jana susu nikani.
Paragraph (păr'â-grâf), *n*. Adita kata gimikni tong ba bak.
Parallel (păr'al-lĕl), *n*. Apsan chel·grike salgimin lain. *a*.
Parallelogram (păr'al-lĕl'o-grăm), *n*. Mikkangchakgrikgipa samgni apsan ong·e riking sambri gnanggipa.
Paralysis (pâ-răl'ĭ-sĭs), *n*. An·ma goka ong·ani.
Paralytic (păr'â-lĭt'ĭk), *n*. An·ma goka ong·gipa.
Paralyze (păr'â-līz), *v*. Goka ong·ata.
Paramount (păr'â-mount), *a*. Chubatgipa.
Paraphrase (păr'â-frāz), *v*. Dingtang dingtang katachi ortoko mesoka.
Parasite (păr'â-sīt), *n*. Janggi gnanggiparango ba bolrango tanggipa.
Parasol (păr'â-sŏl), *n*. Chata chongipa.
Parboil (pär'boil'), *v*. Mingitanga.
Parcel (pär'sĕl), *v*. Bak daka, suala. *n*. Katom.
Parch (pärch), *v*. Jo·å; ran·ata.
Parchment (pärch'ment), *n*. Sechakani matbigil.
Pardon (pär'd'n), *v*. Wata, kema ka·a.
Pare (pâr), *v*. Repa, bigil rae gala.
Parent (pâr'ent), *n*. Ma·a ba paa.
Parentage (pâr'ent-aj), *n*. Ma·-a paa ong·ani.
Parenthesis (pâ-rĕn'the-sĭs), *n*. Sentensni ning·o mesokani ba talatani, kata donggipa kata aro uko mosokani chinrang; (') iandakgipa.
Paring (pâr'ing), *n*. Repe galani bigil.
Parish (păr'ĭsh), *n*. Kamalni ba mondolini ning·o donggipa manderangni song.
Park (pärk), *n*. Songjinmao rona bakra dake dongimin biap.

Parley (pär'ly), *n.* Agangrikani ba jegrikani.
Parliament (pär'li-ment), *n.* England songni niamko dakgipa dal·gipa melaani.
Parlour (pär'lêr), *n.* Sokgipako grongani kutori.
Paroquet (păr'o-kĕt), *n.* Do·sik chonbegipa ma·sa.
Parricide (păr'rĭ-sīd), *n.* Paako so·otgipa.
Parrot (păr'rŭt), *n.* Do·sik.
Parse (pärs), *v.* Gramarni niam gita katani bakrangko agana.
Parsee (pär'sē ba pär-sē'), *n.* Parsini toromko ra·gipa, wa·alko olakigipa.
Parsimony (pär'sĭ-mo-ny), *n.* Rubeani, kirpin dəkani.
Parsley (pärs'ly), *n.* Samjak ma·sa.
Parsnip (pärs'nip), *n.* Bita dakgipa samjak ma·sa.
Parson (pär's'n), *n.* Mondolini pamong.
Parsonage (pär's'n-aj), *n.* Mondolini pamongni nok.
Part (pärt), *v.* Bak daka, dingtang daka. *n.* Bak mitam.
Partake (pär-tāk'), *v.* Bak ra·paa, bak man·paa.
Partial (pär'shal), *a.* Chu·sokgijagipa, adora, mikkang nigipa.
Participate (pär-tĭs'i-pāt), *v.* Gipinrang baksa bak man·paa.
Participle (pär'tĭ-si-p'l), *n.* Verb aro adjectiveni ortoko mesokgipa ba bilko man·gipa kata; matchotsranggijagipa kata.
Particle (pär'tĭ-k'l), *n.* Chonbegipa, bisemsem.
Particular (pär-tik-u-lêr), *a.* Dingtangmancha, mongsong.
Partisan (pär'tĭ-zan), *n.* Baksa ong·pagipa, chakpagipa.
Partition (pär-tish'ŭn), *n.* Dingtang dakani, champengani, pakma.
Partner (pärt'nêr), *n.* Bak man·pagipa.
Partridge (pär'trĭj), *n.* Do·bekrot dal·gipa jat ma·sa.
Party (pär'ty), *n.* Dol, ma·mal, adita jinma.
Pass (pȧs), *v.* Re·a, bata, re·paka.
Pass (pȧs), *n.* Re·china ba dakchina on·gimin hukum; a·bri gisepni apchangipa rama.
Passage (pȧs'saj), *n.* Re·ani rama; saniba agangimin kata tong·sa.
Passenger (păs'sĕn-jêr), *n.* Gari ba jahato gakate re·gipa.
Passion (păsh'ŭn), *n.* Ka·onangani, duk chakani, gisik nangbeani.
Passionate (păsh'ŭn-at), *a.* Ka·onangrakgipa.
Passive (păs'siv), *a.* Dakako man·gipa, chakchikna amgipa.
Passover (păs'ō-vêr), *n.* Jihudirangni alani, watchangani alani.
Passport (pȧs'pōrt), *n.* Re·na on·ani hukum ba chiti.
Past (pȧst), *a.* Re·anggimin, batanggimin, bon·anggimin.
Paste (pāst), *n.* Ma·gapatani, stapatani. *v.*
Pasteboard (pāst'bōrd'), *n.* Lekako rake aro ritchae kingsan gita stapatgimin.
Pastime (pas'tīm'), *n.* Salko re·atani, kal·grikani, rororoani.

Pastor (pås'têr), *n*. Mondolini pamong. -**al**, *a*.
Pastry (pās'try), *n*. Moidako dakgimin cha·anirang.
Pasture (pås'tur), *n*. Jillani·rangni cha·amani bakra.
Pat (păt), *v*. Doktopa.
Pat (păt), *a*. Kraa.
Patch (pătch), *v*. Kodapa; *n*. Kodapgimin.
Pate (pāt), *n*. Sko patal, sko.
Patent (păt'ent ba pā't·nt), *n*. Kolko dakchenggipana una agre gipin dakna man·jana gita on·gimin hukum.
Patent (păt'ent ba pā'tent), *a*. Uininggni, parak.
Paternal (pā-têr'nal), *a*. Paa gita chacha, ba paani biding.
Path (påth), *n*. Rama chon·gipa.
Pathetic (pă-thĕt'ik), *a*. Ka·saatgni, ka·saachi gisiko nangatgni.
Pathology (pă-thŏl'o-jy), *n*. Saako uiani.
Pathos (pā'thŏs), *n*. Ka·sachakatani, gisiko nangchakatani.
Patience (pā'shens), *n*. Chakchikani.
Patient (pā'shent), *a*. Chakchikgipa, neng·ningnikgijagipa, sontol.
Patient (pā'shent), *n*. Samko ringgipa, sagipa.
Patriarch (pā'tri-ärk), *n*. Ma·chongni skotong.
Patrimony (păt'ri-mo-ny), *n*. Paani gam.
Patriot (pā'tri-ŏt), *n*. Songtangninamgniko am·gipa mande. -**ism**, *n*.
Patriotic (pā'tri-ŏt'ik), *a* Songtangni namgnina ska gnang.
Patrol (pă-trōl'), *n*. Walo re·roroe nitimgipa.
Patrol (pă-trōl'), *v*. Walo nina re·roroa.
Patron (pā-trun), *n*. Aldugipa, dakchakgipa.
Patronize (păt'rŭn-īz), *v*. Aldue dakchaka, gaorade·e dakchaka.
Patter (păt'têr), *v*. Toktak toktak gam·a.
Pattern (păt'têrn), *n*. Mesokani, nomuna.
Paucity (pô'si-ty), *n*. Bang·gija ong·ani.
Pauper (pô'pêr), *n*. Bi·ame cha·gipa; a·tongko aldugijagipa.
Pave (pāv), *v*. It ba ro·ongchi ana.
Pavement (pāv'ment), *n*. It ba ro·ongchi angimin.
Pavilion (pă-vil'yŭn), *n*. Dongchakani tambu, ra·rorona man·gipa nok.
Paw (pô), *n*. Matgipa jakskil gnanggipa matburungrangni jakpa ba ja·pa.
Pawn (pôn), *v*. Bondok dona.
Pawnbroker (pôn'brō'kêr), *n*. Bondok dontimgipa mahajon.
Pay (pā), *n*. Dormaha.
Pay (pā), *v*. Gro chota, dam on·a.
Payment (pā'ment), *n*. Chota ba on·ani.
Pea (pē), *n*. Motol.
Peace (pēs), *n*. Tom·tomani, nangrimani.
Peaceable (pēs'ă-b'l), *a*. Tom·tomgip-a, warachakgijagipa.
Peace-offering (pēs'ŏf'fêr-ing), *n*. Nangrimani boli.
Peach (pēch), *n*. Te·gatchu bilati, pich bol.

Peacock (pē'kŏk), *n.* Do·de bipa.
Peahen (pē'hĕn), *n.* Do·de bima.
Peak (pēk), *n.* Ku·chot, kambe bon·chotani.
Peal (pēl), *n.* Gam·beani, mikka kima ba top goani gam·a.
Pear (pâr), *n.* Bol bite ma·sa.
Pearl (pêrl), *n.* Mukta.
Pearlash (pêrl'ăsh), *n.* Tarisogimin katchi.
Peasant (pĕz'*a*nt), *n.* A·a gamgipa, game cha·gipa.
Pease (pēz), *n.* Motolrang.
Pebble (pĕb'b'l), *n.* Chongipa rong·te.
Peck (pĕk), *v.* Sua. suteta.
Peck (pĕk), *n.* Toani ma·sa.
Peculiar (pe-kūl'yêr), *a.* Gipin gita ong·gijagipa; dingtang mancha.
Pecuniary (pe-kun'ya-ry), *a.* Gamni biding.
Pedal (pĕ'd*a*l ba pĕd'*a*l), *n.* Maiba kolko re·atna ja·a ga·chakani.
Pedant (pĕd'*a*nt), *n.* On·tisa lekaporao gaora de·gipa mande.
Peddle (pĕd'd'l), *v.* Re·roroe pala, paldinga.
Peddler (pĕd'd'lêr), *n.* Paldinggipa.
Pedestal (pĕd'ĕs-t*a*l), *n.* Bimang dakgiminni, maiba songdogiminni ja·pang.
Pedestrian (pe-dĕs'trĭ-*a*n), *n.* Ja·achi re·gipa.
Pedigree (pĕd'ĭ-grē), *n.* Ma·gitcham pagitchamrangni riting.
Pedobaptist (pē'do-băp'tĭst), *n.* Bi·sako napbolatani pal chi satkikigipa.
Peek (pēk), *v.* Niua, sriksrik nia.
Peel (pēl), *v.* Bigilko kika ba repa.
Peel (pēl), *n.* Bikap, bigil.
Peep (pēp). *v.* Nachenga; niua; chipchip ine mikoa.
Peer (pēr), *n.* Dal·a ma·chongni mande.
Peer (pēr), *v.* Niona, niua, nicholua.
Peerless (pēr'lĕs), *a.* Pilakna batgipa.
Peevish (pē'vĭsh), *a.* Namnikgijako aganninggipa, ka·onangninggipa.
Peg (pĕg), *n.* Bolni gojal.
Pelican (pĕl'ĭ-k*a*n), *n.* Chioni rajahas ma·sa.
Pelt (pĕlt), *v.* Nange gotata. *n.* Kimil gnang kikgimin bigil.
Pelvis (pĕl'vĭs), *n.* Ki·sangteni greng dalgap dal·gipa, ki·singkopni greng.
Pen (pĕn), *n.* Seani pen ba kolom.
Penal (pē'n*a*l), *a.* Sastini biding.
Penalty (pĕn'*a*l-ty), *n.* Sasti, saja.
Pencil (pĕn'sĭl), *n.* Seani pensil.
Pend (pĕnd), *v.* Kadea; maibaona kingking tik ong·gija donga.
Pendant (pĕnd'*a*nt), *n.* Kadegimin.
Pending (pĕnd'ĭng), *a.* Tik ong·kujagipa.
Pendulum (pĕn'du-lŭm), *n.* Ringrenggipa bostu, gorio kadegipa wingwanggipa.
Penetrate (pĕn'e-trāt), *v.* Napa, bu·a. -**ion**, *n.*
Peninsula (pĕn'ĭn'su-lâ), *n.* Chichi dulnasigipa a·a.

Penitent (pĕn'ĭ-tent), *a.* Papni gimin kalime gisik pil·gipa.
Penitentiary (pĕn'ĭ-tĕn'shâ-ry), *n.* Patok nok.
Penknife (pĕn'nīf'), *n.* Chakku, churi chongipa.
Penman (pĕn'man), *n.* Kolomchi segipa.
Penniless (pĕn'nĭ-lĕs), *a.* Gam grigipa, tangka grigipa.
Penny (pĕn'ny), *n.* England songni paisa.
Pennyweight (pĕn'ny-wāt'), *n.* Toani ma·sa, roti kolgrik brini pal jrimgipa.
Pension (pĕn'shŭn), *n.* Kam ka·a ruutani gimin sikujana kingking indin on·a dormaha, pensin.
Pensive (pĕn'sĭv), *a.* Chanchibegipa; dukko chanchigipa.
Pentagon (pĕn'tå-gŏn), *n.* Ki·tik aro rikam bongagipa.
Pentateuch (pĕn'tå-tūk), *n.* Moseni sea ki·tap kingbonga, sastroni skanggipa ki·tap king bonga.
Pentecost (pĕn'te-kŏst), *n.* Jihudirangni alani ge·sa, sotbongani sal.
Penult (pē'nŭlt ba pe-nŭlt'), *n.* Katani bon·kamgipana skang donggipa silebel.
Peon (pē'ŏn), *n.* Pion, peada.
People (pē'p'l), *n.* Manderang, jat.
Pepper (pĕp'pêr), *n.* Ja·lik, sagipa, pempli.
Peppermint (pĕp'êr-mĭnt'), *n.* Smilgipa sam ma·sa, podina ma·sa.
Peradventure (pĕr'ăd-vĕn'tur), *adv.* Haida, ong·naba donga.
Perambulate (pêr-ăm'bu-lāt), *v.* Re·roroa, roroa.
Perceive (pêr-sēv'), *v.* Uia, masia.
Percentage (pĕr-sĕnt'aj), *n.* Ritchaprakni bak.
Perception (pêr-sĕp'shŭn), *n.* Nikani, ma·siani, uiani.
Perch (pĕrch), *n.* Do·o ma·bakchakani go·ol; na·tok ma·sa mik chi·sani pal ro·gipa toani.
Perch (pĕrch), *v.* Ma·baka.
Perchance (pêr-châns'), *adv.* Ong·naba donga, haida.
Percolate (pêr'ko-lāt), *v.* Ka·sne ka·sne chipanga.
Perdition (pêr-dĭsh'ŭn), *n.* Gimasrangani, nisisrangani, jringjrotni siani.
Peremptory (pêr'ĕmp-to-ry), *a.* Jechakna amgijagipa.
Perennial (pĕr-ĕn'nĭ-al), *a.* Jring jring ong·gipa, dongdikgijagipa.
Perfect (pêr'fĕkt), *a.* Chu·sokgipa, matchotgipa, namsranggipa. **-ion,** *n.*
Perfidious (pêr-fĭd'ĭ-ŭs), *a.* Ku·rachakako pe·gipa, kakketgijagipa.
Perforate (pêr'fo-rāt), *v.* Pua, su·prota. **-or, -ion,** *n.*
Perforce (pêr-fōrs'), *adv.* Bilchi, bilake.
Perform (pêr-fôrm'), *v.* Dakata, chu·sokata. **-ance,** *n.*
Perfume (pêr'fūm ba pêr-fūm'), *n.* Smilgigipa biba ba bitchi.
Perhaps (pêr-hăps'), *adv.* Ong·naba donga, haida.
Peril (pĕr'ĭl), *n.* Gimaani ong·benaba dongani, gimabeani ong·naba dongani. **-ous,** *a.*
Perimeter (pĕr-ĭm'e-têr), *n.* Dul.

Period (pē'rĭ-ŭd), *n.* Matchotgipa dondikani, (dari); adita salrangko minggopani.

Periodical (pē'rĭ-ŏd'ĭk-*a*l), *a.* Somoi apsano ong·taitaigipa. *n.* Songbat.

Perish (pĕr'ĭsh), *v.* Gimara, bon·a; soa.

Perjure (pêr'jur), *v.* Tol·e mikcheta. **-y,** *n.*

Permanence (pêr'mȧ-nens), *n.* Dingtang ong·gijani.

Permanent (pêr'mȧ-nent), *a.* Kimkimgipa, pangnangipa, dongkamgnigipa, baigipa.

Permission (pêr-mĭsh'ŭn), *n.* Dakchina on·ani hukum.

Permit (pêr-mĭt'), *v.* Dakna hukum on·a.

Perpendicular (pêr'pĕn-dĭk'u-lêr), *a.* Srongsronggipa, chadengsronggipa.

Perpetual (pêr-pĕt'u-*a*l), *a.* Pangnangipa, matchotgijagipa, jringjring ong·gipa.

Perplex (pêr-plĕks'), *v.* Jajaata.

Persecute (pêr'se-kūt), *v.* A·rika, sanala. **-ion,** *n.*

Persevere (pêr'se-vēr'), *v.* Dongdikgija joton ka·a. **-ance,** *n.*

Persist (pêr-sĭst'), *v.* Kimkim ong·a, dongdikgija dakanga, dakchaa. **-ent,** *a.* **-ence,** *n.*

Person (pêr's'n), *n.* Mande; mikkang bimang.

Personage (pêr's'n-aj), *n.* Dal·a mande.

Personal (pêr's'n-al), *a.* Mandeni; an·tangni.

Personate (pêr's'n-āt), *v.* Uiatgija dake daka, sakgipin ong·a gita daka.

Perspiration (pêr'spĭ-rā'shŭn), *n.* Ding·ol, gramchi.

Perspire (pêr'spīr'), *v.* Ding·ola, gramchia.

Persuade (pêr-swād'), *v.* Mol·molachi ba mesokachi skata ba ra·chakata.

Persuasion (pêr-swā'zhŭn), *n.* Chanchiako ba aganako ra·chakgimin, bebe ra·gimin.

Pert (pêrt), *a.* Mande mingija.

Pertain (pêr-tān'), *v.* Nangrimpaa.

Peruse (pe-ruz'), *v.* Gisik nange poraia.

Pervade (pêr-vād'), *v.* Pilakchinan gipa ba chipa.

Perverse (pêr-vêrs'), *a.* Namgija dakanggipa, skiako ra·chakgijagipa, bamgijagipa.

Pervert (pêr-vêrt'), *v.* Namaoni ekata, ortoko dingtangata, ba choletata.

Pest (pĕst), *n.* Nisiatani biati; namnikgija ong·atani; jajrengatani.

Pester (pĕs'têr), *v.* Duk on·a, ettala, jongkaia, ka·onangata.

Pestle (pes''l), *n.* Rimol, imol.

Pet (pĕt), *n.* Mikmalgimin.

Petal (pĕt'*a*l), *n.* Bibalni bijak.

Petition (pē-tĭsh'ŭn), *n.* Mol·molani, bi·ani; dorkasto. *v.*

Petrifaction (pĕt'rĭ-făk'shŭn), *n.* Ro·ong pil·ani.

Petrify (pĕt'rĭ-fī), *v.* Ro·ong pil·ata.

Petroleum (pe-trō'le-ŭm), *n.* A·ani to, tarikujagipa kerosin.

Petticoat (pĕt'tĭ-kōt), *n.* Ning·o kruani saia.

Petty (pĕt'ty), *a.* Chongipa, chonnikgni.

Petulant (pĕt'u-l*a*nt), *a.* Matnangninggipa, ka·onangninggipa.

Pew (pū), *n*. Gilja nokni asongchakani rokomsa.

Pewter (pū'tėr), *n*. Dosta, sisa aro rang bringimin sil.

Phantom (făn'tŭm), *n*. Mamungba ong·gijako nikani, me·mang, put.

Pharisee (făr'ĭ-sē), *n*. Porisi, Jihudini ma·mal·sa.

Pharmacy (făr'mȧ-sy), *n*. Samko dakani; samko dakani nok.

Phase (fāz), *n*. Bostu mingsanko dingtang dingtang nikani.

Pheasant (fĕz'*a*nt), *n*. Burungni do·o, do·rerap, do·grik, do·de iarang.

Phenomenon (fe-nŏm'e-nŏn), *n*. Nikronggijaniko nikani.

Philanthropist (fĭ-lăn'thro-pĭst), *n*. Pilakni namgniko am·gipa ba sikgipa.

Philology (fĭ-lŏl'o-jy), *n*. Ku·sikni ja·pangko sandie uiani.

Philosophy (fĭ-lŏs'o-fy), *n*. Ong·arangni ja·pangko uiani.

Phlegm (flĕm), *n*. Ku·sikoni ginggre.

Photograph (fō'to-grȧf), *n*. Seng·achi tiktak dakgimin noksa.

Phrase (frāz), *n*. Sentensni tong ba bak.

Physic (fĭz'ĭk), *v*. Julap on·a. *n*.

Physician (fĭ-zĭsh'*a*n), *n*. Sam on·gipa, daktor.

Physics (fĭz'ĭks), *n*. Pilak bostuni gimin uiani.

Piano (pe-ä'no). *n*. Balwa grigipa bajona ma·sa.

Piazza (pĭ-ăz'zȧ), *n*. Baranda, pindapgimin rama.

Pick (pĭk), *v*. Su·dika, sea, kolama, aka.

Pick (pĭk), *n*. A·a rakako su·ani.

Pick axe (pĭk'ăks'), *n*. Gaiti.

Picket (pĭk'ĕt), *n*. Killa ba bariko su·dulgipa ritchok; bobilna nitimgipa sipai.

Pickle (pĭk'k'l), *n*. Maiba biteko mesengatgimin.

Picture (pĭk'tur), *n*. Noksa.

Pie (pī), *n*. Maiba be·en ba biteko ning·chi brae dakgimin cha·ani; pelsani bakgitamni baksa.

Piece (pēs), *n*. Tong, ba chong·-dok.

Piece (pēs), *v*. Ritchua, nangdimata.

Pier (pēr), *n*. It ba ro·ongko dakgimin krong ba guare; jahat kana chiona rikanggimin.

Pierce (pērs), *v* Su·a, pua.

Piercing (pērs'ĭng), *a*. Sua gita dakgipa, napprotgipa, gisiko nanggni, ka·tongo nanggni.

Piety (pī'e-ty), *n*. Isolna ka·sae uni namnikako dakani.

Pig (pĭg), *n*. Wak bi·sa.

Pigeon (pĭj'ŭn), *n*. Do·kru, paroa, do·rek aro do·pilgim iarang.

Pigeonhole (pĭj'ŭn-hōl'), *n*. Baksko kutori kutori dake dakgimin.

Pile (pīl), *v*. Dandaka, chong·-a.

Pile (pīl), *n*. Dandakgimin, dal·begipa milong.

Piles (pīlz), *n*. Ki·sangchiko an·chi jokgipa ba ripimgipa saa ma·sa.

Pilfer (pĭl'fėr), *v*. Chonchonarangko cha·ua.

Pilgrim (pĭl'grĭm), *n*. Re·gipa, songregipa.

Pill (pĭl), *n*. Changprak ringna guli dake tom·gimin sam.

Pillage (pĭl'laj), *n*. Ra·sekani, cha·uani, ra·sekgimin. *v*.

Pillar (pĭl'lêr), *n*. Krong.

Pillow (pĭl'lo), *n*. Kodam, balis. *v*.

Pilot (pī'lŭt), *n*. Jahatko dilgipa, rama mesokgipa. **-age,** *n*.

Pimple (pĭm'p'l), *n*. Gangma minani, mintotani.

Pin (pĭn), *n*. Pin; herpin; silni bu·su. *v*. Pin teka.

Pincers (pĭn'sêrz), *n*. Kepani, dang·kep, sildangkep.

Pinch (pĭnch), *v*. Se·eta, tikota.

Pine (pīn), *n*. Bol ma·sa; slongket.

Pine (pīn), *v*. Duk ong·e ram·sisia, gisiko duk ong·e ram·anga.

Pine apple (pīn'ăp'p'l), *n*. Anaros, te·rik sagil.

Pin feather (pĭn'fĕтн-êr), *n*. Grang dambe, grang namitubachenggipa.

Pinion (pĭn'yŭn), *n*. Do·oni grang.

Pink (pĭngk), *n*. Gitchak gipbok bringipa bibal ma·sa. *a*. Gitchakmrang.

Pink eye (pĭngk-ī), *n*. Mikron saani, mikgitchak saani.

Pinnacle (pĭn'nå-k'l), *n*. Nokni ku·chot, protchong.

Pint (pīnt), *n*. Toani ma·sa, matchu sok ong·ode adha selni pal.

Pioneer (pī'o-nēr'), *n*. Songko ochenggipa.

Pious (pī'ŭs), *a*. Isolna kengipa, toromi.

Pipe (pīp), *n*. Bolni ba silni wa·singtok; bangsi; ka·srang.

Pirate (pī'rat), *n*. Sagalo ra·seke ra·gipa.

Piss (pĭs), *v*. Su·bua, a·pal bi·sa re·a.

Pistil (pĭs'tĭl), *n*. Bibalni bitchri ra·chakgipa.

Pistol (pĭs'tŭl), *n*. Jepo chipe ra·bitna man·gipa chongipa slai ma·sa.

Pit (pĭt), *n*. A·ani tu·gipa a·kol.

Pitch (pĭch), *n*. Ritgimin alkatra.

Pitch (pĭch), *v*. Onata gita goa.

Pitcher (pĭch'êr), *n*. Tikili ma·sa, chi ra·chakani.

Pitch fork (pĭch'fôrk'), *n*. Gariona mi ba samko ra·gatatani silchonggeng.

Pitiable (pĭt'ĭ-å-b'l), *a*. Duk man·gipa, ka·sachaka man·na kragipa.

Pith (pĭth), *n*. Bolni nom·gipa ga·brong.

Pitiful (pĭt'ĭ-ful), *a*. Ka·sachakako man·na kragipa.

Pittance (pĭt-tans), *n*. On·titi on·ani.

Pity (pĭt'y), *v*. Ka·sachaka.

Pivot (pĭv'ŭt), *n*. Wilwilchakani ku·chot.

Place (plās), *n*. Biap.

Place (plās), *v*. Dona.

Placid (plăs'ĭd), *a*. Tom·tomgipa, rinokgipa, gisik moninggijagipa.

Plague (plāg), *n*. Sabisi, jeo mande bang·en sia.

Plain (plān), *n*. A·kawe.

Plain (plān), *a*. Dalgapgipa; apsan; ramram.

Plaint (plānt), *n*. Kalimani kata; dukko janapani; nalis ka·ani.

Plaintiff (plān'tĭf), *n*. Nalis ka·gipa.

Plait (plāt), *v*. Wata, saka, tem·skema.

Plan (plăn), *n.* Chanchiani; mesokani, noksa.
Plane (plān), *n.* Apsangipa; renda.
Plane (plān), *v.* Apsan daka, renda on·a.
Planet (plăn'ĕt), *n.* A·a aro ugita salko wilwilgiparang.
Plank (plănk), *n.* Tokta, bolpleng.
Plant (plănt), *v.* Ge·a.
Plant (plănt), *n.* Bol bi·sa, samjak, chagipa.
Plantain (plăn'tan), *n.* Te·rik̊.
Plantation (plăn-tā'shŭn), *n.* Dal·gipa bari ba bagija.
Plaster (plăs'têr), *n.* Repiani, parirango pa·ani stapgipa.
Plaster (plăs'têr), *v.* Repia, pa·dapa.
Plate (plāt), *n.* Tala, bason, dalgapgipa sil.
Plateau (plå-tō'), *n.* Chugipa a·kawe.
Platform (plăt'fôrm'), *n.* Adita chue rikgimin chadengani biap.
Platter (plăt'têr), *n.* Dal·begipa tala.
Play (plā), *v.* Kal·grika; doka dam·a, ba sala.
Plea (plē), *n.* Jechakani ba dorkastoni ja·pang.
Pleader (plēd'êr), *n.* Ukil, aganchakgipa.
Plead (plēd), *v.* Aganchaka, man·na mol·mola.
Pleasant (plĕz'ant), *a.* Nitoa, namnikatgni.
Please (plēz), *v.* Namnikata, kusi ong·ata.
Pleasing (plēz'ĭng), *a.* Nitoa, namnikatgni.
Pledge (plĕj), *v.* Bondok dona.
Pleiades (plē'yå-dēz), *n.* Do·sadipil aski.
Plenty (plĕn'ty), *n.* Chu·ongani, bang·ani.
Pleura (plū'rå), *n.* Kaprang.
Pliable (plī'å-b'l), *a.* Dol·ninggipa, nom·gipa; bamninggipa.
Pliers (plī'êrz), *n.* Chongipa kepani, dang·kep.
Plod (plŏd), *v.* Neng·e dakanga ba re·anga.
Plot (plŏt), *n.* A·a tong·sa; namgijako dakna ku·mongani.
Plot (plŏt), *v.* Namgijana ku·monga
Plough (plou), *v.* Aru wea.
Plough, plow (plou), *n.* Nanggri.
Pluck (plŭk), *v.* Aka.
Plug (plŭg), *v.* A·kolko mitua ba teka.
Plug (plŭg), *n.* A·kolko mituani ba tekani.
Plum (plŭm), *n.* Angkil ba angkil gita dakgipa.
Plumage (plūm'aj), *n.* Do·oni kimil.
Plumb (plŭm), *a.* Srongdingding songdogipa. *n.*
Plume (plūm), *n.* Do·oni kimil jeko manderang tarina jakkala.
Plump (plŭmp), *a.* Milgipa, poragipa.
Plunder (plun'dêr), *v.* Ra·seke ra·a. *n.*
Plunge (plŭnj), *v.* Chio songchoke chokona.
Plural (plū'ral), *a.* Ge·sana batako mesokgipa.
Plus (plŭs), *a.* Chandimgni ba chandapgni.
Ply (plī), *v.* Kamko watgija ka·a; dakronga, jakkala.

Pneumonia (nu-mō'nĭ-å), *n.* Bhutguti saa.

Pocket (pŏk'ĕt), *n.* Jep.

Pod (pŏd), *n.* Bitchri donchakani bikap.

Poem (pō'ĕm), *n.* Poear ba poido dake segimin, git, poitri dake segimin.

Poet (pō'ĕt), *n.* Poitriko segipa.

Poetry (pō'ĕt-ry), *n.* Poido, poitri.

Point (point), *n.* Ku·chot, su·tot.

Point (point), *v.* Chin daka, ku·chot daka, petchoka; jaksi ote mesoka.

Poison (poi'z'n), *n.* Bisi.

Poke (pōk), *n.* Bario napna man·jana gita matchu ba do·bokni gitoko kadegipa go·ol.

Poke (pōk), *v.* Otroka, su·roka.

Poker (pōk'ēr), *n.* Wa·al otrokani sil.

Pole (pōl), *n.* A·ani ganduri.

Police (po-lēs'), Pulis.

Polish (pŏl'ĭsh), *v.* Nata, ehing·ata.

Polite (po-līt'), *a.* Ka·sae dakgipa.

Politician (pŏl'ĭ-tĭsh'*a*n), *n.* Govermentni kamo chanchibegipa ba gisik nanggipa.

Poll (pōl), *n.* Sko ba sko chanani.

Pollute (pŏl-lūt'), *v.* Ong·siata.

Poltroon (pŏl-trōōn), *a.* Kenrakgipa, ka·pong.

Polygamy (po-lĭg'å-my), *n.* Jik bang·e kimgipa.

Polygon (pŏl'ĭ-gŏn), *n.* Rikam brina agre ong·gipa, rikam bang·gipa.

Polysyllable (pŏl'ĭ-sĭl'lå-b'l), *n.* Selebel bang·gipa kata.

Pomegranate (pŭm'grăn'at), *n.* Dalim bite.

Pomp (pŏmp), *n.* Rasong chabee mesokani.

Pond (pŏnd), *n.* Pokri, chibol.

Ponder (pŏn'dêr), *v.* Gisik on·e chanchia.

Ponderous (pŏn'dêrŭ-s), *a.* Jrimbea.

Pony (pō'ny), *n.* Gure chongipa.

Pool (pụl), *n.* Pokri, chibol, chiklok.

Poor (pụr), *a.* Kangal.

Pop (pŏp), *v.* Wa·ani sintuluk ba maiba goani gam·a.

Pope (pōp), *n.* Roman Katolik mondolini pamong dal·batgipa.

Poppy (pŏp'py), *n.* Apingni bibal.

Populace (pŏp'u-las), *n.* Manderamramrang.

Popular (pŏp'u-lêr), *a.* Manderamramni namnikgni.

Populate (pŏp'u-lāt), *v.* Mandeko jelata ba donata.

Population (pŏp'u-lā-shŭn), *n.* Songni mande gimik.

Populous (pŏp'u-lŭs), *a.* Mande bang·e gnanggipa.

Porcelain (pôr'se-lĭn), *n.* Janera gita a·ako dakgimin.

Porch (pōrch), *n.* Chongipa baranda.

Porcupine (pôr'ku-pīn), *n.* Okupu.

Pore (pōr), *v.* Miksonge poraia.

Pore (pōr), *n.* Ding·ol ong·katani a·kol.

Pork (pōrk), *n.* Wak be·en.

Porpoise (pôr'pŭs), *n.* Susu.

Porridge (pŏr'rĭj), *n.* Chio ritgimin ginde.

Port (pōrt), *n.* Jahat karam, bondor; draka bitchi ma·sa.

Portable (pōrt'ā-b'l), *a.* Ra·ru-rana man·gipa.
Portal (pōr'tal), *n.* Chongipa cholguga ba do·ga.
Portend (pōr-tĕnd'), *v.* Ong·gni-mesoksoa ba uisoata.
Porter (pōr'têr), *n.* Cholguga ko dongtimgipa.
Porthole (pōrt'hōl'), *n.* Jahat-ni oksambengo donggipa ker-ki.
Portion (pōr'shŭn), *n.* Bak, ong·gimin bak.
Portrait (pōr'trat), *n.* mandeni noksa.
Portray (pōr-trā'), *v.* Noksa dake ba katachi tiktak dake mesoka.
Position (po-zĭsh'ŭn), *n.* Dong-ani biap.
Possess (pŏz-zĕs' ba pŏssĕs'), *v.* Nokgipa ong·a.
Possessive (pŏz-zĕs'- ba pŏs-sĕs'-ĭv), *a.* Nokgipa ong·ako me-sokgipa.
Possible (pŏs'sĭ-b'l), *a.* Ong·na amgni.
Post (pōst), *n.* Krong; kamni biap; dak.
Postage (pōst'aj), *n.* Dakni masul.
Postal (pōs'tal), *a.* Dakni bi-ding.
Post haste (pōst' hāst'), *adv.* Gong·rakbee.
Posterity (pŏs-têr'ĭ-ty), *n.* De-rutchu, su·rutchu, de su·u.
Postman (pōst'man), *n.* Dak-wala ba pion.
Postmaster (pōst'mås'têr), *n.* Daknokni nokgipa, dak ba-bu.
Postmeridian (pōst'me-rĭd'ĭ-an), *a.* Saljatchi paksa, atam-chibara.
Postmortem (pōst-môr'tĕm), *a.* Siani ja·mano.
Post office (pōst'ŏf'fis), *n.* Dak nok.
Postpone (pōst-pōn'), *v.* Den-tonga.
Postscript (pōst'skrĭpt), *n.* Se-dapgimin.
Posture (pŏs'tur), *n.* Mandeni dongani rokom.
Pot (pŏt), *n.* Ra·chakani ba songchakani.
Potash (pŏt'ăsh), *n.* Bolni kat-chi ma·sa.
Potato (po-tā'to), *n.* Alu.
Potent (pō'tent), *a.* Bilakgipa, bil man·gipa.
Potter (pŏt'têr), *n.* Me·dik sam·dik dakgipa, hira.
Pouch (pouch), *n.* Chongipa dokra ba mona; petop, pechu.
Poultice (pōl'tis), *n.* Pario nom·gipa kadapani.
Poultry (pōl'try), *n.* Noko jilla do·orang.
Pounce (pouns), *v.* Chapaka.
Pound (pound), *n.* Adha serni pal jrimgipa toani ma·sa; silling kolgriko pound sa; jilarangko chipchangani nol, koar.
Pound (pound), *v.* Dokå, dok-chaa, dokpneka.
Pour (pōr), *v.* Ruå, paka.
Pout (pout), *v.* Ku·chilko pe·t-ka·onangako mesoka.
Poverty (pŏv'êr-ty), *n.* Kangal ong·ani, gam griani.
Powder (pou'dêr), *n.* Ginchi; barud, baruk.
Power (pou'êr), *n.* Bil.
Practical (prăk'tĭ-kal), *a.* Jak-kalani biding.
Practice (prăk'tis), *v.* Dakrong-a, ranta ka·a.

Prairie (prā'rĭ), *n.* Apalbegipa bakra, agalgrim.

Praise (prāz), *v.* Mitela.

Prance (prȧns), *v.* Gaora de'e bilchokchoka.

Prank (prănk), *n.* Kal'ake dakani.

Prate (prāt), *v.* Bokboka, bol'bola.

Prattle (prăt't'l), *v.* Bi'sa chongipani dipet dipet ina.

Prawn (prôn), *n.* Na'tik ma'sa

Pray (prā), *v.* Bi'a. mol'mola.

Preach (prech), *v.* Aganpraka, prochar ka'a.

Precarious (pre-kā'rĭ-ŭs), *a.* Tik ong'gija, gimanaba donggipa, jeko tik ong'jasusu ba gimasusu nika.

Precaution . (pre-kô'shŭn), *n.* Gisik raksoani.

Precede (pre-sēd'), *v.* Skango ba mikkango re'a, re'soa.

Precedence (pre-sēd'*e*ns), *n.* Batani, skang ong'ani.

Precedent (pre-sēd'*e*nt), *n.* Dakgimin maiba ja'rikgni ba ra'gatgni.

Precept (prē'sĕpt), *n.* Ge'eta, niam.

Preceptor (prē-sĕp'tēr), *n.* Skulni skigipa.

Precious (prĕsh'ŭs), *a.* Gamchata.

Precipice (prĕs'ĭ-pĭs), *n.* A'kuang.

Precipitate (pre-sĭp'ĭ-tāt), *v.* A'kuangchi galonata ; ong'kujaon rang'san daka.

Precise (pre-sīs'), *a.* Tiktak. -ion, *n.*

Preclude (pre-klūd'), *v.* Champengsoa.

Precocious (pre-kō'shŭs), *a.* Sal sokgija brigipa ba mingipa ; sal sokgija brigipa gisik.

Preconceive (prē kŏn-sēv'), *v.* Skang uisoa, chanchichipsoa.

Predecessor (prĕd e-sĕs-sēr), *n* Skang dongchenggipa ba ka'chenggipa.

Predestinate (pre-dĕs'tĭ-nāt), *v.* Skangon tik ka'soa.

Predicate (prĕd-ĭ-kāt), *n.* Sentensni ja'panggipa verb.

Predict (pre-dĭkt), *v.* Agansoa. -ion, *n.*

Predominate (pre-dŏm'ĭ-nāt), *v.* Bilakbatgipa ong'a.

Preeminent (pre-ĕm'ĭ-n*e*nt), *a.* Pilakna bate batgipa.

Preen (prēn), *v.* Do'oni grang tar'a.

Preface (prĕf'as), *n.* Pora'soani.

Prefer (pre-fēr'), *v.* Namnikbata. -ence, *n.*

Prefix (pre-fĭks'), *v.* Skangchi on'dapa.

Prefix (prē-'fĭks), *n.* Skangchi on'dapani oikor ba silebel.

Pregnant (prĕg'n*a*nt), *a.* Oko gnang ; gapa.

Prejudge (pre-jŏj'), *v.* Katako knasrangkujaon bichal ka'a.

Prejudice (prĕj'u-dĭs), *n.* Chanchisrangkujaon namniksogijani.

Prejudicial (prĕ'ju-dĭsh'*a*l), *a.* Champengatgipa.

Preliminary (pre-lĭm'ĭ-na-ry), *a.* Kamko dakna tarisoani, ba daksoani.

Prelude (prē'lūd ba prĕl'ŭd), *n.* A'bachengna skang ong'ani.

Premature (prē'mȧ-tūr'), *a.* Sal sokgija bria ba mina.

Premeditate (pr-mĕd'ĭ tāt), *v.* Skangon chanchisoa. -ion, *n.*

Premier (prē′mī-êr), *n.* Montri dal·batgipa.

Premises (prĕm′ĭ-sĕz), *n.* Ja·-pangrang; mandeni a·a ba nokrang.

Premium (prē′mī-ŭm), *n.* Bata ra·ani.

Preoccupy (prē-ŏk′ku-pī), *v.* Skangon dongsoa.

Prepare (pre-pâr′), *v.* Taria, tarisoa. **-ation,** *n.*

Preposterous (pre-pŏs′têr-ŭs), *a.* Ong·na amgijagipa, goka.

Prerequisite (pre-rĕk′wĭ-zĭt), *a.* Nangsogipa.

Presbyter (prĕz′bĭ-têr ba prĕs′-), *n.* Mondolini me·apa.

Prescribe (prē-skrīb′), *v.* Ge·eta, dakgni ba ka·gniko mesoksoa.

Prescription (pre-skrĭp′shŭn), *n.* Samko tariani niam.

Present (prĕz′ent), *n.* Ka·sai on·ani boksis.

Present (pre-zĕnt′), *v.* Donsoa, on·a.

Present (prĕz′ent), *a.* Ong·eng-gipa, ba dongenggipa.

Preserve (pre-zêrv′), *v.* Rakia, jokata.

Preside (pre-zīd′), *v.* Pamongni kam ka·a, dakdila.

President (prĕz′ĭ-dent), *n.* Pa-mong.

Press (prĕs), *n.* Sinjetani kol; chapa ka·ani kol.

Press (prĕs), *v.* Sinjeta. **-ure,** *n.*

Prestige (prĕs′tĭj), *n.* Cholon ba kam chu·sokani bil.

Presume (pre-zūm′), *v.* Chan-chichipa; agre ka·soka.

Presumption (pre-zŭmp′shŭn), *n.* Ong·susu nikani. **-tuous,** *a.* Agre ka·sokgipa, gaorade·a gnang chonnike dakgipa.

Pretend (pre-tĕnd′), *v.* Dak-maia; dakmika.

Pretense (pre-tens′), *n.* Dak-maiani, pa·sikani.

Pretext (pre-tĕkst′ ba prē′-tĕkst), *n.* Tol·nape mesokani, pa·sikani.

Pretty (prĭt′ty), *a.* Nitoa.

Prevail (pre-vāl′), *v.* Ama, chea; cholia.

Prevalent (prĕv′ā-lent), *a.* Choligipa.

Prevalence (prĕv′ā-lens), *n.* Choliani.

Prevent (pre-vĕnt′), *v.* Cham-penga, champengsoa. **-ion,** *n.*

Previous (prē′vĭ-ŭs), *a.* Skang ong·gipa.

Prey (prā), *n.* Sikar, jeko gogen ba chikgen; chikgimin; ra·sekgimin.

Price (prīs), *n.* Dam.

Prick (prĭk), *v.* Su·dika, bu·a.

Pride (prīd), *n.* Gaora de·ani.

Priest (prēst), *n.* Kamal.

Priesthood (prēst′ hụd), *n.* Kamal ong·ani.

Primary (prī′ma-ry), *a.* Skang-gipa, ong·chenggipa.

Prime (prīm), *n.* Bimiting ong·-ani. *a.* Skanggipa, nambe-gipa.

Primer (prĭm′êr), *n.* Skang skiani ki·tap.

Primeval (pri-mē′val), *a.* Skanggipa salni biding.

Primitive (prĭm′ĭ-tĭv), *a.* Skang dongchenggipa ba ong·chenggipa.

Prince (prĭns), *n.* Rajani de.

Princess (prĭn′sĕs), *n.* Rajani demechik.

Principal (prĭn′sĭ-pal), *n.* Chu-batgipa, skotonggipa, mong-songgipa.

Principle (prĭn'sĭ-p'l), *n.* Ja·pang, a·bachengani, dakani niam.
Prior (prī'êr), *a.* Skang ong·gipa.
Prism (prĭz'm). *n* Samgitam-chin rikam apsangipa janera.
Prison (prĭz''n), *n.* Patok nok.
Prisoner (prĭz''n-êr), *n.* Koidi, rim·gimin mande.
Private (prī'vat), *a.* Saksanni, mitingipa.
Privacy (pri'vå-sy), *n.* Mitin, sriksrik; nikgijani.
Privation (pri-vā'shŭn), *n.* Donggijani, kangal ong·ani.
Privilege (prĭv'ĭ-lĕj), *n.* Dakna on·ani ba on·gimin chol.
Privily (prĭv'ĭ-ly), *adv.* Parak-gija.
Prize (prīz), *n.* Susaani boksis.
Prize (prīz), *v.* Gamchatnika, damchata.
Probably (prŏb'å-bly), *adv.* Ong·naba donga, ong·susu, kon.
Probation (pro-bā'shŭn), *n.* Cholon ba dakako niani.
Problem (prŏb'lĕm), *n.* Tik ka·gni, chanehie ba hisab ka·e aganchakgni.
Proboscis (pro-bŏs'sĭs), *n.* Sun-dul ba ro·gipa gingting.
Proceed (pro-sēd'), *v.* Dakanga; ong·kata.
Proceeding (pro-sēd'ing), *n.* Dakangani, re·angani.
Process (prŏs'ĕs), *n.* Dakani be-wal.
Procession (pro-sĕsh'ŭn), *n.* Tarie re·angenggipa jinma.
Proclaim (pro-klām'), *v.* Agan-prakata, pilaknan uiata.
Procrastinate (pro-krăs'tĭ-nāt), *v.* Dorikrike ruutata.
Procreate (prō'kre-āt), *v.* Ong·-katata, atchiata.
Procure (pro-kūr'), *v.* Man·a, joton ka·e man·a.
Prodigal (prŏd'ĭ-gal), *a.* Agre koroch ka·gipa, rusigipa.
Produce (pro-dūs'), *v.* Ong·kat-ata, atchiata, dakata.
Produce (prŏd'ūs), *n.* Ong·kat-atgimin, nanggimin biterang.
Product (prod'ŭkt), *n.* Ong·kat-atgimin bite; chantaitaiani pol, ba gimik.
Profane (pro-fān'), *a.* Rongtal-gija, marang gnang, torom ong·gija.
Profane (pro-fān'), *v.* Marang nangata, rongtalgija ong·ata.
Profess (pro-fĕs'), *v.* Bebe ra·-ako parakata, ba ku·rachaka.
Profession (pro-fĕsh'ŭn), *n.* Gisikni kamko ka·rongani.
Professor (pro-fĕs'êr), *n.* Skul dal·ao skigipa; bebe ra·ako ku·rachakgipa.
Proffer (prŏf'fêr), *v.* On·a ba on·na ku·rachaka.
Proficient (pro-fĭsh'ent), *a.* Changgipa, sapgipa.
Profit (prŏf'ĭt), *n.* Man·dapani, lab.
Profligate (prŏf'lĭ-gat), *a.* Namgijako dakgipa, parake namgijako dakgipa.
Profound (pro-found'), *a.* Ning·tuako nigipa; ning·tu-gipa.
Profuse (pro-fūs'), *a.* Bang·en, agrea, agre jaksramgipa.
Progenitor (pro-jĕn'ĭ-têr), *n.* Pagitcham.
Progeny (prŏj'e-ny), *n.* De su·u.
Progress (prŏg'rĕs), *n.* Mik-kangchi bariangani. **-ion,** *n.*

Progress (prŏ-grĕs'), *v*. Mikkangchi baria.
Prohibit (pro-hĭb'ĭt), *v*. Beng·a, champenga.
Project (proj'ĕkt), *n*. Dakna mangsongani ba chanchiani chol.
Project (pro-jekt'), *v*. Goa, gala; batanga, chutinga.
Prolific (pro-lĭf'ik), *a*. Bite nangbegipa, bi·sa ba·begipa.
Prolong (pro-lŏng'), *v*. Bakroata, ruutata.
Promenade (prŏm'e-näd' ba -näd'), *n*. Hawa cha·e roani biap.
Prominent (prŏm'ĭ-nent), *a*. Chugipa, niksenggipa.
Promise (prŏm'ĭs), *v*. Dakgen ba on·gen ine ku·rachaka.
Promising (prŏm'ĭs-ĭng), *a*. Ka·dongani gnang.
Promissory note (prŏm'ĭs-so-ry nōt'), *n*. Ku·rachake seani, kot ba tomusuk.
Promontory (prŏm'ŭn-to-ry), *n*. Chugipa a·kuchot.
Promote (pro-mōt'), *v*. Dal·ata, namata, bariata.
Promotion (pro-mō'shŭn), *n*. Kam doani ba chuani.
Prompt (prŏmpt), *a*. Tik somoio dakronggipa.
Promulgate (pro-mŭl'gāt), *v*. Uiata, gipata.
Prone (prōn), *a*. Tujole donggipa; daknirggipa.
Prong (prŏng), *n*. Silchonggengni jaksi.
Pronoun (prō'noun), *n*. Nounni pal ra·gipa kata.
Pronounce (pro-nouns'), *v*. Minga, gam·ata.
Proof (prụf), *n*. Saki ba bebeko mesokani.
Proof (prụf), *a*. Mangrakgipa.
Propagate (prŏp'ā-gāt), *v*. Ong·ata, bang·ata, jelata.
Propel (opĕl'), *v*. Mikkangchi re·ata
Proper (prŏp'ēr), *a*. Kraa, tik.
Property (prŏp'ēr-ty), *n*. Gam; gun.
Prophecy (prŏf'e-sy), *n*. Katchinike agangimin.
Prophesy (prŏf'e-si), *v*. Katchinike agana.
Prophet (prŏf'ĕt), *n*. Katchinikgipa.
Propitiate (pro-pĭsh'ĭ āt), *v*. Namnikata, gisikko rongdimata.
Proportion (pro-pōr'shŭn), *n*. Apsan nangrimgipa bakrang.
Proposal (pro-pōz'al), *n*. Naatani ba janapani kata.
Propose (pro-pōz'), *v*. Chanchiatna janapa ba naata. **-ition**, *n*.
Proprietor (pro-prī'e-tēr), *n*. A·a nokgipa.
Propriety (pro-prī'e-ty), *n* Kraani, tik ong·ani.
Prose (prōz), *n*. Poido ong·gija katachi segimin.
Prosecute (prŏs'e-kūt), *v*. Ja·rika; nalis ka·a. **-or, -ion**, *n*.
Proselyte (prŏs'e-līt), *n*. Toromtangko wate gipin toromko ra·gipa.
Prospect (prŏs'pĕkt), *n*. Ka·dongani ja·pang ba a·sel' niwatani.
Prosper (prŏs'pēr), *v*. Sila, chu·soka. **-ous**, *a*. **-ity**, *n*.
Prostitute (prŏs'ti-tūt), *n*. No ti, dari.
Prostrate (prŏs'trat), *v*. A·ao tujola. *a*. **-ion**, *n*.

Protect (pro-tĕkt'), *v.* A·sel nangaoniko rakia. **-or, ion,** *n.*
Protest (pro-tĕst'), *v.* Katachi wasrachaka.
Protestant (prŏt'ĭs-tant), *n.* Romni mondoliko jechakgipa.
Protract (pro-trăkt'), *v.* Ruutata.
Protrude (pro-trūd'), *v.* Mikkangchi sikchepa.
Proud (proud), *a.* Gaorade·gipa, a·tangko dal·nikgipa.
Prove (prūv), *v.* Tik ka·a; saki on·a.
Provender (prŏv'ĕn-dêr), *n.* Jilarangni cha·ani, ran·gimin jeng ba me·gap.
Proverb (prŏv'êrb), *n.* Skiani kata, aganme·apaani kata.
Provide (pro-vīd'), *v.* Donsoa; alduaniko on·a, tarisoc dona.
Provided that (pro-vid'ĕd-thăt), *conj.* Ode, ba uan ong·ode.
Providence (prŏv'ĭ-dens), *n.* Tarisoani, donsoani; Isolni mandeko alduani ba sandiani.
Province (prŏv'ins), *n.* A·songni dal·gipa bak.
Provision (pro-vĭzh'ŭn), *n.* Chimongsogimin cha·ani; daksoani, donsoa.
Provoke (pro-vōk'), *v.* Ka·onangata.
Provocation (prŏv'o-kā'shŭn), *n.* Ka·onangatani.
Prowl (proul), *v.* Cha·aniko am·e re·roroa, malua.
Proximity (prŏks-im'ĭ-ty), *n.* Sepang dongani.
Proxy (prŏks'y), *n.* Sakgipinni pal kam ka·gipa.
Prudence (prū'dens), *n.* Uiani ba niksoani. **-ent,** *a.*
Prune (prūn), *v.* Bol cheksiko den·krea.
Prune (prūn), *n.* Ran·gimin *plumb* bite.
Pry (prī), *v.* PRIED, PRYING. Nikna nanggijako srikerik niua; manggolchi jila.
Psalm (säm), *n.* Daudni git.
Pshaw (shô), *intj.* Phu ba chi· ine chonnikani ba mitchiako mesokani.
Public (pŭb'lĭk), *n.* Mande gimikni ba sorkari.
Publication (pŭb'lĭ-kā'shŭn), *n.* Ki·tapko chapa ka·ani.
Publish (pŭb'lĭsh), *v.* Parakata, gipata; ki·tap chapa ka·a.
Pucker (pŭk'ĕr), *v.* Skemata.
Pudding (pud'dĭng), *n.* Matchusok, moida, do·chi aro chini brine dakgimin cha·ani.
Puddle (pŭd'd'l), *n.* Kimonggipa chiklok.
Puerile (pū'ĕr-ĭl), *a.* Bi·sa gita dakgipa.
Puff (pŭf), *v.* Spoa; gaora de·e gangbinga.
Pug (pŭg), *n.* Chongipa achak ma·sa.
Pugilist (pū'jĭl-ist), *n.* Jaktom·achi dokgrikgipa.
Pugnacious (pŭg-nā'shŭs), *a.* Dakgrikna sikgipa.
Pull (pul), *v.* Sala.
Pullet (pul'lĕt), *n.* Do·o bitra.
Pulley (pul'ly), *n.* Kobikol, budu salruraani gila.
Pulp (pŭlp), *n.* Biteni nom·gipa bak.
Pulpit (pul'pit), *n.* Gilja noko skichakani biap.
Pulse (pŭls), *n.* Jak ja·dil cha·-suani, motor.
Pulverize (pŭl'vêr-īz), *v.* Natkninga, bnekata.
Pump (pŭmp), *n.* Chiko salopani ba saldoani kol.

Pump (pŭmp), *v.* Kolehi chiko salopdoa.
Pumpkin (pŭmp'kin), *n.* Jogonot, jogonot ma'sa, akkaru, gominda.
Pun (pŏn), *n.* Etalani kata, aganchoktani.
Punch (pŭnch), *v.* Su'prua, su'tinga.
Punctual (pŭngk'tu-al), *a.* Tik somoi gita dakronggipa.
Punctuate (pŭngk'tu-āt), *v.* Chinchi katako dingtang daka.
Puncture (pŭngk'tur), *n.* Su'prugimin a'kol. *v.*
Punish (pun'ish), *v.* Sasti on'a.
Pup (pŭp), *v.* Achak dua.
Pup, puppy (pŭp), *n.* Achak bi'sa.
Pupil (pūpĭl), *n.* Chatro, chatri, skulo poraigipa; mikron birong.
Puppet (pŭp'pĕt), *n.* Maichiba ii'engatna amgipa mande gita dakgimin.
Purchase (pêr'chas), *v.* Brea.
Pure (pūr), *a.* Grikå, rongtala, bringija.
Purge (pêrj), *v.* Rongtalata; julap re'a ba ok re'bea.
Purify (pū'ri-fī), *v.* Rongtalata.
Puritan (pū'ri-tan), *n.* Kristianni toromna simsakgipa. *a.*
Purity (pū'ri-ty), *n.* Rongtalani.
Purple (pêr'p'l), *a.* Gitchakmrang.
Purpose (pêr'pŭs), *n.* Manggongani. *v.* Manggonga.
Purr (pêr), *v.* Menggo gita gitok gam'a.
Purse (pêrs), *n.* Tangka donsai, mona.
Purser (pêrs'ĕr), *n.* Jahatni tangka dontimgipa.
Pursue (pêrs-ū'), *v.* Ja'rika, rika; dakanga.
Pursuit (pêr-sūt'), *n.* Ja'rikani, rikani; dakangani.
Purvey (pêr-vā'), *v.* Cha'aniko am'e on'a.
Pus (pŭs), *n.* Minsu.
Push (push), *v.* Jitpaka, sinata, sikdidia.
Puss, pussy (pus), *n.* Menggo.
Put (put), *v.* Dona.
Put off (put'ôf'), *v.* Kamko dontonga, gipin somoina manchia.
Put out (put'out'), *v.* Kimita, galata.
Putrefy (pū'tre-fī), -FIED, -FYING, *v.* Soa, jronga.
Putrid (pū'trĭd), *a.* Sogimin.
Putty (pŭt'ty), *n.* Do'ga ba kerkio ainako rakatani bokgipa stapgipa.
Puzzle (pŭz'z'l), *n.* Jajaatani, bil'dikbil'dak dakatani. *v.*
Pygmy (pĭg'my), *n.* Chakandikgipa, gantiagipa.
Pyramid (pĭr'å-mĭd), *n.* Ro'ongko dal'bee chubee rikdogimin.
Pyre (pīr), *n.* Mande so'ani ganchi.
Python (pī'thŏn), *n.* Chipu nokma.

Q.

Quack (kwăk), *n.* Do'gepni mikoa; changgijagipa oja.
Quadrangle (kwŏd'răng-g'l), *n.* Rikam sambri ki'tikbri gnanggipa.
Quadruped (kwŏd'ru-pĕd), *n.* Ja'sambrigipa matrang.
Quadruple (kwŏd'ru-p'l), *a.* Duna bri.
Quaff (kwåf), *v.* Ku'sik gape ringa, bang'e ringa.

Quail (kwāl), *v.* Duk ba saknaako nike wamisila, misila, an·skita.
Quail (kwāl), *n.* Do·bekrot.
Quake (kwāk), *v.* Moa, til·tila.
Quaker (kwāk'êr), *n.* Kristian ma·malsa.
Qualification (kwŏl'ĭ-fĭ-kā'-shŭn), *n.* Kraani, gun gnangani.
Qualify (kwŏl'ĭ-fī), *v.* Kamna kraata, tariata.
Quality (kwŏl'ĭ-ty), *n.* Nama ba namgija ong·ani, gun.
Quantity (kwŏn'tĭ-ty), *n.* Jeko bang·atna, komiatna ba tona ama.
Quarantine (kwŏr'*an*-tēn), *n.* Sagipa songoni katbagipa mandeko gipin songo napna beng·ani.
Quarrel (kwŏr'rĕl), *v.* Ka·-onange jegrika, ba saigrika. *n.*
Quarrelsome (kwŏr'rĕl-sŭm), *a.* Saigrikninggipa.
Quarry (kwŏr'ry), *n.* Nok rikani ro·ongko bikotram.
Quart (kwôrt), *n.* Toani ma·sa, sel sani pal.
Quarter (kwôr'têr), *n.* Bak brini bak sa.
Quarter deck (kwôr'têr-dĕk'), *n.* Jahatni kosakgipa gadang.
Quarterly (kwôr'têr ly), *a.* Ja gitam gitam ong·gipa.
Quartet, quartette (kwôr-tĕt'), Sulni bak bri, ba ring·gipa sakbri.
Quarto (kwôr'to), *n.* Ki·tapni dal·a ma·sa, leka kinggimikko tem·bri dakgimin.
Quartz (kwôrts), *n.* Ro·ong ma·sa.
Quay (kē), *n.* Ring karam, ghat.

Queen (kwēn), *n.* Rajani jik, rani me·chik; bija ba a·kinni bimadot.
Queer (kwēr), *a.* Nikronggija ba ong·ronggijagipa.
Quell (kwĕl), *v.* Bamata, tom·-tomata.
Quench (kwĕnch), *v.* Kimita; ringna skako namata, ka·sin-ata.
Querist (kwē'rist), *n.* Sing·-rakgipa, sandirakgipa.
Query (kwē'ry). *n.* Sing·ani.
Quest (kwĕst), *n.* Amani, sandiani.
Question (kwĕs'chŭn), *n.* Sing·-ani.
Queue (kū), *n.* Kni kochura.
Quibble (kwĭb'b'l), *v.* Sing·ako aganchakgija aganchholeta.
Quick (kwĭk), *a.* Bakbakgipa; janggi gnang; gisik rak-gipa.
Quicklime (kwĭk'līm'), *n.* Ding·-gnigipa ba cha·gnigipa chun.
Quicksand (kwĭk'sănd'), *n.* A·-bel gipugipa.
Quicksilver (kwĭk'sĭl'vêr), *n.* Para, parot, mikkang niani janerao nonggipa.
Quiet (kwī'ĕt), *a.* Tom·tomgipa.
Quill (kwĭl), *n.* Do·grang.
Quilt (kwĭlt), *n.* Lep.
Quince (kwĭns), *n.* Bite ma·sa.
Quinine (kwī'nin ba kwi-nīn'), *n.* Ka·gipa sam ma·sa.
Quinsy (kwĭn'zy), *n.* Gitoko pari dakani ma·sa.
Quire (kwīr), *n.* Lekani dista.
Quit (kwĭt), *v.* Dondika, wat-gala.
Quite (kwīt), *adv.* Sranga, -srang.
Quiver (kwĭv'êr), *v.* Moa, til·-tila.

Quorum (kwō'rŭm), *n*. Kamko chu·sokatna nanga gita chu·onggipa mande.
Quotation (kwo-tī'shŭn), *n*. Gipinni katako segimin, uko mesokani chin.
Quote (kwōt), *v*. Gipinni katako agana.
Quoth (kwōth or kwŭth), *v*. Aganaha.
Quotient (kwō'shent), *n*. Suale man·gimin bak.

R

Rabbi (răb'bī ba răb'bī), *n*. Robi, Jihudirangni skigipa.
Rabbit (rab'bĭt), *n*. Sapau.
Rabble (răb'b'l), *n*. Jikjakgipa jinma.
Rabid (răb'id), *a*. Pagila; ka·onangbegipa.
Race (rās), *n*. Ma·chong; katsusaani; boi, dongge.
Rack (răk), *n*. Datkrangani ba badalchakani.
Rack (răk), *v*. Kranga, datkranga.
Racket (răk'ĕt), *n*. Golmal ba jikjakani.
Radiant (rā'dĭ-ant), *a*. Ching·gipa, teng·sugipa.
Radiate (rā'dĭ-āt), *v*. Teng·suata, pipraata, gipata.
Radical (răd'ĭ-kal), *a*. Ja·pangni biding.
Radish (răd'ish), *n*. Mula ma·sa.
Radius (rā'dĭ-ŭs), *n*. Dulni jatchioni rikamona toani.
Raft (råft), *n*. Wa·a ba bolko kagimin chap.
Rafter (råft'ĕr), *n*. Bolko dotgimik dake ragimin reil.
Rail (rāl), *n*. Bolni pitgimin; reil gari re·na angipa sil.
Railroad (rāl'rōd'), *n*. Reilni rama.
Raiment (rā'ment), *n*. Ganani ba·rarang.
Rain (rān), *n*. Mikka.
Rain (rān), *v*. Mikka waa.
Rainbow (rān'bō'), *n*. Sundare.
Rainy (rān'y), *a*. Mikka gnang, badria gnang.
Raise (rāz), *v*. Chuata; chakatata; bariata; ong·katata.
Raisin (rā'z'n), *n*. Draka bite ran·gimin, kismis.
Rake (rāk), *n*. Sam sarokani silchonggeng.
Rake (rāk), *v*. Silchonggengchi saroka.
Rally (răl'ly), *v*. Chimonge tariata.
Ram (răm), *n*. Mes bipa.
Ramble (răm'b'l), *v*. Rororoa.
Rampart (răm'pärt), *n*. Killani guare.
Ramrod (răm'rŏd), *n*. Slai su·rokani sil, slai gos.
Ran (răn), *v*. Daariaha, kataha. *Run*ko nibo.
Ranch (rănch), *n*. Jillarangni cha·amani dal·begipa a·ba.
Rancid (răn'sĭd), *a*. To ba mitim soangenggipa.
Random (răn'dŭm), *a*. Mangsonga gri ba bingbang.
Range (rānj), *v*. Niroroa.
Ranger (rānj'ĕr), *n*. Nirorogipa, burungko nitimgipa.
Rank (rangk), *n*. Riting; mande ra·gnini.
Rank (rangk), *a*. Agre silgipa.
Ransack (răn'săk), *v*. Am·rikkita.

Ransom (răn'sŭm), *n.* Piokani, on·chakani.
Rant (rănt), *v.* Gam·bee gaora de·e agana.
Rap (răp), *v.* Doktiktika, kakkaka.
Rapacious (rå-pā'shŭs), *a.* Mikbokgipa, ra·gopgipa.
Rapacity (rå-păs'ĭ ty), *n.* Agre mikbokani.
Rape (rāp), *n.* Bilchi ra·sekani.
Rapid (răp'ĭd), *a.* Gong·rakgipa, ta·rakgipa.
Rapids (răp'ĭds), *n.* Ro·ongrango nangtinge onding ondang dake ta·rakgipa chi.
Rapture (răp'tur), *n.* Katchaan gapani.
Rare (râr), *a.* Ong·ronggijagipa, nikronggijagipa. **-ity,** *n.*
Rascal (răs'kal), *n.* Denggu. **-ity,** *n.*
Rash (răsh), *a.* Chanchigija dakninggipa.
Rasp (råsp), *n.* Dal·gipa ret ma·sa.
Raspberry (răz'bĕr-ry), *n.* Bite ma·sa.
Rat (răt), *n.* Mese.
Ratchet (răch'ĕt), *n.* Korat ba ugita maiba wagam gnanggipani wilwilako wagamo sikteka gita rakatrikna dakgiminsil.
Rate (rāt), *n.* Tik ka·gimin kajana, dam; re·ani.
Rather (răTH'ĕr), *adv.* Batesa -na bate ...... bata.
Ratify (răt'ĭ-fī). *v.* Bil man·gipachi tik ka·ata ba mangrakata.
Ratio (rā'shĭ-o ba rā'sho), *n.* Apsangipa bakrang.
Ration (rā'shŭn ba răsh'ŭn), *n.* Salantini cha·ani.
Rational (răsh'ŭn-al), *a.* Gisik grang.
Rattan (răt-tăn'), *n.* Ré, rebet.
Rattle (răt't'l), *v.* Mororoka ba roktakani gam·a.
Rattlesnake (răt't'l-snāk), *n.* Amerikani bisi bang·begipa chipu ma·sa.
Rattoon (rat-tōōn'), *n.* Grit ja·gu.
Ravage (răv'aj), *n.* Ra·sekani ba gimaatani. *v.*
Rave (rāv), *v.* Pagi'a ong·a, ka·onange bokboka.
Ravel (răv'ĕl), *v.* Grua, enggrua.
Raven (rā'v'n), *n.* Do·ka re·chim.
Ravenous (răv''n-ŭs), *a.* Cha·na sikbegipa.
Ravine (råv-ēn'), *n.* Chikol, chikare, a·kong.
Ravish (răv'ĭsh), *v.* Ra·seka, cha·ua, bilchi ra·seke ra·anga.
Raw (rô), *a.* Gitang, song·gija, mingija; gilskokgipa.
Ray (rā), *n.* Sal ja·dil.
Raze (rāz), *v.* Nisiata, rua.
Razor (rā'zĕr), *n.* Kure. mrid, mrid ma·sa.
Reach (rēch), *v.* Jaksoka, soka, man·a.
Reaction (re-ăk'shŭn), *n.* Dakpilani, nangchakpilani.
Read (rēd), *v.* Poraia.
Readily (rĕd'ĭ-ly), *adv.* Ske, gong·rake, namnika gnang, ba namnike.
Readiness (rĕd'ĭ-nĕs), *n.* Tarie ong·ani, changani, sapani.
Reading (rēd'ĭng), *n.* Poraiani.
Readmission (rē'ăd-mĭsh'ŭn), *n.* Nappiltaiani, rimnaptaiani.

Ready (rĕd'y), *a*. Tarigimin.
Realize (rē'al-īz), *v*. Chong·mot ine uia.
Realm (rĕlm), *n*. Songnok.
Ream (rēm), *n*. Leka dista kolgriko ream sa ong·a.
Reanimate (re-ăn'i-māt), *v*. Tang·pilata.
Reap (rēp), *v*. Mi raa, chimonga.
Reaping hook (rēp'ing hųk'), *n*. Atchili.
Reappear (rē'ăp-pēr'), *v*. Mikkang pa·taia. **-ance,** *n*.
Rear (rēr), *n*. Sipairangni ki·sangchini bak, ki·sang.
Rear (rēr), *v*. Jila, dal·ata, rika; gureni ja·a sangnio ga·e chadenga.
Rear Admiral (rēr'ăd'mĭ-ral), *n*. Dakgrikani jahatni pamong.
Reason (rē'z'n), *n*. A·sel, Ja·pang; chanchiani bil.
Rebel (re-bĕl'), *v*. Rajani kosako bobil daka ba chakata.
Rebel (rĕb'ĕl), *n*. Rajani kosako bobil dakgipa. **-lion,** *n*. **-lious,** *a*.
Rebuff (re-bŭf'), *v*. Beng·a, champenga.
Rebuke (re-bųk'), *v*. Manenga.
Recall (re-kôl'), *v*. Okampila.
Recant (re-kănt'), *v*. Agangiminko ra·pila ba jepila.
Recapitulate (rē'kă-pĭt'u-lāt), *v*. Minggope agantaia. **-ion,** *n*.
Recede (re-sēd'), *v*. Ki·sang bitina, pil·anga.
Receipt (re-sēt'), *n*. Ra·a ba man·ako ku·rachakani chiti.
Receive (re-sēv'), *v*. Man·a, ra·a, ra·chaka.
Recent (rē'sent), *a*. Gital, ruutkujagipa, daldalgipa.
Receptacle (re-sĕp'tă-k'l), *n*. Ra·chakani.
Reception (re-sĕp'shŭn), *n*. Ra·chakani, rimnapani.
Recess (re-sĕs') *n*. Neng·takani somoi; nokdringo tuna dim·tikgimin, guareo kongrue on·tisa nokdring dakgimin.
Recipe (rĕs'i-pe), *n*. Sam ba cha·aniko dakani niam, maikoba brinani niam.
Recipient (re-sĭp'i-ent), *n*. Ra·chakgipa.
Reciprocal (re-sĭp'ro-kal), *a*. Ong·grikgipa, sakgni ba ma·malgnini ong·grikgipa, dakgrikgipa.
Reciprocate (re-sĭp'ro-kāt), *v*. On·pilskaa. **-ion,** *n*.
Recite (re-sīt'), *v*. Parako minga ba aganata. **-ation,** *n*.
Reckless (rĕk'lĕs), *a*. Gisik on·gijagipa, simsakgijagipa.
Reckon (rĕk''n), *v*. Channa hisab ka·a, chanchia.
Reclaim (re-klām'), *v*. Man·pila, man·pilna ama, namatpila.
Recline (re-klīn'), *v*. Dengdala, dan·dana.
Recognize (rĕk'ŏg-nīz), *v*. Nike uipila, uiako ku·rachaka, ra·chaka.
Recoil (re-koil'), *v*. Tang·pila, kom·totpila.
Recollect (rĕk'ŏl-lĕkt'), *v*. Gisik ra·pila.
Recommend (rĕk'kŏm-mĕnd'), *v*. Nama ine aganata. **-ation,** *n*.
Recompense (rĕk'ŏm-pĕns), *v*. Man·na nangako on·a; on·skaa, on·pilskaa.
Reconcile (rĕk'ŏn-sīl'), *v*. Nangrimgrikattaia, namgrikattaia.
Record (re-kôrd'), *v*. See donrika.

Record (rĕk'ērd), *n.* See donrikani.
Recount (re-kount'), *v.* Sulsul pilakkon tale agana.
Recover (re-kŭv'ĕr), *v.* Man·pila; an·sengako man·pila, nampila.
Recreate (rē'kre-āt'), *v.* Neng·takata, bilakdapattaia. **-ion,** *n.*
Recruit (re-krūt'), *n.* Sipai gital.
Recruit (re-krūt'), *v.* Gimagiminni pal bil ba an·sengaiko man·piltaia.
Rectangle (rĕk'tăng'g'l), *n.* Ki·tik apsan rikam sain brigipa.
Rectify (rĕk'tĭ-fī), *v.* Gualako namata.
Rectitude (rĕk'tĭ-tūd), *n.* Bebe ong·ani, kakket ong·ani.
Rector (rĕk'tēr), *n.* Mondolini ba skulni maiba pamong.
Rectum (rĕk'tŭm), *n.* Ki·sangkol, ki·sangkolchibaragipa bibik dal·gipani bak.
Recumbent (re-kŭm'bent), *a.* Tuatgimin, tudengdalgipa.
Recuperate (re-kū'pēr-āt), *v.* An·sengtaia.
Recur (re-kēr'), *v.* Ong·taia. **-rence,** *n.*
Red (rĕd), *a.* Gitchåk.
Redden (rĕd'd'n), *v.* Gitchakata.
Reddish (rĕd'ish), *a.* Gitchakmranga.
Redeem (re-dēm'). *v.* Pioka.
Red hot (rĕd'hŏt'), *a.* Wal·chagipa.
Red lead (rĕd'lĕd'), *n.* Sindur.
Redouble (re-dŭb''l), *v.* Duna gni dakata.
Redress (re-drĕs'), *v.* Taritaia; namattaia.
Reduce (re-dūs'), *v.* Komiata, chonata; bamata. **-tion,** *n.*
Redundant (re-dŭn'dant), *a.* Agregipa, gitchagipa.
Re-echo (rē-ĕk'o), *v.* Ku·rangko ra·chakgrika.
Reed (rēd), *n.* Tillu, gin·cheng.
Reef (rēf), *n.* Sagal ning·o chi kosakona nabregija donggipa rong·brak.
Reek (rēk), *n.* Biba, wal·ku.
Reel (rēl), *n.* Kilding ba maikoba wenchakani.
Reel (rēl), *v.* Wenchakanio wena; rokrek chokchek ra·a.
Refectory (re-fĕk'to-ry), *n.* Cha·ram.
Refer (re-fēr'), *v.* Gipinna pakwata, bichal ka·na ba tik ka·na pakwata. **-ence,** *n.*
Refine (re-fīn'), *v.* Rongta'ata, namata.
Refit (re-fĭt'), *v.* Tariata.
Reflect (re-flĕkt'), *v.* Jagring ba mikkangko nikatpiia, teng·suskaa; chanchia. **-ion,** *n.*
Reform (rē-fôrm'), *n.* Dingtang ba gital dakatani, namatpiltaiani. **-ation,** *n.*
Refract (re-frăkt'), *v.* Gonggeata, mongsongde teng·suachi.
Refrain (re-frān'), *v.* A·tangko salrikpila. *n.* Ring·taitaiani.
Refresh (re-frĕsh'), *v.* Neng·takata, okkaata.
Refreshment (re-frĕsh'ment), *n.* Cha·ani.
Refuge (rĕf'uj), *n.* Katnapani, dongnapani.
Refugee (rĕf'u-jē'), *n.* Katnapgipa, dongnapgipa.
Refund (re-fŭnd'), *v.* On·pila, gro chota.
Refuse (re-fūz'), *v.* Jechaka. **-al,** *n.*
Refuse (rĕf'us), *n.* Jechakgimin, galgimin, jabol.

Refute (re-fūt'), *v.* Bebe ong·ja ine jechake mesoka. **-ation,** *n.*

Regain (rē-gān'), *v.* Man·pila, man·daptaia.

Regal (rē'gal), *a.* Rajani biding.

Regard (re-gärd'), *v.* Gisik on·a; mander a·a.

Regenerate (re-jĕn'ĕr-āt), *v.* Atch taiata, gital dakata. **-ion,** *n.*

Regent (rē'jent), *n.* Rajani kamko ka·gipa.

Regicide (rĕj'i-sīd), *n.* Rajako so·otani; rajako so·otgipa.

Regiment (rĕj'i-ment), *n.* Sipai hajalsamang, kotokni.

Region (rē'jūn), *n.* Jol.

Register (rĕj'is-tĕr), *v.* Gimajana gita see dona.

Register (rĕj'is-tĕr), *n.* Registerko segipa ba rakigipa.

Registration (rĕj'is-trā shun), *n.* See donani.

Registry (rĕj'is-try), *n.* See donani.

Regret (re-grĕt'), *v.* Duk man·a, skima.

Regular (rĕg'u-lĕr), *a.* Niam gita ong·ronga, dakronga gita.

Regulate (rĕg'u-lāt), *v.* Niam gita dakata, tarisoe donata.

Rehearse (re-hĕrs'), *v.* Tarisoa gita agane nia, ranta ka·e agantaia.

Reign (rān), *v.* Raijo ka·a, sason ka·a. *n.*

Rein (rān), *n.* Gureni lagam, gureko moatani.

Reiterate (re-it'ĕr-āt), *v.* Pil·nipil agana, agantaitaia.

Reject (re-jĕkt'), *v.* Jachaka, ra·chakja, chonnika.

Rejoice (rē-jois'), *v.* Kusi ong·a, katchaa ka·sroka.

Relapse (re-lăps'), *v.* Sataia; papo ga·aktaia.

Relate (re-lāt'), *v.* Katako sulsul agana; nangrimata. **-or, -tion,** *n.*

Relative (rĕl'ā-tiv), *n.* Ma·drang, bak.

Relax (re-lăks'), *v.* Olduata, olgrokata.

Relay (rē-lā'), *n.* Bodol on·na donsogimin. *v.*

Release (rē-lēs'), *v.* Wata, watpila.

Relent (re-lĕnt'), *v.* Ka·tong rakako wate nom·pila, ka·saka·gipa ong·a.

Reliable (re-li'ā-b'l), *a.* Pangchakna ba ka·dongna kragipa.

Reliance (re-li'ans), *n.* Pang, chakani, ka·dongani.

Relic (rĕl'ik), *n.* Dongspa, sogimin ba gimagiminni dongspa.

Relieve (re-lēv'), *v.* Ka sinata ritchengata.

Relief (re-lēf'), *n.* Ka·sinatani ritchengatani.

Religion (re-lij'ŭn), *n.* Torom. **-ist,** *n.*

Relinquish (re-lin'kwish), *v.* Wata, watgala. **-ment,** *n.*

Relish (rĕl'ish), *v.* Su·unika, cha·tonika, namnika.

Reluctance (re-lŭk'tans), *n.* Sikgijani, gong·gijani, namnikgijani.

Rely (re-li'), *v.* Pangchaka, ka·donga.

Remain (re-mān'), *v.* Dongrika.

Remainder (re-mān'dĕr), Bangki.

Remains (re-mānz), *n*. Cha'spa, dongspa, bangki; manggisi.
Remark (re-märk'), *n*. On'tisa janapani kata.
Remedy (rĕm'e-dy), *n*. An'sengatani, namatani.
Remember (re-mĕm'bêr), *v*. Gisik ra'a. **-brance**, *n*.
Remind (re-mīnd'), *v*. Gisik ra'ata.
Reminiscence (rĕm'ĭ-nĭs'sens), *n*. Gisik ra'ani, gisiko naani.
Remiss (re-mĭs'), *a*. Simsakgijagipa, aratgipa.
Remission (re-mĭsh'ŭn), *n*. Kema ka'ani, watani.
Remit (re-mĭt'), *v*. Watata, on'ata. **-ment**, *n*.
Remittance (re-mĭt'tans), *n*. Watatgimin ba on'atgimin tangka.
Remnant (rĕm'nant), *n*. Dongspa, bangki.
Remonstrate (re-mŏn'strāt), *v*. Dakjana skia ba mol'mola.
Remorse (re-môrs'), *n*. Skimani, sinteani.
Remote (re-mōt'), *a*. Chel'a.
Remove (re-mo͞ov), *v*. Jita, apjita. **-al**, *n*.
Remunerate (re-mū'nêr-āt), *v*. Dormaha on'a; gimaani gimin on'skaa. **-ion**, *n*.
Rend (rĕnd), *v*. Chita.
Render (rĕn'dêr), *v*. On'a, on'pila.
Rennet (rĕn'nĕt), *n*. Matchu bi'sani ran'gimin bimema.
Renounce (re-nouns'), *v*. Jechaka. **-ment**, *n*.
Renovate (rĕn'o-vāt), *v*. Gital gita daktaia, namattaia.
Renown (re-noun'), *n*. Mingsingani.
Rent (rĕnt), *n*. Grina, kolgipuo; keria ba bhara.
Renunciation (re-nŭn'sĭ-ā'sh n), *n*. Nokgipa ong'akwatani.
Repair (re-pâr'), *v*. Taritaia, namattaia.
Repast (re-pȧst'), *n*. Cha'aniko cha'ani.
Repay (re-pā'), *v*. On'pila. **-ment**, *n*.
Repeal (re-pēl'), *v*. Ge'eta niam ba seako gimata, manina nanggijani dakata.
Repeat (re pēt'), *v*. Agantaia, mingtaia, daktaia.
Repel (re-pĕl'), *v* Jecha'a, champenga, warachaka, a'rikata. **-lent**, *a*.
Repent (re-pĕnt'), *v*. Gisik pil'a, skima
Repetition (rĕp'e-tĭsh'ŭn), *n*. Agantaiani, mingtaiani, daktaiani.
Repine (re-pīn'), *v*. Jajrenga, mangnenga.
Replace (re-plās'), *v*. Donpila. **-ment**, *n*.
Replenish (re-plĕn'ish), *v*. Gapattaia. **-ment**, *n*.
Replete (re-plēt'), *a*. Gapsranggimin. **-ion**, *n*.
Reply (re-plī'), *v*. Aganchaka.
Report (re-pōrt'), *v*. Riport on a, ong'gimin ba man'giminko mesoka.
Repose (re-pōs'), *v*. Neng'taka, tom'toan donga, tue neng'taka.
Represent (rĕp're-zĕnt'), *v*. Mesokata; gipinni pal dakata ba maichiba mesokata. **-ation**, *n*.
Repress (re-prĕs'), *v*. Sinjetpila, bamata. **-ion**, *n*.

Reprieve (re-prēv'), *v.* So·otna ge·etmano aditana dondikata. *n.*

Reprimand (rĕp'ri-mănd), *v.* Manengbea.

Reproach (re-prōch'), *v.* Saia, manenga.

Reproof (re-prōōf'), *n.* Manengani.

Reprove (re-prōōv'), *v.* Manenga

Reptile (rĕp'til), *n.* Ka·bakchi re·gipa, chipu aro u·ita dakgipa

Republic (re-pŭb'lik), *n.* Mande jinmachi sason ka·ani. **-an,** *a.*

Repudiate (re-pū'di-āt'), *v.* Watgala, chel·ata. **-ion, -or,** *n.*

Repugnance (re-pŭg'nans), *n.* Namnikgijani, mitchiani.

Repulse (re-pŭls'), *v.* Jechaka; rikatpila.

●**Repulsive** (re-pŭl'siv), *a.* Mitchigni.

Reputation (rĕp'u-tā'shŭn), *n.* Mingsingani, mande ra·ani.

Request (re-kwĕst'), *v.* Bi·a, mol·mola.

Require (re-kwīr'), *v.* Nanga; on·bo ine ge·eta.

Requisite (rĕk'wi-zit), *n.* Narg·ani bostu.

Requite (re-kwīt'), *v.* On·skaa; dormaha on·a. **-al,** *n.*

Rescue (rĕs'ku), *v.* Jokata.

Research (rē-sêrch'), *n.* Uina sandiani, namedake niani am·beani. *v.*

Resemble (re-zĕm'b'l), *v.* Gita ong·a.

Resent (re-zĕnt'), *v.* Nanggijani ong·a gita nike ka·onanga.

Reserve (re-zêrv'), *v.* Ra·rika. **-ation,** *n.*

Reservoir (rĕz'êr-vwôr), *n.* Chiko donchakani dal·begipa biap, pokri.

Reside (re-zīd'), *v.* Dongkama.

Residence (rĕz'i-dens), *n.* Dongkamchakani biap ba nok.

Resident (rĕz'i-dent), *n.* Dongkamgipa.

Residue (rĕz'i-dū), *n.* Bangki.

Resign (re-zīn'), *v.* Kam ba chakri ka·ako wata, watgala.

Resin (rĕz'in), *n.* Cha·chat ma·sa.

Resist (re-zist'), *v.* Warachaka, champenga.

Resolute (rĕz'o-lūt), *a.* Kimkim mangsonggipa, gisiko kimkimgipa.

Resolution (rĕz'o-lū'shŭn), *n.* Kimkim mangsongani ba ka·dongani gisik.

Resolve (re-zŏlv'), *v.* Jrongata; mangsonga.

Resort (re-zôrt'), *v.* Re·rurarонga, pil·nipil re·ronga

Resound (re-zound'), *v.* Gam·chaka, ku rangko ra·chaka.

Resource (re-sōrs'), *n.* Chol, nangarangko man·na pingchakani.

Resources (re-sōrs'ĕs), *n.* Gamrang.

Respect (re-spĕkt'), *v.* Manda ra·a.

Respecting (re-spĕkt'ing), *prep.* Gimin, nangrimani gnang.

Respective (re-spĕkt'iv), *a.* An·tangtangni; jeni je.

Respire (re-spīr'), *v.* Rang·sita, biba wata. **-ation,** *n.*

Respite (res'pit), *n.* Neng·takani, dondikani.

Respond (re-spŏnd'), *v.* Aganchaka. **-ent,** *a.*

Respondent (re-spŏnd'ent), *n*. Aganchakgipa, ra chakgipa.
Response (re-spŏns'), *n*. Aganchakani, jechakani.
Responsible (re-spŏn'sĭ-b'l), *a*. Kamko chu·sakatna bil gnanggipa.
Rest (rĕst), *n*. Bangki; nengtakani.
Rest (rĕst), *v*. Neng·taka, dondika, tom·tom ong·a; dengdala; pangchaka, ka·donga.
Restless (rĕst'lĕs), *a*. Tom·tomgija, neng·ta·kgija.
Restaurant (rĕs'to-rant), *n*. Mi bree cha·ani nok.
Restitution (rĕs'tĭ-tū'shŭn), *n*. Gamko on pilani, on·skaani.
Restoration (rĕs'to-rā'shŭn), *n*. On·pilani; an·sengpilani.
Restorative (res-tō rā-tĭv), *a*. An·sengatgipa, bilakatgipa.
Restore (re-stōr'), *v*. On·pila, an·sengattaia.
Restrain (re-strān), *v*. Salrika, ·ra·rika, rim·rika, champenga.
Restrict (re-strĭkt'), *v*. Chipchanga. **-ion**, *n*.
Result (re-zŭlt'), *n*. Kamni bite, ong·ani bite.
Resume (re-sūm'), v. Ra·pila, a·bachengtaia.
Resurrection (rĕz'ŭr-rĕk'shŭn), *n*. Chakatpilani.
Retail (retāl'), *v*. Pe·e ba rotrot pala. (rē'tāl), *n*. Rotrot palani.
Retain (re-tān), *v*. Rakia, ra·rika.
Retake (re-tāk'), *v*. Ra·pila, ra·ta·a
Retaliate (re-tăl'ĭ-āt), *v*. Jakbikpila, a·jak soka. **-ion**, *n*.
Retard (re-tärd'), *v*. Ruutata, ka·sinata.
Retention (re-tĕn'shŭn), *n*. Rim·e ra·rikani, rim·rikani.
Retentive (re-tĕn'tĭv), *a*. Gisiko ra·rikna amgipa.
Reticent (rĕt'ĭ-sent), *a*. Aganron·gija, jrip jrip donggipa. **-cence**, *n*.
Retina (rĕt'ĭ-nă), *n*. Mikron nonorio ba·gipa bigil.
Retire (re-tīr'), *v*. Re·pila, kamko wata, mitinchi re·anga. **-ment**, *n*.
Retort (re-tôrt'), *v*. Bakbak aganchaka. *n*.
Retrace (re-trās'), *v*. Ja·koltangko re·pila; sandipila. **-ion**, *n*.
Retreat (re-trēt'), *v*. Amchakgija katpila.
Retrench (re-trĕnch'), *v*. Korochko komiata. **-ment**, *n*.
Retribution (rĕt'rĭ-bū'shŭn), *n*. On·pilani, jakbikpilani, on·skaani.
Return (re-têrn), *v*. Re·pila; on·pila.
Reunion (re-ūn'yŭn), *n*. Nangdimtaiani.
Reveal (re-vēl'), *v*. Parape·ata, parakata, mesokata.
Revel (rĕv'ĕl), *v*. Cha·e ringe chrokmesara.
Revelation (rĕv'e-lā'shŭn), *n*. Ong·gniko mesoksoa ba aganseani, pa·rape·ani.
Revenge (re-vĕnj'), *v*. Jakbikpila, a·jak soka.
Revenue (rĕv'e-nū), *n*. Man·gimin kajana; gamchi man·dapani.
Reverberate (re-vêr'bêr-āt), *v*. Ku·rangko ra·chakgrika.
Revere (re-vēr'), *v*. Mande ra·bea. **-ence**, *n*.
Reverend (rĕv'êr-end), *a*. Mande ra·ako man·na kragipa; ordain ka·giminna on·dapa bimung.

Reverse (re-vêrs'), *v.* Bikpilata. -al, *n.*

Reverse (re-vêrs'), *n.* Samsachi.

Revert (re-vêrt'), *v.* Re·pila, dakpila.

Review (re-vū'), *v.* Name dake niroka, nipila.

Revile (re-vīl'), *v.* Saia, man-enga.

Revise (re-vīs'), *v.* Nitaia, nam-attaia. -ion, *n.*

Revive (re-vīv'), *v.* Tangpila, tangpilata, ka·dim·ata. -al, *n.*

Revoke (re-vōk'), *v.* Ge·etako gimaata.

Revolt (re-vōlt' ba re-vŏlt'), *v.* Rajana bamgija daka, bobil daka.

Revolution (rĕv'o-lū'shŭn), *n.* Wilwilani, dingtangat-sranga.

Revolve (re-vŏlv'), *v.* Wilwila, wilwilata.

Revulsion (re-vŭl'shŭn), *n.* Mitchiani gimin an·skitani, tang·pilani.

Revolver (re-vŏlv'êr), *n.* Changprako guli rong bonga ba rong dok dake sike wilwile gona man·gipa slai, pistol ma·sa.

Reward (re-wôrd), *n.* Boksis, on·skaani.

Rhetoric (rĕt'o-rĭk), *n.* Ku·sikko jakkalna changani.

Rheumatism (rụ'mă-tĭz'm), *n.* Biritchurango saani biati ma·-sa.

Rhinoceros (rī-nŏs'e-rŏs), *n.* Gondu.

Rhyme (rīm), *n.* Poiar seao rit-ingrangni bon·kamgipa katarangni apsan gam·ani.

Rib (rĭb), *n.* Guasu.

Ribbon (rĭb'bŭn), *n.* Resomni ro·dingding dakgipa ba·ra, resomi pita.

Rice (rīs), *n.* Mi, merong.

Rich (rĭch), *a.* Gam gnanggipa, man·e cha·gipa; cha·ani gimin ong·ode chi·a, mitima ba toa ong·a.

Rickets (rĭk'ĕts), *n.* Nama cha·-aniko man·jani gimin bi·sa chongipani grengko nom·atani biati.

Rid (rĭd), *v.* Maiba namgijako gale noni jakgitel ong·a.

Riddle (rĭd'd'l), *n.* Sompiani.

Riddle (rĭd'd'l), *v.* Pintingpintang napongata, mongsongde slaini gulichi.

Ride (rīd), *v.* RODE, RIDDEN. Gakate re·a.

Ridge (rĭj), *n.* Kimbri, a·kim-bri.

Ridicule (rĭd'ĭ-kūl), *v.* Ka·dingsteka.

Ridiculous (rĭ-dĭk'u-lŭs), *a.* Ka·dingstekgni.

Rifle (rī'f'l), *n.* Nolningchi pes raa gnanggipa slai ma·sa.

Rifle (rī'f'l), *v.* Ra·sekanga.

Rift (rĭft), *n.* Aram gisepko nikatani.

Right (rīt), *a.* Kakket, krara, songa, bebe; jakra.

Right (rīt), *n.* Nokgipa ong·-ani bil, jakra.

Righteous (rī'chŭs), *a.* Kakketgipa, toromi, bebegipa.

Rigid (rĭj'ĭd), *a.* Rakgipa, dol·-na ba bamatna man·gijagipa. -ity, *n.*

Rigor (rĭg'êr), *n.* Dol·na man·-gija rakani, il·engatna man·gi-jani.

Rile (rīl), *v.* Kimongata.

Rill (rĭl), *n.* Chonbegipa chiring.

Rim (rĭm), *n.* Rikam, a·sam.

Rind (rīnd), *n.* A·palchini bigil ba bikap.

Rinderpest (rĭn'dêr-pĕst), *n.* Matchuni chobka saani.

Ring (rĭng), *n.* Jakstem; maikoba dol·e kon·gimin.

Ring (rĭng), *v.* RANG, RUNG, Konta doka.

Ringleader (rĭng'lēd'êr, *n.* Namgija dakna jinmako dilgipa.

Ringworm (rĭng'wêrm), *n.* Kat, kat cha·ani.

Rinse (rĭns), *v.* Ringranga, mororoka.

Riot (rī'ŭt), *v.* Bang·a mande golmal daka, jinma niamko pe·a. *n.* **-ous,** *a.*

Rip (rĭp), *v.* Enggrua; chita.

Ripe (rīp), *a.* Mingipa.

Ripple (rĭp'p'l), *n.* Chonchonbegipa chipakkore.

Rise (rīz), *v.* ROSE, RISEN, Chákata; naa; doanga; dal·roroanga.

Risk (rĭsk), *n.* A·sel nangnaba donga ine uioba uko dakani.

Rite (rīt), *n.* Maniani niam.

Ritual (rĭt'u-*a*l), *n.* Niamko maniani dakbewalrang.

Rival (rī'v*a*l), *v.* Susara. *n.*

River (rĭv'êr), *n.* Chibima.

Rivet (rĭv'ĕt), *n.* Silni tekani.

Rivulet (rĭv'u-lĕt), *n.* Chongipa chiring.

Roach (rōch), *n.* Selu, seluk, karo bima.

Road (rōd), *n.* Rama, sorok.

Roam (rōm), *v.* Re·roroa, rororoa.

Roan (rōn), *a.* Bigilo toka bang·gipa.

Roar (rōr), *v.* Randinga, gam·a.

Roast (rōst), *v.* So·a, wa·alo ange minata.

Rob (rŏb), *v.* Ra·seka, cha·ua.

Robber (rŏb'bêr), *n.* Dokprete ra·gipa, ra·sekgipa, cha·ugipa.

Robe (rōb), *n.* Kosako ganani ba·ra ba bigil.

Robust (ro-bŭst'), *a.* Bilakgipa, an·senggipa.

Rock (rŏk), *n.* Ro·ong, rong·brak.

Rock (rŏk), *v.* Ringrenga, il·enga.

Rock salt (rŏk'sôlt'), *n.* Ro·ongni kari ma sa.

Rod (rŏd), *n.* Go·ol, gol·dik; put (foot) chi·dok samsako rod sa minga.

Rode (rōd), *v. Ride*ko nibo.

Rodent (rō'dent), *n.* Mese gita tingipani jatrang.

Roe (rō), *n.* Balgitchak ba matchok bima; na·tok bitchi.

Rogue (rōg), *n.* Namgijagipa, denggu.

Roil (roil), *v.* Kimongata.

Roll (rōl), *v.* Romtoma, dol·a, romroma, romromjeta.

Roll (rōl), *n.* Romtomani, romtomgipa; bimungko sulsul seani; dol·gimin.

Roman (rō'm*a*n), *n.* Rom songni mande. *a.*

Romance (ro-măns'), *n.* Aganaia kata, kata a·jong.

Romantic (ro-măn'tĭk), *a.* Ong·jasusu nikpilgipa, aiao inmangni.

Romp (rŏmp), *n.* Tom·tomgijagipa me·chik. *v.*

Roof (ru̥f), *n.* Nokking.

Rook (ru̥k), *n.* Do·ka.

Room (ru̥m), *n.* Biap; nokdring, kutori.

Roost (ru̥st), *n.* Do·oni ma·bakchakani bol. *v.*

Root (ru̥t), *n.* Ja·dil.

Root up (rṳt'ŭp'), *v*. Ja·pang pika, pangpika.

Rope (rōp), *n*. Budu, paga.

Rose (rōz), *n*. Golap bibal.

Rose (rōz), *v*. *Riseko* nibo.

Rosin (rŏz'in), *n*. Cha·chat ma·sa.

Rot (rŏt), *v*. Sŏa, sojronga.

Rotation (rō-tā'shŭn), *n*. Wil-wilani.

Rotten (rŏt't'n), *a*. Sogimin.

Rough (rŭf), *a*. Ga·nanggija-gipa, skakgipa.

Round (round), *a*. Tom·beta, bo·rota.

Round (round), *adv*. Pilakchin, dula, samtangtango.

Round about (round'ā-bout), *a*. Dulgipa, srongggija.

Rouse (rouz), *v*. De·mesàa, mik-rakata.

Rout (rout), *v*. Amata, a·rikata.

Route (rṳt), *n*. Re·ani.

Routine (rṳ-tēn'), *n*. Kam ka·rongani bewal ba dakrongani.

Rove (rōv), *v*. Re·roroa, rororoa.

Row (rō), *n*. Riting, sari.

Row (rō), *v*. Ring chòa.

Row (rou), *n*. Jikjakani golmal.

Rowdy (rou'dy), *n*. Golmal dakatronggipa.

Rowel (rou'ĕl), *n*. Pari dakatna siktekani.

Royal (roi'al), *a*. Rajani biding. **-ty**, *n*.

Royalist (roi'al-ist), *n*. Rajachi chakgipa.

Rub (rŭb), *v*. Nata, nol·a, mo-lia.

Rubber (rŭb'bêr), *n*. Rangket, robol.

Rubbish (rŭb'bish), *n*. Itroke galgimin moila, re·cham.

Ruby (rṳ'by), *n*. Gitchakgipa ro·ong ma·sa.

Rudder (rŭd'dêr), *n*. Ringni ki·me, ringko pil·atani.

Rude (rṳd), *a*. Mande ra·bregi-jagipa, rakgipa.

Rudiment (rṳ'di-ment), *n*. A·-bachengani, ong·chengani.

Rue (rṳ), *v*. Dakmanahao sintea.

Ruffian (rŭf'yan ba rŭf'fi-an), *n*. Namgijagipa, mande so·ot-gipa.

Rug (rŭg), *n*. Wa·seo anani rit-chagipa ba·ra.

Rugged (rŭg'gĕd), *a*. Ga·nang-gijagipa.

Ruin (rṳ'in), *v*. Gimata, rurong-ata, bon·ata, nisiata. **-ation, -ous**, *n*.

Ruins (rṳ'ins), *n*. Gimagimin ba ruronggiminni dongspa-rang.

Rule (rṳl), *n*. Niam; rul salani go·ol.

Rule (rṳl), *v*. Sason ka·a; rul sala.

Rum (rŭm), *n*. Chu ma·sa.

Rumble (rŭm'b'l), *n*. Banggri-ani ba chel·ao mikka kimani gam·a gita gam·beani.

Ruminant (rṳ'mi-nant), *n*. Chobaitaigipani jat.

Ruminate (rṳ'mi-nāt), *v*. Cho-baitaia. **-ion**, *n*.

Rummage (rŭm'maj), *v*. Am·-rikkita.

Rumour (rṳ'mêr), *n*. Mande-rangni jangani.

Rump (rŭmp), *n*. Ki·sangte.

Rumple (rŭm'p'l), *v*. Skemata, skem skem dakata.

Run (rŭn), *v*. RAN, RUN. Kata, daaria, jokanga; guli rua.

Runaway (rŭn'ā-wā), *n*. Ka-tanggipa.

Rung (rŭng), *v*. *Ringko* nibo. *n*. Jang·ke teng·prak.

Rupee (ru̥-pē′), *n.* Tangka.
Rupture (rŭp′tur), *n.* Bretani.
Rural (ru̥′ral), *a.* Songjinma ong·gijagipa.
Rush (rŭsh), *v.* Chapinapa.
Rush (rŭsh), *n.* Chonchonbegipa tilu ma·sa.
∧ **Rust** (ru̥st), *v.* *Maram* cha·a. **-y,** *a.*
Rustic (rus′tĭk), *n.* Pilakni giminba mandeska baksa dakpana changgijagipa, gaine cha·gipa. *a.*
Rusticate (rŭs′tĭ-kāt), *v.* Jinmaoni eke donga ba dongata.
Rustle (rŭs′t′l), *v.* Siksak siksak gam·a.
Rut (r t), *n.* Gari ja·kolni chikare.
Rye (rī), *n.* Mi ma·sa.
Ryot (rī′ŏt), *n.* Raiot.

S.

Sabbath (săb′bath), *n.* Neng·takani sal.
Saber, sabre (sā′bêr), *n.* Tonual ma·sa.
Sack (săk), *n.* Chalja, tolia.
Sack (săk), *v.* Chaljao chipa; ra·seke nisiata.
Sackcloth (săk′klŏth′), *n.* Chaljani ba·ra.
Sacrament (săk′râ-ment), *n.* Mikchetani; Kristoni dongimin toromko dakani, Gitelni meatam.
Sacred (sā′krĕd), *a.* Rongtala, Isolni ba toromni biding.
Sacrifice (săk′rĭ-fīz), *v.* Boli on·a, namgnina pakwate on·a. *n.*
Sad (săd), *a.* Gisikni jrima ba duk gnang.
Saddle (săd′d′l), *n.* Gureni jin.
Safe (sāf), *n.* Donchakani, rakchakani.
Safe (sāf), *a.* A·sel nangani gri, ka·dongani gnang, jokgimin. **-ty,** *n.*
Sag (săg), *v.* Jrimani gimin dol·a ba oldua.
Sagacious (sâ-gā′shŭs), *a.* Gisik sramgipa, chalak. **ity,** *n.*
Sage (sāj), *a.* Uigipa, gisik gnanggipa.
Sage (sāj), *n.* Gisik gnangbegipa; sam ma·sa.
Sago (sā′go), *n.* Sagu.
Said (sĕd), *v.* *Sayko* nibo.
Sail (sāl), *n.* Ringo ping·e choani ba·ra. *v.*
Sailor (sāl′êr), *n.* Jahat chogipa, kalasi.
Saint (sānt), *n.* Rongtalgipa mande.
Sake (sāk), *n.* -ni gimin, a·sel.
Salad (săl′ad), *n.* Samjak gitangko dakgimin bijak.
Salary (săl′â-ry), *n.* Dormaha, beton.
Sale (sāl), *n.* Palani.
Saleratus (săl′e-rā′tŭs), *n.* Tin·dakgimin katchi.
Saline (sā′līn), *a.* Kari nanggipa, kari gnang.
Saliva (sâ-lī′vâ), *n.* Ku·chi, stu.
Salivate (săl′ĭ-vāt), *v.* Samchi ku·chi ong·ata. **-ion,** *n.*
Sallow (săl′lo), *a.* Saa gnange bokdalgepgep dakgipa.
Sally (săl′ly), *v.* Dakgrikna ong·katpraka, rang·san ong·katprake chaanga.
Salmon (săm′ŭn), *n.* Na·tok ma·sa.
Saloon (sâ-lo̤n′), *n.* Mande jinmana dal·gipa nokdring; chu ringani nok.
Salt (sôlt), *n.* Kari.

Salt cellar (sôlt'sĕl'lêr), *n*. Kari donchakani.

Saltpetre ba **-ter** (sôlt'pē'têr), *n*. Sora, songra.

Saltrheum (sōlt'rụm'), *n*. Bigil joljol cha·gipa kat ma·sa.

Salubrious (så-lū'brĭ-ŭs), *a*. An·sengatani, an·sengatgni.

Salutary (săl'u-ta-ry), *a*. Namgni ong·atgipa.

Salute (så-lụt'), *v*. Salam ka·a, ku·dimå. **-ation**, *n*.

Salvation (săl-vā'shŭn), *n*. Jokatani.

Salve (säv), *n*. Pario tapani sam.

Same (sām), *a*. Apsan, dingtang ong·gija.

Samp (sămp), *n*. Me·raku ginchiko ritgimin.

Sample (sám'p'l), *n*. Mesokani, nomuna.

Sanctify (sĭngk'tĭ-fī), *v*. Rongtalata. **-fication**, *n*.

Sanction (săngk'shŭn), *v*. Namnike ra·chaka; hukum on·a.

Sanctuary (săngk'tu-a-ry), *n*. Rongtala ba toromni biap.

Sand (sănd), *n*. An·cheng.

Sandal (săn'dal), *n*. Ja·kop, korom.

Sandal wood (săn'dal-wụd'), *n*. Chondon bol, smilgipa bol ma·sa.

Sand paper (sănd'pā'pêr), *n*. An·cheng ma·gapatgimin leka.

Sane (sān), *a*. Gisik an·senggipa. **-ity**, *n*.

Sang (săng), *v*. *Sing*ko nibo.

Sanguinary (săn'gwĭ-na-ry), *a*. An·chi ong·atna ska gnang.

Sanguine (săn'gwĭn), *a*. An·chi gapgipa; an·saogipa, ka·dongani gnang.

Sanitary (săn'ĭ-ta-ry), *n*. An·sengatani biding.

Sank (săngk), *v*. *Sink*ko nibo.

Sap (săp), *n*. Bolni biski ba bitchi.

Sap (săp), *v*. Kongrue ba srik srik gimaata.

Sapient (sā'pĭ-ent), *a*. Gisik gnanggipa, uigipa.

Sapling (săp'lĭng), *n*. Bol bi·sa.

Sapphire (săf'ĭr ba săf'êr), *n*. Tangsimgipa ro·ong ma·sa, ripok do·katchi.

Saracen (săr'å-sĕn), *n*. Arab songni musolman.

Sarcasm (sär'kăz'm), *n*. Kal·stape mitelani.

Sarcastic (sär-kăs'tĭk), *a*. Kal·stape mitelgipa.

Sarcophagus (sär-kŏf'å-gŭs), *n*. Manggisi donchakani ro·ong.

Sardine (sär'dēn ba sär-dēn'), *n*. Tino chipgimin na·tok ma·sa.

Sardonyx (sär'do-nĭks), *n*. Gamchatgipa ro·ong ma·sa.

Sarsaparilla (sär'så-på-rĭl'lå), *n*. Salsa minggipa sam ma·sa, an·chiko rongtalatani.

Sash (săsh), *n*. Kang·kare katongani ba·ra ro·dinggipa ki·sangchi biritchu dongipa; kerki ba do·gao janerako rakatani bol.

Sat (săt), *v*. *Sit*ko nibo.

Satan (sā'tan), *n*. Soitan, Satan.

Satchel (săch'ĕl), *n*. Ki·tap donani chongipa dokra.

Sate (sāt), *v*. Okkaata.

Satellite (săt'ĕl-līt), *n*. Chongipa upogroho, aski ma·sa.

Satiate (sā'shĭ-āt), *v*. Okkaata.

Satin (săt'ĭn), *n*. Ching·gipa resomi ba·ra ma·sa.

Satisfaction (săt'ĭs-făk'shŭn), *n*. Chu·ongnikani.
Satisfy (săt'ĭs-fī), *v*. Chu·ongnikata, okkaata, namnikata.
Saturate (săt'u-rāt), *v*. Sosiata, chijimata. **-ion**, *n*.
Saturday (săt'ŭr-da), *n*. Sonibar.
Saturn (săt'ŭrn), *n*. Soni minggipa groho.
Sauce (sôs), *n*. Cha·ani maiba bijak, su·uatani.
Saucepan (sôs'păn), *n*. Song·-chakani ma·sa, saspen.
Saucer (sô'sêr), *n*. Ba·ranggipa piala ma·sa.
Saucy (sô'sy), *a*. Mande ra·gija aganpilgipa, kratcha·gijagipa.
Saunter (sän'têr), *v*. Arate ka·-sin ka·sin re·a.
Sausage (sô'saj), *n*. Mosla brine bneke natgimin be·en.
Savage (săv'aj), *a*. Mikmalgijagipa, chikrakgipa, burungo donggipa.
Save (sāv), *v*. Jokata, rakia, chimonga.
Save (sāv), *prep*. -na agre.
Saving (sāv'ing), *a*. Chimonggipa, koroch ka·gijagipa.
Savior, Saviour (sāv'yêr), *n*. Jokatgipa.
Savour (sā'vêr), *n*. Su·uani.
Saw (sô), *n*. Korat.
Saw (sô), *v*. *See*ko nibo; koratchi raa.
Sawmill (sô'mĭl'), *n*. Toktako raani kolni nok.
Sawdust (sô'dŭst'), *n*. Bol raani biginchi.
Saxon (săks'ŭn ba -'n), *n*. England songni mande skangni jatsa.
Say (sā), *v*. SAID, SAID. Agana.
Saying (sā'ing), *n*. Agana kata.
Scab (skăb), *n*. Parini bisingkap.
Scabbard (skăb'bêrd), *n*. Tonualni bikop.
Scaffold (skăf'fold), *n*. Chugipa gan·sang.
Scald (skôld), *v*. Chi ding·achi chibila.
Scale (skāl), *v*. Bisingkapko gala; jang·keko gakata.
Scale (skāl), *n*. Na·tokni bisingkap; jrimako toani; gadang, jang·ke.
Scalp (skălp), *n*. Sko kochurani bigil.
Scamp (skămp), *n*. Denggugipa mande.
Scamper (skăm'pêr), *v*. Katangbea.
Scan (skăn), *v*. Namedake nia.
Scandal (skăn'dal), *n*. Kratcha·-atani, namgija ong·atani. **-ize**, *v*. **-ous**, *a*.
Scant (skănt), *a*. Chu·onggija, bang·gija.
Scanty (skănt'y), *a*. Chu·onggija, bang·gija.
Scantling (skănt'ling), *n*. Bolgro dake ragimin reil.
Scapula (skăp'u-lâ), *n*. Pakreni greng.
Scar (skär), *n*. Namgimin parini chin.
Scarce (skârs), *a*. Bang·gija, man·na neng·gni.
Scarcely (skârs'ly), *adv*. Neng·-edike, jenten.
Scare (skâr), *v*. Kenata.
Scarecrow (skâr'krō'), *n*. Do·-orangko kenatna dongimin.
Scarf (skärf), *n*. Chongipa chinani ba·ra.

Scarlet (skär'lĕt), *n.* Gitchak-srang.
Scatter (skăt'tĕr), *v.* Bilding bildang dakata.
Scene (sēn), *n.* Niani, nikani. -**ry**, *n.*
Scent (sĕnt), *n.* Bisak.
Scent (sĕnt), *v.* Smilgipa, gingsika.
Scepter, sceptre (sĕp'tĕr), *n.* Rajani gol·dik.
Schedule (skĕd'ụl), *n.* Sulsul seani.
Scheme (skēm), *n.* Mangsongani; noksa.
Scholar (skŏl'ĕr), *n.* Sninggipa, poraigipa, chatro.
Scholarship (skŏl'ĕr-ship), *n.* Changa ba man·ani gimin on·a koraki.
School (skụl), *n.* Skul, poraiani biap; na·tok jinma.
Schooling (skụl'ing), *n.* Leka pora skiani.
Schooner (skụn'ĕr), *n.* Rokomsa jahat.
Science (sī'ens), *n.* Bida ba uiani.
Scion (sī'ŭn), *n.* Ritim gitalbagipa cheksi, bimitu; depante ba demechik.
Scissors (sĭz'zĕrz), *n.* Ba·ra raani, kesi.
Scoff (skŏf), *v.* Ka·dingsteka.
Scold (skŏld), *v.* Manenga, saia.
Scoop (skụp), *v.* Koncholichi we·waka. *n.*
Scope (skŏp), *n.* Mangsongani, nikgopa ba rim·gopani.
Scorch (skôrch), *v.* Kamsraka. kamskoka, kamretreta.
Score (skōr), *n.* Chanani chin; kolgrik.
Scorn (skôrn), *v.* Chonnika.
Scorpion (skôr'pĭ-ŭn), *n.* Mangkisang, me·konchek.
Scotch (skŏch), *n.* Scotland songni mande. *a.*
Scot-free (skŏt'frē'), *a.* Kajana gri, a·sel gri.
Scoundrel (skoun'drĕl), *n.* Namgijagipa ba denggugipa mande.
Scour (skour), *v.* Nata.
Scourge (skĕrj), *v.* Betsmitchi doka.
Scout (skout), *v.* Chonnike jechaka; bobilko nina re·roroa.
Scow (skou), *n.* Ki·sang dalgapgipa ring.
Scowl (skoul), *v.* Mikskeme nia.
Scrabble (skrăb'b'l), *v.* Chadenge akbritgrika.
Scramble (skrăm'b'l), *v.* A·aoniko akbritgrika, malama.
Scrap (skrăp), *n.* Chong dok.
Scrape (skrāp), *v.* Neng·e chimonga; siksika, rikota, saroka.
Scratch (skrătch), *v.* Ku·aka, brika; salchrita.
Scrawl (skrôl), *v.* Sena changgijani sea.
Scrawny (skrô-ny), *a.* Grengraragipa, ram·sisigipa.
Scream (skrēm), *v.* Chrika.
Screech (skrēch), *v.* Chrika.
Screen (skrēn), *n.* Pindapani ba donpengani porda.
Screw (skrụ), *n.* Pes gnanggipa gojal.
Screw driver (skrụ'drīv'ĕr), *n.* Pes tekani.
Scribble (skrĭb'b'l), *v.* Gong·rake ba simsakgija sea.
Scribe (skrīb), *n.* Jakchi segipa.
Scrimp (skrĭmp), *v.* Chu·onggija ba sokgija dakata.

Scrip (skrĭp), *n.* Chongipa mona; chongipa chiti.
Script (skrĭpt), *n.* Jakchi seani.
Scripture (skrĭp'tur), *n.* Kristianni sastro, Baibel.
Scrofula (skrŏf'u-lȧ), *n.* Ripime sagipa biati, mongsongde gitoko.
Scrub (skrŭb), *v.* Rake nata, talatna rake nata.
Scruple (skrṳ'p'l), *n.* Namja ine chanchie dakna sikgijani; roti chetni pal jrimgipa toani ma·-sa.
Scrupulous (skrṳ'pu-lŭs), *a.* Namja ine chanchie dakna sikgijagipa.
Scud (skŭd), *v.* Balwachi ta·-rake balpakanga.
Scuffle (skŭf'f'l), *n.* Jakchi rim·-chakgrikani.
Scull (skŭl), *n.* Ring choani kan·dikgipa boita.
Sculptor (skŭlp'têr), *n.* Bimang dake ro·ongko sol·gipa.
Scum (skŭm), *n.* Ka·spu, chini kosako balbogipa moila.
Scythe (sɪᴛʜ), *n.* Sam raani dal·-gipa atchili.
Sea (sē), *n.* Apalgipa kari nanggipa chi, sagal.
Seaboard (sē'bōrd'), *n.* Sagal rikam jolo donggipa a·a.
Sea coast (sē'kōst'), *n.* Sagal rikam jol jol.
Seafaring (sē'fâr'ing), *a.* Sagalo reruragipa.
Seal (sēl), *n.* Sagalo donggipa matburung gita dakgipa ma·-sa; mohor su·gimin.
Seal (sēl), *v.* Mohor su·a, donue dona, mohor su·e bon ka·a.
Sealing-wax (sēl'ing-wăks'), *n.* Mohor su·ani laha.
Seam (sēm), *n.* Koani biritchu.
Seaman (sē'mən), *n.* Kalasi, jahat chogipa.
Seaport (sē'pōrt'), *n.* Bondor, sagal rikamo donggipa songjinma.
Sear (sēr), *v.* Kamsraka.
Search (sêrch), *v.* Am·a.
Seashore (sē'shōr'), *n.* Sagal rikam.
Seasick (sē'sĭk), *n.* Ringo re·ani ka·reke saa, sagalo re·ani saa.
Season (sē'z'n), *n.* Bilsini kari.
Season (sē'z'n), *v.* Su·uata, kari pua.
Seat (sēt), *n.* Asongchakani, choki.
Seat (sēt), *v.* Asongata, donata.
Seaward (sē'wêrd), *adv.* Sagalchipak.
Secede (se-sēd'), *v.* Dingtang dakata, ekanga, dingtang donata.
Secession (se-sĕsh'ŭn), *n.* Dingtang dakatani, ekangani, dingtang donatani.
Second (sĕk'ŭnd), *a.* Gnigipa.
Second (sĕk'ŭnd), *n.* Minitni bak sotdokni bak sa.
Secondhand (sĕk'ŭnd-hănd'), *a.* Gipinni jakkalgimin.
Secondhand (sĕk'ŭnd-hănd'), *n.* Kontani sekenko mesokgipa.
Secret (sē'krĕt), *n.* Dongnugimin, parakgijani.
Secretary (Sĕk're-ta-ry), *n.* Setimgipa.
Secrete (se-krēt'), *v.* Dongnua; dingtangate ong·katata. -ion, *n.*
Sect (sĕkt), *n.* Maiba toromko ra·gipani ma·mal.
Section (sĕk'shŭn), *n.* Ratonggimin tong, chong·dok; oidai.
Secular (sĕk'u-lêr), *a.* Toromni ong·gija a·gilsakni biding.

Secure (se-kūr'), *a.* Kenani gri.
Secure (se-kūr'), *v.* Tik ka·a, rakia. **-ity**, *n.*
Sedan (se-dăn'), *n.* Palki gita dakgipa mande ripeani choki.
Sedate (se-dāt'), *a.* Gisik tom·-tomgipa, mogijagipa.
Sedative (sĕd'ā-tĭv), *a.* Tom·-tomatgipa.
Sediment (sĕd'ĭ ment), *n.* Ki·-tikchi skonggimin.
Sedition (se-dĭsh'ŭn), *n.* Raja-ni kosako bobil dakani.
Seduce (se-dūs'), *v.* Tol·nape ong·gijako dakata. **-ment**, *n.*
Seduction (se-dŭk'shŭn), *n.* Tol·nape ong·gijako dakatani.
See (sē), *v.* SAW, SEEN Nika, nia.
Seed (sēd), *n.* Bitchri.
Seedling (sēd'lĭng), *n.* Bitchri-oni chabagipa chonchongipa bol.
Seek (sēk), *v.* SOUGHT, SOUGHT. Am·a.
Seem (sēm), *v.* Gita nika.
Seemly (sēm'ly), *a.* Krara.
Seen (sēn), *v.* *See*ko nibo.
Seer (sēr), *n.* Katchinikgipa, uigipa.
Segment (sĕg'ment), *n.* Tong, chong·dok, mongsongde dul-gipani.
Segregate (sĕg're-gāt), *v.* Dingtang dingtang ong·ata. **-ion**, *n.*
Seine (sēn ba sān), *n.* Na·tok rim·ani dal·begipa chek.
Seize (sēz), *v.* Rim·a.
Seldom (sĕl'dŭm), *adv.* Ong·-rongbreja, basakoba basakoba-san.
Select (se-lĕkt'), *a.* See ra·gimin.
Select (se-lĕkt'), *v.* See ra·a. **-ion**, *n.*
Self (sĕlf), *a.* An·tang.
Self-applause (sĕlf'ăp-plôs'), *n.* A·tangko rasong chaatani ba de·mitelani.
Self-defence (sĕlf'de-fĕns'), *n.* A·tangko rakiani.
Self-existent (sĕlf'ĕgz-ĭst'ent), *a.* A·tangni bilchi ong·aigipa.
Selfish (sĕlf'ĭsh), *a.* A·tangna-san ehanchiaigipa.
Self-righteous (sĕlf'rī'chŭs), *a.* A·tangko toromi nikgipa.
Selfsame (sĕlf'sām'), *a.* Apsan, tiktak, uan.
Self-willed (sĕlf'wīld'), *a.* Ska-tang dakgipa.
Sell (sĕl), *v.* Pala.
Selves (sĕlvs), *n.* A·tangmang.
Semblance (sĕm'blans), *n.* Gita ba apsan ong·ani.
Semi (sĕm'ĭ), *a.* Samsa; ian gipin katani a·bachengani ong·a, aro iani orto samsa ba adha ong·ronga.
Semicolon (sĕm'ĭ-kō'lŏn), *n.* Sea ba poraiao katani tong·ko me-sokani chin (;) ian.
Seminal (sĕm'ĭ-nal), *a.* Bitchrini biding.
Seminary (sĕm'ĭ-na-ry), *n.* Skul ma·sa.
Senate (sĕn'at), *n.* Sason ka·ani kamko dakna tom·ani. **-or**, *n.* (United States aro France songo donga).
Send (sĕnd), *v.* SENT. Watata, on·ata.
Senior (sēn'yēr), *a.* Bilsi batgip-a.
Sensation (sĕn-sā'shŭn), *n.* Be·-enchi uiani; gisikni ong·ako uiani. **-al**, *a.*
Sense (sĕns), *n.* Uiani.
Sensible (sĕn'sĭ-b'l), *a.* Gisik gnanggipa, namedake uigip-a.

Sensitive (sĕn′sĭ-tĭv), *a.* Ui-inggipa.
Sensual (sĕn′shụ-*a*l), *a.* Be·enni sukko am·gipa.
Sent (sĕnt), *v.* *Send*ko nibo.
Sentence (sĕn′t*e*ns), *n.* Matchotgipa kata; sastina ge·etani.
Sentiment (sĕn′tĭ-m*e*nt), *n.* Gisik nangani, gisik nanganiko janapani kata. **-al**, *a.*
Sentinel (sĕn′tĭ-n*e*l), *n.* Nitimgipa ba pohora on·gipa sipai.
Sentry (sĕn′try), *n.* Nitimgipa ba pohora on·gipa sipai.
Separate (sĕp′å-rāt), *a.* Dingtang ong·gipa.
September (Sĕp-tĕm′bêr), *n.* Bilsini skugipa ja.
Septuagint (sĕp′tu-a-jĭnt), *n.* Greek ku·siko seskagimin sastro gitcham.
Sepulcher, sepulchre (sĕp′ŭl-kêr), *n.* Gopram.
Seraph (sĕr′*a*f), *n.* Dal·batgipa salgini sa·gre,
Seraphim (sĕr′å-fĭm), *n.* Ibri ku·siko sa·grerang.
Serene (se-rēn′), *a.* Mogijagipa, tom·tomgipa.
Serf (sêrf), *n.* Gipinni ning·o donggipa, nokol, a·a gamgipa nokol.
Sergeant (sär′j*e*nt ba sêr′j*e*nt), *n.* Captainni ning·o donggipa sipaini pamong.
Serial (sē′rĭ-*a*l), *a.* Sulsul donani biding.
Series (sē′rēz ba sē′rĭ-ēz), *n.* Sulsul donani.
Serious (sē′rĭ-ŭs), *a.* Gisiko nangbeani, kenani jrimani.
Sermon (sêr′mŭn). *n.* Sastroni katako ra·e skiani. **-ize**, *n.*
Serpent (sêr′p*e*nt), *n.* Chipu.
Servant (sêr′v*a*nt), *n.* Chakol, nokol.
Serve (sêrv), *v.* Gipinna kam ka·a ba dangdike on·a.
Service (sêrv′ĭs), *n.* Chakolni kamko ka·ani, chakri ka·ani, dakchakani.
Servile (sêrv′ĭl), *a.* Nokol gita.
Servitude (sêrv′ĭ-tud), *n.* Nokol ong·ani.
Session (sĕsh′ŭn), *n.* Skul, soba ba maiba kam ka·na tom·ani changsa.
Set (sĕt), *n.* Tom·dak, gimik.
Set (sĕt), *v.* Dona; salnapa.
Settle (sĕt′t′l), *v.* Dongkama; tik ka·a mangrakata; grikata, skonga.
Seven (sĕv′n), *a.* Sni, ge·sni.
Sevenfold (sĕv′′n-fōld′), *a.* Duna sni.
Seventeen (sĕv′′n-tēn), *a.* Chi·-sni, ge·chisni.
Seventeenth (sĕv′′n-tēnth′), *a.* Chi·snigipa.
Seventh (sĕv′′nth), *a.* Snigipa, ge·snigipa.
Seventieth (sĕv′′n-tĭ-ĕth), *a.* Sotsnigipa.
Seventy (sĕv′′n-ty), *a.* Sotsni.
Sever (sĕv′êr), *v.* Rasota, rae dingtangata.
Several (sĕv′êr-*a*l), *a.* Gnina bata, indiba bang·beja.
Severally (sĕv′êr-*a*l-ly), *adv.* Ge·prakprak, dingtang dingtang ong·e.
Severe (se-vēr′), *a.* Rakgipa, ka·sinninggijagipa.
Sew (sō), *v.* SEWED, SEWN. Sika, koa.
Sewer (sū′êr), *n.* Moilako salange galani chikare.
Sex (sĕks), *n.* Bima ba bipa ong·ani.

Sexton (sĕks'tŭn), *n*. Gilja nokni dopdori; mande gopna a·kol cho·timgipa.
Sexual (sĕks'u-*al* ba sĕk'shu-*al*), *a*. Bima bipani biding.
Shabby (shăb'by), *a*. Ba·ra suri ba ba·ra gringiminkc gangipa.
Shackles (shăk'k'ls), *n*. Sildeng, beri.
Shade (shād), *n*. Salakim.
Shadow (shăd'o), *n*. Jagring.
Shaft (shȧft), *n*. Bra ga·tong; krong bitong; gariko salani bipong.
Shaggy (shăg'gy), *a*. Kimil chabegipa, kokaksisi dakgipa.
Shah (shä), *n*. Paroisoni raja.
Shake (shāk), *v*. SHOOK, SHAKEN. Moata, il·engata, ringrengata.
Shall (shăl), *v*. SHOULD. -gen; dakna nanga.
Shallow (shăl'lo), *a*. Ba·gipa, tu·gija; uigijagipa.
Shalt (shălt), *v*. *Shall* gita second persono jakkala.
Sham (shăm), *n*. Ong·gijako ong·a gita dakatani.
Shamble (shăm'b'l), *v*. Ga·bingbange re·a.
Shame (shām), *n*. Kratcha·ani.
Shamefaced (shām'fāst'), *a*. Kratcha·rakgipa.
Shank (shănk), *n*. Ja·skuoni ja·gitokona gimikko minggopa.
Shanty (shăn'ty), *n*. Jamdap, chongipa nok.
Shape (shāp), *n*. Bimang.
Shape (shāp), *v*. Bimang daka.
Share (shâr), *n*. Bak.
Shark (shärk), *n*. Hanggor minggipa sagalni na·tok ma·sa; gamko man·na sikbegipa; ma·mantiko dakani cha·aniko man·begipa.
Sharp (shärp), *a*. Mata, srama; su·a gita sagipani biding.
Shave (shāv), *v*. Roka, si·roka, sol·oka.
Shaving (shāv'ing), *n*. Roka, sol·oka ba renda on·ani bisemsem.
Shawl (shôl), *n*. Sal minggipa chinani ba·ra rokomsa.
She (shē), *pro*. Bimako mesokani pronoun, Nominative case.
Sheaf (shēf), *n*. Metal.
Sheaves (shēvs), *n*. Metalrang.
Shear (shēr), *v*. SHEARED, SHORN. Kesichi rasota.
Shears (shērs), *n*. Kesi dal·gipa.
Sheath (shēth), *n*. Tonualni bikop, chukop.
Shed (shĕd), *v*. Ruronga, singsola.
Shed (shĕd), *n*. Paja, jamdap.
Sheep (shēp), *n*. Mes, mesrang.
Sheep-fold (shēp'fōld'), *n*. Mes nol.
Sheepish (shēp'ish), *a*. Maikoba dakahani gimin kratcha·e mesokgipa.
Sheet (shēt), *n*. Palango andapani ba·ra; lekani king; maiba ba·ranggipa apalgipa.
Shelf (shĕlf), *n*. Pakma baksa dakkapgipa almari, ki·tap ba maiba bosturangko donani.
Shelves (shĕlvs), *n*. *Shelf*ni plural.
Shell (shĕl), *n*. Bikrok, biking.
Shell (shĕl), *v*. Bikapko oa, rongroka.
Shellac (shĕl'lăk'), *n*. Jrongate daktaigimin laha.
Shellfish (shĕl'fish'), *n*. Etchaluk ba ugita bikrok gnanggipa.
Shelter (shĕl'têr), *n*. Pindapani, ma·chakani.

Shepherd (shĕp'êrd), *n*. Mes nirikgipa.
Sheriff (shĕr'ĭf), *n*. Adita songrangni pamong, bichal ka·gipa.
Sherry (shĕr'ry), *n*. Spain songoni draka bitchi ma sa.
Shield (shēld), *n*. Danil, rakiani.
Shift (shĭft), *v*. Biapsaoni biapsaona dingtangata.
Shiftless (shĭft'lĕs), *a*. Simsakgijagipa, aratgipa, changgijagipa, a·tangko alduna amgijagipa.
Shilling (shĭl'ĭng), *n*. England songni tangka ma·sa, ana chi·gnini pal.
Shin (shĭn), *n*. Ja·riking.
Shin (shĭn), *v*. Bolko maldoa.
Shine (shīn), *v*. SHONE, SHONE. Ching·a, teng·sua.
Shingles (shĭng'g'ls), *n*. Nokking rapani tokta ba silrang.
Ship (shĭp), *n*. Sagalo ba·ra ping·e chogipa dal·gipa jahat.
Shipboard (shĭp'bōrd'), *n*. Jahato, jahatni kosak.
Shire (shīr, ba shēr, ba shĭr, ba shêr), *n*. England songni jilla chongipa, district.
Shirk (shêrk), *v*. Dakna nangako dakgija kamoni jokna sikgipa.
Shirt (shêrt), *n*. Chola kamij.
Shiver (shĭv'êr), *v*. Til·tila, moa.
Shiver (shĭv'êr), *v*. Bnekata, be·kningata.
Shoal (shōl), *n*. Na·tok jinma; chi tu·gijagipa.
Shoat (shōt), *n*. Wak bitra, wak bi·sa.
Shock (shŏk), *v*. Chatinga, rang·san kena ba kusi ong·achi dil·dil ong·ata.
Shod (shŏd), *v*. *Shoe*ko nibo.
Shoe (shụ), *n*. Juta. *v*. SHOD, SHOD. Jutako ga·ata.
Shone (shōn ba shŏn), *v*. *Shine*ko nibo.
Shoo (shụ), *int*. Siah ine do·oko a·rikani.
Shook (shọk), *v*. *Shake*ko nibo.
Shoot (shụt), *n*. Bijak jakgital, me·a.
Shoot (shụt), *v*. SHOT, SHOT. Slaini goa; manchoka; soksola.
Shop (shŏp), *n*. Dokan; mistrini kam ka·ani nok, karkana.
Shore (shôr), *n*. Sagaloi rikam.
Shorn (shôrn), *v*. *Shear*ko nibo.
Short (shôrt), *a*. Kan·dikgipa; ruutgija, chu·sokgija, sokmangija.
Shorten (shôrt''n), *v*. Kan·dikata.
Shortlived (shôrt-līvd'), *a*. On·tisasan tangaigipa.
Shorthand (shôrt'hănd'), *n*. Chinchi kan·dikate seani.
Shortsighted (shôrt'sīt'ĕd), *a*. Chel·e niksokgijagipa, sepangonikosan nikaigipa.
Shot (shŏt), *n*. Saraguli, goani; gosoka kakket.
Should (shụd), *v*. *Shall*ko nibo.
Shoulder (shōl'dêr), *n*. Pakre.
Shout (shout), *n*. Inchroani. *v*.
Shove (shŭv), *v*. Jitpaka, sinchepa.
Shovel (shŭv''l), *n*. A·a cho·ani chamos dal·gipa. *v*.
Show (shō), *v*. Mesoka.
Shower (shou'êr), *n*. Rang·san wae tipgipa mika, wapakaigipa mika.
Shrank (shrănk), *v*. *Shrink*ko nibo.
Shred (shrĕd), *n*. Tong, chong·dok, chong·dik.

Shrew (shrṳ), *n.* Menggotchi chotchonchi; ku·namgijagipa me·chik.
Shrewd (shrṳd), *a.* Gisik seng·gipa, nikninggipa.
Shriek (shrēk), *v.* Chrika.
Shrill (shril), *a.* Chrikani gam·agita.
Shrine (shrīn), *n.* Rongtalako donram, ganchi.
Shrink (shrĭnk), *v.* SHRANK, SHRUNK. Kom·tota, kom·pila, salpila, tang·pila.
Shrimp (shrĭmp), *n.* Na·tik.
Shrivel (shrĭv''l), *v.* Sikrepa, kom·tota.
Shroud (shroud), *n.* Pindapani ba wenani dal·gipa ba·ra.
Shrub (shrŭb), *n.* Chongipa bol, boldim.
Shuck (shŭk), *n.* Rakgipa bikap, bikrok.
Shudder (shŭd'dêr), *v.* Til·tila, an·skita, an·tesrengsreng daka.
Shuffle (shŭf'f'l), *v.* Brinbawe daka, brinata.
Shun (shŭn), *v.* Gela, a·tangko chel·e rakia.
Shut (shŭt), *v.* Chipa.
Shutter (shŭt'têr), *n.* Kerkini kosako pindapani.
Shuttle (shŭt't'l), *n.* Ba·ra dakani maku.
Shy (shī), *a.* Kratcha·ninggipa.
Shy (shī), *v.* SHYING, SHIED, Kenani gimin gele re·a.
Sick (sĭk), *a.* Saa.
Sickle (sĭk'k'l), *n.* Mi raani atchili.
Side (sīd), *n.* Rikam; samba; oksambeng.
Side (sīd), *v* Chaka, samsa pak ong·a.
Sideways (sīd'wāz'), *adv.* Rikamchi, ketchie.
Siege (sēj), *n.* Songjinma ba killako bamatna dongdulani.
Sieve (sĭv), *n.* Ginde moani, gitchera, wakginde.
Sift (sĭft), *v.* Ginde moa.
Sigh (sī), *v.* Rang·spita. *n.*
Sight (sīt), *n.* Nikani bil; nikgimin, niani; slaini nisan.
Sign (sīn), *n.* Chin.
Sign (sīn), *v.* Chin on·a, bimung soi ka·a ba bimungtangko sea.
Signal (sĭg'nal), *n.* Uiatani chin.
Signature (sĭg'nā-tur), *n.* Bimungtangko segimin.
Signet (sĭg'nĕt), *n.* Rajani mohor.
Significant (sĭg-nĭf'ĭ-kant), *a.* Orto gnang. **-ance,** *n.*
Signify (sĭg'nĭ-fī), *v.* SIGNIFYING, SIGNIFIED. Uiata, ortoko mesoka.
Silence (sī'lens), *v.* Jrip donga, tom·tom donga.
Silk (sĭlk), *n.* Muga, eria ba resomni kilding ba ba·ra.
Silk worm (sĭlk wêrm), *n.* Muga, eria ba resomni jo·ong.
Sill (sĭl), *n.* Sing·kam.
Silly (sĭl'ly), *a.* Goka, gisik gri, indin ka·dinggipa, bi·sa gita dakgipa.
Silver (sĭlvêr), *n.* Rupa, tangkani sil.
Similar (sĭm'ĭ-lêr), *a.* Gita.
Simile (sĭm'ĭ-le), *n.* Mesokani, toani.
Simmer (sĭm'mêr), *v.* Ka·sne rita.
Simple (sĭm'p'l), *a.* Ge·sangipa, brina grigipa; uininggni.

Simplify (·ĭm′plĭ·fī), *v.* Srongata, talata.

Simply (sĭm′plȳ), *adv.* Mangmang.

Simultaneous (sī′mŭl-tā′ne-ŭs), *a.* A psangipa sal.

Sin (sĭn), *n.* Pap, Isolni niamko pe·ani, dakna nanggijako dakani.

Since (sĭns), *adv.* Intaltal; uni gimin.

Sincere (sĭn-sēr′), *a.* Kakketgipa, sronggipa, cha·chipila grigipa.

Sinew (sĭn′u), *n.* Be·enni ja·-dil.

Sing (sĭng), *v.* SANG, SUNG. Ring·a, mikoa.

Singe (sĭnj), *v.* Kamsraka, kamskoka.

Single (sĭng′g′l), *a.* Ge·sangipa, saksangipa; bringijagipa; kimgijagipa.

Singular (sĭng′gu-lêr), *a.* Ong·-ronggijagipa; sanko mesokgipa.

Sink (sĭngk), *v.* SANK, SUNK. Sripa, dubia; rooka; daapa; bilgri ong·a.

Sink (sĭnk), *n.* Chi jokatani nol.

Sinner (sĭn′nêr), *n.* Papi, pap dakgipa.

Sip (sĭp), *v.* Ringota, salope cha tota.

Sir (sêr), *n.* Mande ra·ani kata, hujur inani pal.

Sire (sīr), *n.* Pagipa, atchiatgipa.

Sister (sĭs′têr), *n.* Nogipa ba abitang, ma·sanni demechik.

Sister-in-law (sĭs′têr-ĭn-lô), *n.* Se ba jikni nogipa ba abitang, jonggipa ba adatangni jik, saritang, nosari.

Sit (sĭt), *v.* SAT, SAT. Asonga; bama.

Site (sīt), *n.* Biap, maikoba rikani biap.

Situate (sĭt′u-at), *v.* Dona, donga.

Situated (sĭt′u-ā′tĕd), *part.* Dongimin, donggimin.

Situation (sĭt′u-ā′shŭn), *n.* Dongani biap; ong·ani, obosta; dongimin kam.

Six (sĭks), *a.* Dok, ge·dok.

Sixth (sĭksth), *a.* Dokgipa, ge·-dokgipa.

Sixfold (sĭks′fōld′), *a.* Dunadok.

Sixpence (sĭks′pens), *n.* Anadokni pal gamchatgipa Englishni tangka.

Sixteen (sĭks′tēn′), *a.* Chi·dok.

Sixteenth (sĭks′tēnth′), *a.* Chi·-dokgipa.

Sixtieth (sĭks′tĭ-ĕth), *a.* Sotdokgipa.

Sixty (sĭks′ty), *a.* Sotdok.

Size (sīz), *n.* Dal·ani, bimang.

Skate (skāt), *n.* Suurini kosako ga·e re·ani sil.

Skein (skān), *n.* Kilding apale wengimin.

Skeleton (skĕl′e-tŭn), *n.* Be·enni korokgimin greng gimik.

Skeptic, sceptic (skĕp′tĭk), *n.* Bebeo ka·donggijagipa, kenchakgipa.

Sketch (skĕch), *v.* Gimikni mongsongrangko noksa daka, kata ja·pangrangko uina see ra·a.

Skiff (skĭf), *n.* Chongipa ring.

Skill (skĭl), *n.* Changani, sapani.

Skim (skĭm), *v.* Kosak joljol we·e ra·a.

Skin (skĭn), *n.* Janggi gnanggipani aro biteni ba·gipa bigil

Skin (skin), *v*. Bigil kika.
Skip (skĭp), *v*. Bilchroka.
Skirmish (skêr'mĭsh), *n*. Mande bang·gija dakgrikani, on·tisa dakgrikani. *v*.
Skirt (skêrt), *n*. Saia.
Skulk (skŭlk), *v*. Dongnue re·a.
Skull (skŭl), *n*. Sko korokgimin, sko bikrok.
Sky (skī), *n*. Salgi, kosakchini bangbang.
Sky-rocket (skī'rŏk'ĕt), *n*. Salgichi wa·al watani.
Slab (slăb), *n*. Rong·pleng; bigilchinibaragipa bolpleng.
Slack (slăk), *a*. Olgrokgipa; ka·-singipa, simsakgijagipa.
Slacken (slăk''n), *v*. Olgrokata.
Slake (slāk), *v*. Tipata; ringna skako namata.
Slam (slăm), *v*. Rake chipata; maiba dalgapgipako rake dona.
Slander (slăn'dêr), *v*. Tol·e mitaka.
Slant (slănt), *v*. Chongkrenga.
Slap (slăp), *v*. Satkapa, doktapa. *n*.
Slash (slăsh), *v*. Den·bingbinga.
Slat (slăt), *n*. Chongipa ba·-gipa tokta ba sil.
Slate (slāt), *n*. Sechakani, silet, slat.
Slattern (slăt'têrn), *n*. Noktang ba ba·ratangni gimin simsakgijagipa me·chik.
Slaughter (slô'têr), *n*. So·otbeani, bang·en so·otani. *v*.
Slave (slāv), *n*. Nokol, bregimin nokol. **-ry**, *n*. **-ish**, *a*.
Slay (slā), *v*. SLEW, SLAIN. So·-ota.
Sled (slĕd), *n*. Chaka grigipa gari ma·sa.
Sledge (slĕj), *n*. Chaka grigipa gari ma·sa.
Sledge hammer (slĕj'hăm'mêr), *n*. Dal·gipa turi.
Sleek (slēk), *a*. Rimiltrita, mnenga.
Sleep (slēp), *v*. SLEPT, SLEPT. Tusia.
Sleeper (slēp'êr), *n*. Ka·machba ja·pango dongipa bol; tuisigipa.
Sleepy (slēp'y), *a*. Tusina ska gnang.
Sleet (slēt), *n*. Suuri ba stilmisi bringipa mika.
Sleeve (slēv), *n*. Pakreoni jakgitokona pindapani.
Sleigh (slā), *n*. Suuri kosako re·ani chaka gripipa gari.
Slender (slĕn'dêr), *a*. Ram·a, chona, chongkalenga, joldengsia.
Slept (slĕpt), *v*. *Sleep*ko nibo.
Slew (slū), *v*. *Slay*ko nibo.
Slice (slīs), *n*. Ragimin kaprang. *v*. Raplenga.
Slick (slĭk), *a*. Rimiltrita, mnenga.
Slide (slīd), *v*. Sol·sola, sol·tapa, ga·soltapa.
Slight (slīt), *v*. Simsakgija dak-a, mangrakja.
Slim (slĭm), *a*. Joldengsigipa, cha·soldenggipa.
Slime (slīm), *n*. A·dubekni ata; ginggre.
Sling (slĭng), *v*. SLUNG. Pakskea, skea; bengjuri goa.
Sling (slĭng), *n*. Bengjuri, skeani ba·ra ba matbigil.
Slink (slĭngk), *v*. SLUNK. Dongnue katanga, mitin mitin katanga.
Slip (slĭp), *v*. Skona, tapskoka, sol·tapa; guala.
Slipper (slĭp'pêr), *n*. Sliper juta, choti juta.

Slippery (slĭp′pĕr-y), *a*. Rimila.
Slit (slĭt), *n*. Ragroani.
Sliver (slĭv′ĕr ba sʼī vĕr), *n*. Bichrit, bisring.
Sloop (slọọp), *n*. Ba·ra ping·e choani jahat chongipa.
Slop (slŏp), *v*. Pokpeke nasia.
Slope (slōp), *v*. A·solsol daka. *n*.
Sloppy (slŏp′py), *a*. Snekbnekg pa.
Slot (slŏt), *n*. Chongipa ro·gipa a·kol, du·rok.
Sloth (slŏth), *n*. Ka·sinani, aratani; ka·singipa matburung ma·sa.
Slothful (slŏth′fụl), *a*. Aratgipa.
Slough (slou), *n*. A·bel dakgipa a·a.
Slough (slŭf), *v*. Gilsrea, sorur onga.
Slough (slŭf), *n*. Soe jronggimin, gilsreani bigil.
Sloven (slŭv′′en), *n*. Rongtalgijagipa, moilagipa, nok ba ba·rani gimin simsakgijagipa.
Slow (slō), *a*. Ka·singipa, ruutgipa, gong·rakgija.
Slug (slŭg), *n*. Etchaluk ma·sa; aratgipa; slaini guli ma·sa.
Sluggard (slŭg′gĕrd), *n*. Aratgipa, tusidumugipa.
Sluggish (slŭg′gĭsh), *a*. Aratgipa, olgrokgipa.
Sluice (slūs), *n*. Chi jokruraani biap, chikare.
Slum (slŭm), *n*. Namgijagipa moilagipa manderangni dongram songjinmani biap.
Slumber (slŭm′bĕr), *v*. On·tisa tusia. *n*.
Slump (slŭmp), *v*. Giputroma.
Slung (slŭng), *v*. *Sling*ko nibo.
Slunk (slŭnk), *v*. *Slink*ko nibo.
Slur (slĕr), *n*. Chonnikani kata; gitni iachinrang.
Slush (slŭsh), *n*. Suurini a·dubek.
Slut (slŭt), *n*. Achak bima; rongtalgijagipa me·chik.
Sly (slī), *a*. Chalak.
Small (smôl), *a*. Chona.
Small-pox (smôl′poks′), *n*. Uri dal·gipa.
Smart (smärt), *v*. Bibrao dake kama gita saani. *a*. Ta·rake dakgipa, gisik seng·gipa.
Smash (smash), *v*. Ripik kning dakata, bnekata.
Smear (smēr), *v*. Nongmraka, repia.
Smell (smĕl), *n*. Seenga ba smilani bisak.
Smell (smĕl), *v*. SMELLED ba SMELT. Gingsika.
Smelt (smĕlt), *v*. SMELT. A·koloni man·a silko jronge rongtalata.
Smile (smīl), *v*. Ka·dingsika.
Smite (smīt), *v*. SMOTE, SMITTEN. Doka; so·ota.
Smith (smĭth), *n*. Sil dakgipa kamal.
Smoke (smōk), *v*. Wal·ku ong·kata; tamaku ringa; wal·kusio ripoa.
Smoke-stack (smōk′stăk′), *n*. Jahat ba maiba kolni karkanaoni wal·ku jokatani.
Smooth (smọọth), *a*. Rinoka, apsan.
Smote (smōt), *v*. *Smite*ko nibo.
Smother (smŭth′ĕr), *v*. Kang·sitna man·jana gita pindapa, wa·al dipua.
Smolder, smoulder (smōl′dĕr), *v*. Ning·joljol kama.

Smudge (smŭj), *n.* A·ki a·ki dake wal·ku; nangmrikgimin.

Smuggle (smŭg'g'l), *v.* Masul on·a nanga badingani bostuko masul on·gija sriksrik ra·-anga.

Smut (smŭt), *n.* Dim·ak, dikmak.

Snag (snăg), *n.* Chi ning·o donggipa bolritchong, bolchongdik.

Snail (snāl), *n.* Gap, gaptek.

Snake (snāk), *n.* Chipu.

Snap (snăp), *v.* Doknaka: chika; be·rikkepa.

Snare (snâr), *n.* Ja·ga.

Snarl (snärl), *v.* Achak gita randinga.

Snatch (snătch), *v.* Ra·seka.

Sneak (snēk), *v.* Mitin mitin re·anga.

Sneer (snēr), *n.* Gingting songga.

Sneeze (snēz), *v.* Atchinga.

Snicker (snĭk'ẽr), *v.* Pit dake ka·dinga.

Sniff (snĭf), *v.* Gingsika.

Snooze (snooz), *v.* Tusisranggija adita tusia.

Snore (snōr), *v.* Enggok ra·a.

Snort (snôrt), *v.* Gure gita pru pru ine ina.

Snout (snout), *n.* Wak gita ro·-gipa gingting.

Snow (snō), *n.* Mikka gita ga·-akgipa suui.

Snuff (snŭf), *v.* Gingsika; *n.* Ta·maku ginchi; kampongimin sorta.

Snug (snŭg), *a.* Chapchap dongtoa.

So (sō), *adv.* Indake; ugita; uni gimin; namen.

Soak (sōk), *v.* Chio dim·a.

Soap (sop), *n.* Sabon.

Soar (sōr), *v.* Kosakchi bila; chuna joton ka·a.

Sob (sŏb), *v.* Ka·siksika.

Sober (sō'bẽr), *a.* Tom·tomgipa; chu ringgijagipa. *n.* **Sobriety.**

Social (sō'shal), *a.* Rorimna namnikgipa, rorimbegipa; rorimani biding.

Society (so-sī'e-ty), *n.* Nangrimgimin manderang; uibatgipa rangni nangrimgrikani.

Sock (sŏk), *n.* Kan·dikgipa muja.

Socket (sŏk'ĕt), *n.* Maikoba sikkrokchakani, wa·singtok.

Sod (sŏd), *n.* Samsi panggimik, ja·dil ja·pang aro a·a gnang samsi.

Soda (sō'då), *n.* Tarigimin katchi bitin, katchi nanggipa, soda.

Sofa (so'få), *n.* Nom·gipa asongchakani ba tuchakani.

Soft (sŏft), *a.* Nom·a, rinoka.

Soil (soil), *v.* Moila nangata.

Soil (soil), *n.* Kosakgipa a·a, a·sal, ki·i.

Sojourn (sō'jẽrn ba so-jẽrn'), *v.* Adita salna songgipino donga. *n.*

Solace (sŏl'as), *v.* Ka·dimeata, tom·tomata. *n.*

Solar (sō'lẽr), *v.* Salni biding.

Solder (sŏd'ẽr ba sŏl'dẽr), *n.* Ritchuani. *v.*

Soldier (sōl'jẽr), *n.* Dakgrikgipa, sipai.

Sole (sōl), *n.* Ja·pa; jutani ka·-bak; na·tok ma·sa.

Sole (sōl), *a.* Sasan.

Solemn (sŏl'ĕm), *a.* Toromni gimin gisiko nanga. **-ity,** *n.* **-ize,** *v.*

Solicit (so-lĭs'ĭt), *v.* Bi·a, mol·-mola. **-er**, *n.*
Solid (sŏl'ĭd), *a.* A·kara, ma·-keta. raka, jronggijagipa. **-ity**, *n.* **ify**, *v.*
Solitary (sŏl'ĭ-ta-ry), *a.* Mande gri, saksan ong·ani biding.
Solo (sō'lo), *n.* Saksan ring·ani.
Soluble (sŏl'u-b'l), *a.* Chio jronggnigipa.
Solution (so-lū'shŭn), *n.* Jrong-atgimin.
Solve (sŏlv), *v.* Katani ortoko pe·a, uigijako tale pe·a ba uiata.
Somber, Sombre (sŏm'bèr), *a.* Katchaa gri; dimela, rong-dima.
Somehow (sŭm'hou'), *adv.* Mai-ba ka·e.
Something (sŭm'thing), *n.* Maiba.
Sometime (sŭm'tīm'), *adv.* Ba-sakoba, changsao.
Sometimes (sŭm'tīms'), *adv.* Basakoba basakoba, gisep gi-sep.
Somewhat (sŭm'whăt'), *adv.* On·tisa, adita.
Somewhere (sŭm'whâr), *adv.* Banoba.
Son (sŭn), *n.* Depante.
Song (sŏng), *n.* Git, ring·ani.
Songster (sŏng'stêr), *n.* Ring·-gipa.
Son-in-law (sŭn'ĭn-lô), *n.* Cha-wari.
Soon (sụn), *adv.* Bakbak, ruut-gija.
Soot (sụt), *n.* Dim·ak, wal·kusi.
Soothe (sụTH), *v.* Ka·sinata, tom·tomata.
Sop (sŏp), *n.* Chio sim·bolgim-in; chi chipatgimin cha·ani. *v.*
Sorcerer (sôr'sêr-êr), *n.* Montol dakgipa, bheliki dakgipa.
Sorcery (sôr'sêr-y), *n.* Montol, bheliki.
Sordid (sŏr'did), *a.* Chongipa, ongipa, mikbokgipa.
Sore (sōr), *n.* Pari.
Sore (sōr), *a.* Saa gnang, sa-knaa·gnang.
Sorghum (sôr'gŭm), *n.* Grit ma·sa.
Sorrow (sŏr'ro), *n.* Gisikni duk, kalimani sinteani.
Sorry (sŏr'ry), *a.* Duk ong·ani biding; duk ong·a gnang.
Sort (sôrt), *n.* Rokom.
Sort (sôrt), *v.* Basea, rosea.
Sot (sŏt), *n.* Chu pekronggipa.
Sought (sôt), *v.* *Seek*ko nibo.
Soul (sōl), *n.* Be·en ning·o donggipa mande, gisik, janggi.
Sound (sound), *a.* An·senggipa, saa ding·a gri; soa sima gri.
Sound (sound), *n.* Gam·a; tu·-gijagipa sagal.
Soup (sụp), *n.* Sorua ritgimin, ringani bitchi.
Sour (sour), *a.* Mesenggipa.
Source (sōrs), *n.* Ong·katram, a·bachengram, nabaram.
South (south), *n.* Salgipeng.
Southern (sŭTH'ērn), *a.* Salgi-pengchigipa.
Southward (south-wērd), *adv.* Salgipengchi pak.
Sovereign (sŭv'êr-in ba sŏv-), *n.* Raja; England songni tangka ma·sa, poundsa, gong·chibong-ani pal.
Sow (sō), *v.* Bitchri sata.
Sow (sou), *n.* Wak bima.
Space (spās), *n.* Gisepgrikni biap.
Spacious (spā'shus), *a.* Apalani biding.

Spade (spād), *n.* Chamos dal·gipa ma·sa, sobol.

Span (spăn), *n.* Krusa; fathom sani bak chetni bak sa ba inch sku; gongdule rikgimin ja·pangni chel·grikani.

Spanish (spăn'ish), *a.* Spain songni biding.

Spank (spăngk), *v.* Ki·sango doktopa.

Spare (spâr), *a.* Gitchagipa; ram·gipa, mangchenggram-gipa. *v.* On·a, wata, kema ka·a.

Spark (spärk), *n.* Wal·misi.

Sparkle (spär'k'l), *v.* Ching·cheta.

Sparrow (spăr'ro), *n.* Do·chok ma·sa.

Spasm (spăz''m), *n.* Ja·dilrangni salkomtotani.

Spat (spăt), *v.* Ka·sine doktopa; on·tisa jegrika.

Spatter (spăt'têr), *v.* A·dubek satdapa, chi satchima.

Spawn (spôn), *n.* Na·tok bitchi. *v.*

Speak (spēk), *v.* SPOKE, Agana.

Spear (spēr), *n.* Sel·u. *v.* Sel·uchi su·a.

Special (spĕsh'al), *a.* Dingtang-manchagipa, mongsonggipa.

Specie (spē'shĭ), *n.* Silni tangka-rang.

Species (spē'shēz), *n.* Ma·a, ro-kom.

Specific (spe-sĭf'ik), *a.* Ding-tangmancha tik ka·gimin.

Specify (spĕs'ĭ-fī), *v.* Tikko me-soka. **-ication,** *n.*

Specimen (spĕs'ĭ-men), *n.* Bo-komko niatna mesokani; no-muna.

Speck (spĕk), *n.* Chonchonbe-gipa dak.

Spectacle (spĕk'tă-k'l), *n.* Nik-ronggijagipa maiba niani.

Spectacles (spĕk'tă-k'ls), *n.* Mikrono niani janera, chosma.

Spectator (spĕk-tā'têr), *n.* Ni-gipa.

Specter, Spectre (spĕk'têr), *n.* Me·mang. **Spectral,** *a.*

Speculate (spĕk'u-lāt), *v.* Dam rakbato palskana bree dona; gisiko chanchie niroka. **-ive,** *a.*

Speech (spēch), *n.* Jinmana aganani kata; aganani bil; ku'sik.

Speed (spēd), *n.* Gong·rakani, ta·rakani.

Speed (spēd), *v.* SPED, Gong·rakata, ta·rakata.

Spell (spĕl), *v.* SPELLED, SPELT, Banan ka·a; gipinko neng·takatoa on·tisa ka·skaa; bodol nang·takata.

Spend (spĕnd), *v.* SPENT, SPENT, Re·ata; koroch ka·a.

Spendthrift (spĕnd'thrĭft'), *n.* Rusigipa, koroch ka·begipa.

Spew (spū), *v.* Chisata, el·bua, wakala.

Sphere (sfēr), *n.* Tom·betgipa.

Sphinx (sfĭngks), *n.* Misor songni ro·ongko sol·gimin, mikkang me·chik gita aro be·en singho gita dakgipa.

Spice (spīs), *n.* Smilgipa mo-sla.

Spider (spī'dêr), *n.* Guang.

Spike (spīk), Gojal dal·gipa; mini bidang.

Spill (spĭl), *v.* SPILT, Nasiata.

Spin (spĭn), *v.* SPAN, SPUN, Kil-ding rika; bakroata; wilwil-ata.

Spinal (spī'nal), *n.* Janggil bol-groni biding.

Spindle (spĭn'd'l), *n*. Kilding rikani takuri.

Spine (spīn), *n*. Janggil bolgro.

Spinning-wheel (spĭn'ning whēl'), *n*. Kilding rikani jontol, charrangga.

Spinster (spĭn'stĕr), *n*. Se kimkujagipa me'chik.

Spiral (spī'ral), *a*. Wendogipa, wenani biding.

Spire (spīr), *n*. Gilja nokni protchong, ku'chot.

Spirit (spĭr'ĭt), *n*. Gisik katchi, janggi.

Spirited (spĭr'ĭt-ĕd), *n*. Nachilarigipa; kal'grikani gisik gapgipa.

Spirits (spĭr'ĭts), *n*. Pekgatipa churang; kal'grikani ba nachilakani gisik.

Spiritual (spĭr'ĭt u-al), *a*. Isol ba toromni biding.

Spit (spĭt), *v*. SPIT, Stua, ku'chi ong'a. *n*. Stu; gosura gol'sok.

Spite (spīt), *n*. Miknengani, jakbikpilna skani.

In spite of (ĭn-spīt'ŏv), *adv*. Minggija.

Spittle (spĭt't'l), *n*. Stu.

Splash (splăsh), *v*. Sãtchima.

Spleen (splēn), *n*. Pilai, okpil.

Splendor -our (splĕn'dĕr), *n*. Nitoani, ching'beani.

Splice (splīs), *v*. Ritchua, joraa. *n*.

Splinter (splĭn'tĕr), *n*. Bichrit.

Splinter (splĭn'tĕr), *v*. Pitsria, pitmisia, *n*.

Split (splĭt), *v*. SPLIT, Pita.

Spoil (spoil), *v*. Gimaata, nisiata, soe gimara.

Spoke (spōk), *v*. *speak*ko nibo.

Spoke (spōk), *n*. Gari chakao peng'pange datgipa bol.

Sponge (spŭnj), *n*. Sagalo chagipa ma'sa, chi sepdape auna jeko jakkalronga.

Spool (spōōl), *n*. Kilding wenani bol.

Spoon (spōōn), *n*. Chamos.

Sport (spōrt), *n*. Kal'grikani, sikar ka'ani.

Sportsman (spōrts'man), *n*. Sikar ka'gipa.

Spot (spŏt), *n*. Dak, chia; biap.

Spotted (spŏt'tĕd), *a*. Toka gnanggipa.

Spouse (spouz), *n*. Jik se kimgimin mande.

Spout (spout), *n*. Chi jokatani ku'mang.

Spout (spout), *v*. Tang'doeong'kata.

Sprawl (sprôl), *v*. Tue ja'a jakko gowingwange il'eng pileng daka.

Sprain (sprān), *n*. Be'enko sakmrenani, biritchu ringretani.

Sprang (sprăng), *v*. *Spring*ko nibo.

Spray (sprā), *n*. Chipakkore ratani chi.

Spread (sprĕd), *v*. Badala, gipa.

Spring (sprĭng), *n*. Sam bolrang ritimbachengani kari, March, April aro May ia jaarang; bildoani, sikchepna aro badalna ba tang'doatna tang'onatna man'gipa maiba kon'gimin; chimik.

Spring (sprĭng), *v*. SPRANG, SPRUNG, Bimik naa, ong'kata; bildoa, bilchroka.

Sprinkle (sprĭngk''l), *v*. Satkikia; wasisia; pudrapa.

Sprout (sprout), *n*. Bimik, bijak jakgital. *v*. Bimik naa.

Sprung (sprung), *v*. *Spring*ko nibo.

Spry (sprī), *a*. Mamungkoba dakna ta·rakgipa.
Spun (spŭn), *v*. *Spin*ko nibo.
Spunk (spŭnk), *n*. Jeba ong·-chong dakani, mamungkoba minggija dakani.
Spur (spêr), *n*. Do·o ja·sing, do·o ja·ching ; su·ani ba·su.
Spurious (spū'rĭ-ŭs), *a*. Bebe ong·gijani biding.
Spurn (spêrn), *v*. Ga·tinga ; chonnika.
Spurt (spêrt), *v*. Tang·srota.
Sputter (spŭt'têr), *v*. Talsrang-gija agana, to·tara.
Spy (spī), *n*. Nirikkigipa.
Spyglass (spī'glås'), *n*. Chel·-aoniko niani durbin.
Squabble (skwŏb'b'l), *n*. Jegrik-ani, ra·sekgrikani.
Squad (skwŏd), *n*. Bang·gija sipaini kotok, chongipa kotok.
Squadron (skwŏd'rŭn), *n*. Si-pai kotok ; dakgrikani jahat jinma.
Squalid (skwŏl'id), *a*. An·-chuek bang·begipa, moilabe-gipa.
Squall (skwôl), *n*. Chrika ; rang·-san ta·rake bal balani. *v*.
Squander (skwŏn'dêr), *v*. Rusia, sate gala, simsakgija tangka-ko koroch ka·a.
Square (skwâr), *n*. Mistrirang-ni toani ma·sa ; borgo.
Square (skwâr), *a*. Ki·tik bri aro rikam sambri apsangipa.
Squash (skwŏsh), *n*. Akkaru ma·sa.
Squash (skwŏsh), *v*. Nol·emu dalgapata.
Squat (skwŏt), *v*. Asong chong·-prua.
Squawk (skwôk), *v*. Gam·e chrika.
Squeak (skwēk), *v*. Tengkrange chrika.
Squeal (skwēl), *v*. Ku·sikchi chrika.
Squeeze (skwēz), *v*. Sinjeta, rim·jeta.
Squint (skwĭnt), *v*. Mikkelai dake nia.
Squirm (skwêrm), *v*. Gong·geng bakeng daka.
Squirrel (skwêr'rĕl), *n*. Mat, gredong.
Squirt (skwêrt), *v*. Serka maria, satchima.
Stab (stăb), *v*. Su·a, jotprota.
Stable (stā'b'l), *n*. Gure donani nok, gure ba matchu nol.
Stack (stăk), *n*. Megap ba am·-prangni tongbol.
Staff (ståf), *n*. Go·ol, gol·dik.
Stag (stăg), *n*. Matchok bipa.
Stage (stāj), *n*. Rama re·ani tong·sa ; chue rikgimin agan-gipani a·songani ba chadengani.
Stage coach (stāj'kōch'), *n*. Ba-ra on·ani gari, keria on·ani gari.
Stagger (stăg'gêr), *v*. Ching-reng chingpeng ba gitching gitchong daka.
Stagnant (stăg'nant), *a*. Jok-gijagipa chi moila, chiklokni chi gita.
Stain (stān), *v*. Marang nanga, dak nanga. *n*.
Stairs (stârs), *n*. Kosakgipa ga-dangchina re·angani ro·gipa jang·ke.
Staircase (stâr'kās'), } *n*. Ko-
Stairway (stâr'wā'), } sakchi-na gakatangani jang·ke.
Stake (stāk), *n*. Gol·chong chongli, milong.
Stale (stāl), *a*. Gitcham ; soba-enggipa ; simgimin.

Stalk (stôk), *v.* Be·enko dal·ate re·a.

Stall (stôl), *n.* Gure mangprakni kutori, antidamo sakprakprakni palram biap.

Stallion (stăl'yŭn), *n.* Kasigijagipa gure.

Stalwart (stŏl'wêrt ba stôl'), *a.* Dal·gipa, bilakgipa.

Stammer (stăm'mêr), *v.* Ku·sik to·tara.

Stamp (stămp), *n.* Mohor ; tiket ; mohor su·gimin.

Stamp (stămp), *v.* Ga·tima ; mohor su·a.

Stampede (stăm'pēd'), *v.* Matchu ba gureni kenne katgrima.

Stand (stănd), *n.* Chadengani ba donani biap, chongipa tebil, *table.*

Stand (stănd), *v.* STOOD, Chadenga, donga, dongdika.

Standard (stănd'êrd), *n.* Nisan ; namsranggipa ; je baksa gipinko toa.

Staple (sta'p'l), *n.* Bisring, silni nabak.

Star (stär), *n.* Aski.

Starch (stärch), *n.* Men·di.

Stare (stâr), *v.* Nitata.

Start (stärt), *v.* Re·chakata ; a·bachenga ; to·tro ong·a.

Startle (stär't'l), *v.* Kenata, to·tro ong·ata.

Starve (stärv), *v.* Cha·aniko man·jani gimin okkrie sia.

State (stāt), *n.* Ong·ani, obosta ; raijo.

State (stāt), *v.* Katako agana.

Statesman (stāts'man), *n.* Governmentni niamko uigipa.

Station (stā'shŭn), *n.* Dongani, donani ba dongdikani biap ; mandeni dongani obosta.

Stationary (stā'shŭn-a-ry), *a.* Kimkim ba uan uan dongaigipa.

Stationer (stā'shŭn-êr), *n.* Leka, kali, kolom, iarangko palgipa.

Stationery (stā'shŭn-êr-y), *n.* Leka, kali, kolom iarang.

Statuary (stăt'u-a-ry), *n.* Bimang dakako sol·gimin ba sol·gipa.

Statue (stăt'u), *n.* Sol·gimin bimang.

Stature (stăt'ur), *n.* Bimangni chua.

Statute (stăt'ut), *n.* Niam ge·etarang.

Stanch, Staunch (stănch), *v.* Tipata ; bon ka·a ; *a.* Raka, bilaka, mangraka, kimkim.

Stave (stāv), *v.* STAVED ba STOVE, Dokprua, pe·e gala.

Stave off (stāv ŏf), *v.* Jitpakata.

Stay (stā), *v.* STAYED ba STAID, Donga, dongrika ; pangchaka ; champenga, dongdikata.

Stead (stĕd), *n.* Pal ; biap.

Steadfast (stĕd'fast), *a.* Kimkim, mangraka.

Steady (stĕd'y), *a.* Il·enggija ; mogija ; uan uan ; tom·tom.

Steak (stāk), *n.* Jo·na ba so·na tarigimin be·en bitin.

Steal (stēl), *v.* STOLE, Cha·ua.

Steam (stēm), *n.* Biba.

Steamer (stēm'êr), *n.* Bibachi re·gipa jahat ; bibachi song·chakani.

Steed (stēd), *n.* Namgipa gure.

Steel (stēl), *n.* Silchi.

Steep (stēp), *v.* Chio dim·a.

Steep (stēp), *a.* A·solsol ba dare dakgipa.

Steeple (stē'p'l), *n.* Gilja nokni protchong.

Steer (stēr), *n*. Matchu bolot, bidom.
Steer (stēr), *v*. Ki·me pe·ata.
Steerage (stēr'aj), *n*. Jahatni ki·sangchini bara mande dongram.
Stem (stĕm), *n*. Bibalni ga·tong, ga·tong.
Stench (stĕnch), *n*. Seengbeani bisak babiba.
Step (stĕp), *n*. Ja·ku; jang·ke; jang·ke teng·prak.
Step (stĕp), *v*. Ja·ku ga·a.
Step-brother (stĕp'brŭтн'ẽr), *n*. De gnanggipa tanggitikrang kimgrikode saksani depante sakgipinni deni step-brother ong·a.
Step-daughter (stĕp'dô'tẽr), *n*. Jik gitcham ba se gitchamni demechik kimtaigipa me·asa ba me·chickni step-daughter ong·a.
Step-father (stĕp' fäтнẽr), *n*. Wanggipa, pachong·motni simano ma·ani kimtaigipa paa.
Step-mother (stĕp'mŭтн'ẽr), *n*. Ma·detang, ma·a chong·motni simano pani kimtaigipa ma·a.
Step-sister (stĕp'sĭs'tẽr), *n*. De gnanggipa tanggitikrang kimgrikode saksani demechik sakgipinni deni step-sister ong·a.
Step-son (stĕp'sŭn'), *n*. Jikgitcham ba segitchamni depante kimtaigipa me·asa ba me·chikni step-son ong·a
Stereopticon (stē're-ŏp'tĭk-ŏn), *n*. Wa·alchi noksako mesokatani.
Stereoscope (stē're-o-skōp), *n*. Mikron ronggnina niani donggipa noksa niani.
Sterile (stĕr'ĭl), *a*. Bite nanggijagipa; a·sal grigipa; bañijagipa.
Sterling (stẽr'lĭng), *n*. Tik ong·gipa tangka, mongsongde England songni tangka.
Stern (stẽrn), *n*. Jahatni ki·sangchinigipa. *a*. Rakgipa, mangnamgijagipa.
Stethoscope (stĕth'o-skōp), *n*. Be·en ning·chini gam·ako knatimani.
Stew (stū), *v*. Ka·sne ka·sne rita ba minata.
Steward (stū'ẽrd), *n*. Nokni nokol pamong; on·timgipa.
Stick (stĭk), *n*. Go·ol; gol·dik; bolcheksi; bol chongipa.
Stick (stĭk), *v*, STUCK, Ma·gapa, stapa.
Stiff (stĭf), *a*. Raka, dol·na amgijagipa.
Stiffen (stĭf'n), *v*. Rakata, dol·na amgija dakata.
Stile (stīl), *n*. Jang·batra.
Still (stĭl), *a*. Il·enggija; tom·tom; jripjrip.
Still (stĭl), *v*. Jripata; tom·toma·a.
Still (stĭl), *adv*. Piti, -ku- .
Stilts (stĭlts), *n*. Ja·bengbang ga·ani wa·a.
Stimulate (stim'u-lāt), *v*. Didiata; bilakdapata. -**or**, -**ion**, *n*.
Sting (sting), *v*. STUNG, STUNG, Birichi dela, saknaata. *n*. Biri.
Stingy (stĭn'jy), *a*. Gipinna on·na sikgijagipa, man·gopna sikgipa.
Stink (stĭngk), *n*. Seengani biba.
Stink (stĭngk), *v*. STANK, STUNK. Seenga.

Stipend (sti'pĕnd), *n*. Koraki, beton.

Stipendiary (sti-pĕn'di-a-ry), *n*. Korak cha·gipa.

Stipulate (stĭp'u-lat), *v*. Dakna nangako tiktak agansoa, tik ka·griksoa.

Stir (stêr), *v*. Jingjengata, wingwangata, il·engata, il·enga.

Stirrup (stŭr'rŭp ba stir'rŭp), *n*. Gure jinni ja·a ga·chakani.

Stitch (stĭtch), *n*. Koani ge·sa.

Stock (stŏk), *n*. Ja·pang; bipang; tangka bima; jilarang; donsogimin; slai kunda.

Stocks (stŏks), *n*. Ja·king tekani.

Stockade (stŏk-ād'), *n*. Bolchi kagimin guare ba killa.

Stocking (stŏk'ing), *n*. Muja, ja·o kruani.

Stole (stōl), *v*. *Steal*ko nibo.

Stomach (stŭm'ak), *n*. Bimema.

Stone (stōn), *n*. Ro·ong, rong·te.

Stone (stōn), *v*. Ro·ongchi goa ba gotata.

Stony (stō'ny), *a*. Ro·ongrara, rong·grim.

Stood (stụd), *v*. *Stand*ko nibo.

Stool (stụl), *n*. Am·pok.

Stoop (stụp), *v*. Bamgopa, gonggonga.

Stop (stŏp), *v*. Dongdika, neng·taka; dondikata, dongtongata.

Store (stōr), *n*. Chimonge donram, gudam; dokan.

Store (stōr), *v*. Chimonge donsoa.

Store-house (stōr'hous'), *n*. Bandal, gudam, jam.

Stork (stôrk), *n*. Halgila do·o ma·sa.

Storm (stôrm), *n*. Ta·rakbegipa mika balwa.

Storm (stôrm), *v*. Bilake chaa.

Story (stō'ry), *n*. Kata, golpo; gadang.

Stout (stout), *a*. Bilaka; mila.

Stove (stōv), *n*. Wa·al sikani ba mi song·chakani chankol.

Stove (stōv), *v*. *Stave*ko nibo.

Stow (stō), *v*. Simsake dona, chimonge dona.

Straddle (străd'd'l), *v*. Ja·ako ga·krange re·a; ja·pak sepe gakata.

Straggle (străg'g'l), *v*. Iachi uchi re·roroa.

Straight (strāt), *a*. Sronga, dingbrenga; tongtong.

Straightway (strāt' wā'), *adv*. Da·on, bakan.

Strain (strān), *v*. Salkringa; sakmrena; cheka.

Strait (strāt), *n*. Chi apgitok, apgitok.

Strait (strāt), *a*. Apchona, apchangket.

Straiten (strāt''n), *v*. Apchonata, apchangket dakata.

Strand (strănd), *n*. Chi rikam; budu sakani gun.

Strange (strānj), *a*. Nikronggija, uigija; aiao inmangni.

Stranger (strān'jêr), *n*. Songgipinni mande; uigija mande; mande a·gital.

Strangle (străng'g'l), *v*. Rim·eke so·ota, rang·sitaniko bon ka·e so·ota.

Strap (străp), *n*. Tarigimin ro·dinggipa matbigil.

Stratagem (străt'a-jêm), *n*. Bobilko bingbangatna ba gualatna chol dakani.

Strategy (strătе-jy), *n*. Chanchina changgipani chol dakani, chalaki dakani.

Straw (strô), *n*. Megap.

Strawberry (strô'bĕr-ry), *n*. Chongipa bite ma·sa.

Stray (strā), *v*. Branga.

Streak (strēk), *n*. Ro·ding ro·ding dake nanggipa moila ba salsretani.

Streaked (strēkt ba strēk'ĕd), *a*. Tongtonggija salsrete toka, bakroe mrikmrak daka.

Stream (strēm), *n*. Chibima; jokgipa chiring.

Stream (strēm), *v*. Jokruraa; joksolsola.

Street (strēt), *n*. Songjinmani sorok.

Strength (strĕngth), *n*. Bil.

Strengthen (strĕngth''n), *v*. Bilakata, bilakdapata.

Stretch (strĕtch), *v*. Badala; gipata; salkringa.

Strew (strŏ ba strō), *v*. Satpripraa, satbildanga.

Stricken (strĭk''n), *a*. Dokgimin.

Strict (strĭkt), *a*. Tiktak dakgipa.

Stride (strīd), *n*. Ja·ku ro·begipa. *v*.

Strife (strīf), *n*. Jegrikani, dakgrikani, susagrikani.

Strike (strīk), *v*. STRUCK, STRUCK, Doka.

Striking (strīk'ing), *a*. Aiao inmangni; miksongatgni.

String (strĭng), *n*. Chongipa budu, kilding, bisring.

String (strĭng), *v*. STRUNG, STRUNG. Ripok sika, rengsi sika.

Stringer (strĭng'ĕr), *n*. Ripok sikgipa; jang·rang ning·chi chanbatgipa bol.

Strip (strĭp), *n*. Maibani ro·dinggipa bichrit.

Strip (strĭp), *v*. Kika. nagande dakata, bigil kika.

Stripe (strīp), *n*. Bet dokani chin, maiba ro·gipa chin; ro·dingding salgipa.

Stripling (strĭp'ling), *n*. Brikujagipa paute, mangchenggramgipa.

Strive (strīv), *v*. STROVE, STRIVEN, Tikkela.

Stroke (strōk), *n*. Dokani, salani.

Stroke (strōk), *v*. Rim roka.

Stroll (strōl), *v*. Re·roroa, rororoa.

Strong (strŏng), *a*. Bilakgipa, an·senggipa.

Stronghold (strŏng'hōld'), *n*. Kila, rakgipa guarechi kadulgimin.

Strove (strōv), *v*. *Strive*ko nibo.

Struck (strŭk), *v*. *Strike*ko nibo.

Structure (strŭk'tur), *n*. Rikgimin, nok.

Struggle (strŭg'g'l), *v*. Joton ka·bea, gogoteka, gojrona.

Strung (strŭng), *v*. *Strike*ko nibo.

Strut (strŭt), *v*. Gaorade·e be·enko dal·ate re·a, gangbinge mesoka.

Strychnine (strĭk'nĭn ba -nēn), *n*. Matcha bisi ma·sa.

Stub (stŭb), *n*. Be·tongspa, chong·dok.

Stubble (stŭb'b'l), *n*. Den·spa, ja·pang.

Stubborn (stŭb'bêrn), *a*. Skatang dakaina mangsonggipa.

Stud (stŭd), *n*. Jelatna jilgipa gure jinma; songdogipa reil, chongipa krong; kamijni butam.

Student (stū'dent), *n*. Ki·tapko poraibegipa, skulo poraigipa, chatro.
Study (stŭd'y), *v*. Poraia, chanchia.
Stuff (stŭf), *n*. Jeoniko bosturangko dakna man·a; nanggija galani, jabol.
Stuff (stŭf), *v*. Siktentene gapata, namen gapata.
Stuffing (stŭf'fing), *n*. Be·enko su·uatani ba gapatani.
Stumble (stŭm'b'l), *v*. Ja·gidota.
Stumbling-block (stŭm'bling-blŏk'), *n*. Ja·gidotani, champengani.
Stump (stŭmp), *n*. Den·gimin bolni ja·pang, bolchongdik.
Stun (stŭn), *v*. Doke sibokata.
Stung (stŭng), *v*. *Sting*ko nibo.
Stunk (stŭnk), *v*. *Stink*ko nibo.
Stunt (stŭnt), *v*. Dal·gniko champenga, chonata.
Stupendous (stu-pĕn'dŭs), *a*. Aiao inmane dal·gipa, dal·begipa.
Stupefy, Stupify (stū'pe-fī), *v*. Goka ong·a·a, uigija dakata.
Stupid (stū'pĭd), *a*. Gokagipa, uininggijagipa.
Sturdy (stêr'dy), *a*. Bilakgipa, rakgipa.
Stutter (stŭt'têr), *v*. To·tara.
Sty (stī), *n*. Mikil to·sok mina; wak nol.
Style (stīl), *v*. Bimung minga, bimung dona.
Style (stīl), *n*. Katako aganani ba seani bewal, dakani, ganani ba aganani bewal.
Sub- (sŭb), A·bachengao segipa *prefix*rangko nibo.
Subdivide (sŭb'dĭ-vīd'), *v*. Sualtaia, chone bak daktaia.
Subdue (sŭb-dū'), *v*. Bamata.
Subject (sŭb'jĕkt), *n*. Raiot; kata ma·chong.
Subject (sŭb'jĕkt), *a*. Gipinni ning·o donggipa.
Subject (sŭb-jĕkt'), *v*. Bamata, ning·o ong·ata. **-ion**, *n*.
Subjugate (sŭb'ju-gāt), *v*. Bamata.
Sublime (sŭb-līm'), *a*. Dal·gipa, chugipa.
Submerge (sŭb-mêrj'), *v*. Chiningo napa, dubia.
Submission (sŭb-mĭsh'ŭn), *n*. Ge·eta ra·ani, bamani.
Submit (sŭb-mĭt'), *v*. Bama, mania; ona.
Subordinate (sŭb-ôr'dĭ-nat), *a*. Ning·o donggipa. *v*.
Subscribe (sŭb-skrīb'), *v*. Maiba katako ku·rachake bimungko sea, ku·rachaka.
Subsequent (sŭb'se-kwent), *a*. Ja·man ong·gipa.
Subside (sŭb-sīd'), *v*. Komia, rooka; tipa; ka·sina.
Subsist (sŭb-sĭst'), *v*. Janggi tanga.
Subsistence (sŭb-sĭst'ens), *n*. Janggi tangani.
Substance (sŭb'stans), *n*. Bicham, maiba ong·ani ba katani ja·pang.
Substantial (sŭb-stăn'shal), *a*. Ja·pang gnanggipa, mangrakgipa.
Substitute (sŭb'stĭ-tūt), *v*. Bodol dona, pal dona. *n*.
Subterranean (sŭb'tĕr-rā'nean), *a*. A·a ning·onigipa.
Subtile (sŭb'tĭl ba sŭt''l), *a*. Chongipa; ba·gipa; chalaki.
Subtract (sŭb-trăkt'), *v*. Bang·aoniko ra·anga, biog ka·a. **-ion**, *n*.

Subtrahend (sŭb'trâ-hĕnd'), *n.* Chonatgipa, biog ka·gnigipa, re·angatgnigipa.
Suburbs (sŭb'êrbs), *n.* Songjinmani sepango donggipa songrang.
Subway (sŭb'wā'), *n.* A·a ning·ko dakgipa rama.
Succeed (sŭk-sēd'), *v.* Ja·chong donga ; chu·sokata.
Success (sŭk-sĕs'), *n.* Chu·sokatani.
Succession (sŭk-sĕsh'ŭn), *n.* Riting riting ong·ani, ja·rikrikani.
Succor (sŭk'kêr), *n.* Dakchakani, *v.* Dakchaka.
Succumb (sŭk-kŭm'), *v.* Warachakako wata, bima.
Such (sŭch), *a.* Indake ba ugita.
Suck (sŭk), *v.* Opa, salopa.
Suckle (sŭk'k'l), *v.* Sok kana.
Suckling (sŭk'lĭng), *a.* Sok cha·gipa bi·sa, bakgitchak.
Suction (sŭk'shŭn), *n.* Salopani.
Sudden (sŭd'dĕn), *a.* Rang·san.
Suds (sŭds), *n.* Sabon aro chini ka·spu.
Sue (sū), *v.* Mol·mola ; nalis ka·a.
Suet (sū'ĕt), *n.* Mitim, gilani sepango donggipa mitim.
Suffer (sŭf'fêr), *v.* Chakchika, ongna on·a.
Sufficient (sŭf-fĭsh'ent), *a.* Chu·ong·a, bang·a.
Suffix (sŭf'fiks), *n.* Suffixni gimin a·bachengachi seako nibo.
Suffocate (sŭf'fo-kāt), *v.* Rang·sitaniko peng·ata.
Suffuse (sŭf-fūz'), *v.* Gipata, chipata.
Sugar (shụg'êr), *n.* Chini.
Sugarcandy (shụg'êr-kăn'dy), *n.* Misri.
Sugarcane (shụg'êr-kān'), *n.* Grit.
Suggest (sŏg'jĕst' ba sŭd-jĕst'), *v.* Janapa, naata.
Suicide (sū'ĭ-sīd), *n.* A·tangko so·otani ; a·tangko so·otgipa.
Suit (sūt), *n.* Mokordoma ; mol·molani.
Suit (sūt), *v.* Krara, ma·gapa.
Sully (sŭl'ly), *v.* Moila nangata.
Sulk (sŭlk), *v.* Ning·joljol ka·onanga.
Sulphur (sŭl'fŭr), *n.* Gondok.
Sultan (sŭl'tan Arabic sụl-tän'), *n.* Turusko songni raja.
Sum (sŭm), *n.* Chandimani gimik.
Summary (sŭm'mâ-ry), *n.* Kan·dikate ra·chimonggimin, mangsongako ba ja·pangrangko mesokani.
Summer (sŭm'mêr) *n.* Ding·kari, June, July, August ia jarang.
Summit (sŭm'mĭt), *n.* Ku·chot, a·kimbri.
Summon (sŭm'mŭn), *v.* Okamata, somon on·a, okamchimongata.
Sun (sŭn), *n.* Sal.
Sunbeam (sŭn'bēm'), *n.* Sal teng·suani ja·dil, sal ja·dil.
Sunburnt (sŭn'bêrnt), *a.* Sal kamgimin.
Sunday (sŭn'da), *n.* Robibar.
Sunder (sŭn'dêr), *v.* Dingtang dakata.
Sundial (sŭn'dī-al), *n.* Salni salakimchi bajiko mesokani.
Sundry (sŭn'dry), *a.* Ma·manti.
Sundown (sŭn'doun), *n.* Sal napmanahani.
Sung (sŭng), *v.* *Singko* nibo.

Sunk (sŭngk), *v.* *Sinkko* nibo.
Sunlight (sŭn'līt'), *n.* Salni teng·a.
Sunrise (sŭn'rīz'), *n.* Sal naani.
Sunset (sŭn'sĕt'), *n.* Sal napani.
Sunshine (sŭn'shīn'), *n.* Salni teng·sua.
Super (sū'pêr), *n.* Kosakgipa, kosakni ; *prefix* rangkoba nibo.
Superabundance (sū'pêr-ā-bŭn'-*da*ns), *n.* Namen agreani.
Superb (su-pêrb'), *a.* Dal·gipa, namgipa, nitogipa, aiao inmangni.
Superficial (sū'pêr-fĭsh'*a*l), *a.* A·palchinigipa, kosaknigipa.
Superfine (sū'pêr-fīn), *a.* Namen nambegipa, nambatbegipa.
Superfluous (su-pêr'flu-ŭs), *a.* Agregipa, nangana agregipa.
Superintendent (su'-pêr-ĭn-tĕn'd*e*nt), *n.* Kamko mesoktimgipa, nirokgipa.
Superior (su-pē'rĭ êr), *a.* Nambatgipa, chubatgipa.
Superlative (su-pêr'lā-tĭv), *a.* Pilakna bate batgipa.
Supernatural (sū'pêr-năt'u-r*a*l), *a.* Ong·ronggija, ong·rongana bate batgipa.
Superscribe (sū'pêr-skrīb'), *v.* Kosako ba a·palo sedapa.
Superstition (sū'pêr-stĭsh'ŭn), *n.* Ong·gijani torom, ong·gija bebe ra·arang.
Superstructure (sū'pêr strŭk'-tur), *n.* Kosako rikani.
Supervise (sū'pêr-vīs'), *v.* Pamong daka, niroka, mesoktima.
Supper (sŭp'pêr), *n.* Meatam, atamo cha·ani.
Supplant (sŭp'plănt'), *v.* Maiba cholchi biap ba kamko man·skaa.
Supple (sŭp'p'l), *a.* Dol·ning gipa, kon·na man·gipa.
Supplement (sŭp'ple-m*e*nt), *n.* On·dapani ba matchotatani tong·sa.
Supply (sŭp-plī'), *v.* Ra·bac on·a, nangako on·a.
Support (sŭp-pōrt'), *v.* Aldua, rim·chaka. ra·chaka.
Suppose (sŭp-pōz'), *v.* Chanchichipa.
Suppress (sŭp-prĕs'), *v.* Rim·-penga, sinjeta, bon·ata.
Supreme (sū-prēm'), *a.* Chubatgipa, dal·batgipa.
Sure (shụr), *a.* Chong·motgipa, uichong·motgipa, kenchaka grigipa.
Surety (shụr'ty), *n.* Jamin ; pangchakani.
Surf (sêrf), *n.* Rikamchina satpekgipa sagalni chipakkore.
Surface (sêr'fas), *n.* A·palni, kosakni.
Surgeon (sêr'j n), *n.* Mandeni be·enko rana changgipa daktor.
Surly (sêr'ly), *a.* Ning·joljol ka·onangako mesokgipa.
Surmise (sêr'mīz'), *v.* chanchichipa. *n.*
Surmount (sêr-mount'), *v.* Batanga, gakata, ama.
Surname (sêr'nām'), *n.* Ma·-chongni bimung. *v.*
Surpass (sêr-pȧs'), *v.* Bata.
Surprise (sêr-prīz'), *v.* Aiao inmanata ; chachipa, rang·san rim·a.
Surrender (sŭr-rĕn'dêr), *v.* Bama, a·tangko bobilni jako on·a.
Surround (sŭr-round'), *v.* Dula.
Survey (sŭr-vā'), *v.* Namedake nia ; a·ako toa.

Survive (sŭr-vīv'), *v.* Gipinni simano tange dongrika, tange dongkua.

Suspect (sŭs-pĕkt'), *v.* Kenchak-a, chanchichipa, donga ine chanchia.

Suspend (sŭs-pĕnd'), *v.* Kadingdea; dondikata.

Suspension (sŭs-pĕn'shŏn), *n.* Adita salna dondikatani; kadingdeani.

Suspicion (sŭs-pĭsh'-ŭn), *n.* Kenchakani. *Suspect*ni *n.*

Sustain (sŭs-tān'), *v.* Rim'chak-a. chakchika, aldua.

Swab (swŏb), *n.* Soriate moilako ipakani, wagam natani.

Swallow (swŏl'lo), *v.* Minoka.

Swallow (swŏl'lo), *n.* Do'rong, do'matchi.

Swam (swăm), *v.* *Swim*ko nibo.

Swamp (swŏmp), *n.* Chibitek, chidipek, chibol, drop.

Swan (swŏn), *n.* Rajahas ma'sa.

Swap (swŏp), *v.* On'srea.

Swarm (swôrm), *n.* Jak jinma, ma'dima. *v.*

Swash (swŏsh), *v.* Chiko wingwangata.

Sway (swā), *n.* Nokgipa ong'-ani, sason ka'ani.

Sway (swā), *v.* Wingwanga, moata.

Swear (swâr), *v.* SWORE, SWORN, Mikcheta.

Sweat (swĕt), *n.* Ding'ol, gramchi. *v.*

Sweep (swēp), *v.* SWEPT, Itroka.

Sweet (swēt), *a.* Chi'a, toa, smila, nitoa, knatoa.

Sweeten (swēt''n), *v.* Chi'ata.

Sweetheart (swēt härt)', *n.* Jena ka'saboa.

Sweetmeat (swēt'mēt), *n.* Chi'a' cha'ani, mitairang.

Swell (swĕl), *v.* SWELLED, SWOLLEN. Gangbua, ripima.

Swept (swĕpt), *v.* *Sweep*ko nibo.

Swift (swift), *a.* Gong'raka.

Swim (swim), *v.* SWAM, SWUM, Jroa, chio jroa.

Swindle (swin'd'l), *v.* Togia, cha'ua.

Swine (swīn), *n.* Wak.

Swing (swing), *v.* SWUNG, Wingwanga.

Switch (swĭtch), *n.* Gol'sri; silni ramao gari re'aniko dingtang dakatani.

Swivel (swĭv''l), *n.* Silitingni wilwilchakani.

Swollen (swōl''n), *v.* *Swell*ko nibo.

Swoon (swōōn), *v.* Siboka.

Swoop (swōōp), *v.* Chapake rim'-a.

Sword (sōrd), *n.* Tonual, mil'-am.

Swore (swōr), *v.* *Swear*ko nibo.

Swum (swŭm), *v.* *Swim*ko nibo.

Swung (swŭng), *v.* *Swing*ko nibo.

Syllable (sĭl'lă-b'l), *n.* Adita oikorrangko damsan gam'atani, silebil.

Symbol (sĭm'bŏl), *n.* Mesokani, toani, niani, chin.

Symbolize (sĭm'bŏl-īz), *v.* Toanichi uiata.

Symmetry (sĭm'me-try), *n.* Bakrangni krae nangrimani.

Sympathize (sĭm'pă-thīz), *v.* Gipinni duk suk ong'ao ong'-para

Sympathy (sĭm'pă-thy), *n.* Duk suk ong'paani.

Symptom (sĭm'tŭm), *n.* Chin, be'en saani chin.

Synagogue (sĭn'ă-gŏg), *n.* Jihudirangni olakiram nok.
Synonym (sĭn'o-nĭm), *n.* Orto sepanggrikgipa kata ge·sa.
Synopsis (sĭn-op'sĭs), *n.* Kan·dike ra·dimgimin.
Syringe (sĭr'ĭnj), *n.* Selka.
System (sĭs'tĕm), *n.* Adita bang·ani niam gita nangrimgimin.
Systematic (sĭs'tĕm-ăt'ĭk), *a.* Nangrimani niam gita.

T.

Tabernacle (tăb'ĕr-nă-k'l), *n.* Olakiani tambu.
Table (tā'b'l), *n.* Mej, tebil.
Table-cloth (tā'b'l klŏth'), *n.* Mej ba tebilo anani ba ra.
Tack (tăk), *n.* Chongipa petchokgipa gojal.
Tackle (tăk'k'l), *n.* Jrimako de·doani kol.
Tact (tăkt), *n.* Kraako dakna changani.
Tadpole (tăd'pōl'), *n.* Alaring.
Tag (tăg), *n.* Chongipa kadapani, mongsongde bimungko seani.
Tail (tāl), *n.* Ki·me.
Tailor (tāl'ĕr), *n.* Ba·ra kogipa dorji.
Tailor-bird (tāl'ĕr-bĕrd'), *n.* Bol bijakko soksole ba kachepe sa·gipa do·pinchep.
Taint (tānt), *v.* Sopingata, bisi ba maiba namgija nape ong·siata.
Take (tāk), *v.* TOOK, TAKEN, Ra·a.
Tale (tāl), *n.* Golpo, maiba agane roani kata.
Talent (tăl'ent), *n.* Ba·kapani gisik; adita tangkani jrimako tik mesokani.
Talk (tôk), *v.* Agana, agangrika. *n.*
Talkative (tôk'ă-tiv), *a.* Aganrakgipa, betbetgipa.
Tall (tôl), *a.* Changroa, chùa.
Tallow (tăl'lo), *n.* Mes, do·bok aro matchurangni mitim.
Talon (tăl'ŭn), *n.* Chikgipa do·oni ja·skil.
Tamarind (tăm'ă-rĭnd), *n.* Cheng.
Tame (tām), *a.* Mikmala. *v.* mikmalata.
Tamper (tăm'pĕr), *v.* Nanggijako jakkala.
Tan (tăn), *v.* Bigilko taria.
Tangle (tăng'g'l), *v.* Bingbanga, stita, ja·gao ke·a, nanga.
Tank (tăngk), *n.* Pokri.
Tanner (tăn'nĕr), *n.* Bigil tarigipa.
Tannery (tăn'nĕr y), *n.* Bigil tariani biap.
Tantalize (tăn'tă-līz), *v.* Ka·donggramata, nachilaka.
Tap (tăp), *v.* Chiko jokatna su·pua; doktika; ja·pao ka·dapa. *n.* Ja·pao ka dapani.
Tape (tāp), *n.* Ro·dinggipa chongipa ba·ra.
Tapestry (tăp'ĕs-try), *n.* Ma·manti tokgipa pul de·gipa ba·ra ma·sa, kadeani.
Tapworm (tāp'wĕrm'), *n.* Okningo donggipa dal·rorogipa jo·ong ma·sa.
Tapioca (tăp'ĭ-ō'kă), *n.* Sagu gita dakgipa cha·ani ma·sa.
Tar (tär), *n.* Alkatra.
Tardy (tär'dy), *a.* Ka·singipa, srapgijagipa, aratgipa.
Tare (târ), *n.* Maran, jengge; chalja ba maiba chipchakani jrima.

Target (tär'gĕt), *n*. Nisan, jeko gogen.
Tarnish (tär'nĭsh), *v*. Moila nanga, maram cha·a.
Tarry (tăr'ry), *v*. Dongrika, ruuta, senga.
Tart (tärt), *a*. Mesenggipa.
Tartar (tär'têr), *n*. Tartar songni mande.
Task (tåsk), *n*. Kam, dakna nangani kam.
Tassel (tăs's'l), *n*. Tupi ba maioba kadena dakgimin kĭldingni bo·rotgipa.
Taste (tāst), *n*. Nama ba namgija su·uani.
Taste (tāst), *v*. Cha·tota.
Tattle (tăt't'l), *v*. Bokboka, agangrika, knaako aganskaa, aganjojoa.
Tattoo (tăt'tọ), *v*. Be·eno dim·ak aro tochi napate gimajana gita toka
Taught (tôt), *v*. *Teach*ko nibo.
Taunt (tänt), *v*. Ka·dingsteka, maiba gualako janaptaitaia.
Taut (tôt), *a*. Kringa.
Tax (tăks), *n*. Kajana.
Tax (tăks), *v*. Agre gatata, jrimata; kajana on·na, nangata.
Tea (tē), *n*. Cha.
Teach (tēch), *v*. TAUGHT, Skia.
Teacher (tēch'êr), *n*. Skigipa.
Teak (tēk), *n*. Segun bol.
Teal (tēl), *n*. Grang tangsekgipa do·gep ma·sa.
Team (tēm), *n*. Gari ge·sanko salgipa matchu ba gurerang.
Tear (tēr), *n*. Mikchi.
Tear (târ), *v*. TORE, TORN. Chita, grinata.
Tease (tēs), *v*. Jongkaia, kal·aka.
Teat (tēt), *n*. Sokkute.
Tedious (tē'dĭ-ŭs ba tēd'yŭs), *a*. Jak ruutgipa, neng·atgipa.
Teem (tēm), *v*. Gipa, gapa.
Teeth (tēth), *n*. Wagamrang.
Telegraph (tĕl'e-grȧf), *n*. Katako watat·ani kol.
Telephone (tĕl'e-fōn), *n*. Chel·ao donge agangrikani kol.
Telescope (tĕl'e-skōp), *n*. Chel·aoniko nikani kol.
Tell (tĕl), *v*. TOLD, TOLD, Agana, maikoba agana.
Temper (tĕm'pêr), *n*. Gisikni bewal.
Temper (tĕm'pêr), *v*. Nom·ata, brine apsan dakata, chiripa.
Temperance (tĕm'pêr-*a*ns), *n*. Kraa gita dakani ba cha·ani.
Temperate (tĕm'pêr-at), *a*. Agregija.
Temperature (tĕm'pêr-ā-tur), *n*. Sin·a ba ding·ani.
Tempest (tĕm'pĕst), *n*. Mikka balwa rakbegipa.
Temple (tĕm'p'l), *n*. Mite nok, olakiani nok; nateng, natengni greng.
Temporal (tĕm'po-r*a*l), *a*. A·gilsakni jringjrotna dongkamgijagipa.
Temporary (tĕm'po-ra-ry), *a*. Dikdiksa ba adita salna dong-aigipa.
Tempt (tĕmpt), *v*. Mikbokata, dakmajoa, ruraa.
Ten (tĕn), *a*. Chikung.
Tenant (tĕn'*a*nt), *n*. Bara on·gipa raiot, bara on·e ba kajana on·e donggipa.
Tend (tĕnd), *v*. Nitima, nirika; sandia; dakanga.
Tendency (tĕnd'*e*n-sy), *n*. Dakangani.
Tender (tĕnd'êr), *a*. Nom·gipa rinokgipa; ka·sagipa.
Tender (tĕnd'êr), *v*. On·a, on·na ku·rachaka.

Tendon (tĕn'dŭn), *n*. Ja·dil.
Tendril (tĕn'drĭl), *n*. Buduni jak.
Tenement (tĕn'e-ment), *n*. Bara on·ani nok ba dongani biap.
Tenfold (tĕn'fōld'), *a*. Duna chikung.
Tennis (tĕn'nĭs), *n*. Kal·ani ma·sa.
Tenon (tĕn'ŭn), *n*. Nangrimatsani bol.
Tenor (tĕn'ĕr), *n*. Me·asani tengkranggipa ku·rang.
Tense (tĕns), *a*. Krenggipa, kringgipa.
Tense (tĕns), *n*. Verbni somoiko mesokani.
Tension (tĕn'shŭn), *n*. Kringani, krengani.
Terrace (tĕr'ras), *n*. Gat gat ba gadang gadang dake a·ako gatgimin.
Terrestrial (tĕr-rĕs' trĭ-al), *a*. A·gilsakni biding.
Terrible (tĕr'rĭ-b'l), *a*. Namen kenbeani.
Terrific (tĕr-ĭf'ĭk), *a*. Kenchakbeani ba kenbeani gnang.
Terrify (tĕr'rĭ-fī), *v*. Kenata.
Territory (tĕr'rĭ-to-ry), *n*. A·song, nokgipa saksanni a·a.
Terror (tĕr'rĕr), *n*. Namen kenbeani.
Test (tĕst), *v*. Porika ka·e nia, dake nia.
Testament (tĕst'ā-ment), *n*. Sastroni bak gni.
Testify (tĕs'tĭ-fī), *v*. Saki on·a.
Testimony (tĕs'tĭ-mony), *n*. Saki on·ani.
Tether (tĕTH'ĕr), *n*. Cha·amtona gita matchu ba do·bokko ka·ani budu. *v*.
Tetrarch (tē'trärk), *n*. Romrangni pamong ma·sa, a·songni bak brini bak sani nokgipa.
Tetter (tĕt'tĕr), *n*. Kat cha·arang.
Text (tĕkst), *n*. Kata ba skiani ja·pang.
Texture (tĕks'tur), *n*. Ba·rani rokom.
Than (THăn), *conj*. Tosusaani kata.
Thank (thăngk), *v*. Mitela, namgnini gimin namnikako agana.
Thanksgiving (thăngks'gĭv'-ĭng), *n*. Kusi ong·e mitelani.
That (THăt), *pr*. Ua.
That (THăt), *conj*. Ine ; maikai.
Thatch (thăch), *n*. Am·prang.
Thaw (thô), *v*. Jronganga, suurichi tin·kae rakgipako ding·achi nom·ata ba jrongata.
The (THē), *art*. Ua, ua ine tiktak mesokani kata.
Thee (THē), *pr*. Nang·ko ; ia katako sastroo jakkala.
Theft (thĕft), *n*. Cha·uani.
Their (THâr), *pr*. Uamang·ni.
Them (THĕm), *pr*. Uamang·ko, uarangko.
Theme (thēm), *n*. Aganani ba se·ani ja·pang.
Themselves (THĕm-sĕlvz'), *pr*. Uamang·an, a·tangtangan.
Then (THĕn), *adv*. Unikoa, unon ; indide.
Thence (THĕns), *adv*. Unoni.
Thenceforth (THĕns'fōrth'). *adv*. Ua sal intal, uantaltal.
Thenceforward (THĕns-fôr'-wĕrd), *adv*. Ua sal intal, uantaltal.
Theologian (thē'o-lō'jĭ-an), *n*. Torom sastroko uigipa.

Theology (the-ŏl′o-jy), *n.* Isolni gimin uiani.
Theory (thē′o-ry), *n.* Chanchichipani, ong·arangko nie uarangni ja·pangko chanchichipani.
There (THâr), *adv.* Uano.
Thereabout (THâr′ȧ-bout′), *adv.* Uni sepango, uni jolo.
Thereafter (THâr-ȧf′têr), *adv.* Uni ja·mano.
Thereat (THâr-ăt′), *adv.* Uno, uni gimin.
Thereby (THâr-bī′), *adv.* Uachi.
Therefore (THêr-fōr ba THâr′fōr), *conj.* aro *adv.* Uni gimin, -ni gimin.
Therein (THâr-ĭn′), *adv.* Uno, uni ning·o.
Thereof (THâr-ŏf′ ba -ŏv′), *adv.* Uoni.
Thereon (THâr-ŏn′), *adv.* Uno, uni kosako.
Therewith (THâr -wĭth′ ba -WĭTH′), *adv,* Un baksa.
Thermometer (thêr-mŏm′e-têr), *n.* Sin·a ba ding·ako toani.
These (THēz), *pr.* Iarang.
They (THā), *pr.* Uamang, uarang.
Thick (thĭk), *a.* Ritchara; bing·a; dika; tin·kaa.
Thief (thēf), *n.* Cha·ugipa.
Thigh (thī), *n.* Ja·ping.
Thimble (thĭm′b′l), *n.* Ba·ra koo jaksio sikkrokani.
Thin (thĭn), *a.* Ba·a, ritchaja; eng·a; ram·a.
Thing (thĭng), *n.* Bostu; ong·gimin.
Think (thĭngk), *v.* THOUGHT, Chanchia.
Third (thêrd), *a.* Gitamgipa.
Thirst (thêrst), *n.* Ringna ska, sikbeani.
Thirteen (thêr′tēn′), *a.* Chi·gitam.
Thirty (thêr′ty), *a.* Kolatchi.
This (THĭs), *pr.* Ia.
Thistle (thĭs′s′l), *n.* Bu·su chagipa sam ma·sa.
Thither (THĭTH′êr), *adv.* Uano, uchin.
Thong (thŏng), *n.* Bigilni budu chongipa, barat.
Thorn (thôrn), *n.* Bu·su.
Thorough (thŭr′o), *a.* Gimikan, pilakchin, -srang.
Thoroughfare (thŭr′o-fâr′), *n.* Jinmani rama.
Those (THōz), *pr.* Uarang.
Thou (THou), *pr.* Na·a; ia katako sastroo jakkala.
Though (THō), *conj.* -oba.
Thought (thôt), *v.* *Think*ko nibo. *n.* Chanchiani.
Thousand (thou′zand), *a.* Ritcha chikung, hajal sa.
Thrash (thrăsh), *v.* Doka mi naka.
Thrashing-floor (thrăsh′ĭng-flōr′), *n.* Mi nakram, mi moram.
Thread (thrĕd), *n.* Kilding.
Threat (thrĕt), *n.* Duk on·gen ine agànani, ka·mikenatani.
Threaten (thrĕt′′n), *v.* Ka·mikenata.
Three (thrē), *a.* Gitam.
Threefold (thrē′fōld′), *a.* Duna gitam.
Threescore (thrē′skōr), *a.* Kolchang gitam.
Thresh (thrĕsh), *v.* Mi naka, mi moa.
Threshold (thrĕsh′ōld), *n.* Cholgugani ga·batram, cholgugao donggipa ga·batani.

Threw (thrū), *v.* *Throw*ko nibo.
Thrice (thrīs), *adv.* Chang gitam.
Thrift (thrĭft), *n.* Silani, man·e cha·baani. -y, *a.*
Thrill (thrĭl), *n.* Til·tilani.
Thrive (thrīv), *v.* Sila, man·e cha·a.
Throat (thrōt), *n.* Gitokbu.
Throb (thrŏb), *v.* Ka·tong cha·sua gita til·ika.
Throne (thrōn), *n.* Singhason.
Throng (thrŏng), *n.* Mande jinma.
Through (thrū), *prep.* Jatchiko, gisepko.
Throw (thrō), *v.* THREW, THROWN, Galåta, gålata.
Thrush (thrŭsh), *n.* Do·o ma·sa.
Thrust (thrŭst), *v.* Jitpaka, sinchepa.
Thug (thŭg), *n.* Mandeko se·otgipa Hindûni jat ma·sa.
Thumb (thŭm), *n.* Jaksi ma·mong.
Thump (thŭmp), *n.* Doktopani gam·a, jrima ga·akani gam·a.
Thunder (thŭn'dêr), *n.* Mikka kimpreta.
Thunderbolt (thŭn'dêr-bōlt'), *n.* Goera goani.
Thunderstruck (thŭn'dêr-strŭk'), *a.* Dil·dil ong·a.
Thursday (thêrz'da), *n.* Brihospotibar, bristibar.
Thus (THŭs), *adv.* Indake.
Thy (THī), *pr.* Nang·ni.
Thwart (thwôrt), *v.* Champenga, donpenga.
Thyself (THī-sĕlf'), *pr.* Na·a an·tangan.
Tick (tĭk), *n.* Ghori re·ani gam·a.
Ticket (tĭk'ĕt), *n.* Tikit, maikoba mesokani leka chongipa.
Tickle (tĭk'k'l), *v.* Mengmenga, jukjuka.
Ticklish (tĭk'klĭsh), *a.* Ka·jikgipa.
Tide (tīd), *n.* Chi dal·baa ba rookangani, (joar bhata).
Tidings (tī'dĭngz), *n.* Knaani kata.
Tidy (tī'dy), *a.* Rongtalgimin, tarigimin.
Tie (tī), *v.* Kaå.
Tiffin (tĭf'ĭn), *n.* Mesal.
Tiger (tī'gêr), *n.* Matcha.
Tight (tīt), *a.* Ketket.
Tile (tīl), *n.* It pleng.
Till (tĭl), *prep.* -na king king.
Till (tĭl), *v.* Wea, gama.
Till (tĭl), *n.* Tangka donani,'gipin baksni ning·o donskagipa chongipa baks.
Tillage (tĭl'aj), *n.* A·a gamani.
Tiller (tĭl'êr), *n.* Ringni ki·meko pe·ani bol.
Tilt (tĭlt), *v.* Gitchinga, chingkrenga.
Timber (tĭm'bêr), *n.* Sol·gimin bolrang, tum ba sirirang.
Time (tīm), *n.* Somoi.
Timepiece (tīm'pēs'), *n.* Salko niani ghori.
Timid (tĭm'ĭd), *a.* Kenninggipa, ka·pong.
Tin (tĭn), *n.* Sil ma·sa, tin.
Tincture (tĭngk'tur), *n.* Maiba bitchio on·tisa simata; on·tisa namgijani napa.
Tinder (tĭn'dêr), *n.* Kamningipa, wa·al cha·bakninggipa.
Tine (tīn), *n.* Sil ki·chong ba mainiba jaksi.
Tinge (tĭnj), *v.* Rongo sim·ata.
Tingle (tĭng'g'l), *v.* Bibrao daka.
Tinker (tĭngk'êr), *n.* Silni me·dik sam·dikrangko taritaigipa.

Tinkle (ting'k'l), *v.* Gaanti chongipani gam a.
Tinsel (tin'sĕl), *n.* Rangpata, gun gri nitoatani.
Tiny (ti'ny), *a.* Chonbegipa.
Tip (tip), *v.* Samsading gitchinga, chingkrenga.
Tip (tip), *n.* Ku·chot.
Tippet (tip'pĕt), *n.* Golabon.
Tipsy (tip'sy), *a.* Chu pektimanga, pekmilanga.
Tip-toe (tip'tō'), *n.* Ja·si ku·chot.
Tiptop (tip'tŏp'), *n.* Chubatgipa ku·chot. *a.* Nameŋ nambea.
Tire (tīr), *n.* Gari chakao datdulgipa sil.
Tire (tīr), *v.* Neng·ata.
Tiresome (tīr'sŭm), *a.* Neng·atgipa.
Tissue (tish'u), *n.* Ba·begipa ka·prang.
Titbit (tit'bit'), *n.* Cha·ani nambatgipa.
Tithe (tīTH), *n.* Bak chikungni bak sa.
Title (tī't'l), *n.* Kam ba manderaˑako mingani.
To (tụ), *prep.* -na,-chi,-ona.
Toad (tōd), *n.* Beng·blok kakappru ba janggilripu.
Toast (tōst), *n.* Wa·alo anggimin ruti.
Tobacco (to-băk'ko), *n.* Ta·maku.
Today (tụ-dā'), *adv.* Da·alo.
Toe (tō), *n.* Ja·si.
Together (tụ-gĕTH'ĕr), *adv.* Damsan.
Toil (toil), *n.* Neng·ani kam. *v.*
Toilet (toi'lĕt), *n.* Be·entangko tariani.
Token (tō'k'n), *n.* Chin, gisik ra·ani.
Told (tōld), *v.* *Tell*ko nibo.
Tolerable (tŏl'ĕr-ā-b'l), *a.* Chakchikna amgni.
Tolerate (tŏl'ĕr-āt), *v.* Ong·na ba donna chakchika.
Toll (tōl), *n.* Masul ba kerea.
Toll (tōl), *v.* Ruuŋ rute changprak doka.
Tomato (to-mā'to ba to-mä'to), *n.* Baring bilati.
Tomb (tụm), *n.* Mandeko gopna rikgimin.
Tom-boy (tŏm'boi'), *n.* Tom·tomgijagipa me·chik bi·sa.
Tom-cat (tŏm'kăt'), *n.* Menggo bipa.
Tomorrow (tụ-mŏr'ro), *n.* Knalo, knapo.
Ton (tŭn), *n.* 'Muan kolgrik bongamang jrimgipa.
Tone (tōn), *n.* Ku·rang ba gam·ani rokom ; an·sengani.
Tongs (tŏngz), *n.* Wa·al otani sildangkep.
Tongue tŭng), *n.* Sre, ku·sik.
Tonic (tŏn'ik), *n.* Milatgipa, mangrakatgipa.
To-night (tụ-nīt'), *n.* Da·a wal. *adv.*
Too (tụ), *adv.* Ba, agre.
Took (tụk), *v.* *Take*ko nibo.
Tool (tụl), *n.* Silchidare, jakkalani.
Toot (tụt), *v.* Singga sika.
Tooth (tụth), *n.* Wagam.
Toothache (tụth'āk'), *n.* Wagam saani.
Toothpick (tụth'pik), *n.* Wagam jotrokani.
Top (tŏp), *n.* Kosak, ku·chot ; latum.
Topaz (tō'păz), *n.* Gamchatgipa ripok ma·sa.
Tope (tōp), *n.* Olakianirangko donram, bolgrim, te·gatchugrim.

Toper (tŏ'pêr), *n.* Chu pekrakgipa.
Topknot (tŏp'nŏt'), *n.* Do·oni kimchol, basu ; knitom.
Topmost (tŏp'mōst'), *a.* Kosakbatgipa, chubatgipa.
Torch (tôrch), *n.* Bilcham.
Tore (tōr), *v.* *Tear*ko nibo.
Torment (tôr'mĕnt'), *v.* Namen saknaata.
Tornado (tôr-nā'do), *n.* Ta·rakbegipa balminduri.
Torpedo (tôr-pe'do), *n.* Jahatko gopretani ma·sa.
Torpid (tôr'pĭd), *a.* Goka ong·-gipa. **-ity,** *n.*
Torpor (tôr'pêr), *n.* Goka ong·-ani.
Torrent (tŏr'rent), *n.* Ta·rakani.
Torrid (tŏr'r'd), *a.* Ding·begipa, ran·gipa.
Tortoise (tôr'tĭs ba -tŭs), *n.* Ki·sing.
Torture (tôr'tur), *v.* Namen saknaata. *n.*
Toss (tŏs), *v.* Godoa.
Total (tō'tăl), *n.* Gimik. *a.*
Totter (tôt'têr), *v.* Ringrenga, il·engpileng daka.
Toucan (tụ'kăn), *n.* Renggok ma·sa.
Touch (tŭch), *v.* Nangdika, dangtapa.
Touching (tŭch'ing), *a.* Chanchiatgipa, gisiko nangatgipa.
Tough (tŭf), *a.* Su·uta, chotninggijagipa.
Tour (tụr), *n.* Songko re·roroani.
Tourist (tŭr'ist), *n.* Songko re·-rorogipa.
Tow (tō), *v.* Chio salanga.
Towards (tō'ĕrdz), *prep.* -chipak.
Tow-boat (tō'bōt'), *n.* Salgimin ring, gipin ringko salani jahat chongipa.
Towel (tou'ĕl), *n.* Jaron, be·en ipakani ba·ra.
Tower (tou'êr), *n.* Chugipa nok ba maiba rikgimin.
Towline (tō'līn'), *n.* Ringko salani budu.
Town (toun), *n.* Chongipa songjinma.
Townhall (toun'hôl'), *n.* Songjinmani manderangni tom·ani nok.
Tow-path (tō'păth'), *n.* Chisamjoljol ringko salani rama.
Toy (toi), *n.* Kal·ani.
Trace (trās), *n.* Ja·kol, chin.
Trace (trās), *v.* Ja·kol sanna, sandia.
Track (trăk), *n.* Ja·kol, chin, rama ; reilni ramao angipa silrang.
Tract (trăkt), *n.* Chongipa ki·-tap ; chongipa a·song ba chi.
Trade (trād), *v.* Badinga.
Tradesman (trādz'man), *n.* Badinggipa mande.
Tradition (trā-dish'ŭn), *n.* Aganrikrika kata.
Traffic (trăf'fik), *n.* Badingani, mande ba bosturangko reil ba jahato ra·angani.
Tragedy (trăj'e-dy), *n.* Maiba signini a·sel ong·ani.
Tragical (trăj'i-kal), *a.* Duk ong·begni, maiba signini a·sel ong·ani biding.
Trail (trāl), *v.* Salbrita, bisakko sandie ja·rika.
Trail (trāl), *n.* Dongrikgipa bisak ba maikoba salangani chin.
Train (trān), *v.* Skia, tarisoa, ranta ka·a.

Train (trān), *n*. Adita bang·a mande ja·rikgiparang; ritchugrikgipa, adita reilni garirang.
Train oil (trān′oil′), *n*. Timi na·tokni to.
Traitor (trā′tẽr), *n*. Rajana bobil dakgipa, tol·napgipa.
Tram (trăm), *n*. Songjinmao gurechi ba kolchi salruragipa gari.
Trample (trăm′p′l), *v*. Ga·bel bela.
Tramp (trămp), *v*. Ja·achi re·a.
Tramp (trămp), *n*. Ja·ku gam·ani, ja·achi re·ani; ja·chi re·gipa, re·rorogipa.
Trance (trȧns), *n*. Sibokani, mikjumang gita ong·ani.
Tranquil (trăng′kwĭl), *a*. Tom·tomgipa.
Tranquillize (trăng′kwĭl-īz), *v*. Tom·tomata.
Transact (trăns-ăkt′), *v*. Kamko dakata, chu·sokata.
Transcribe (trăn-skrīb′), *v*. Seskaa.
Transfer (trăns-fẽr′), *v*. On·skaa, donskaa.
Transfigure (trăns-fĭg′ūr), *v*. Mikkang nambataona dingtang ong·ata.
Transform (trăns-fôrm′), *v*. Bimangko dingtang dakata.
Transgress (trăns-grĕs′), *v*. Niamko pe·a, pap daka.
Transient (trăn′shĕnt), *a*. Dikdiksana dongaigipa.
Transit (trăns′it), *n*. Batsotani, battongani.
Transition (trăn-sĭzh′ŭn), *n*. Dingtang ong·ani.
Transitory (trăn′sĭ-to-ry), *a*. Dikdiksana dongaigipa.
Translate (trăns-lāt′), *v*. Gipin ku·siko donskaa, seskaa, ba aganskaa.
Transliterate (trăns-lĭt′ẽr-āt), *v*. Gipin oikorchi seskaa.
Translucent (trăns-lū′sent), *a*. Seng·ako mangmang nikprotaigipa.
Transmigrate (trăns′mī-grāt), *v*. Gipino songdongna re·anga.
Transmit (trăns-mĭt′), *v*. Watata, on·skaa.
Transparent (trăns′pâr′ent), *a*. Grika, rongtala.
Transpire (tran′spīr′), *v*. Parak ong·a.
Transplant (trăns-plănt′), *v*. Pike ge·skaa.
Transport (trăns-pōrt′), *v*. Jitata, gipinchi ra·anga, sasti on·ani pal gipin biapchi watata.
Transport (trans′pōrt), *n*. Sipairangko gipin biapchi ra·angani jahat.
Transpose (trăns-pōz′), *v*. Biap srea, donskaa.
Trap (trăp), *n*. Ja·ga.
Trap-door (trăp′dōr′), *n*. Wa·seo ba nokkingchi donggipa do·ga.
Trappings (trăp′pĭngs), *n*. Tarianirang.
Trash (trăsh), *n*. Jabol, nanggija choligija bostu.
Travail (trăv′al), *v*. An·pakani saknaako man·a.
Travel (trăv′ĕl′), *v*. Songgipinchi re·roroa.
Traveller (trăv′ĕl-ẽr), *n*. Songregipa.
Tray (trā), *n*. Maikoba ra·chakani ba dangdike on·ani tala.
Treacherous (trĕch′ẽr-ŭs), *a*. Nampinikgipa, tol·napgipa.

Treacle (trē'k'l), *n*. Mitai bitchi.

Tread (trĕd), *v*. TROD. Gå·a, gá·dapa, ga·bela.

Treason (tre z'n), *n*. Nampinike rajana bobil dakani.

Treasure (trĕzh'ur), *n*. Chimonggimin gam, gamchatb·a bostu.

Treasury (trĕas'ur-y), *n*. Gam ba tangka donram.

Treat (trēt), *v*. Mandena daka bostuko jakkala; cha·aniko ala.

Treat (trēt), *n*. Alani, kusi ong·atani.

Treaty (trē'ty), *n*. Ku·rachakgrike ba namgrike seani.

Treble (trĕb''l), *a*. Duna gitam.

Tree (trē), *n*. Bol.

Tremble (trĕm'b'l), *v*. Til·tila, moa.

Tremendous (tre-mĕn'dŭs), *a*. Aiao inmane dal·a.

Tremor (trē'mŏr ba trĕm'ŏr), *n*. An·dildilani.

Trench (trĕnch), *n*. Chikare, dongge.

Trend (trĕnd), *v*. Bachiba dakanga.

Trespass (trĕs'pas), *v*. Gipinni a·achi batanga; dos daka.

Trestle (trĕs''l), *n*. Jang·rangko ra·chakna krongni pal sil ba bolko chengsri dake watgimin.

Trial (trī'al), *n*. Nina dakani; joton ka·ani; bichal ka·ani.

Triangle (trī'ang'g'l), *n*. Ki·tik gitam aro rikam gitam gnanggipa.

Tribe (trīb), *n*. Ma·chong ba jat.

Tribulation (trĭb'u-lā'shŭn), *n*. Duk ong·beani.

Tribunal (tri-bū'nal), *n*. Bichal ka·ram, bichal ka·giparang.

Tributary (trĭb'u-ta-ry), *n*. Kajana on·skagipa, gipino braskagipa chi.

Tribute (trĭb'ut), *n*. Gipin songna on·a kajana.

Trick (trĭk), *n*. Chalaki ba bheliki dakani.

Trickle (trĭk'k'l), *v*. Tingtota, tottak tottak dake gr·aka.

Tricycle (trī'si-k'l), *n*. Chaka ge·gitamgipa ja·achi ga·e re·ani gari.

Trident (trī'dent), *n*. Jaksi ge·gitam gnanggipa silni gol·dik.

Triennial (tri-ĕn'nĭ-al), *a*. Bilsi gitam gitamprak.

Trifle (trī'f'l), *n*. Chonbegipa, gamchatgijagipa bostu.

Trigger (trĭg'gêr), *n*. Slaini kora.

Trill (trĭl), *n*. Ku·rang til·tilani.

Trim (trĭm), *v*. Apsan rasote taria; nitoata.

Trip (trĭp), *v*. Ja·a ritchenge re·a; ja·gitotata, ga·skokata.

Trip (trĭp), *n*. Adita salna songree roani.

Tripe (trīp), *n*. Matchu bimemani bigilni ning·oni be·enko cha·na song·gimin.

Triple (trĭp''l), *a*. Duna gitam.

Tripod (trī'pŏd), *n*. Ja·a ge·gitamgipa maiba donchakani.

Triumph (trī'umf), *n*. Ama ba cheani rasong.

Triumphant (trī-um'fant), *a*. Amgipa, chegipa.

Trivial (trĭv'i-al), *a*. Gamchatgijagipa, simsakna nanggijagipa.

Triweekly (trī'wēk'ly), *a*. Anti gitam gitamprak.

Troop (trup), *n*. Sipai kotok.

Trooper (trọp'ẽr), *n.* Gureo gakatgipa sipai.
Trot (trŏt), *v.* Katjokjoke re·a.
Trough (trŏf), *n.* Kingkong.
Trousers (trou'zẽrz), *n.* Pantaloon, ja·o kruani jama.
Trout (trout), *n.* Na·tok ma·sa.
Trowel (trou'ĕl), *n.* Mistrirangni repiani sil danggap; a·a cho·ani.
Truant (trọ'ant), *n.* Watako man·gija dongchipgipa, roaigipa.
Truce (trọs), *n.* Ku·monggrikna dakgrikao dondikani.
Truck (trŭk), *n.* Palani me·su samjakrang; jrimako salani mangrakgipa gari.
Trudge (trŭj), *v.* Ga·timtime re·a.
True (trọ), *a.* Bebe. kakket.
Trumpet (trŭmp'ĕt), *n.* Singga, begul ma·sa.
Trunk (trŭngk), *n.* Ba·ra donani baks; sundul; bitong.
Trust (trŭst), *v.* Bebera·a, pangchaka, ka·donga.
Trustee (trŭs-tē'), *n.* Gipinni gamko rakina dongimin mande.
Trusty (trŭst'y), *a.* Ka·dongna ba bebera·na kraa.
Truth (trọth), *n.* Bebe ong·ani, kakket ong·ani.
Try (trī), *v.* Joton ka·a.
Tub (tŭb), *n.* Bolko daka dal·gipa chi ra·chakani.
Tube (tūb), *n.* Noli, wa·singtok.
Tuck (tŭk), *v.* Bil·tingata, sikchipilata.
Tuesday (tūz'dā), *n.* Mongolbar.
Tug (tŭg), *v.* Salkingkinga.
Tuition (tu-ĭsh'ŭn), *n.* Skulo poraiani masul.
Tumble (tŭm'b'l), *v.* Romtome ga·aka.
Tumor (tū'mẽr), *n.* Katchi goa.
Tumult (tū'mŭlt), *n.* Golmal.
Tune (tūn), *n.* Gitni sul.
Tunnel (tŭn'nĕl), *n.* A·ningko cho·e dakgimin rama; chubegipa wal·ku jokani; ruchakani.
Turban (tẽr'ban), *n.* Kotip, paguri.
Turbid (tẽr'bĭd), *a.* Moilagipa, kimonggipa.
Turbulent (tẽr'bu-lent), *a.* Saigrikgipa, jegrikgipa, golmal dakgipa.
Turf (tẽrf), *n.* Samsi a·a gnang ja·pang gimik.
Turk (tẽrk), *n.* Turosko songni mande.
Turkey (tẽr'ky), *n.* Turosko song; dal·gipa do·nok ma·sa.
Turn (tẽrn), *v.* Bikpila, an·pila, wilwila; dingtang ong·ata.
Turn (tẽrn), *n.* Gonggeatani; pal.
Turnip (tẽr'nĭp), *n.* Salgum, mula ma·sa.
Turnstile (tẽrn'stīl'), *n.* Saksasan napna man·aigipa wilwilgipa cholguga.
Turpentine (tẽr'pĕn-tīn), *n.* Tarpin to, to ma·sa.
Turtle (tẽr't'l), *n.* Ki·sing.
Turtle-dove (tẽr't'l-dŭv'), *n.* Do·kru ma·sa.
Tusk (tŭsk), *n.* Waching, mongma wagam.
Tut (tŭt), *interj.* Dut ba che ine inani pal.
Tutor (tū'tẽr), *n.* Skigipa, nitimgipa.
Tweezers (twē'zẽrs), *n.* Silskep.
Twelfth (twĕlfth), *a.* Chignigipa.
Twelve (twĕlv), *a.* Chigni.

Twentieth (twĕn'ti-ĕth), *a.* Kolgrikgipa.
Twenty (twĕn'ty), *a.* Kolgrik.
Twice (twīs), *adv.* Changgni.
Twig (twĭg), *n.* Chongipa cheksi.
Twilight (twī'līt). *n.* Seng·mit·chimitchi ba walsimsim.
Twin (twĭn), *a.* Jonja.
Twine (twīn), *v.* Budu wea, saka ba sakmrona.
Twine (twīn), *n.* Budu chongipa.
Twinge (twĭnj), *n.* Dikdiksa saknaani. *v.*
Twinkle (twĭng'k'l), *v.* Ching·chet ching·chet daka.
Twirl (twêrl), *v.* Wilwila, mitila.
Twist (twĭst), *v.* Saka, sakmrena.
Twit (twĭt), *v.* Ka·dingsteka, maiba guala ba dosko janaptaitaia.
Twitch (twĭch), *v.* Til·iket dakata.
Twitter (twĭt'têr), *v.* Chekchak chekchak ina.
Two (tụ), *a.* Gni, ge·gni.
Twofold (tụ'fōld'), *a.* Duna gni.
Type (tīp), *n.* Chapani oikor; chin.
Typewriter (tīp'rīt'êr), *n.* Seani kol.
Tyrannical (ti-răn'nĭ-kal), *a.* Raiotko duk on·gipa.
Tyranny (tĭr'an-ny), *n.* Raja ba nokgipani ka·saninggija kam.
Tyrant (tī'rant), *n.* Namgija, ka·saniggijagipa raja ba nokgipa.
Tsar, tzar (zär), *n.* Rusiani raja.

U.

Udder (ŭd'dêr), *n.* Matchuni sok ba sokkute.
Ugly (ŭg'ly), *a.* Nitogijagipa, daknanggijagipa.
Ulcer (ŭl'sêr), *n.* Pari.
Ultimate (ŭl'tĭ-mat), *a.* Chon·kamgipa, chel·batgipa.
Umbrella (ŭm-brĕl'lȧ), *n.* Chata.
Umpire (ŭm'pīr), *n.* Namgrikatgipa, tik ka·gipa, katako pe·e on·gipa.
Un- (ŭn), Katani a·bachengo donani, uni orto ong·ja ba griko mesoka.
Unable (ŭn-ā'b'l), *a.* Amgija.
Unacceptable (ŭn'ăk-sĕpt'ȧ-b'l), *a.* Ra·chakna kragija.
Unanimous (u-năn'ĭ-mŭs), *a.* Ku·cholsan, gisiksan.
Unarmed (ŭn-ärmd'), *a.* Silchidare gri, taria gri.
Unbalanced (ŭn-băl'anst), *a.* Gisik tom·tomgijagipa.
Unbar (ŭn-bär'), *v.* Kang·ako enga, kang·a gri dakata.
Unbind (ŭn-bīnd'), *v.* Enga, kagija dakata.
Unbolt (ŭn-bolt'), *v.* Teka gri dakata, tekako oa.
Unborn (ŭn-bôrn'), *a.* Atchigijagipa, atchikujagipa.
Unbosom (ŭn-bụz'ŭm), *v.* Gisikko oe agana.
Unburden (ŭn-bêrd'd'n), *v.* Bal gri dakata, balko ra·gala, ritchengata.
Unceasing (ŭn-sēs'ĭng), *a.* Matchotgija, dondikgija, bon·changgija.
Uncertain (ŭn-sêr'tĭn), *a.* Tik gri.

Uncivil (ŭn-sĭv'ĭl), *a.* Mandera·na changgijagipa.

Uncivilized (ŭn-sĭv'ĭl-īzd), *a.* Uigijagipa ; skia man·gijagipa.

Uncle (ŭng'k'l), *n.* Wanggipa, pajongtang, mamatang, ma·a aro pani jonggipa aro adatangrang.

Unclean (ŭn-klēn'), *a.* Rongtalgija.

Uncommon (ŭn-kŏm'mŭn), *a.* Ramram ong·gija, ong·ronggija.

Unconcerned (ŭn'kŏn-sêrnd'), *a.* Simsakgija.

Unconditional (ŭn'kŏn-dĭsh'ŭn-al, *a.* Agandapani gri.

Unconscious (ŭn-kŏn'shŭs), *a.* Siboka ; uiani gri.

Uncouth (un-kṳth), *a.* Daknanggija, skia man·gija.

Undaunted (ŭn-dänt'ĕd), *a.* Kengijagipa, kenmangijagipa.

Undeceive (ŭn'de-sēv'), *v.* Togia ba tol·ako uiata.

Undecided (ŭn'dē-sī'dĕd), *a.* Mangsongkujagipa, tik ka·kujagipa.

Under (ŭn'dêr), *prep.* Ning·o, kokkimao, ka·mao.

Under (ŭn'dêr), *adv.* Ka·mao.

Underbrush (ŭn'dêr-brŭsh'), *n.* Ning·o chagipa burung.

Underdone (ŭn'dêr-dŭn'), *a.* Song·a mingija.

Undergo (ŭn'dêr-gō'), *v.* Chaka chakchika.

Undergrowth (ŭn'dêr-grōth'), *n.* Ning·o chagipa chongipa burung.

Underhand (ŭn'dêr-hănd'), *a.* Sriksrik, tol·napa gnang.

Underlease (ŭn'dêr-lēs'), *v.* Bhara ra·gipani bhara on·skaa.

Underlet (ŭn'dêr-lĕt'), *v.* Bhara ra·gipani bhara on·skaa.

Underline (un'dêr-līn'), *v.* Ka·mao salsreta.

Undermine (ŭn'dêr-mīn'), *v.* Kongrua, ning·joljol oniako daka.

Undermost (ŭn'dêr-mōst'), *a.* Kokkimabatgipa.

Underneath (ŭn'dêr-nēTH' ba nēth'), *adv.* Ka·mao, kokkimao.

Underrate (ŭn'dêr-rāt'), *v.* Chonnika, gamchatnikja.

Underscore (ŭn'dêr-skōr'), *v.* Kokkimao salsreta.

Undersell (ŭn'dêr-sĕl'), *v.* Dam kome pala.

Undershot (ŭn'dêr-shŏt'), *a.* Kokkimako chi jokate wilwilatgipa chaka.

Undersized (ŭn'dêr-sīzd'), *a.* Bewal gita dal·gijagipa.

Understand (ŭn'dêr-stănd'), *v.* Uia, ma·sia.

Understanding (ŭn'dêr-stănd'ĭng), *n.* Uiani, ku·rachakani.

Undertake (ŭn'dêr'tāk'), *v.* Joton ka·a.

Undertaker (ŭn'dêr-tāk'êr), *n.* Manggisiko goptimgipa.

Undertone (ŭn'dêr-tōn'), *n.* Ku·rang ka·sina.

Undervalue (ŭn'dêr-văl'u), *v.* Gamchatnikja, chonnika.

Undigested (ŭn'dĭ-jĕst'ĕd), *a.* Jrongija, goligija.

Undiscovered (ŭn'dĭs-kŭv'êrd). *a.* Nikkujagipa, parakkujagipa, uikujagipa.

Undo (un-dṳ'), *v.* UNDID, UNDONE. Enggrua, enga.

Undress (ŭn-drĕs'), *v*. Ganako enga.
Undue (ŭn-dū'), *a*. Agrea, bang·bea; on·na nangkuja.
Undulate (ŭn'du-lāt'), *v*. Onding ondang daka.
Unearth (ŭn-êrth'), *v*. Parakata, oprakata.
Unearthly (ŭn-êrth'ly), *a*. A·gilsakni ong·gija.
Uneasy (ŭn-ēz'y), *a*. Dongtogija, tom·tomgija, suk gri, jajrenga gnang.
Unequal (ŭn-ē'kwal), *a*. Apsangipa gri, soman ong·gijagipa.
Unerring (ŭn-êr'rĭng ba -ĕr'rĭng), *a*. Guala gri, tik.
Uneven (ŭn-ē'v'n), *a*. Apsan ong·gijagipa.
Unexampled (ŭn'ĕgz-ăm'p'ld), *a*. Ugita gipin gri, toka amgija.
Unexpected (ŭn'ĕks-pĕkt'ĕd), *a*. Nichaksogija, rang·san.
Unfair (ŭn'far'), *a*. Kakket ong·gija.
Unfasten (ŭn-fås''n), *v*. Enga, tekako oa.
Unfavourable (ŭn fā'vêr-å-b'l), *a*. Namnikani ong·gija, champenggipa.
Unfeeling (ŭn-fel'ĭng), *a*. Uininggijagipa, ka·saninggijagipa.
Unfinished (ŭn-fĭn'ĭsht), *a*. Matchotgija, chu·sokgija.
Unfit (ŭn-fĭt'), *a*. Kragija, nitogija.
Unfold (ŭn-fōld'), *v*. Paraka, oa, badala.
Unfortunate (ŭn-fôr'tu-nat), *a*. Rasong gri, kopal gri.
Unfounded (ŭn-found'ĕd), *a*. Ja·pang gri.
Unfriendly (ŭn-frĕnd'ly), *a*. Ka·sagijagipa, ripeng ong·gijagipa.
Unfruitful (ŭn-frụt'fụl), *a*. Bite gri, a·sal gri, banji.
Unfurl (ŭn-fêrl'), *v*. Dol·giminko engata, badalata.
Ungainly (ŭn-gān'ly), *a*. Skia man·gija.
Ungodly (ŭn-gŏd'ly), *a*. Isol gita ong·gija, otoromi, papi.
Unguarded (ŭn-gärd'ĕd), *a*. Nirokgipa gri, nitimgipa gri; mikrakgija.
Unhandy (ŭn-hănd'y), *a*. Kamna choligijagipa, changgijagipa.
Unhappy (ŭn-hăp'py), *a*. An·senggijagipa, katchaa grigipa, kusi ong·gijagipa.
Unhealthy (ŭn-hĕlth'y), *a*. Be·enni an·senggijagipa.
Unheard (ŭn-hêrd'), *a*. Knakujagipa.
Unhitch (ŭn-hĭch'), *v*. Garioniko gureko enga.
Unholy (ŭn-hō'ly), *a*. Rongtalgija.
Unhurt (ŭn-hêrt), *v*. Mata bu·a gri.
Uniform (ū'nĭ-fôrm), *n*. Apsan ong·ani, sipairangni posak. *a*.
Unify (ū'ni-fī), *v*. Apsan dakata, nangdimata.
Union (ūn'yŭn), *n*. Nangrimani.
Unique (ū-nēk'), *a*. Ugita gipin grigipa.
Unit (ū'nĭt), *n*. Ge·sa.
Unite (u-nīt'), *v*. Nangdimata, damsan dakata.
Unity (ū'nĭ-ty), *n*. Ku·cholsan ong·ani, gisiksan ong·ani.
Universal (ū ni vêr'sal), *a*. Pilakchin donggipa.

Universe (ū'nĭ-vêrs), *n.* A'gilsak, sal, ja, aski aro pilak dakgiminrang.
University (ū'nĭ-vêr'sĭ-ty), *n.* Ma'mantini gimin skiani skul dal'gipa.
Unjust (ŭn-jŭst'), *a.* Kakketgijagipa.
Unkind (ŭn-kīnd'), *a.* Ka'sagijagipa.
Unlade (ŭn-lād'), *v.* Balko ra'-ona.
Unlawful (ŭn-lô'ful), *a.* Niam gita ong'gija.
Unlearned (ŭn-lêrn'ĕd), *v.* Skia man'gijagipa.
Unleavened (ŭn-lĕvn'd), *a.* Wanti gri.
Unless (ŭn-lĕs'), *conj.* -jaode.
Unlike (ŭn-līk'), *a.* Apsana ong'-gija.
Unlikely (ŭn-līk'ly), *a.* Ong'jawakon, ong'janaba donga.
Unlimited (ŭn-lĭm'ĭt-ĕd), *a.* Sima gri, ari gri.
Unload (ŭn-lōd), *v.* Balko ra'-ona.
Unlock (ŭn-lŏk'), *v.* Tekako oa, kulia.
Unloose (ŭn-lus), *v.* Enga.
Unlucky (ŭn-lŭk'y), *a.* Rasong gri, kopal gri.
Unman (ŭn-măn'), *v.* Ka'donggija dakata.
Unmerciful (ŭn-mêr'sĭ-ful), *a.* Ka'sachaka grigipa.
Unmindful (ŭn-mīnd'ful), *a.* Gisik on'gijagipa, gualgipa, simsakgijagipa.
Unnatural (ŭn-năt'u-ral), *a.* Ba'kapani bewal ong'gija.
Unnecessary (ŭn-nĕs'ĕs-sa-ry), *a.* Nanggija.
Unpack (ŭn-păk'), *v.* Katomako enga, sikgiminko orara.
Unparalleled (ŭn-păr'al-lĕld), *a.* Apsangipa gri.
Unpopular (ŭn-pŏp'u-lêr), *a.* Jinmani namnikgija.
Unpretending (ŭn'prē-tĕnd'-ing), *a.* Gaorade'gija, rasong chagija, sontol dakgipa, dal'-nikgijagipa.
Unquiet (ŭn-kwī'ĕt), *a.* Tom'-tomgijagipa.
Unravel (ŭn-răv'l), Enggrua.
Unready (ŭn-rĕd'y), *a.* Tarisogija.
Unreal (ŭn-rē'al), *a.* Bebe ong'-gija.
Unrevealed (ŭn're-vēld'), *a.* Parakkujagipa.
Unremitting (ŭn're-mĭt'ting), *a.* Dondikgija.
Unreserved (ŭn-re-zêrvd'), *a.* Cha'chipila gri, ra'rikgija.
Unrighteous (ŭn-rī'chŭs), *a.* Otoromi, kakketgijagipa.
Unripe (un-rīp'), *a.* Mingija, gitang.
Unroll (ŭn-rōl'), *v.* Dol'ako badala.
Unroof (ŭn-roof'), *v.* Nokkingko kika.
Unruly (ŭn-rool'y). *a.* Manigijagipa, bamgijagipa.
Unsafe (ŭn-sāf'), *a.* Kenchakani gnang.
Unscrew (ŭn-skru'), *v.* Skruko oka.
Unscrupulous (ŭn-skru'pul-ŭs), *a.* Namana namja simsakgijagipa.
Unseal (ŭn-sēl'), *v.* Mohorko oa.
Unseasonable (ŭn-sē'z'n-ā-b'l), *a.* Kragijani salo ong'gipa.
Unseemly (ŭn-sēm'ly), *a.* Ong'-togija, kragija, nitogija.

Unseen (ŭn-sēn'), *a.* Nikna man·gija.
Unsettle (ŭn-sĕt'tl), *v.* Dingtangata, golmal dakata, moata.
Unsound (ŭn-sound'), *a.* An·senggija, kakketgija, sea gnang.
Unsteady (ŭn-stĕd'y), *a.* Tom·tomgija, kimkimgija.
Unsuitable (ŭn-sūt'a-b'l), *a.* Kragija.
Untie (ŭn-tī'), *v.* Kaako enga.
Until (ŭn-tĭl'), *adv.* Kingking, dipet.
Untimely (ŭn-tīm'ly), *a.* Kragipa salo ong·gijagipa.
Unto (ŭn'tọ), *prep.* -ona, kingking.
Untoward (ŭn-tō'ĕrd), *a.* Jajrengatgipa, champenggipa.
Untold (ŭn-tōld'), *a.* Aganna ampilgija.
Untrue (ŭn-trụ'), *a.* Bebegija, tol·a.
Untruth (ŭn-trụth'), *n.* Tol·a.
Untwist (ŭn-twĭst'), *v.* Sakako balgrenga.
Unusual (ŭn-ū'zhu-al), *a.* Ong·ronggija.
Unwary (ŭn-wā'ry), *a.* Gisik rakgija.
Unwearied (ŭn-wē'rid), *a.* Neng·nikgija, watgalgija, dondikgija.
Unwell (ŭn-wĕl'), *a.* An·senggija.
Unwieldy (ŭn-wēld'y), *a.* Dal·begipa, jrimgipa, jakkaltobregija.
Unwilling (ŭn-wĭl'ling), *a.* Sikgija, gong·gija.
Unwise (ŭn-wīz'), *a.* Gisik bang·e dongbregijagipa, goka.
Unwittingly (ŭn-wĭt'ting-ly), *adv.* Uigija, mangsonggija.
Unworthy (ŭn-wer'thy), *a.* Kragija.
Unwritten (ŭn-rĭt't'n), *a.* Segijagipa, sea grigipa, sea donggijagipa.
Unyoke (ŭn-yōk'), *v.* Pakripeko ra·gala.
Up (ŭp), *adv.* Kosak, kosako, kosakchi.
Upbraid (ŭp-brād'), *v.* Man-enga, ma·nanga.
Uphold (ŭp-hōld'), *v.* Rim·e rakia, mangrak ta, dakchaka.
Upholster (ŭp-hōl'stĕr), *v.* Tappuata, so·opata.
Upland (ŭp land), *n.* Chugipa a a.
Uplift (ŭp-lĭft'), *v.* Kosakchi de·doa.
Upon (ŭp-ŏn'), *prep.* Kosak.
Upper (ŭp'pêr), *a.* Kosakgipa.
Uppermost (up'pêr-mōst'), *a.* Kosakbatgipa.
Upraise (ŭp-rāz'), *v.* De·doa, chuata.
Upright (ŭp'rīt), *a.* Sronge chadenggipa, kakketgipa.
Uproar (ŭp'rōr), *n.* Jikjakani, golmal ong·ani.
Uproot (ŭp-rọt) *v.* Ja·pang pika.
Upset (ŭp-sĕt'), *v.* Pangpilata, bikpilata.
Upward (ŭp'wĕrd), *a.* Kosakchi.
Urchin (ĕr'chin), *n.* Okupu, nachil dakbegipa, chongipa bi·sa.
Urge (ĕrj), *v.* Didiata.
Urgent (ĕr'jent), *a.* Nangbegipa, bakbak nanggipa.
Urine (ū'rīn), *n.* Su·bu.
Urinate (ū'ri-nāt), *v.* Su·bua.
Us (ŭs), *pro.* Chingko, a·chingko.
Use (ūz), *v.* Jakkala, dakronga.

Use (ūs), *n*. Jakkalani, dakrongani.
Useful (ūs'ful), *a*. Kamna nanggipa, choligipa.
Usher (ŭsh'ẽr), *n*. Manderangko asongattimgipa.
Usual (ū'zhu-al), *a*. Bewalgita, ong·ronga gita.
Usurp (u-zẽrp'), *v*. Onia ka·e bilko ra·seka.
Usury (ū'zhu-ry), *n*. Agre sud ra·ani.
Utensil (u-tĕn'sil), *n*. Jakkalani, ra·chakani.
Utility (u-til'i-ty), *n*. Choligipa ong·ani, jakkalani ong·ani, dakchakani ong·ani.
Utilise (ū'til-iz), *v*. Jakkalani ong·ata.
Utmost (ŭt'mōst'), *a*. Amadipet, sokadipet, chel·batgipa.
Utter (ŭt'tẽr), *v*. Minga, gam·-ata. -ance, *n*.
Utter (ŭt'tẽr), *a*. -srang.

V.

Vacant (vā'kant), *a*. Bangbang, arara. -cy, *n*.
Vacate (vā'kāt), *v*. Ong·kate wata, bangbang dakata.
Vacation (va-kā'shŭn), *n*. Adita neng·takani sal, huti.
Vaccinate (văk'ci-nāt), *v*. Tika su·a.
Vacillate (văs'il-lāt), *v*. Tom·-tomgija ong·a, tik ong·gija ong·a.
Vacuum (văk'u-ŭm), *n*. Balwa aro mamungba grigipa biap.
Vagabond (văg'a-bŏnd), *n*. Re·-rorogipa, kam grigipa.
Vague (vāg), *a*. Tik ong·sranggija, mringmrang dake jeko talsrange uija.
Vail (vāl), *n*. Illuruani.
Vain (vān), *a*. Gaora de·gipa, dal·nikgipa.
Vale (vāl), *n*. A·bri gisepni a·kawe.
Valiant (val'yant), *a*. Bilakgipa, kengijagipa, ka·donggipa.
Valid (val'id), *a*. Bebe, kakket, nama saki gnanggipa.
Valley (văl'li), *n*. A·bri gisepni a·kawe, a·kong.
Valour (văl'ẽr), *n*. Ka·dongani.
Valuable (văl'u-a-b'l), *a*. Gamchatgipa.
Value (val'u), *n*. Dam ba gamchatani.
Valve (vălv), *n*. Oruraa gita dakgipa peng·ani.
Van (văn), *n*. Sipai kotokni skanggipa, malko ra·angani pindapani donggipa gari.
Vane (vān), *n*. Balwa bachini bala uko tik ka·ani, ba mesokani.
Vanish (văn'ish), *v*. Nikgija ong·e gimaa ong·a.
Vanity (văn'i-ty), *n*. Ong·gramaiani.
Vanquish (văn'kwish), *v*. Bobilko ama, bamata.
Vapour (vā'pẽr), *n*. Biba.
Variable (vā'ri-a-b'l), *a*. Dongkamgija, tom·tomgija, dingtang dingtang ong·gipa.
Variation (vā'ri-ā'shŭn), *n*. Dingtang dingtang ong·ani.
Variety (va-ri'e-ty), *n*. Ma·-manti rokom, rokom rokom.
Various (vā'ri-ŭs), *a*. Ma·manti.
Varnish (vär'nish), *n*. Bolko imilatani ba ching·atani to ma·sa.
Varnish (vär'nish), *v*. Imilata, barnis ka·a.

Vary (vā'ry), *v.* Dingtang ong·a ba ong·ata.

Vase (vās ba väz), *n.* Donchakani, mongsongde pulko donchakani.

Vaseline (văs'e-lin), *n.* Kerasinoniko man·a, nongani sam ma·sa.

Vassal (văs'sal), *n.* Raiot, gipinni ning·o donggipa nokol.

Vast (våst), *a.* Apalbegipa, dal·begipa.

Vat (văt), *n.* Chi ra·chakani tu·gipa chikong.

Vatican (văt'ī-kan), *n.* Rom songo popni dongram.

Vault (vôlt), *v.* Bilbata, bilchroka.

Vault (vôlt), *n.* A·a ning·chi kite nokkingchina gongdole rikgimin.

Vaunt (vänt ba vônt), *v.* Gaorade·e agana.

Veal (vēl), *n.* Matchu bi·sani be·en.

Vegetable (vĕj'e-tå-b'l), *n.* Me·su samjak.

Vegetation (vĕj'e-tā'shŭn), *n.* A·ao chagipa sam bolrang.

Vehement (vē'he-ment), *a.* Ta·rakgipa.

Vehicle (vē'hī-k'l), *n.* Ma·mantiko ra·angchakani.

Veil (vāl), *n.* Mikkang pindapani, illuruani.

Vein (vān), *n.* An·chi jokruraani ja·dil.

Velocity (ve-lŏs'i-ty), *n.* Ta·rakani, gong·rakani.

Velvet (vĕl'vĕt), *n.* Mokmol ba resomini ba·ra ma·sa.

Vend (vĕnd), *v.* Pala.

Venerable (vĕn'ĕr-å-b'l), *a.* Mandera·ako man·na kragipa.

Venerate (vĕn'ĕr-āt), *v.* Mandera·a, olakia.

Vengeance (vĕnj'ans), *n.* Jakbikpilani.

Venison (vĕn'ī-z'n ba vĕn'z'n), *n.* Matchok ba balgichak be·en.

Venom (vĕn'ŭm), *n.* Chipu, snare ba ugita mainiba ku·sikoni bisi.

Vent (vĕnt), *n.* Ong·katani cholrama. *v.* Ong·katata.

Ventilate (vĕn'tī-lāt), *v.* Bal balata -**ion**, *n.*

Venture (vĕn'tur), *v.* Kenani gnangoba daka.

Veracity (ve-răs'ī-ty), *n.* Kakket ong·ani, bebe ong·ani.

Veranda (ve-răn'då), *n.* Baranda, srek.

Verb (vĕrb), *n.* Daka ba ong·ako mesokani kata.

Verdant (vĕr'dant), *a.* Samsi gnanggipa, tangsekgipa.

Verdict (vĕr'dīkt), *n.* Bichal ka·mano rae on·ani.

Verdigris (vĕr'dī-grēs), *n.* Paisani silni tangsekgipa maram.

Verdure (vĕr'dur), *n.* Bol ba samsirangni tangseka.

Verge (vĕrj), *n.* Sima, rikam, dramni riking.

Verify (vĕr'ī-fī), *v.* Bebe ong·a ine mesoka.

Verily (vĕr'ī-ly), *adv.* Beben chong·mot.

Vermin (vĕr'min), *n.* Mese, tik, su·tik, ru·dat aro ugita chongipa janggi gnanggiparang.

Vernacular (vĕr-năk'u-lĕr), *n.* Songtangni ku·sik. *a.* An·tang songni ba songtangni.

Verse (vĕrs), *n.* Poear, poido dake segimin.

Version (vĕr'shŭn), *n*. Gipin ku'siko segimin.
Versed (vĕrst), *a*. Changgipa, sapgipa.
Versus (vĕr'sŭs), *prep*. Warachaka.
Vertebra (vĕr'te-brā), *n*. Bolgroni greng.
Vertex (vĕr'tĕks), *n*. Chubatgipa ku'chot.
Vertical (vĕr'tĭ-kal), *a*. Sronge songdogipa.
Vertigo (vĕr'tĭ-gō), *n*. Miksula.
Very (vĕr'y), *a*. Beben, uan, chong'mot.
Very (vĕr'y), *adv*. Namen, bang'en, -be-.
Vessel (vĕs'sĕl), *n*. Maiba donchakani ; jahat.
Vest (vĕst), *n*. Jakkandagipa chola ma'sa.
Vestige (vĕs'tij), *n*. Ja'kol, ong'-gimin ba gimagiminni maiba chin.
Vestibule (vĕs'tĭ-būl), *n*. Nok ning'ni baranda.
Vestry (vĕs'try), *n*. Gilja nok baksa nangchapgipa nok ba nokdring, gilja nokni ma'-manti bosturangko donram.
Veteran (vĕt'ĕr-an), *n*. Maiba kamko ruute ka'gipa, budepa sipai.
Veterinary (vĕt'ĕr ĭ-na-ry), *a*. Jillarangni saani samni biding.
Veto (vē'to), *n*. Champengani ba beng'ani bil. *v*. Champenga, beng'a.
Vex (vĕks), *v*. Jajrengata.
Via (vī'ā), *adv*. -ko re'a.
Viaduct (vī'ā-dŭkt), *n*. Rama ba chiko battongna kosako rikgimin.
Vial (vī'al), *n*. Botol chonbegipa.
Viands (vī'andz), *n*. Cha'ani.
Vibrate (vī'brāt), *v*. Il'enga, ichi uchi moa.
Vice (vīs), *n*. Namgija, dos, pap dakrongani, denggu dakrongani, matnangani.
Vice (vīs), *v*. Naunna skang donsoani kata uni, orto pal ong'ronga.
Vice-president (vīs'prĕz ĭ-dent), *n*. Pamongni man'jaona dongimin mande.
Viceroy (vīs'roi), *n*. Rajani pal dongimin mande.
Vicinity (vĭ-sĭn'ĭ-ty), *n*. Sepang ong'ani, sepangjol.
Vicious (vish'ŭs), *a*. Namgijako dakgipa, otoromi, papi.
Victim (vik'tĭm), *n*. So'ota ba duk on'ako man'gipa.
Victor (vĭk'tĕr), *n*. Amgipa, che ipa.
Victory (vĭk'to-ry), *n*. Amani, cheani.
Victuals (vĭt''lz), *n*. Chaani.
View (vū), *n*. Niani, niwatani ba nikgimin. *v*. Nia.
Vigil (vĭj'ĭl), *n*. Mikrake nitimani.
Vigilant (vĭj'ĭ-lant), *a*. Mikrakgipa, gisik rakgipa.
Vigour (vĭg'ĕr), *n*. Bil, bilakani. **-ous**, *a*.
Vile (vīl), *a*. Mitchigni ba namgija.
Vilify (vĭl'ĭ-fī), *v*. Saia, mitaka, matnanga.
Village (vĭl'laj), *n*. Song, gitim.
Villain (vĭl'lin), *n*. Denggubegipa.
Vindicate (vĭn'dĭ-kāt), *v*. Dos gri dakata, dos gri ine mesoka.

Vindictive (vīn-dĭk'tīv), *a*. A·-jak sokninggipa, a·jak sokna sikgipa.
Vine (vīn), *n*. Draka budu, ba gipin maiba wegipa budu.
Vinegar (vĭn'e-gėr), *n*. Meseng, sirka.
Vine-yard (vĭn'yêrd), *n*. Draka bari.
Violate (vī'o-lāt), *v*. Niamko pe·a, draa, manigija daka.
Violent (vī'o-lent), *a*. Ta·rake dakgipa. **-lence**, *n*.
Violet (vī'o-lĕt), *n*. Smilgipa bibal ma·sa.
Violin (vī'o-lĭn), *n*. Behela.
Viper (vī'pêr), *n*. Bisi gnangbegipa chipu.
Virgin (vêr'jĭn), *n*. Me·tra, se kimkujagipa.
Virgin (vêr'jĭn), *a*. Rongtalgipa, gital, marang nanggijagipa.
Virile (vī'rīl ba vĭr'īl), *a*. Me·-asani biding.
Virtual (vêr-tu-*a*l), *a*. Tik ong·-jaoba ong·a gita dakgipa.
Virtue (vêr'tu), *n*. Namani, gun, bil, ong·sigijani. **-ous**, *a*.
Visage (vĭz'aj), *n*. Mikkangko jekai nika.
Viscount (vī'kount'), *n*. England songni dal·a mande.
Vise (vīs), *n*. Rake kepani sil.
Visible (vĭz'ĭ-b'l), *a*. Jeko nikna man·a.
Vision (vĭzh'ŭn), *n*. Nikani.
Visit (vĭz'ĭt), *v*. Gronga ba roa. *n*.
Vital (vī'tal), *a*. Janggini biding, nangchongmotgipa.
Vitals (vī'talz), *n*. Janggio nangninggni·rang, bika, kan·-chok, ka·sop, iarang.
Vitriol (vĭt'rĭ-ŭl), *n*. Tutia.
Vivacity (vī-văs'ĭ-ty), *n*. Kusi ong·ani katchaani, janggi gnangani.
Vivid (vĭv'ĭd), *a*. Ching·a, rongchinga, ching·bea.
Vixen (vĭks''n), *n*. Sairakgipa me·chik.
Viz (vĭz), *adv*. Chong·motan.
Vizier (vĭz'yêr ba vĭ-zēr), *n*. Turosko songni montri.
Vocabulary (vo-kăb'u-la-ry), *n*. Chongipa obhidhan.
Vocal (vo'kal), *a*. Ku·rangni biding.
Vocation (vo-kā'shŭn), *n*. Ka·-rongani ba dakrongani.
Vociferate (vo-sĭf'êr-āt), *v*. Rakke agana, chrika.
Voice (vois), *n*. Ku·rang; verbni rokomko mesokgipa kata.
Void (void), *a*. Bangbang, indinari.
Void (void), *v*. Bangbangata, watgala.
Volcano (vŏl-kā'no), *n*. Wa·alni a·bri.
Volume (vŏl'um), *n*. Ki·tap; dal·ani.
Voluntary (vŏl'ŭn-ta-ry), *a*. Ska gita, namnika gita.
Volunteer (vŏl'ŭn-tēr'), *n*. Skatang sipai donggipa.
Vomit (vŏm'ĭt), *v*. Wakala, chisata.
Voracious (vo-rā'shŭs), *a*. Cha·-betbonggipa, okkribegipa.
Vote (vōt), *n*. Namnikako mesokani. *v*.
Vouch (vouch), *v*. Saki on·a.
Voucher (vouch'êr), *n*. Sakini sea, saki on·ani chiti.
Vow (vou), *n*. Isolna maikoba ku·rachaka, ku·rachakbea.
Vowel (vou'ĕl), *n*. An·tangan gam·na amgipa.

Voyage (voi'aj), *n.* Chiko re·ani, chiko songreani.
Vulgar (v l'gêr), *a.* Ramram, onnikgni.
Vulture (vŭl'tur), *n.* Sogin.

W.

Wabble (wŏb'b'l), *v.* Rongreng-a.
Wad (wŏd), *n.* Kartuso su·sikani wad, barutko rakatna su·-sikani.
Waddle (wŏd'd'l), *v.* Chingkreng bakreng re·a.
Wade (wād), *v.* Chiko ja·achi re·a.
Wafer (wā'fêr), *n.* Ba·begipa ruti.
Waft (wȧft), *v.* Chi ba balwachi balpakanga.
Wag (wăg), *v.* Il·enga, gong·-genga.
Wages (wā'jĕz), *n.* Dormaha.
Wagon, waggon (wăg'ŭn), *n.* Mal salani gari.
Wagtail (wăg'tāl'), *n.* Do·pasi.
Wail (wāl), *v.* Kalima, grapa, ma·ama.
Waist (wāst), *n.* Changkichon.
Waistcoat (wāst'k t), *n.* Kotni ning·o kruani chola.
Wait (wāt), *v.* Senga. sengsoa.
Waiter (wāt'êr), *n.* Dangdike on·gipa.
Waive (wāv), *v.* Dongdikata, Watgala.
Wake (wāk), *v.* Mikraka, mikrakata, mikrake donga.
Wake (wāk), *n.* Ring ba jahat re·ani chin, ringni ja·kol; mangtuani.
Waken (wāk''n), *v.* De·misaa, mikrakata.

Walk (wòk), *v.* Ja·achi re·a' roa.
Wall (wôl), *n.* Guar·, pakma.
Wallet (wŏl'lĕt), *n.* Tangka keani chongipa mona.
Wallow (wŏl'lo), *v.* A·dubeko romroma.
Walnut (wŏl'n t), *n.* Bikrok dakgipa bite ma·sa.
Wander (wŏn'dêr), *v.* Branga, re·roroa.
Wane (wān), *v.* Komianga, chonanga.
Want (wônt), *n.* Nangani, am·-ani.
War (wôr), *n.* Dakgrikani.
Warble (wôr'b'l), *n.* Do·oni til·-tile mikoani.
Ward (wôrd), *n.* Rakiani, rim·-rikani, rim·rikgipa.
Wardrobe (wôrd-rōb'), *n.* Ganding chinding, ganding chinding donani.
Warehouse (wâr'hous'), *n.* Gudamkana.
Warfare (wôr'fâr'), *n.* Dakgrik-ani.
Warily (wā'ri-ly), *adv.* Gisik rake.
Warm (wôrm), *a.* Ding·a.
Warn (wôrn), *v.* Gisik rakata.
Warning (wôrn'ing), *n.* Gisik rakatani.
Warp (wôrp), *v.* Sikongkrenga.
Warp (wôrp), *n.* Ba·rani groni kilding.
Warrant (wôr'rant), *n.* Rim·-ani poroana.
Warrior (wôr'yêr ba wŏr'ri-êr), *n.* Dakgrikgipa s·pai.
Wart (wôrt), *n.* An·te.
Wary (wā'ry), *a.* Gisik rak-gipa.
Was (wŏs), *v.* *Beko* nibo.
Wash (wŏsh), *v.* Su·sranga.

Washerman (wŏsh'ĕr-mon), *n.* Ba·ra su·gipa, dhobi.

Wasp (wŏsp), *n.* A·meng.

Waste (wāst), *v.* Gimaata, rusia, cham·ata.

Watch (wŏch), *n.* Nitimgipa, pohora on·gipa; baji niani ghori chongipa.

Watch (wŏch), *v.* Nitima, pohora on·a.

Water (wô'têr), *n.* Chi.

Waterfall (wô'têr-fôl'), *n.* Chi dare.

Water-fowl (wô'têr-foul), *n.* Chio rogipa do·orang.

Watermelon (wô'têr-mĕl'ŭn), *n.* Te·raja, tormuj.

Waterproof (wô'ter-prūf'), *n.* Chi napgijagipa, robolni ba·ra.

Water-wheel (wô'têr-whēl), *n.* Chichi wilwilatgipa chaka.

Wattle (wŏt't'l), *n.* Do·bipani ka·machini gingmat.

Wave (wāv), *n.* Chipakore.

Wave (wāv), *v.* Jipa ba balchi moa.

Wax (wăks), *n.* Ste, tarigimin laha.

Wax-cloth (wăks'klŏth'), *n.* Mom ba·ra, ste nonggimin ba·ra.

Way (wā), *n.* Rama, chol.

Wayfarer (wā'fâr'ĕr), *n.* Rama re·gipa.

Waylay (wā'lā'), *v.* Mandeni ramasamo tima.

Wayside (wā'sīd'), *n.* Rama samba.

Wayward (wā'wērd), *a.* Skatangko dakgipa, manigijagipa.

We (wē), *pr.* Chinga, an·ching.

Weak (wēk), *a.* Bil gri, bilakgijagipa.

Weaken (wēk"n), *v.* Bil gri ong·ata.

Wealth (wĕlth), *n.* Gam.

Wean (wēn), *v.* Sok wata.

Weapon (wĕp'ŭn), *n.* Dakgrikani silchidare.

Wear (wâr), *v.* Gana china, cham·a

Weariness (wē'ri-nĕss), *n.* Neng·ani.

Weary (wē'ry), *a.* Neng·a.

Weary (wē'ry), *v.* Neng·ata.

Weather (wĕth'ĕr), *n.* Salni ksin·a ba ding·ani.

Weather-glass (wĕth'ĕr-glâss), *n.* Balwako toani kol.

Weave (wēv), *v.* Ba·ra daka, wata.

Weaver-bird (wēv'ĕr-bĕrd), *n.* Do·chok.

Web (wĕb), *n.* Watgimin ba sringgimin; guang sringa.

Web-footed (wĕb'fut'ĕd), *a.* Nangchapgipa ja·a dakgipa.

Wed (wĕd), *v.* Bia ka·a, do·sia.

Wedding (wĕd'ding), *n.* Bia ka·ani.

Wedge (wĕj), *n.* Bolko pitna bretao siksepani sil ba bol.

Wednesday (wĕnz'da), *n.* Budbar.

Weed (wēd), *n.* Dange ba game galgni sam.

Week (wēk), *n.* Anti.

Week-day (wēk'da'), *n.* Robibarna agre antini gipin sal.

Weekly (wēk'ly), *a.* Anti anti, sal sni prak.

Weep (wēp), *v.* WEPT, Grapa, mikchi ong·a.

Weigh (wā), *v.* Jrimako toa.

Weight (wāt), *n.* Jrimani.

Welcome (wĕl'kŭm), *v.* Rimchaksoa, namnike ra·chaksoa.

Weld (wĕld), *v.* Dokpelgape ritchua.

Welfare (wĕl'fâr), *n.* Namgni·ni, name ong·ani.

Well (wĕl), *n.* Chiakol.

Well (wĕl), *a*. An·senga, nama.
Well (wĕl), *adv*. Namedake.
Well-bred (wĕl'brĕd'), *a*. Nama skiako man·gipa.
Well-favoured (wĕl'fā'vêrd), *a*. Bimang nama, nitoa.
Well-nigh (wĕl'nī'), *adv*. -nasia.
Welsh (Wĕlsh), *a*. Wales songni.
Went (wĕnt), *v*. *Goko* nibo.
Wept (wĕpt), *v*. *Weepko* nibo.
Were (wêr), *v*. Chim, *wasni* plural.
West (wĕst), Saliram.
Westward (wĕst'wêrd), *adv*. Saliramchi.
Westerly (wĕst'êr-ly), *adv*. Saliramchi.
Wet (wĕt), *a*. Sosia.
Wether (wĕтн'êr), *n*. Mes kasi.
Whale (hwāl), *n*. Timi na·tok, sagalni dal·begipa na·tok ma·-sa.
Wharf (hwôrf), *n*. Jahatoniko mal ra·gatani ghat.
Wharfage (hwôrf-aj), *n*. Ghatni bhara, masul.
What (hwŏt), *pr*. Mai je, maisa.
Whatever (hwŏt-ĕv'êr), *pr*. Jeba, jekoba.
Whatsoever (hwŏt'so-ĕv'êr), *pr*. Jeba, jekoba.
Wheat (hwēt), *n*. Gom mī.
Wheel (hwēl), *n*. Chaka.
Wheelbarrow (hwēl'băr'ro), *n*. Chaka ge·sangipa, jakchi salani gari.
Wheeze (hwēz), *v*. Rang·sitna man·bregija rang·sitani gam·a.
Whelp (hwĕlp), *n*. Matburungrangni chongipa bi·sa.
When (hwĕn), *adv*. Jensalo, basako.
Whence (hwĕns), *adv*. Baoni, banoni.
Whenever (hwĕn'ĕv'êr), *adv*. Jensaloba.
Where (hwâr), *adv*. Bano, jeo.
Whereabouts (hwêr'ă-bouts'), *adv*. Ban biapo, badia jolo.
Whereas (hwâr'ăs'), *adv*. Uni gimin, jeni gimin.
Whereat (hwâr-ăt'), *adv*. Jeo, uno.
Whereby (hwâr-bī), *adv*. Jechi.
Wherefore (hwâr'fōr), *adv*. Maina, maini gimin.
Wherein (hwâr-ĭn'), *adv*. Jeo, maio.
Whereof (hwâr-ov'), *adv*. Jeni, maini.
Wherever (hwâr-ĕv'êr), *adv*. Jeoba, je biapoba.
Wheresoever (hwâr'so-ĕv'êr), Jeoba, je biapoba.
Whereupon (hwâr'ŭp-ŏn'), *adv*. Unon, uni gimin.
Whereto (hwâr-tu), *adv*. Jechi.
Whet (hwĕt), *v*. Wil·la, matata.
Whether (hwĕтн'êr), *conj*. Gnini gisepo ia ba ua.
Whetstone (hwĕt'stōn'), *n*. Rong·chi.
Whey (hwā), *n*. Matchu sok tin·kaaoni ong·katgipa chi.
Which (hwĭch), *pr*. Badia.
Whichever (hwĭch ĕv'êr), *pr*. Jeba.
Whiff (hwĭf), *n*. Balpakgipa bisak, biba ba wal·ku.
While (hwīl), *n*. On·tisa somoi ba sal.
While (hwīl), *adv*. Miting.
Whilst (hwīlst), *adv*. Miting.
Whim (hwĭm), *n*. Dikdiksani kragijani ska.
Whimper (hwĭm'pêr), *v*. Ka·sne ka·sne grapa.
Whine (hwīn), *v*. Agane mol·-mole ba sae grapa.

Whinny (hwĭn'ny), *v.* Gureni kusi ong·e ba namnikako mesoke mikoa.
Whip (hwĭp), *v.* Betsmitchi dok-a.
Whip (hwĭp), *n.* Betsmit, gol·-smit, buduko ba bigilko daka betsmit.
Whirl (hwêrl), *v.* Wilwila.
Whirlpool (hwêrl'pul'), *n.* Chi sikwilwilgipa.
Whirlwind (hwêrl'wind), *n.* Balmanduri.
Whisk (hwĭsk), *v.* Dokponga, satponga.
Whisker (hwĭsk'êr), *n.* Ku·-simang, pedawel.
Whisky (hwĭs'ky), *n.* Chu ma·-sa.
Whisper (hwĭs'pêr), *v.* Aganmitua.
Whist (hwĭst), *int.* Jrip, tom·-tom.
Whistle (hwĭs'l), *v.* Ku·simika.
White (hwīt), *a.* Gibok.
White ant (hwīt'ănt'), *n.* A·kin, kinma.
Whitewash (hwīt'wŏsh), *v.* Chunchi repia. *n.*
Whither (hwĭth'êr), *adv.* Bachi, jeachi.
Whitish (hwīt'ish), *a.* Gibokmrang.
Whittle (hwĭt't'l), *v.* Churichi repe ba sol·e roa.
Whiz (hwĭz), *v.* Guli tang·ani gita gam·a.
Who (hṳ), *pr.* Sa, sawa, je.
Whoever (hṳ-ĕv'êr), *pr.* Jeba.
Whole (hōl), *a.* Gimik; an·-senga.
Wholesale (hōl'sāl'), *n.* Paldimani.
Wholesome (hōl'sŭm), *a.* Cha·-na namgipa, an·sengatgipa.
Wholly (hōl'ly), *adv.* -srang.
Whom (hṳm), *pr.* Sako, jeko.
Whoop (hṳp), *v.* Chrika, hohoa.
Whore (hōr), *n.* Noti, dari.
Whose (hṳz), *pr.* Sani, jeni.
Whosesoever (hṳz'so-ĕv'êr), *pr.* Jeniba.
Why (hwī), *adv.* Maina, main gimin.
Wick (wĭk), *n.* Chakio so·an solta ba ba·ra suri.
Wicked (wĭk'ĕd), *a.* Namgija gipa, kakketgijagipa, denggu gipa.
Wicket (wĭk'ĕt), *n.* Chongipa cholguga, kelki.
Wide (wīd), *a.* Apala.
Widen (wīd''n), *v.* Apalata.
Widow (wĭd'o), *n.* Segri, randi se simangimin.
Widower (wĭd'o-êr), *n.* Jik gri, randi, jik simangimin.
Width (wĭdth), *n.* Gipeng.
Wield (wēld), *v.* Change jakkala.
Wife (wīf), *n.* Jik, jikgipa.
Wig (wĭg), *n.* Kadapani dakgimin kni.
Wiggle (wĭg'g'l), *v.* Dil·dila, til·tila, moa.
Wiggler (wĭg'glêr), *n.* Chio donggipa gangguani jo ong.
Wigwam (wĭg'wŏm), *n.* Jamdap, paja.
Wild (wīld), *a.* Burungni, mikmalgijagipa.
Wilderness (wĭl'dêr-nĕss), *n.* Mande gri song, bakra.
Will (wĭl), *n.* Ska, mangsonga; sinasio see donangani.
Will (wĭl), *v.* -gen; mangsonga.
Wilful (wĭl'ful), *a.* Skatang dakgipa.

Willing (wĭl'ing), *a*. Ska ba nannika guang, namnikgijani ong·ja.

Willow (wĭl'lo), *n*. Bol ma·sa, jhao bol.

Wilt (wĭlt), *v*. Odorea, oldawea.

Win (wĭn), *v*. Ama, man·a, chea.

Wince (wĭns), *v*. Saknae to·tro on·a gita daka.

Winch (wĭnch), *n*. Maiba wenchakani go·ol.

Wind (wĭnd), *n*. Bal, balwa.

Wind (wind), *v*. WOUND. Wenwena, remrema.

Windmill (wĭnd'mĭl'), *n*. Balwachi moa·ani kol.

Window (wĭn'do), *n*. Kelki.

Windpipe (wĭnd'pīp'), *n*. Rang·sitani noli.

Windward (wĭnd'wẽrd), *adv*. Balwachipak.

Windy (wĭnd'y), *a*. Balwa gnang.

Wine (wīn), *n*. Draka bitchi.

Wing (wĭng), *n*. Grang, gangching.

Winged (wĭngd), *a*. Grang gnanggipa.

Wink (wĭngk), *v*. Mikjapa, mikjipa.

Winner (wĭn'nẽr), *n*. Amgipa, man·gipa, chegipa.

Winning (wĭn'nĭng), *a*. Mikmalatgipa, namnikatgipa.

Winnow (wĭn'no), *v*. Choe rongtalata, choponga.

Winter (wĭn'tẽr), *n*. Sin·kari.

Wipe (wīp), *v*. Ipaka.

Wire (wīr), *n*. Siliting, silni budu.

Wiry (wīr'y), *a*. Silni budu gita rangipa, ba·begipa.

Wisdom (wĭz'dŭm), *n*. Uiani.

Wise (wīz), *a*. Uigipa, gisik gnanggipa, seng·gipa.

Wish (wĭsh), *v*. Ska. *n*.

Wishful (wĭsh'fụl), *a*. Sikbegipa.

Wit (wĭt), *n*. Gisik sramani, ka·dingatani bil ba kata, ka·dingatna changani.

Witch (wĭch), *n*. Skal me·chik.

Witchcraft (wĭch'krȧft'), *n*. Skal dakani, snakani.

With (wĭth), *prep*. Baksa ; -chi; -mu.

Withe (wĭth), *n*. Sakgimin kaani.

Withdraw (wĭth-drô'), *v*. Jepila, ra·pila, ekanga.

Wither (wĭth'ẽr), *v*. Sikrepa.

Withhold (wĭth-hōld'), *v*. Dondika, ra·rika.

Within (wĭth-in'), *prep*. Ning·o, gisepo.

Without (wĭth-out'), *prep*. A·palo, gri.

Withstand (wĭth-stănd'), *v*. Warachaka.

Witness (wĭt'nĕss), *n*. Saki, saki on·gipa.

Witty (wĭt'ty), *a*. Nachil dakgipa, ka·dingatgipa.

Wizard (wĭz'ẽrd), *n*. Skal me·asa.

Woe (wō), *n*. Skimani, ma·amani, duk ong·ani.

Wolf (wụlf), *n*. Se·el ma·sa.

Woman (wụm'an), *n*. Me·chik.

Womanhood (wụm'an-hụd'), *n*. Me·chik ong·ani.

Womb (wụm), *n*. Oko kechakani sa·tip, atom.

Wonder (wŭn'dẽr), *v*. Aiao inmanpila.

Wonderful (wŭn'dẽr-fụl), *a*. Aiao inmanani.

Wondrous (wŭn'drŭs), *a*. Aiao inmanani.

Wont (wŭnt), *n*. Bewal, -rongani.

Woo (wụ), *v.* Namnikatna joton ka·a, ka·saako man·na am·a.
Wood (wụd), *n.* Bol, am·bol.
Woodbine (wụd'bīn'), *n.* Budu ma·sa.
Wooded (wụd'ĕd), *a.* Bolgrim gnang.
Wooden (wụd''n), *a.* Bolko dak-a.
Woodman (wụd'man), *n.* Bol den·gipa.
Woodpecker (wụd'pĕk'ẽr), *n.* Do·tileng.
Woodwork (wụd'wẽrk'), *n.* Bolni dakgimin.
Woof (wụf), *n.* Ba·ra gipengni kilding.
Wool (wụl), *n.* Mes kimil.
Woollen (wụl'ĕn), *a.* Mes kimil-ko dakgimin, posomi.
Word (wẽrd), *n.* Kata.
Work (wẽrk), *n.* Kam.
Workhouse (wẽrk'hous'), *n.* Aratgipa, roaigipa, kangalgip-a mandeko kam ka·na chipa-ni nok.
Workshop (wẽrk'shop'), *n.* Kam ka·ani nok, karkana.
World (wẽrld), *n.* A·gilsak, a·gimik.
Worldly (wẽrld'ly), *a.* A·gilsak-ni gita ba biding.
Worm (wẽrm), *n.* Malgipa jo·-ong.
Worm-wood (wẽrm'wụd), *n.* Ka·gipa samjak ma·sa.
Worn (wōrn), *a.* Surigimin, jronggimin, cham·gimin, *wear*ko nibo.
Worry (wŭr'ry), *v.* Jongkaia, jajrengata; jajrenga.
Worse (wẽrs), *a.* Namjabat-a.
Worship (wẽr'shĭp), *v.* Mania, olakia.
Worst (wẽrst), *a.* Pilakna bate namjabatgipa.
Worth (wẽrth), *n.* Gamchatani, dam.
Worthily (wẽr'THi-ly), *adv.* Krae.
Worthy (wẽr'THy), *a.* Kraa, nitoa, gun gnang.
Would (wụd), *v.* -genchim, *will*ko nibo.
Wound (wụnd ba wound), *n.* Mata, ba bu·ani.
Wound (wound), *v.* *Wind*ko nibo.
Wove (wōv), *v.* WOVEN. *Weave*-ko nibo.
Wrangle (răng'g'l), *v.* Ka·-onange jegrika.
Wrap (răp), *v.* Remrema.
Wrapper (răp'ẽr), *n.* Pindapa-ni, remremchakani.
Wrath (räth), *n.* Ka·onangbea-ni.
Wreathe (rēTH), *v.* Saka, sak-mrena.
Wreath (rēth), *n.* Bijak ba bi-balko ripok ba mukut dake sikgimin.
Wreck (rĕk), *v.* Gimara, be·a, nisiata.
Wreck (rĕk), *n.* Nisiatgimin, rugimin.
Wrench (rĕnch), *v.* Saksela. *n.* Sakselatani kol.
Wrestle (rĕs''l), *v.* Sikgrika.
Wretch (rĕch), *n.* Duk man·-gipa, namen namgija mande, denggu.
Wretched (rĕch'ĕd), *a.* Duk man·gipa, namgijagipa, deng-gugipa.
Wriggle (rĭg'g'l), *v.* Ichi uchi il·enga.
Wring (rĭng), *v.* WRUNG, Ba·ra sepa, sakselata, saknaata.

Wrinkle (rĭng'k'l), *v*. Skemata.
Wrinkle (rĭng'k'l), *n*. Skemani.
Wrist (rĭst), *n*. Jakgitok.
Write (rīt), *v*. WROTE, WRITTEN, Sea.
Writhe (rīTH), *v*. Il·eng pileng daka.
Wrong (rŏng), *a*. Namgija, kakketgija, guala gnang.
Wrote (rōt). *v*. *Write*ko nibo.
Wroth (rôth), *a*. Ka·onanga.
Wrung (rŭng), *v*. *Wring*ko nibo.
Wry (rī), *a*. Gonggea, gitchinga.

X.

X English oikorni 24 gipa; chikungko mesokani.

Y.

Y (wī), *n*. English oikorni 25 gipa.
Yacht (yŏt), *n*. Maljuri gnanggipa chongipa ring ma·sa.
Yak (yăk), *n*. Tibet songni matchu.
Yam (yăm), *n*. Ta·a ma·sa.
Yankee (yăng'ke), *n*. United Stateso atchigipako mingani bimung.
Yard (yärd), *n*. Mik gni, goj sa; sara.
Yarn (yärn), *n*. Ba·ra dakna rikgimin kilding.
Yawn (yôn), *v*. Ajama. *n*.
Ye (yē), *pr*. Na·mang, na·simang.
Yea (yā ba yē), *adv*. Oe, beben, chong·mot.
Year (yēr), *n*. Bilsi.
Yearling (yēr'ling), *a*. Bilsisa dal·gipa. *n*.
Yearly (yēr'ley), *adv*. Bilsianti.
Yearn (yêrn), *v*. Sikbea, ka·pakbea.
Yeast (yēst), *n*. Wanti, chuwanti.
Yelk (yĕlk), *n*. Do·chi birimit.
Yell (yĕl), *v*. Chrika, chrike inwata.
Yellow (yĕl'lo), *a*. Rimita.
Yelp (yĕlp), *v*. Duk ba saknaani gimin achakni grapa.
Yes (yĕs), *adv*. Oe, beben.
Yesterday (yĕs'tèr-da), *adv*. Mejalo. *n*.
Yet (yĕt), *conj*. Indiba, -piti, -ku.
Yield (yēld), *v*. Ong·katata, atchiata, on·a, naata, nanga.
Yoke (yōk), *n*. Pakripe.
Yoke-fellow (yōk'fĕl'lo), *n*. Dakrimpagipa, nokolska.
Yolk (yōlk ba yōk), *n*. Do·chi birimit.
Yore (yōr), *adv*. Skangon.
Yonder (yŏn'dêr), *a*. Uachi.
You (yū), *pr*. Na·a, na·simang.
Young (yŭng), *a*. Bilsi bang·gijagipa, dambe, pante.
Young (yŭng), *n*. Jilani ba matburungni bi·sa.
With-young (wĭTH yŭng), *a*. An·o gnang, bi·sa gnang.
Youngster (yŭng'stêr), *n*. Me·a bi·sa, pante bi·sa.
Your (ūr), *pr*. Nang·ni; na·simangni.
Yourself (ūr-sĕlf'), *pr*. Na·a an·tangan.
Youth (ūth), *n*. Pante, panteni sal.

Z.

Zeal (zēl), *n*. Sikbeani, gong·ani.
Zealot (zĕl'ŭt), *n*. Agre gong·gipa, agre bimchipgipa.

Zebra (zē'brȧ), *n*. Africa songni burungni gure ma·sa salmrake toka gnanggipa.

Zebu (zē'bu), *n*. India songni matchu.

Zenith (zē'nĭth), *n*. Sko kambe dingdingni salgi.

Zephyr (zĕf'ẽr), *n*. Balsrisri balgipa balwa, saliramni balwa.

Zero (zē'ro), *n*. Suino, al gri ongko.

Zest (zĕst), *n*. Ske ba namnike dakani.

Zigzag (zĭg'zăg'), *a*. Gongge gongdang dake ichiba uchiba ki·tik dake dakgipa.

Zinc (zĭngk), *n*. Sisa aro rang bringipa dosta minggipa sil.

Zone (zōn), *n*. A·gilsakni sin·a aro ding·ani biaprangko dingtang dingtang ma·ate katongani.

Zoology (zo-ŏl'o-jy), *n*. Janggi gnanggiparangni gimin uiani.

Published by

Facsimile Publisher
Ashok Vihar, Delhi-110052 (India)
Website: www.facsimilepublishers.com

Distributed by

Gyan Books Pvt. Ltd.
5, Ansari Road, Daryaganj, New Delhi-110002 (India)
E-mail: books@gyanbooks.com, Website: www.gyanbooks.com

9 789333 368766